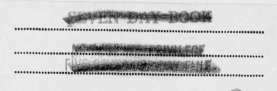

MOLDERS OF THE MODERN MIND

111 BOOKS THAT SHAPED WESTERN CIVILIZATION

ROBERT B. DOWNS

BARNES & NOBLE, INC.   ·   NEW YORK

Publishers   ·   Booksellers   ·   Since 1873

2-290

011
015

ACKNOWLEDGMENTS

For aid in selecting titles for inclusion and valuable criticism of the plan of the book, special acknowledgment is due the following:

Historians of science, social historians, and literary critics: Denis W. Brogan, Cambridge University; I. Bernard Cohen, Harvard University; Malcolm Cowley; David Dietz, Science Editor, Scripps-Howard Newspapers; Herbert M. Evans, University of California; John T. Flanagan, University of Illinois; Harris F. Fletcher, University of Illinois; Max Lerner; John Lydenberg, Hobart and William Smith Colleges; Allan Nevins, Huntington Library; Duane H. D. Roller, University of Oklahoma; A. L. Rowse, Oxford University; S. R Shapiro, rare book dealer; Richard H. Shryock, American Philosophical Society; John T. Winterich.

Librarians: Harry C. Bauer, University of Washington; Charles H. Brown, Iowa State College; Dorothy M. Crosland, Georgia Institute of Technology; Charles W. David, Longwood Library; William S. Dix, Princeton University; Leslie W. Dunlap, State University of Iowa; Oliver C. Dunn, Purdue University; Zoltan Haraszti, Boston Public Library; Richard B. Harwell, American Library Association; Herman H. Henkle, John Crerar Library; Louis Kaplan, University of Wisconsin; Herman W. Liebert, Yale University; Arthur McAnally, University of Oklahoma; Jens Nyholm, Northwestern University; Stanley Pargellis, Newberry Library; Lawrence Clark Powell, University of California; William Ready, Marquette University; Frank B. Rogers, National Library of Medicine; Russell A. Scully, Boston Public Library; Lawrence S. Thompson, University of Kentucky; Frederick H. Wagman, University of Michigan; Carl M. White, Columbia University.

Appreciation should be expressed also to Harry Shaw, of Barnes & Noble, Inc., who conceived the idea for the book and frequently provided helpful advice; and to Elizabeth C. Downs, who did much of the basic research. The preparation of the manuscript was in the highly capable hands of Clarabelle Gunning, University of Illinois Library.

Robert B. Downs

Urbana, Illinois

iii

FOR
BETTY
CLARISSA
AND
BERT

CONTENTS

Contents   xv

ILLUSTRATIONS

INTRODUCTION

The central idea of the present work was perfectly expressed in 1871 by Walt Whitman in his *Democratic Vistas*:

> It is strictly true, that a few first-class poets, philosophs, and authors have substantially settled and given status to the entire religion, education, law, sociology, etc., of the hitherto civilized world, by tinging and often creating the atmospheres out of which they have arisen.

With the keenness of perception characteristic of a great poet, Whitman recognized that the culture and civilization of modern man have been guided and shaped by the thought of a limited number of individuals—sometimes in constructive, occasionally in destructive, directions. Almost without exception, these persons have expressed themselves and spread their doctrines through the medium of the printed word. It will be the purpose here to identify and to analyze the world-shaking books of the past five hundred years, approximately, whose wide influence can be clearly demonstrated and evaluated.

At the outset, certain restrictions were placed on the selection of titles. Emphasis is primarily on the sciences and social sciences, especially the biological and physical sciences, economics, political science, history, education, and sociology. The general area of belles-lettres is omitted, unless the cultural or sociological impact of a book is readily apparent—for example, Montaigne's *Essays*, Shakespeare's *Hamlet*, Defoe's *Robinson Crusoe*, Swift's *Gulliver's Travels*, Dickens' *Hard Times*, Stowe's *Uncle Tom's Cabin*, and Hugo's *Les Misérables*. Also generally excluded are great works of religion and theoretical philosophy—not because of any failure to discern their importance, but because of the intangible, all-pervasive nature of their influence, an element hardly susceptible to measurement. Again, there are a few exceptions for works of social significance, such as, Bunyan's *Pilgrim's Progress*, Luther's *Address to the Christian Nobility of the German Nation*, and Calvin's *Institutes of the Christian Religion*.

To bring the undertaking within reasonable proportions, several additional limitations were decided upon. The first was to confine the list to the period since the invention of printing (actually, it begins with Columbus' discovery of the New World), thereby eliminating the great classics of the ancient and medieval eras. Furthermore, only books of the Western world—European and American—are included, omitting the notable works of religion, literature, and philosophy and other classics of the East, many of which have also profoundly influenced the West.

It should be stressed that there is no intention here to offer another list of "great" books, or "best" books. The basic principle of selection is to discover those books that have directly influenced the history, economics, government, law, scientific thought, and other aspects of Western life since the beginning of the Renaissance in Europe. Many of the books that made the greatest impact during these five hundred years are badly written works, lacking in literary style, but presenting revolutionary new concepts or highly emotional appeals.

The arrangement of the titles calls for brief explanation. From Columbus to Freud, titles are arranged chronologically by publication dates, without regard to subject content. It is hoped in this fashion to illustrate the development of scientific and social ideas and their interaction throughout these several centuries. As one reviews the books selected, a striking feature is the continuity of knowledge—the connecting threads that hold them together, with each generation building upon the past. Several period essays emphasize the relationships among these seminal works.

Nevertheless, final "solutions" are perhaps never found. In the sciences, a great discovery simply opens up new worlds to explore. An Einstein raises more questions than he answers, though the boundaries of knowledge are being constantly pushed back. Less optimism may be justified in the social sciences, where man is far from winning control over his own destiny. Unresolved, and possibly insoluble, issues are as alive and as significant today as when they first received attention centuries ago. Note, for example, such problem areas as church versus state, population growth, extent of government control over the individual, race discrimination, women's rights, nationalism, international law and peace, forms of government, the free enterprise system, universal education—all subjects treated in the books chosen for discussion and ever present in current newspaper headlines.

A reader examining the list of works here included may properly question the definition of a "book." Strictly speaking, the titles by Faraday, Lister, Pasteur, Koch, Thoreau, Mendel, Gibbs, Mackinder, and Turner are not books at all. Their original appearance was as periodical articles, though several were later expanded and separately printed. In addition, such writings, as those by Columbus, Kant, Jefferson, and Paine are pamphlet size. The range of the titles is from Diderot's twenty-eight volume *Encyclopédie* down to a four-page journal article. For present purposes, size is virtually without significance. A considerable proportion of the total list consists of multivolume works—refuting Voltaire's assertion that "it is always the little books, packed with emotions, aflame with passion, that do the business." Big books can also change the world.

There is a natural tendency in a work of this character to over-emphasize the contributions of one's own country and language. A conscious effort has been made to avoid that pitfall by omitting, for the most part, material of only local importance and interest. By nationalities, the distribution of authors is as follows: 41 British, 20 American, 18 French, 14 German, 5 Italian, 3 Dutch, 2 Russian, 2 Austrian, and Belgian, Norwegian, Polish, Spanish, Swedish, and Swiss, one each.

Which have been the greatest eras for the creation of ideas molding the modern mind? If the present selection can be regarded as a fair sample, the distribution by centuries runs: fifteenth 1, sixteenth 9, seventeenth 17, eighteenth 29, nineteenth 46, twentieth 9—giving the palm to the eighteenth and nineteenth. The relatively small number included for the twentieth century is due in part to caution —the belief that we do not yet possess sufficient historical perspective to judge which of the books issued in the past sixty years are of wide-spread or lasting significance. In what ways did these men and their books exert their influence? Sometimes, by turning the human mind into new channels, even in some instances creating new sciences or novel points of view; sometimes, by reawakening an appreciation of ancient truths and traditions; sometimes, by appealing to the emotions and biases of readers; and sometimes, by upsetting cherished beliefs in ideas or institutions.

Invaluable advice and assistance were received from the group of historians, scientists, literary critics, librarians, and others listed in the acknowledgments. Accompanying comments frequently expressed points of view worthy of special note. For example, Duane H. D.

Roller, Associate Professor of the History of Science, University of Oklahoma, writes:

> I happen to believe that history is continuous, and as a consequence I disagree wholeheartedly with the idea that this list of books, or perhaps any other, represents "the pioneer and the trail-blazer" or that these books are the ones which first presented ideas. The mere fact that most of these books are actually summaries of many years of work done before their publication, by the author and/or others, points up how difficult it is to find the beginning of anything . . . if I may illustrate with a few examples: Harvey's book represents research that builds upon that of sixteenth-century anatomists and physiologists. Yet it is through the book of Harvey that the idea has its impact. The book of Linneaus is the culmination of some two centuries of explanation of systems of classifying, particularly plants, and cannot by any means be said to represent really the beginning of anything. It is important because of its impact.

Professor Roller's contention that there is nothing essentially new under the sun is in accord with Sir Isaac Newton's remark, after acknowledging his indebtedness to Copernicus, Kepler, Galileo, and other predecessors: "If I have seen further than other men, it is by standing on the shoulders of giants."

Approximately three hundred titles were recommended for consideration by various consultants. Some were dropped as outside the scope of the project; others were too narrowly specialized or restricted in influence. It is patent that a unanimous verdict is exceedingly difficult to obtain on any given book. Among the experts, however, there is considerably more unanimity of choices in the field of science than in the social sciences or the humanities. Selection is unavoidably a subjective matter, and responsibility for the final list has been borne entirely by the author.

PART ONE

RENAISSANCE AND REFORMATION

Until recently, historians regarded the period of the Renaissance as the first chapter of modern history, marking the rebirth of humanism and a revolt against the authoritarianism, asceticism, and submergence of the individual characteristic of the medieval era. As research on the preceding millenium has proceeded, however, the break between the Middle Ages and the Renaissance has appeared less decisive. Scholars now generally recognize that the great intellectual and cultural flowering of Europe starting in the mid fifteenth century did not spring forth full-grown, but was a natural evolution from the Late Middle Ages. In fact, important concepts of modern science, such as the concept of atomic structure formulated by Leucippus and Democritus 2,400 years ago, can be traced back to their roots in antiquity.

Nevertheless, the amazing growth in cultural progress during the era known as the Renaissance represents in many of its aspects a new day in the life of the Western world. Nowhere are the changes better exemplified than in the field of book production. Prior to Gutenberg's invention of movable type in Germany, dated approximately 1450, books were handwritten. Forty-five copyists working for two years under Cosimo de Medici are reported to have produced only two hundred volumes. In striking contrast to the painfully slow, inaccurate manuscript method, during the first half-century after the invention of printing there appeared in Europe approximately ten million books, comprising forty thousand titles, with hundreds of printers busily turning out new works. The accelerated multiplication of books made possible an equally rapid spread of knowledge. Without perfection of the art of printing, the wide dissemination of Greek, Latin, and other classical writings, so closely identified with the Renaissance, would have been impossible.

The intellectual awakening, accompanied by the rise of universities and remarkable developments in art and architecture, produced an unsettling of traditional beliefs, a questioning of religious institutions, and, on occasion, a reversion to almost pure paganism. The road was being paved for the cataclysm of the Protestant Reformation and momentous succeeding events.

Another significant factor in broadening Europe's horizon was the unparalleled era of discovery and exploration that began in the last decade of the fifteenth century with Christopher Columbus' voyages to the New World. Thanks to the printing press, Columbus' own account of his travels was promptly distributed throughout the Continent. Announcement of the discovery had a tremendous impact on Europe. Other voyages followed quickly, resulting in a flood of publications descriptive of the new lands and detailing the exploits of the explorers. The vast expansion of exploration, migration, conquest, trade, and missionary effort that ensued was destined to affect profoundly both the European and non-European worlds.

The intellectual ferment at home, while the European frontier was thus being extended, is well illustrated by the writings of two close friends, Desiderius Erasmus in Holland and Sir Thomas More in England. Erasmus, the foremost man of letters of his time, has been compared to Petrarch in the fourteenth century and Voltaire in the eighteenth. Though ordained a priest, he lived the life of a traveling scholar, becoming intimately acquainted with the intelligentsia of all western Europe. Erasmus' interest in church dogma was slight; moreover, he disliked fanaticism in any form. His sharp satire was directed at the abuses of the time, the corruption of the clergy, and the formalism of religion, but he never deserted the Church. From Erasmus' *In Praise of Folly* and other writings there emerges a program of religious, political, and educational reform, representative of his own humanistic point of view. By holding up to laughter and ridicule the follies of monks, of scholastic doctors, and of meaningless ceremonies, Erasmus contributed mightily to the battle against superstition, cruelty, and dogmatism.

Sir Thomas More's *Utopia* reflects the early sixteenth-century preoccupation with geographical discovery. Like Erasmus, More opposed the abuses and superstitions prevailing among the contemporary clergy, though he, too, feared the disruptive effects of religious controversy. It was as another great humanist that More presented the utopian ideal: a perfect society in which men might be happy, tolerant, and well adjusted throughout their earthly existence.

Two more uncongenial personalities than Erasmus and Martin Luther could hardly be conceived, and their relationship ended in violent disagreement. But despite their complete lack of mutual sympathy, it has been suggested that "Erasmus laid the egg and Luther hatched it." The need for church reform had been recognized by others. Four years before Luther nailed his ninety-five *theses* to the door of the Wittenberg Church, Machiavelli had written, "Whoever examines the principles upon which that religion [Christianity] is founded, and sees how widely different from those principles its present practice and application are, will judge that her ruin or chastisement is near at hand." A generation later, Roman Catholicism had lost half of Europe to the Protestant Reformation.

The underlying causes of the Reformation were complex, and historians have differed in their interpretations. Some have pictured it as a revolt against medieval tyranny and superstition. Political forces unquestionably played a major role, as the emerging nations of Europe inevitably clashed with the secular powers of the Church. In effect, the economic and political interests of the Church as an international state collided with those of the new national states. The chief appeal of Luther's *Address to the Christian Nobility of the German Nation*, it may be noted, stemmed from his arguments supporting the independence of civil power.

The rising tide of nationalism in the sixteenth and seventeenth centuries inspired numerous other political theorists, notably Niccolò Machiavelli in Italy, Jean Bodin in France, Hugo Grotius in Holland, and Thomas Hobbes and John Locke in England. Each of these five eminent political philosophers has, in turn, provided the stimulus for a large library of critical comment.

Sinister connotations, probably undeserved, have grown up around the name of Machiavelli. His *The Prince* was a brutally realistic portrayal of the cruel, corrupt politics of the Renaissance, especially as practiced in Italy. The realities did not coincide with Machiavelli's personal convictions and ideals, for he believed in republican government; the people, he thought, could more safely be entrusted with power than a dictator or oligarchy. In writing *The Prince*, Machiavelli was motivated entirely by his passionate devotion to the city-state of Florence and by his ultimate dream of a unified Italy—realized several centuries later by Mazzini and Cavour.

Bodin and Hobbes developed similar theories of absolute monarchy. There can be no state at all, as Bodin put it, without a sovereign possessing "supreme power over citizens, unrestrained by the laws." Bodin held that the sovereign, as the maker of laws, was also above them, except that morally he was bound by the law of God and the law of Nature. Hobbes reinforced his arguments for absolutism by means of the social contract theory—a prime premise among political scientists up to the French Revolution. As Hobbes interpreted the theory, all civil authority, resting originally in the people, had been bestowed by them on the ruler in order that he might perform certain necessary functions. The only reservation made by Hobbes in his *Leviathan* to the dictum that the individual owes complete, unquestioned obedience to the sovereign applied to the contingency of the state's becoming so disorderly that life was made insecure, in which event the individual would have the right to protect his own life and security in any way possible.

The apologists for monarchical absolutists did not go unchallenged. John Milton's *Areopagitica* presented the basic arguments for freedom of expression. Later, Locke's *Two Treatises of Civil Government* justified the Revolution of 1688 in England and provided arguments in the eighteenth century for the American and French Revolutions. Locke not only refuted the doctrine of absolute monarchy but also believed that government is responsible both to the people and to the moral law of Nature.

Looking beyond national boundaries, the Dutch jurist and statesman, Hugo Grotius, founded the modern concept of international law, a body of principles which were developed in order to regulate competition among sovereign states. Too realistic to believe that warfare between the states could be wholly eliminated, Grotius sought to formulate some code of honor that would establish the idea of "civilized warfare."

Great literary stars dotted the Renaissance firmament. In France, Rabelais' Gargantua and Pantagruel laughed at the shams and hypocrisies of the age. Montaigne, in his *Essays,* turned a searching, inquiring mind on an immense variety of subjects. Subsequently, the impact of the Renaissance was seen in the dramas of Corneille, Racine, and Molière, the fables of La Fontaine, and the *Thoughts* of Pascal. Spain's major contribution was Cervantes, who in *Don Quixote,* one of the greatest of prose satires, effectively ridiculed the romantic excesses of the age of chivalry.

In England, the Renaissance came late, but there it reached its crest, producing the most extraordinarily creative period in literary history, symbolized by the greatest figure of all, William Shakespeare. Among Shakespeare's contemporaries and successors such names stand out as Marlowe, Donne, Bacon, Ben Jonson, Spenser, Dryden, and the amazing genius, Milton. Also belonging to the era is a monument of the English language, the King James version of the *Bible*, most renowned of biblical translations and a masterpiece of literature in its own right.

The Renaissance was essentially a revival of the humanities. In educated circles the natural sciences were largely ignored or scorned. Even Erasmus disliked scientific study, as is shown by the passages in *The Praise of Folly* holding up to ridicule the "natural philosophers" and mathematicians. The Reformation was marked by a still more direct and aggressive hostility to the scientific spirit. Poets and painters far outnumbered great scientific names between 1500 and 1690. Nevertheless, the resurrection of classical learning represented by the Renaissance and the questioning of established beliefs inevitably accompanying the Reformation created an intellectual climate favorable to science. The works of Archimedes, Aristarchus, Hippocrates, Galen, Euclid, Ptolemy, and other ancients enabled early modern scientists to take up where like-minded men had left off centuries before. The results of the scientific revolution of the sixteenth and seventeenth centuries, according to one historian of science, Herbert Butterfield, "outshine everything since the rise of Christianity and reduce the Renaissance and Reformation to the rank of mere episodes, mere internal displacements, within the system of medieval Christendom."

The new advance of science ignored national boundaries. Of the five geniuses who laid the foundations for modern astronomy, Copernicus was a Pole, Brahe a Dane, Kepler a German, Galileo an Italian, and Newton an Englishman.

By common agreement, modern science dates its birth from the publication of Copernicus' epochal *Concerning the Revolutions of the Heavenly Spheres,* in which the earth and the planets were conceived as revolving around the sun; the disturbing effect of the theory upon man's faith and philosophy can scarcely be overestimated. In the same year (1543) was published Vesalius' *The Structure of the Human Body,* equally revolutionary in its field and likewise indicative of a new spirit in scientific investigation. There followed in succession Brahe's accumulation of an immense body of astronomical data, systematically collected over a period of years; Kepler's formulation of three laws of the solar system, based upon Brahe's observations; Galileo's invention of the telescope and fundamental discoveries in dynamics and mechanics; and the work of the most universal genius of all, Sir Isaac Newton's mathematical proof of the discovery and establishment of the physical law by which the whole universe is governed.

In other branches of scientific effort, Sir William Gilbert was describing and experimenting with magnets and magnetism; William Harvey was establishing modern experimental medicine through his discovery of the circulation of the blood; Robert Boyle's laboratory experiments were beginning to separate medieval alchemy from modern chemistry; and Robert Hooke was carrying on pioneer research in microscopy. Two other thinkers, Francis Bacon in England and René Descartes in France, were making theoretical rather than practical contributions to science through their emphasis on scientific method and research. Bacon's enthusiasm for planned experimentation and his proposal for a co-operative research institute had immense influence in bringing about the establishment of scientific societies and of scientific research as a recognized profession. Descartes' great historical achievement was his teaching that, through proper and systematic use of his intelligence, divorced from myth, magic, and superstition, man could penetrate the most hidden secrets of the universe.

Thus did the Renaissance, the Reformation, and the rise of modern science set the stage for the century of Enlightenment and Reason to follow.

1. NEW WORLD EXPLORER

Christopher Columbus' De Insulis Inuentis; Epistola Christoferi Colom (Letter of Christopher Columbus Concerning Newly Discovered Islands)

1493

Overwhelming proofs exist that Christopher Columbus was not the original discoverer of the Americas. In fact, on his first two voyages to the New World, 1492–94, he did not set foot on either continent. Norsemen were in Greenland and probably on the North American mainland by the tenth century; the voyages of Eric the Red and Leif Ericson, among others, are well authenticated. Less reliable accounts antedate even these records, for as Charles Duff, Columbus' biographer, has pointed out, "It is curious to find that almost as far back as we can go in European history, we find a *legend* of the existence of a 'Great Land to the West.'"

Nevertheless, until Columbus' first voyage there was no real knowledge, but only speculation, concerning the Western Hemisphere. Contacts between the Norsemen and America had long since been broken off and largely forgotten. "It was the achievement of Columbus," commented Cecil Jane, editor of Columbus documents for the Hakluyt Society, "to convert conjecture into certainty, to substitute knowledge for hypothesis, and to open a way across the Atlantic which has never since been closed."

Columbus had the good fortune to live in a highly propitious period, in the beginning of the great intellectual awakening known as the Renaissance, then starting to pervade all of Europe. A spirit of adventure was in the air, and the stage was set for an unparalleled era of discovery and exploration. For this spirit, Columbus was to provide no small share of inspiration. Encouragement and support for finding new worlds came, too, from the all-powerful Catholic Church, interested in saving heathen souls and in acquiring material wealth.

The first written and printed description of the New World was contained in Columbus' celebrated *Letter* of March 14, 1493, written

De Jnfulis nuper in mari Jndico repertis

on shipboard and addressed to Luis de Santangel, keeper of the privy purse, who had been instrumental in persuading Ferdinand and Isabella to finance the initial voyage. At the same time, another letter, probably similar in content, had been sent to the King and Queen. The originals of both letters have vanished, but approximately a month later, in April, 1493, the printed version of one of them was available. Of the first edition, in Spanish, done in Barcelona, a unique copy is now in the New York Public Library.

With amazing speed, considering that the printing art was in its infancy, other editions multiplied. A Latin translation appeared and ran through three Roman editions in 1493. Six different editions were printed at Paris, Basel, and Antwerp before the end of 1494. In 1497, the first German edition came off the press, and a Florentine monk issued an Italian translation, in verse. Thus news of the discovery spread throughout Europe. Within five years after Columbus' return, his report had been printed in at least seventeen editions, in four languages, and in six different countries. Probably most of Europe had heard of Columbus' exploit before the end of the century.

When Columbus came back to Spain in the spring of 1493, he was surrounded by fame and glory. His *Letter* announcing the discovery of a new world, with its promise of unlimited wealth for Spain, his colorful account of savage tribes overseas, and his conquest of a fearsome ocean combined to raise him to the status of a great popular hero. Echoes of his reputation soon reached Portugal, France, England, Germany, and Italy. The *Letter* contributed substantially to his renown. Kings and princes, map makers and geographers, merchants and traders, seafaring men, diplomats, churchmen, and scientific and literary circles were excited by the news and eager for further details. Under the stimulus of Columbus' success, a host of other discoverers, explorers, colonizers, and exploiters would soon be roving the seven seas.

On the basis of the information submitted in Columbus' *Letter* and other documents, Ferdinand persuaded Pope Alexander VI to issue a bull, dated May 4, 1493, establishing a new line of demarcation, dividing the world between Spain and Portugal. Spain was given possession of all lands it might discover to the west of an imaginary line drawn from pole to pole; eastward all discoveries belonged to Portugal. Since such an arrangement was not meekly accepted by France, England, and other interested nations, the end result was several centuries of friction and strife.

In its description of the West Indian Islands, visited on the first voyage, the Columbus *Letter* is reasonably accurate on such matters as the explorers actually witnessed, but unreliable on hearsay evidence. From the natives, Columbus picked up, for example, tall tales about one island of people born with tails, another inhabited by cannibals, and still another "in which the people have no hair." Europeans were intrigued by Columbus' report that among the natives "both men and women go as naked as when their mothers bore them." The story had an Adam and Eve quality, suggesting to the romantically inclined a golden age still to be found in these remote places. The *Letter's* highly optimistic promises to Ferdinand and

Isabella, to "give them all the gold they may need . . . and a thousand other valuable things," helped to obtain support for further voyages, but led to Columbus' ultimate downfall and disgrace when he was unable to fulfill his own promises.

Columbus lived and died, of course, under the delusion that he had discovered a western route to Asia, and his declaration that he had reached "The Indies" was generally accepted in Europe—an error which is still reflected in present-day use of the terms "Indians" for American aborigines and "West Indies" for islands of the Caribbean. Not until Magellan circumnavigated the world in 1521 was the misconception corrected.

One spot where Columbus' fame failed to penetrate was a monastery at Saint-Dié in Lorraine, where a young cartographer, Martin Waldseemüller, was preparing a manual of geography, including a map of the world. The printed chronicle of the four voyages of another Italian explorer, Americus Vespucius, however, had fallen into Waldseemüller's hands. Impressed with Vespucius' extravagant claims, Waldseemüller proposed in his *Cosmographia Introductio*, published in 1507, the name "America" for the new world, and, acting on his own recommendation, printed "America" on his map of the Western Hemisphere. The suggestion took the public fancy and was perpetuated, thereby depriving Columbus of an honor rightfully belonging to him.

2. BUGBEAR OF BIGOTS

Desiderius Erasmus' *Encomium Moriae (The Praise of Folly)*

1511

The Praise of Folly, one of the most brilliant satires in the history of literature, was written by Desiderius Erasmus, Dutch humanist, in the short space of seven days, while he was visiting his friend, Sir Thomas More, in England. The Latin title of the work itself is a pun on More's name. Erasmus, "the Voltaire of the sixteenth century," dominated the intellectual scene of his time, but of his voluminous writings only *The Praise of Folly* has escaped obscurity or oblivion. Preserved Smith, noted American historian, characterized the little book as "a witty sermon, an earnest satire, a joke with an ethical purpose."

Erasmus sets the satirical tone in explaining his purpose in writing the book:

> Since the human race insists upon being completely crazy—since everybody from the Pope down to the humblest of village priests— from the richest of men to the most miserable of paupers—from the fine lady in her silks and satins down to the slut in her calico dressing gown—since the whole world has firmly set its heart against using its God-given brain but insists upon letting itself be entirely guided by its greed, its vanity, and its ignorance, why in the name of a reasonable deity should the few really intelligent people waste so much of their time and their effort in trying to change the human race into something it never wanted to be? Let them be happy in their follies. Don't deprive them of that which gives them more satisfaction than anything else—their sovereign power to make fools of themselves.

In *The Praise of Folly,* Erasmus argues that it is the irrational and foolish desires that make the wheels of the world go around. The book is written in the form of an oration or declamation, delivered by Folly in person to an imaginary audience made up of all classes and conditions of men. Wearing an academic gown, but with a fool's cap on her head, Folly mounts the rostrum, attended by her retainers, Self-Love, Forgetfulness, Laziness, Pleasure, Sensuality, Sound Sleep, Intemperance, and Madness. Folly tells us that she is the child of Plutus and of a charming creature called Youth, and was reared by two seductive nymphs, Drunkenness, offspring of Bacchus, and Ignorance, Pan's daughter. In the sweeping satire that follows, Erasmus, speaking through Folly, pokes fun at virtually all institutions, customs, men, and beliefs of his time, including marriage, war, nationalism, lawyers, scientists, academicians, theologians, kings, and popes.

Without her aid Folly claims, society would collapse. No wise man or woman would risk marrying and producing children unless inspired by Folly, and to her therefore "the haughty philosophers, and kings in their scarlet, pious priests, and triply most holy popes" owe their being. "What part of life is not sad, unpleasant, graceless, flat, and burdensome," asks Folly, "unless you have pleasure added to it, that is, a seasoning of folly?" The wisest men are held to be most wretched, while fools and idiots, untormented by dread of impending evils, "not vexed by the thousand cares to which this life is subject," are happiest. Even the most highly respected professions are deeply indebted to Folly, for medicine is mainly quackery and most lawyers are only pettifoggers. Further, governments are successful in proportion to their ability to fool the people, contrary to Plato's belief that philosophers should be kings and kings philosophers.

Some of Erasmus' sharpest barbs are aimed at the academicians or "grammarians" and their peculiar follies:

> When anyone has found out who was the mother of Anchises, or has lighted on some old, unusual word, such as bubsequus, bovinator, manticulator, or other like obsolete, cramped terms, or can, after a great deal of poring, spell out the inscription on some battered monument, Lord! What joy, what triumph, what congratulations upon his success, as if he had conquered Africa or captured Babylon!

Equally ridiculous, thinks Erasmus, are the scientists attempting to unlock the secrets of Nature and to discover the unknown:

> How sweetly they rave when they build themselves innumerable worlds, when they measure the sun, moon, stars, and spheres as though with a tape to an inch, when they explain the cause of thunder, the winds, eclipses, and other inexplicable phenomena, never hesitating, as though they were the private secretaries of creative Nature or had descended from the council of the gods to us, while in the meantime Nature magnificently laughs at them and at their conjectures.

Every pursuit of mankind is thus shown as being attended by Folly. In the theater, "Destroy the illusion and any play is ruined." The hunters "feel an ineffable pleasure in their souls whenever they hear the raucous blast of the horns and the yelping of the hounds . . . and what is so sweet as a beast being butchered?" Equally deluded are those who "flatter themselves beyond measure with the empty title of nobility. One will trace his family back to Aeneas, one to Brutus, and a third to King Arthur. In every room they display pictures and busts of their ancestors." Similarly, the merchant grubbing for money, the poet seeking immortality, the warrior with illusions of greatness, the gamblers whose "hearts leap and begin to beat faster" when they hear the rattle of dice—these and many others have their lives ruled by Folly.

A generous portion of *The Praise of Folly* is reserved for Folly's discourse on the Church and Christian doctrine. The freedom with sacred names and texts led in his own time to accusations that Erasmus was a heretic and an atheistical scoffer, though he never left the Catholic faith. None of the Church's hierarchy escapes satirical treatment from Erasmus' pen, but his particular target is the monks:

They call it a sign of holiness to be unable to read. They bray out the Psalms in the churches like so many jackasses. They do not understand a word of them, but they fancy the sound is soothing to the ears of the saints. The mendicant friars howl for alms along the street. They pretend to resemble the Apostles, and they are filthy, ignorant, impudent vagabonds.

The splendor and worldliness of popes, cardinals, and bishops are mocked at by Erasmus and contrasted with the simplicity of the Galilean fisherman. The follies of superstitions and of the worship of the saints are also made to appear ludicrous and preposterous. "But what shall I say," asks Erasmus, "of the people who so happily fool themselves with forged pardons for sins?" These fools are deluded into thinking they can buy not only all the blessings and pleasures of this life, but heaven hereafter, he suggests, and for the sake of filthy lucre, the priests encourage them in their error.

Among Erasmus' contemporaries, *The Praise of Folly* was greeted with pleasure and praise from some quarters, with angry protest from others. The immense popularity of the work is attested to by the publication of forty-three editions during the author's lifetime.

To expose current church corruption and to censure the most powerful entrenched organization of his era required courage of a high order on Erasmus' part. His attacks were subtle and oblique, but nevertheless extremely effective. Stefan Zweig, for example, points out: "In *Praise of Folly* was, beneath its carnival mask, one of the most dangerous books of its day, and that which appears to us as a witty firework is in reality a bomb whose explosion opened the road to the German Reformation."

3. VISION OF NEVER–NEVER LAND

Sir Thomas More's *Utopia*

1516

Sir Thomas More is reputed to have written his *Utopia* partly as an imaginative literary fantasy, partly as a joke, and partly as an indictment of the evils of the time. The work itself supports this theory, for it is rich in imagination, full of humor, and eloquent in its scathing attack on contemporary social abuses.

England in the reign of Henry VIII, when *Utopia* was written, was the reverse of "merrie." Wool being in high demand, the rich and noble had turned agricultural land into pastures, dispossessing the tenant farmers, and soldiers returning from foreign wars were discharged into idleness and poverty. The historian, John Brewer, comments that there were:

> no poorhouses, no hospitals, though the sweating sickness raged through the land, but the poor left to perish as paupers by the side of the ditches, filling the air with fever and pestilence; houses never swept or ventilated, choked by rotten thatch above and unchanged rushes within, streets reeking with offal and filthy puddles, no adequate supply of water for cleanliness or health, penal laws stringently enforced, more stringently as the crime grew greater . . . justice proud of its executions, and wondering that theft multiplied faster than the gibbet.

This was the backdrop against which More composed *Utopia* (Greek for *Nowhere*). Monarchs of the era were absolute dictators, corrupt and oppressive; in international relations, deceit and trickery were the approved devices of diplomacy; favoritism and injustice prevailed on every side. The contrast between Christian England and More's pagan paradise of Utopia was striking.

More's book was the first of its kind in modern times, but by no means the last. Other famous ideal societies have included those described in *The City of the Sun* (1623) by the Italian monk, Tommaso Campanella, inspired, like More, by Plato's *Republic; The New Atlantis* (1627) by Francis Bacon, which pictured a society run by scientists; and *Oceana* (1656) by James Harrington, which argued for an aristocratic society ruled by intellectuals and landowners.

Utopia originally appeared in Latin and was not translated into English until 1551, sixteen years after More's death. The work is divided into two sections: the first describes the vile conditions of the age and points out the economic and social causes underlying the deplorable state of English life, while the second describes the ideal state know as Utopia.

To tell his story, More uses a simple literary device evidently borrowed from Plato's dialogues. The author, a traveling diplomat, meets in Antwerp Peter Giles, a conservative Dutch citizen, and Raphael Hithlodaye (Greek for *talker of nonsense*), a sailor who had accompanied Americus Vespucius on one of his four voyages. *Utopia* reports the trio's conversation. During his travels, the sailor had accidentally found the mythical island of Amaurote (Utopia), had lived there for five years, and was returning home with news of the perfect state. Highly unfavorable comparisons are drawn by the narrator between the inhabitants of this blessed isle and the people of England.

Pure communism of goods reigns in Utopia, where all possess equal portions of wealth. The whole island is one family or household, divided into various units. The basic units are families of relatives, with a minimum of ten and a maximum of sixteen children under the age of fourteen. Groups of thirty families are ruled by Philarches, whose principal duty is to see that no one is idle. A Chief Philarche heads ten Philarches and their three hundred families, and a Prince is chosen by the Philarches. The people live in fifty-four districts, each composed of an agricultural area surrounding a town. Streets are of equal width, lined with identically constructed houses, each having an attached garden plot.

Agriculture, in which every citizen is expected to be proficient, is the most highly respected occupation among the Utopians. In addition, all citizens learn trades or crafts. No unemployment exists, for every person must work at a useful and needed task during an apportioned six-hour working day.

Laws in Utopia are few, "for such is their constitution the people do not need many." Such laws as are necessary are clearly drawn and easily understood. "For they think it an unreasonable thing to oblige men to obey a body of laws that are both of such a bulk and so dark as not to be read and understood by every one of the subjects." Further, "they have no lawyers among them, for they consider them as a sort of people whose profession it is to disguise matters and wrest the laws."

Punishment in Utopia is regarded as a means of reclaiming criminals, rather than as vengeance upon them. Only the hopelessly irreconcilable are put to death; for others, compulsory labor is the common method of punishment. A major incentive to crime is removed by the abolition of private property: "All things are held in common."

More's views on religious tolerance, predating the Reformation, are astonishingly liberal. There is complete freedom of religious belief and practice in Utopia, even atheists being tolerated: "Let us endure them in this world, and leave their punishment to the judgement of God in the next." The author injects a humorous aside by observing that the priests of Utopia are expected to be "of exceeding holiness, and therefore they are very few in number."

War is abhorred by the Utopians. They recognize only three justifications for declaring war: the defense of their own country, the defense of friendly neighbors, and the delivery of oppressed people anywhere from the yoke and bondage of tyranny. If war is necessary, the Utopians hire mercenaries to do the fighting—savages from the wild woods and high mountains—a reference to the Swiss mercenary soldiers of More's time.

A multitude of other social reforms have been successfully inaugurated in Utopia. Cosmetics are banned; dress for men and women is standardized; the hopelessly ill are encouraged to commit suicide; there is provision for mutual physical inspection by men and women contemplating matrimony (to discover concealed defects); divorce is legal, though divorced persons cannot remarry; and money in the form of gold and silver no longer circulates, since its original purpose is invalid. The Utopians' contempt for gold is so great that they use it for chamber pots and garbage cans.

In their leisure time, the Utopians improve their intellects by a continuous program of education for children and adults. "Of all pleasures they esteem those to be most valuable that lie in the mind." Numerous social centers or community halls are provided, where the people engage in music, conversation, and wholesome games and listen to lectures. All forms of gambling are illegal.

One commentator has suggested that "for ordinary mortals there was a decidedly dull side to More's ideal state." Other critics have objected to the extreme degree of regimentation that the Utopians are forced to endure. Little real freedom exists. For example, if "any man goes out of the city to which he belongs, without leave, and is found rambling without passport, he is severely treated, he is punished as a fugitive, and sent home disgracefully; and if he falls again into the like fault, is condemned to slavery."

Such passages led Robert Hamilton, in an article in the *Hibbert Journal,* to remark of *Utopia:* "Many other things make us think of modern Russia—the drabness of clothing, the use of women in labour and in war, the need for permission to visit another city, the labour camps for prisoners of war, the preference for practical thought rather than metaphysics, and the hedonistic trend of the morals." Incidentally, it is reported that *Utopia* has been adopted as a textbook in Soviet Russia.

In Mary Bradford Whiting's opinion, writing in the *Contemporary Review,* "It is the modernity of More's views that impresses itself upon the reader to-day: town-planning, ventilation, cleanliness, care of the sick, education of the young, religious toleration, provision for old age, reformatory punishment, shortened hours of labour— all the improvements that are slowly and painfully being effected are set forth in his pages."

4. CHURCH VS. STATE

Martin Luther's An den Christlichen Adel Deutscher Nation (An Address to the Christian Nobility of the German Nation) 1520

Though the German Reformation under Martin Luther's inspiration is commonly treated as a tremendous religious upheaval, its political and social manifestations and implications were scarcely less revolutionary. Of all Luther's voluminous writings, the document most influential in the movement for social reform was his *An Address to the Christian Nobility of the German Nation.* Frantz Funck-Brentano, a Luther biographer, states that the *Address* "is, of all Luther's theological publications, the one that has best stood the test of time, the only one possibly that is still read."

The *Address* was written by Luther after his realization that the breach between him and the papal church was complete and likely to be permanent. He wrote as a patriotic German rather than as a churchman or theologian. The entire work breathes anger and sorrow at the tyranny and greed of the pope, the cardinals, and the Roman bureaucracy. Since direct appeals and protests had been in vain, Luther concluded that the time had come to turn to temporal authorities—to Charles V, newly elected German emperor, and the princes and nobility—to urge them to undertake the religious, ethical, social, and economic reformation of Germany. The *Address* is an indictment of the whole papal system, expressed in the most outspoken terms, arraigning Rome for grave abuses and offering proposals for their removal. Luther apparently felt that he needed to justify the violence of his attack:

We wish to fight the Turk, but let us begin by those among our foes who are doing us most harm. With good reason do we hang robbers and cut off the heads of brigands; then why leave at liberty the worst robber and brigand [Leo X] that has ever appeared on earth or ever will appear?

Luther began his frontal assault by making an attempt to demolish what he described as the three walls of defense built up by Rome. The first was the claim that spiritual power is above the temporal, refuted, according to Luther, by the doctrine of the priesthood of all believers. The second wall was the claim that the pope alone is qualified to interpret Scripture, an assertion met by Luther with the argument that the lay mind is fully capable of understanding the mind of Christ. Finally, the third wall was the declaration by Rome that only the pope could call a council, to which Luther answered that in an emergency the civil powers possess the same right and duty.

Church corruption and the pomp and splendor of the Roman court were vigorously condemned by Luther. He made highly unfavorable comparisons between Christ and the pope: Christ traveled on foot, while the pope parades with imperial pageantry, riding in a palanquin with a retinue of three or four thousand mule drivers; Christ washed the disciples' feet, but the pope has his feet kissed. Luther was particularly indignant at the numerous devices by which Rome had enriched itself at the expense of Germany, among them the traffic in indulgences for the remission of punishment for sin, the sale of certificates of confession and of "butter dispensations" (permission to eat butter during Lent), the creation of cardinals solely to hold and to exploit bishoprics, and papal months and golden years (devices for exacting special funds for church officials), improperly claimed for papal followers. The "drunken Germans," as they were known in Rome, were constantly being despoiled, said Luther, by such abuses of the church's function.

Drastic remedies are proposed in the *Address* for the evil practices denounced by Luther. The temporal possessions of the church should be abandoned in order that the pope might devote himself solely to spiritual affairs. The jurisdiction of the pope, bishops, and other church officials must be eliminated in all secular affairs. The church's income should be reduced by banning annates (a year's revenue which every bishop or abbot on being enthroned was obliged to pay to Rome), fees, indulgences, golden years, crusading taxes, reservations, commendations, expectations, and similar contrivances which had developed and been in effect since the late Middle Ages to enrich the papal coffers. The college of cardinals should be reduced in number to no more than twelve members. The German clergy would have a German leader at its head, with litigation in church courts involving Germans to be tried in Germany under a German primate—looking toward the creation of a national church.

Two highly controversial recommendations made by Luther involved lower levels of ecclesiastical organization: the abolition of celibacy and the transfer to congregations of the right to elect pastors. The clergy should be permitted to marry, he maintained, because they need housekeepers, and to place men and women together in this fashion and not to expect them to yield to temptation "is as though one were to put fire and straw together and command that it shall neither smoke nor burn." Minor proposals added by Luther called for a reduction in the number of church festivals, a curb on pilgrimages, and prohibition of the practice of begging for alms.

Luther's ambitions for reform were by no means limited to the church. In the *Address* he demands, for example, a thoroughgoing revision of the system of caring for the poor. Also greatly in need of overhauling, he believes, are the universities, especially their slavish adherence to the "blind heathen master" Aristotle; lectures on Aristotelian logic, rhetoric, and poetics would continue, but the study of classical Greek physics and metaphysics should be banished. In the law faculty the study of the Canon should be abolished, and in the theological faculty the Holy Scriptures should replace the *Sentences* of Peter Lombard, principal text of the time.

In the secular realm, too, Luther enumerates other reforms close to his heart. The *Address* asks for strict laws against luxury in clothing, against excessive eating and drinking, against the spice trade, which was taking much money out of the country, and against the usurious lending of money. Finally, Luther demands the suppression of the common brothels, houses then maintained by the towns with public funds.

From the point of view of political science, the major significance of Luther, and of the Reformation which he led, was the emancipation of the state from clerical control. Before Luther, the state was universally regarded as subordinate to the church. Any state law in conflict with canon or church law was held invalid. Furthermore, state magistrates were considered inferior to the ecclesiastical hierarchy and subject to their commands. The revolt which Luther began on grounds of religious dogma and practices almost immediately began to take on political and social overtones. The Reformation removed Germany from the dominant influence of the Catholic church, liberated the secular German princes from the financial burdens imposed by Rome and gave them the wealth of the church with which to strengthen their regimes, and ultimately resulted in the civil regulation of religion and education. Thus was a long step taken toward complete separation of church and state, occurring in later times in many nations of the world.

Another consequence of the new doctrines is pointed out by Heinrich Boehmer in his *Road to Reformation*. In medieval times, religion was a force unifying all culture, but, Boehmer states, "Wherever Luther's ideas penetrated, this unity of culture, which continued only because of the commanding authority of the church, began to totter. Religion, philosophy, science, and art now went their own several ways."

5. THE REALITIES OF POLITICS

Niccolò Machiavelli's *Il Principe* (The Prince)

1532

For more than four centuries, Niccolò Machiavelli's *The Prince* has been recognized as the foremost exposition of the realistic view of political theory. So much observation on the facts of political life, it has been remarked, has never been compressed in so small a package by anyone else. Virtually every tyrannical ruler and dictator since the mid sixteenth century has received inspiration from Machiavelli's masterpiece. The term "Machiavellian" is, in the popular mind, synonymous with devious and immoral practices in government.

Machiavelli learned his lessons in politics firsthand as a minor official in Renaissance Florence. For eighteen years, he served as a Florentine state secretary and ambassador. The high point of his career came when he was sent as envoy to Cesare Borgia, whose personality fascinated Machiavelli. Never before had he witnessed such an extraordinary combination of political audacity, prudence, cruelty, deceit, firmness and flexibility as that possessed by Cesare. Here was the ideal political character, Machiavelli was convinced, to undertake the stupendous task of creating a united Italy.

Certainly Italy's condition in Machiavelli's lifetime was tragic enough to make any patriot weep. The politics of the time were extraordinarily corrupt. Diplomatic and occasionally military conflicts were chronic among the Italian city-states—Florence, Venice, Pisa, Milan, and Genoa—and internal weaknesses invited recurring foreign invasion. The Church, fully as concerned with maintaining its temporal as its spiritual power was at the most degraded period of its history.

In one of the frequent governmental upheavals, Machiavelli lost his official position and was banished to his small country estate. Thereafter, he devoted his remaining years to recording what he had observed about the political facts of life. One of the results was *The Prince,* the prime purpose of which was to illustrate ways by which a strong man might rescue the Italian people from their desperate situation. No one except a ruthless leader, capable of imposing his authority on the quarreling Italian states, could, in Machiavelli's view, succeed in the formation of a single nation which would be capable of defending itself and of driving the hated foreigners from Italy's sacred soil. *The Prince* presents Machiavelli's conception of the kind of leader required and the tactics such a man would have to employ to gain his ends.

Machiavelli believed that politics have only one object: success. The means by which success is attained are immaterial. The essential argument of *The Prince* is that the welfare of the state justifies any course of action. In political matters necessity overrules ethics, and, consequently, moral standards in public life must be different from those assumed to exist in private life. The Machiavellian doctrine holds that fair dealing may be too costly a luxury for a ruler, who, for the sale of expediency, might have to commit deceitful and violent acts that would be considered intolerable and probably criminal in private transactions. Machiavelli taught, in effect, that the state should have nothing to do with morality. Politics and ethics should be separated from each other.

In offering his series of instructions to princes or other rulers on how to win and to hold power, Machiavelli considered "How Provinces Are To Be Governed." Three methods are suggested by which a state accustomed "to live under its own laws and in freedom . . .

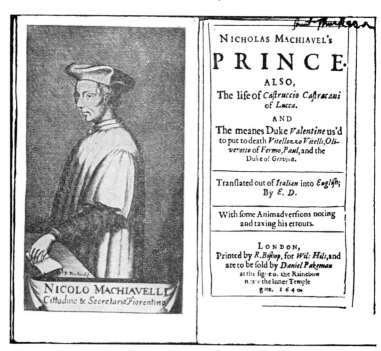

NICOLO MACHIAVELLI
Cittadino & Secretario Fiorentino

NICHOLAS MACHIAVEL's

PRINCE.

ALSO,

The life of *Caftruccio Caftracani*
of *Lucca*.

AND

The meanes Duke *Valentine* us'd
to put to death *Vitellozzo Vitelli,Oli-
verotto* of *Fermo,Paul,* and the
Duke of *Grauina*.

Tranflated out of *Italian* into *English*;
By *E. D.*

With fome Animadverfions noting
and taxing his errours.

LONDON,
Printed by *R.Biſhop,* for *Wil: Hils,*and
are to be fold by *Daniel Pakeman*
at the figure o. the Rainebow
near the Inner Temple
gate. 1 6 4 o.

may be held. The first is to destroy it; the second to go and reside
there in person; the third, to suffer it to live on under its own laws,
subjecting it to tribute, and entrusting its government to a few of
the inhabitants who will keep the rest your friends." Of these methods, the first two are recommended as safest. It is also advised that
any surviving members of the conquered prince's line be "extin-
guished," to make certain that dissident elements will have no natural leader around whom to rally.

Glorifying the personality and career of Cesare Borgia as the ideal
of a strong leader, Machiavelli comments:

> He who considers it necessary to secure himself in his new princi-
> pality, to win friends, to overcome either by force or fraud, to make
> himself beloved and feared by the people, to be followed and revered
> by the soldiers, to exterminate those who had power or reason to hurt
> him, to change the old order of things for new, to be severe and
> gracious, magnanimous and liberal, to destroy a disloyal soldiery, and
> to create new, to maintain friendships with kings and princes in such
> a way that they must help him with zeal and offend with caution,
> cannot find a more lively example than the actions of this man.

A usurper who has seized power in a state "should make haste to inflict what injuries he must, at a stroke, that he may not have to renew them daily. . . . Benefits should be conferred little by little, so that they may be more fully enjoyed." The fear of punishment is, of course, a weapon to be used by a sovereign to control his people, "but a prince who is a man of courage and is able to command, who knows how to preserve order in his state, need never regret having founded his security on the affection of the people." If cruelty is necessary to preserve order, "a few signal examples will in the end be more merciful than too great leniency which permits things to take their course and so to result in rapine and bloodshed." Further, if a choice must be made, "it is far safer to be feared than loved."

The Prince's most notorious chapter is entitled "How Princes Should Keep Faith." Characteristic passages are often cited:

> A prudent prince neither can nor ought to keep his word when to keep it is hurtful to him and if the causes which led him to pledge it are removed. If all men were good, this would not be good advice, but since they are dishonest and do not keep faith with you, you, in return, need not keep faith with them; and no prince was ever at a loss for plausible reasons to cloak a breach of faith. . . . It is well to seem merciful, faithful, humane, religious, and also to be so, but . . . were it needful not to be so, you should be able and know how to change to the contrary. . . . Everyone sees what you seem, but few know what you are.

The Prince ends with an impassioned "Exhortation to Liberate Italy." Unfortunately, over three and a half centuries were to elapse before Machiavelli's dream of a united Italy, free of foreign occupation and domination, was to be realized. Five years after Machiavelli's death, publication of *The Prince* was approved by Pope Clement VII, and numerous editions were issued. Then a storm began to gather. The Council of Trent ordered the works of Machiavelli destroyed, and he was denounced by Catholics and Protestants alike.

Not until the nineteenth century did Machiavelli's reputation win some measure of exoneration and vindication. Revolutionary movements in America, France, Germany, and elsewhere caused an irresistible trend toward secularization in government and separation of church from state. But it was primarily to the Italian people that Machiavelli directed his message, and from him the national patriots of Italy have drawn inspiration for over four centuries. Count Cavour, who led the Italian crusade for freedom in the nineteenth century, is known to have followed closely the Machiavellian precepts in accomplishing his mission. Far less laudable use of Machiavelli's doctrines, however, was made by Louis XIV, Frederick the Great, Napoleon Bonaparte, Bismarck, Benito Mussolini, and Adolf Hitler, all of whom were his avid readers.

It is perhaps an understatement to remark that no writer previous to Karl Marx has had as revolutionary an impact on political thought as has Machiavelli. He has been described appropriately as "The Founder of the Science of Politics." To this day his principles of national sovereignty and "might makes right" have been reflected in the conduct of political affairs within and among nations.

6. MASTER THEOLOGIAN

John Calvin's *Institutio Religionis Christianae* (Institutes of the Christian Religion)

1536

What Newton's *Principia* is to science and Kant's *Kritik* is to philosophy, John Calvin's *Institutes* is to theology—a work comparable in scope to Thomas Aquinas' earlier *Summa Theologiae*. One commentator has asserted that "it would be impossible to make a list of the twenty books which have most influenced the world without including the *Institutes*." More clearly than any other book that came out of the Reformation, it reflects the thought of the entire Protestant movement.

Originally, Calvin had planned the *Institutes* as an elementary manual of doctrine. A fresh outbreak of persecution in France led him instead to write a work that would serve as a vindication of his wronged coreligionists there. The famous Introduction, addressed "to His Most Christian Majesty Francis, King of the French," warns against the false accusations that were being spread abroad concerning Protestants and severely condemns their imprisonments and subsequent tortures and burnings by the French magistrates.

The first edition of the *Institutes*, appearing in print when Calvin was only twenty-six years of age, was a small book of six chapters.

Successive editions produced in Calvin's lifetime culminated in the 1559 edition, containing eighty chapters—the completed masterpiece of a great theologian.

Theology proper is outside the scope of the present work, but the profound influence of Calvinism on subsequent developments in political science and economics can best be interpreted in terms of Calvin's own tenets. The three essential features of his doctrine were: (1) the absolute sovereignty of God; (2) the absolute helplessness and the total depravity of man; (3) the salvation of the elect. The vast majority of men, by nature evil, are destined to be eternally damned; only the elect, predestined by God to be saved, reach heaven. No individual can know whether he is of the chosen few except through an inward sign from God. He should be constantly motivated by moral righteousness in the hope of eternal glory and happiness. One who leads a life of sin demonstrates to the world that he belongs to the damned.

According to Calvin's dogma of predestination, God has created a natural order in the world. This in turn means that people have natural rights and are governed and must be obedient to natural law, the foundation of all legal and moral relations between men.

Calvin's views on the relation of church and state are of basic significance. His position, according to some critics, is that the church should dominate the state and control the lives of its members. Support for this charge was furnished by the theocratic form of government which Calvin was instrumental in establishing over Geneva, where the civil government was subordinated to the ecclesiastical. In his formal doctrine, however, Calvin held that the church and state are co-ordinate institutions, each divinely authorized and each possessing certain inalienable rights.

Broadly speaking, as Calvin defined their respective spheres, the church is concerned with the spiritual and eternal interests of man, while the state is responsible for the care of his material and temporal needs. "He who knows how to distinguish between the body and the soul, between the present and transitory life and the future eternal one," states Calvin, "will find no difficulty in understanding that the spiritual kingdom of Christ and civil government are things very different and remote from one another."

It should never be forgotten, however, Calvin points out, that the supreme purpose of every institution can be nothing except the glory of God. Therefore, both civil and ecclesiastical authority are designed to promote the same end. Calvin firmly believed that it is the duty of government to enforce religious conformity. The concept of religious tolerance is completely alien to his philosophy; and the extreme to which he was willing to go was shown by the infamous case of Servetus, burned at the stake for attacking the doctrine of the Trinity.

Clearly connected with Calvin's predestination theology is his theory of how the subjects of a corrupt government should behave. Tyrants are raised up to their offices by the will of God, Calvin declares, in the same manner as are benevolent governors. While he holds sovereign power, the most iniquitous ruler "ought to be regarded with the same reverence and esteem which they would show to the best of kings." Such evils must be accepted as divine chastisements for sin. The rights of the people as a fundamental truth appear to carry no weight with Calvin. As the English historian W. R. Matthews comments, "We shall search his writings in vain for any recognition of the principle of democracy or any but contemptuous references to the mass of citizens."

Under one condition only, according to Calvin, is there justification for resistance to an established government—namely, if the civil government attempts to exercise authority in things pertaining to God. "We ought to obey God rather than men," if, for example, the governor orders us to join in superstitious worship or otherwise trespasses upon the religious domain. "If they [the rulers] command anything against Him, let us pay not the least regard to it, nor be moved by all the dignity which they possess as magistrates—a dignity to which no injury is done when it is subordinated to the special and truly supreme power of God."

Calvin claims to attach no particular importance to the forms of government, holding that monarchy, aristocracy, and democracy are equally approved by God. Perhaps because of the persecution of his coreligionists in France and England, however, he distrusted monarchy and considered it inimical to the divine sovereignty. His sympathies were with the type of aristocratic government then in control of Geneva. "I readily acknowledge," remarks Calvin, "that no kind of government is more happy than this where liberty is regulated with becoming moderation, and properly established on a durable basis."

Despite the fact that Calvin's teaching was almost entirely on the side of established authority, Calvinism in practice has been an active and radical force, designed to reconstruct church and state, to penetrate with the influence of religion every phase of life and society, and, unintentionally, to provide a powerful impulse toward freedom and democracy. Ironically, in view of Calvin's own conservative leanings, Calvinism in Scotland, Holland, England, and later in America became a liberating political influence. Acting upon Calvin's admonition to obey God instead of men, rather than upon his slavish theory of the duty of submission, Calvinists concluded that saints should rule the earth and that ungodly rulers should be overthrown. American civilization and religious life were directly affected through the New England Puritans and the Scotch Presbyterians, who interpreted Calvin's doctrine of obedience to God's will as complete justification for resistance to earthly tyrants.

Economic historians give major credit to Calvin and his followers for creating the conditions that made possible the rise of modern capitalism. Calvin dignified ordinary economic activities by referring to them as "callings," as tasks set directly by God. Constructive labor was for the glory of God and the general good, and the economic virtues of thrift and industry were identified with moral virtues. Further, Calvin saw that credit and capital were indispensable to society. The profits of trade and finance, therefore, were placed upon the same level of respectability as the earnings of the laborer. Thus, the pursuit of riches came to be regarded as the ally of religion (providing wealth was not misused for self-indulgence), and its consequence, worldly success, was soon recognized as a token of grace.

7. SUN–CENTERED UNIVERSE

Nicolaus Copernicus' *De Revolutionibus Orbium Coelestium* (Concerning the Revolutions of the Heavenly Spheres)

1543

For more than fourteen centuries a system devised by Claudius Ptolemy, second-century Egyptian astronomer, was accepted as the true conception of the universe. Ptolemy held that the world is a fixed and immovable sphere, situated at the center of the universe, about which all celestial bodies, including the sun and the fixed stars, revolve.

The Ptolemaic structure remained intact until the coming of the great era of intellectual awakening in Europe, the Renaissance. Its destruction was the work of a Polish astronomer and churchman, Nicolaus Copernicus. Doubtful of the Ptolemaic conception, Copernicus (perhaps inspired by reading Pythagoras, Aristarchus, and other early Greek astronomers) started testing a new system for the universe. His investigations were carried on quietly and alone, without help or consultation.

For an observatory, Copernicus used a turret, a protective wall built around the cathedral at Frauenberg. Astronomical instruments available to him were crude and primitive. For example, his work was done nearly a century prior to the invention of the telescope. For measuring purposes, he used a sundial; a triquetrum—a three-sided wooden instrument—which he devised to obtain the altitudes of the stars and planets; and an astrolable, a sphere within vertical and horizontal rings. The climate was unfavorable to astronomical observations; proximity to the Baltic Sea and rivers brought fogs and clouds, and clear days and nights were rare. Nevertheless, on every possible occasion, year after year, Copernicus labored over his calculations.

The revolutionary theory which Copernicus was attempting to prove through his prolonged studies went directly contrary to the time-honored and revered Ptolemaic system. In short, he was attempting to demonstrate that the earth is not stationary but rotates on its axis once daily and travels around the sun once each year. So fantastic was such a concept in the sixteenth century that Copernicus did not dare to announce it until he was convinced his data were irrefutable. Consequently, thirty years elapsed before the Copernican system was revealed to the world.

It is conceivable that Copernicus' masterpiece, on which he had toiled for so many years, might never have reached the printing press and therefore would have been lost to posterity except for the efforts of a young German scholar, George Joachim Rheticus. Hearing of Copernicus and his experiments, Rheticus paid him a lengthy visit and was immensely impressed with the aging astronomer's discoveries. In 1540, at Danzig, Rheticus printed the *Narratio prima* (First Account), the first published statement of Copernicus' world-shaking theories.

Previously, Copernicus had been extremely reluctant to permit publication of his complete work. He was a perfectionist who felt that every observation had to be checked and rechecked. Further-more, it is possible that the potential disapproval of the Church may have deterred him. The Protestant Reformation and the intellectual ferment of the Renaissance were making religious authorities sus-picious of revolutionary theories, especially of any thoughts that might upset orthodox teachings. Finally, however, responding to the urgent pleas of Rheticus and other admirers, Copernicus yield-ed. The manuscript was entrusted to Rheticus to take to Nuremberg for printing. While the book was still in press the author suffered a severe stroke. He died a few hours after the first copy of *De Revolu-tionibus Orbium Coelestium* had been placed in his hands.

Diplomatically, Copernicus dedicated his work to Pope Paul III, stating, in part:

> I hesitated for a long time as to whether I should publish that which I have written to demonstrate the earth's motion, or whether it would not be better to follow the example of the Pythagoreans, who used to hand down the secrets of philosophy to their relatives and friends in oral form. . . . I was almost impelled to put the finished work wholly aside, through the scorn I had reason to anticipate on account of the newness and apparent contrariness to reason of my theory.

De Revolutionibus is divided into six "books" or main sections. In the beginning, Copernicus presents his views of the universe, arguments in favor of the heliocentric or sun-centered theory—in-cluding the idea that the earth, like other planets, revolves around the sun—and a discussion of the seasons. The second section deals with the motions of the celestial bodies, measured mathematically, and closes with a catalog of stars, showing the position of each in the sky. The last four "books" present detailed descriptions of the motions of the earth, the moon, and the other planets. In each in-stance, explanation of the motions is accompanied by a geometrical diagram showing the course followed by the sphere on the basis of Copernicus' calculations.

For Copernicus, the sun was inert and passive, stationary amid revolving planets. Its only functions were to supply light and heat. The universe was strictly limited. Outside the sphere of the stars, as Ptolemy had taught, space ceased to exist. Neither did Copernicus abandon Ptolemy's system of epicycles, reaffirming the ancient as-tronomer's assertion that for each of the orbits there was a different center. These features of the Copernican system were to be cor-rected by later astronomers.

Acceptance of the Copernican theories was slow, both among scientists and the general populace. With a few exceptions, expressions of contemporary opinion were in violent opposition. Martin Luther severely criticized Copernicus, and John Calvin was equally emphatic in his condemnation. Not until 1615, however, was the book placed on the Catholic *Index Librorum Prohibitorum*, and there it remained for over two centuries.

In the light of numerous modifications made by scientists in later centuries, the question may reasonably be asked: Is the Copernican theory true? Undeniably, Copernicus left his system incomplete and inaccurate at various points. His conception of the perfectly circular motion of celestial bodies, of a universe with finite limitations, and of other details does not conform to present-day knowledge. But in its essential feature—the choice of the sun as the center of our planetary system—Copernicus discovered a fundamental truth and provided a foundation for modern scientific astronomy.

Copernicus' place in the history of science is permanently established. His influence on his contemporaries and on all subsequent thought entitles him to a preeminent position. Harold C. Urey, one of the great scientists of our own day, agrees:

> All superlatives fail when describing the work of Nicolaus Copernicus. He broke with a conception of the solar system that had stood for one thousand years, and introduced an entirely new concept of the relation of the planets to the sun. In so doing he initiated the whole modern method of scientific thought, and modified our thinking on all phases of human life.

8. FATHER OF SCIENTIFIC ANATOMY

Andreas Vesalius' *De Humani Corporis Fabrica*
(On the Structure of the Human Body)
1543

It is an amazing coincidence that Nicolaus Copernicus' *De Revolutionibus Orbium Coelestium* (May 25, 1543) preceded by only one week publication of another monumental scientific work, Andreas Vesalius' *De Humani Corporis Fabrica* (June 1, 1543). Scholars agree that, as definitely as such events can be traced, these two books represent the end of the medieval era and the birth of modern science. A striking difference may be noted, however, between the ages of the authors: Copernicus was seventy and Vesalius only twenty-eight when their books appeared.

Vesalius came from a Belgian family that had produced five generations of physicians, and he was determined from the outset to follow in their footsteps. His specific interest in anatomy began early. As a boy, he dissected hundreds of small animals—moles, toads, rats, pigs, cats, dogs, and monkeys—fascinated by their physical characteristics. After a preliminary education at Louvain, he chose to go to Paris to study anatomy. The chief attraction there appears to have been a renowned teacher, Jacobus Sylvius. But Vesalius was destined to be bitterly disappointed in Sylvius' lectures and demonstrations.

The teaching of anatomy and the sciences in general was, at the time, highly formalized, a practice handed down from the Middle Ages. The professor of anatomy sat on a raised platform, high above the class, reading appropriately sanctioned passages from Galen, a second-century Greek physician. At his feet was a body, usually of an animal, and beside it a barber-surgeon, who dissected the specimen in crude fashion and pointed out the parts described by the physician.

In the Preface to his celebrated book, Vesalius referred contemptuously to "the detestable procedure now in vogue, that one man should carry out the dissection of the body, and another give the description of the parts." He continued:

> These latter are perched up aloft in a pulpit like jackdaws, and with a notable air of disdain they drone out information about facts they have never approached at first hand, but which they merely commit to memory from the books of others, or of which they have descriptions before their eyes; the former are so ignorant of languages that they are unable to explain their dissections to the onlookers and botch what ought to be exhibited in accordance with the instruction of the physician, who never applies his hand to the dissection, and contemptuously steers the ship out of the manual. Thus everything is wrongly taught, days are wasted in absurd questions, and in the confusion less is offered to the onlooker than a butcher in his stall could teach a doctor.

During the medieval era and until well into the sixteenth century Galen's writings were read with almost idolatrous reverence. For fourteen centuries his treatise on the organization of the human body was the accepted text for the entire medical world. Galen was the final authority in everything relating to anatomy, physiology, diagnosis, therapy, and medical theory. To doubt him might well lead to death for heresy. Scant attention was paid to the work of critics, such as Leonardo da Vinci (1452–1519), whose remarkable anatomical dissections and drawings disproved some of Galen's conclusions. In dissections, if the specimen differed in any particular from Galen's descriptions, the explanation was that the human body had changed since the master's time.

Dissatisfied with the type of instruction he had encountered in Paris, Vesalius concluded that anatomy could be learned only through first-hand dissection of human bodies. Cadavers, however, were extremely difficult to come by. His search for material led him, at great personal risk, to undertake "body-snatching" expeditions. On one occasion, he stole a corpse from the gallows outside the Louvain city walls, the body being that of a criminal who had been left hanging as a warning to other malefactors.

After Paris and a period in Venice, Vesalius was appointed Professor of Surgery and Anatomy at Padua. There he lectured to overflowing classes of students, personally performing all dissections, and unhesitatingly corrected Galen when his own observations showed Galen in error. Meanwhile, work continued on his great anatomical treatise, conceived by Vesalius several years earlier.

By late summer of 1542, Vesalius had ready the text and illustrations for *De Humani Corporis Fabrica*, "On the Structure of the Human Body." The magnificent drawings are believed to have been done under Vesalius' direction by Jan Stephan van Calcar, a pupil of Titian. The *Fabrica*, as one commentator wrote, "is more than a milestone in the history of medicine; it is a great work of creative art." The woodcuts combine scientific exactness and artistic beauty, while the printing is a superb example of the typography of Oporinus of Basel, the Swiss city where the book was produced.

The subject matter in the *Fabrica* was arranged in the same order of topics as Vesalius' lectures: the bones, the muscles, blood vessels and nerves, the internal organs, and the brain. Though Vesalius' anatomical descriptions have great merit, chief interest centers in the plates, frequently described as the finest anatomical drawings ever made. Even the initial letters are works of art, showing cherubs engaged in dissection and other activities. In the frontispiece, Vesalius himself is shown standing beside the dissecting table, on which a

ANDREAE VESALII
BRVXELLENSIS, SCHOLAE
medicorum Patauinæ profefforis, de
Humani corporis fabrica
Libri feptem.

body lies, with a panoramic view of the dissection theatre as a background. Here is depicted the birth of scientific anatomy, man's first clear and accurate knowledge of the foundation stone of medical science and of the whole science of the human body.

The effect of such a radical publication as the *Fabrica* on a superstitious age was explosive. Because it denied concepts of the structure of the human body accepted for centuries and attacked the sacred writings of Galen himself, Vesalius was uncompromisingly condemned by the stubborn forces of tradition. Leading the attack was Sylvius, Vesalius' old teacher at Paris, who spoke of Vesalius as a madman, and added:

> I implore his Majesty the Emperor to punish severely as he deserves, this monster, born and reared in his own home, this most pernicious exemplar of ignorance, ingratitude, arrogance, and impiety: and to suppress him completely lest he poison the rest of Europe with his pestilential breath.

Highly sensitive to criticism, Vesalius resigned his post at Padua, burned all his notebooks, and moved to Spain to become personal physician to Charles V and later to Philip II. His career in anatomical research was finished.

Vesalius was more than the founder of a real science of anatomy; along with Harvey, he was instrumental in establishing sound principles of scientific research—science based on fact rather than tradition. Sir William Osler, the noted Canadian authority, called the *Fabrica* "the greatest medical book ever written—from which modern medicine starts." The famous British physiologist, Sir Michael Foster, concurred:

> This book is the beginning, not only of modern anatomy, but of modern physiology. . . . Upon the publication of the "Fabrica" the pall of authority was once and for ever removed. It ended, for all time, the long reign of fourteen centuries of precedent; it began in a true sense the renaissance of medicine.

9. THE WELL–ORDERED STATE

Jean Bodin's *Les Six Livres de la Republique*
(The Six Books on the State)
1576

Jean Bodin, French lawyer and government official, is rated by a leading political scientist, William M. McGovern, as "the most vigorous and logical of the political theorists of the sixteenth century . . . [who] because of his scholarliness, his clear vision, and his rationality, deserves to be ranked with the great political philosophers of all time." Bodin's *Six Books on the State* is generally accepted as the first truly modern treatise on the science of politics. Though little read now, chiefly because the style is verbose and somewhat ponderous, Bodin continues to be one of the most frequently cited of political theorists.

In the *Six Books,* Bodin attempted to do for modern politics what Aristotle had done nearly two thousand years earlier for classical politics. His aim was to construct a general theory of the state. To this end, he collected much data on the world of his day, gathering his information from the dominions of the Grand Turk to the New World, from accounts of travelers and historians of his own time, and from available diplomatic correspondence, and drawing on his own vast knowledge of the ancient and medieval world. The customs and laws of all peoples, Bodin insisted, had to be studied in order to understand government and history.

Bodin was a political realist, not an ivory tower dweller; he had but little interest in dreaming up an ideal commonwealth. While he hoped to arrive at a universal science of politics, his immediate objective was to aid his native France, then acutely troubled by a series of domestic and foreign crises. National peace and unity were imperiled by the religious conflict that grew out of the Reformation; imminent or actual civil war was for four decades the country's prevailing condition. It was with the hope of restoring France to its former dominance in the hierarchy of nations that Bodin undertook to explore political phenomena and to prepare a statement of policy based upon the principles he discovered.

Among Bodin's outstanding contributions is his idea of the progress of mankind. Classical and medieval thinkers had pictured a mythical golden age in the past, since which time the world and mankind had steadily deteriorated. Bodin, on the other hand—like Condorcet and Emerson later—held that human society is slowly but gradually improving; modern man is superior to his ancestors, and there is no limit to his potential progress.

Another significant addition to political theory is Bodin's idea about the influence of environment upon mankind and its political and social institutions. According to Bodin, mankind, together with its laws and institutions, falls into three main categories which correspond to three climatic zones. The north, cold and dry, produces a mentally stolid but physically vigorous type, leaning toward democratic forms of government; the south, with its hot climate, is populated by intelligent, but lazy and politically passive races, usually governed by some form of despotism; and the central zone, where the climate is temperate, is typified by countries such as France. The people in the last-mentioned zone are especially adapted to legal and political life and favor a monarchical form of government. The environmental theory was revived by Montesquieu in the eighteenth century and by Arnold Toynbee in the twentieth century. In recent years it has influenced the development of the sciences of anthropography and geopolitics.

Bodin's theory of the origin of the state was directly at variance with the concepts held by other political philosophers of his day. Some held that the state was of divine origin, and others believed that it originated in a voluntary social contract between individuals. Bodin asserted that the state originated by force, offering examples from ancient history to show that political organization began when a strong man or group of strong men conquered and established political domination over their neighbors. The theory of the origin of the state by force is now accepted by most social scientists.

Of all Bodin's contributions to political philosophy, his idea of sovereignty is widely regarded as most fundamental. Sovereignty— he was the first to use the word—is defined by Bodin as "the absolute and perpetual power of the state, that is, the greatest power to command." Under Bodin's theory of sovereignty, the state shall have sole ultimate control over all persons and corporations within its territory; and, further, within every state a person or a group of persons shall possess potentially absolute power over the state and its legislative activities.

Bodin distinguished between the government and the state. Forms of government may change, but sovereignty itself is perpetual. Sovereignty exists as long as does the state. Bodin recognized three basic forms of government: monarchy, aristocracy, and democracy, and he has much to say concerning the advantages and disadvantages of each type. Democracies, in his opinion, are the least stable form of commonwealth because the majority of men are ignorant, passionate, and gullible. Aristocracies are also insecure because of constant dissensions between the governed and the governing class and struggles for power within the governing class itself. Bodin's conclusion was that for most countries and most peoples hereditary monarchy is by far the best form of state.

Just as Bodin was partial to the monarchical type of state, he also believed that the patriarchal system is best fitted to preserve the unity of the family. He conceived of a state as an association of families recognizing a sovereign power. The right of property, based on the law of nature, belongs to the family. The relationship of the sovereign to his subjects is similar to that of the patriarch to his family.

While Bodin insisted upon the necessity for absolute sovereignty, he modified this extreme stand with a number of restraints upon excesses in the exercise of sovereign power. For example, though a monarch would not be subject to civil or human law, according to Bodin's doctrines, he is subject to divine and natural laws. Furthermore, the "absolute sovereign" possesses no right to interfere with family life (for example, steal his subjects' womenfolk); "without just cause the sovereign can neither seize nor give away the property of another"; and the right of taxation is limited.

A remarkable feature of Bodin's theory of politics, considering the age, was his insistence upon religious toleration for the preservation of a strong state. Where several religions exist in a state, he contended, any attempt to impose religious conformity will lead to civil war and thus weaken the state. Bodin objected to persecution also, on the ground that it is likely to produce a general skepticism about religion; in his view, any organized system of beliefs is preferable to atheism.

"There are many causes of revolution in the form of the commonwealth," stated Bodin; among those he emphasized the "extreme poverty of the great mass of the people and the excessive wealth of a small handful, or great inequality in the distribution of estates and of honors." Though strongly opposed to the equalization of property, he suggested that through proper legislation a monarch should prevent the growth of unduly large fortunes—advice which, if heeded, might have averted the French Revolution.

William Ebenstein, Professor of Political Science at Princeton University, sums up Bodin's essential thesis as follows:

> Bodin's state is strong but not aggressive; monarchical but not tyrannical. It became the model for the new national state in which the interests of the monarchy were allied with those of the rising merchant and middle classes against church and aristocracy. In this new state the bourgeoisie was willing to accept a strong government under kingly command, provided that it was allowed to make money and enjoy reasonable legal and political security. This alliance was to last over two hundred years, until the French Revolution raised the fundamental issue whether sovereignty should be vested in the king or in the people.

10. DISCOVERER OF MAN

Michel de Montaigne's *Essais*

1580–1595

Michel de Montaigne, who established the essay as a literary form, was a brilliant and complex personality. His leading modern translator, Donald M. Frame, characterizes him as "the first essayist, a skeptic, an acute student of himself and of man, a champion of man-based morality, a vivid and charming stylist. . . ." Montaigne has been described by other critics in such contradictory terms as an atheist, a deist, a Roman Catholic but not a Christian, a radical, an arch-conservative, a Stoic, and an Epicurean. For each of these conclusions a certain amount of justification can be seen in Montaigne's most celebrated work, his *Essays* (1580–1595).

Diverse interpretations of Montaigne's thought are inevitable, because his ideas, written down over a twenty-year period, changed with the passage of time, and he himself was little disturbed by his own inconsistencies and contradictions. Our understanding of Montaigne is aided by these discerning comments from the pen of the eminent French literary critic, Sainte-Beuve:

> With an appearance of making himself out peculiar, of reducing himself to a bundle of odd manias, he has touched each one of us in his

most secret part, and while portraying himself with careless, patient and incessantly repeated strokes, he has cunningly painted the majority of mankind, and all the more successfully as he has the more minutely dissected his single self—'wavering and diverse' as he says. Each one of us finds a morsel of his own property in Montaigne.

In the *Essays*, Montaigne reveals himself more intimately perhaps than any other writer in history, with the possible exceptions of Rousseau and Samuel Pepys. "If the world finds fault with me for speaking too much of myself," he says, "I find fault with the world for not even thinking of itself." There was purpose behind Montaigne's complete self-analysis. As Jean Misrahi, French scholar and literary critic, points out: "He believes that each individual man contains within himself a résumé of the entire human condition, with all its possibilities of wisdom and folly, of virtue and vice. If, then, we examine any one man thoroughly in all his thoughts, emotions and actions, we shall learn a great deal about man in general, his nature and conduct, and be aided thereby in formulating conclusions to guide us in our own lives."

Montaigne's philosophical approach is expressed by his constant question: "What do I know?" In an age when men's beliefs were fixed for them by theological sanction, Montaigne insisted upon objective and skeptical examination. He was impressed by the strange, contradictory customs and ideas reported by explorers of distant lands. He weighed prevailing opinions, customs, creeds, and prejudices—balancing notion against notion, man against man, usage against usage. Believing that all ideas contained elements of truth, Montaigne reviewed the opinions of opposing schools of thought with equal admiration. All knowledge, in his view, is relative, and, since certainties do not exist, tolerance and liberality are essential. Ralph Waldo Emerson, another great essayist, saw Montaigne as the perfect representative of skepticism. But a more accurate evaluation would rate his position as that of an antidogmatist, a firm believer in the spirit of free inquiry and investigation.

Evidence of Montaigne's deep mistrust of dogmatic convictions appears not only in the *Essays* but also in the mottoes which he had inscribed on the rafters of his library: "I take no definite view," "I suspend judgment," "I do not commit myself," "With nothing to choose either way," "To every reason there is as good a counter-reason," "Woe to you that are wise in your own eyes," "Be no wiser than you must so as not to be paralyzed," "It is possible and yet impossible," "It is not more this way than that way, or neither way." Such a code led F. L. Lucas, in his *Studies French and English,* to remark that "The fence seems to Montaigne a pleasanter seat than any armchair. It is as if he felt the Universe capable of anything; and the human mind of nothing, except mares' nests."

A partial explanation of Montaigne's equivocal, yes-and-no attitude, it has been suggested, is that he lived through the worst period of the French religious wars. Witnessing the excesses to which religious bigotry could lead and seeing the horrible spectacle of men killing each other because of religious convictions, Montaigne could not help but review with pessimism the human intellect and its ability to arrive at rational decisions.

Doubtless for the same reason, Montaigne's social and political views had a conservative bent. He was aware that tradition and culture were the most dependable safeguards against barbaric anarchy. In a time of violence and frightful cruelties, he craved peace and prosperity for the French people. Reformers, in his experience, usually combined "supercelestial thoughts and subterranean conduct."

The literary form of a typical Montaigne essay begins with the statement of a simple event or perhaps some thought that struck the author's fancy. Following what modern psychoanalysts would term a free association method, Montaigne then broadens and extends the theme until it has universal significance. The essays, eighty-seven in number, range in length from a couple of pages to more than a hundred. In subject content, they are of infinite variety, covering such themes as these: the affections, idleness, liars, constancy, cowardice, fear, imagination, custom, friendship, moderation, clothes, solitude, drunkenness, conscience, books, cruelty, honesty, repentance, vanity, education, experience, and the classical authors. Montaigne acquaints us with his taste in books, his impressions of men and affairs, his views on education, and his judgment of religious reformers; and he describes, too, matters relating directly to his own person, such as the meats he liked, the wine he drank, his digestion, his hours of sleeping and waking, his marital intimacies and infidelities, the discomforts of his painful malady (kidney stones), his laziness and bad memory. Though some essays deal with man in general, the emphasis is throughout individualistic and self-directed, carrying out the author's prefatory explanation: "Reader, I am myself the subject of this book."

Along with Rabelais, Montaigne laid the foundations which helped to establish French as a literary language. His influence on both French and English literature has been immense. Nearly every great work of French prose reflects the style and method of expression of the *Essays*. Particularly in his debt for this reason are Pascal, La Rochefoucauld, La Bruyère, Rousseau, Montesquieu, Sainte-Beuve, Renan, Anatole France, and Jules Lemaître. Similarly, in English literature, passages from the *Essays* were used in Shakespeare's plays, and Montaigne was quoted by virtually every other notable English writer of the sixteenth and seventeenth centuries. Montaigne did not personally instigate any social revolution, but he was the father of the spirit of inquiry which produced Voltaire and the French Revolution.

Emerson's tribute to Montaigne, his spiritual and literary ancestor, is famous:

> There have been men with deeper insight, but, one would say, never a man with such abundance of thoughts; he is never dull, never insincere, and has the genius to make the reader care for all he cares for. The sincerity and marrow of the man reaches to his sentences. I know not anywhere the book that seems less written. It is the language of conversation transferred to a book. One has the same pleasure in it that we have in listening to the necessary speech of men about their work, when any unusual circumstance gives momentary importance to the dialogue. For blacksmiths and teamsters do not trip in their speech; it is a shower of bullets. Cut Montaigne's words, and they would bleed; they are vascular and alive.

11. CLASSIC OF EXPERIMENTAL SCIENCE

William Gilbert's De Magnete, Magneticisque Corporibus, et De Magno Magnete Tellure (On the Loadstone, Magnetic Bodies, and On the Great Magnet the Earth)

1600

Dr. William Gilbert, personal physician to Queen Elizabeth and James I, has been accorded such laudatory titles as "the father of electricity," "the father of experimental science in England," "the founder of magnetic and electrical sciences," and "the first great man of science in England since Roger Bacon." It is hardly an overstatement to refer to him, as did the German philosopher Kurd Lasswitz, as "the first real physicist and the first trustworthy methodical experimenter," and his *De Magnete* as the first great work of physical science to be published in England.

The intellectual climate of his day was propitious for Gilbert. Fielding H. Garrison, a leading science historian, points out that "the seventeenth century, the age of Shakespeare and Milton, Velasquez and Rembrandt, Bach and Purcell, Cervantes and Molière, Newton and Leibnitz, Bacon and Descartes, Spinoza and Locke, was preeminently a period of intense individualism, intellectual and spiritual." The very first year of the century is made memorable for us by the appearance of Gilbert's epoch-making *De Magnete*.

Medieval superstition still flourished, however, and perhaps nowhere with more damaging effect than in Gilbert's field of interest—magnetism and electricity. Gilbert, an avid reader of books ancient and modern, complained that "the shops of the booksellers are crammed" with scientifically valueless works replete with false ideas handed down from ancient times on alchemy, astrology, and magic.

In the introduction to *De Magnete*, Gilbert reviews some of the innumerable writings on magnetism since the times of Plato and Aristotle, enumerating the manifold errors and exploding the worn-out theories. In particular, Gilbert reviewed the exaggerated fables surrounding the properties of the loadstone and proceeded to destroy the myths through direct and demonstrable scientific data. Prevailing beliefs held that the loadstone's magnetic power, dulled at night, could be restored by a bath in goat's blood; that its power, extending to the area of domesticity, could reconcile husbands to wives and wives to husbands; that if pickled in the salt of a sucking fish the loadstone gained additional power to pick up gold from the deepest wells; and that if rubbed with garlic, or placed where there was a diamond nearby, it could not attract iron. Applying experimental methods to each of these absurd but accepted beliefs, Gilbert proved them to be without foundation.

But he had little hope of converting his opponents. In the Preface to *De Magnete*, he pays his respects to the priggish doctrinaire believers and the anti-intellectuals devoted to their ignorance:

> Why should I submit this noble science and this new philosophy to the judgment of men who have taken oath to follow the opinions of others, to the most senseless corrupters of the arts, to lettered clowns, grammatists, sophists, spouters, and the wrong-headed rabble, to be denounced, torn to tatters, and heaped with contumely! To you alone,

true philosophers, ingenuous minds, who not only in books but in things themselves look for knowledge, have I dedicated these foundations of magnetic science.

The last sentence supplies the key to Gilbert's basic principle: scientific knowledge is valid only if founded on the bases of practical experiment and observation. Idle speculations and theories are worthless unless they are supported by demonstrable evidence. In the modern world, the practice of scientific experimentation has become so commonplace that it is difficult to realize how revolutionary was the concept of experimental evidence in 1600.

De Magnete consists of six sections or "books." In the main body of the volume, Gilbert describes his own experimental work on magnetism. One of the principal pieces of apparatus he used was a large spherical loadstone, which he called a *terrella*—a miniature earth; its magnetic poles were found by using a minute compass needle. Here Gilbert introduced what most historians of science regard as his greatest contribution: his view of the earth itself as one great magnet. He proved that the magnetic nature of the earth accounts for the behavior of the mariner's compass. "There resides, therefore," he says, "a Magnetick force in the earth just as in the terrella." By his theory and experiments on the magnetic nature of the earth Gilbert created the science of terrestrial magnetism.

Through the study of terrestrial magnetism, Gilbert then became a strong advocate—the first in England—of the Copernican system, lending support which required considerable courage during that intolerant era. In the same year *De Magnete* was published, Giordano Bruno was burned at the stake in Italy for promoting Copernicus' theory, and Galileo was shortly to be condemned by the Inquisition. Copies of *De Magnete* reaching Italy were so censored that all mention of the heretical doctrine was effaced.

Most of Gilbert's work is concerned with magnetism, but one section is devoted to the phenomena of electrical attraction. Gilbert was the first scientist to differentiate between electrical and magnetic attraction. Prior to his time, it was thought that only amber could be electrified by friction. Gilbert's experiments revealed that the same phenomena could be observed to take place in more than a score of substances, including glass, sulphur, resin, and such precious stones as the diamond and sapphire, all of which on vigorous rubbing acquired similar properties to those of amber. His proof came with the help of a delicately mounted needle, called a "versorium," now known as an electroscope. Substances showing positive magnetic attraction were classed as "electrics"; those on which the versorium had a negative effect were called "non-electrics"—the equivalents of modern-day conductors and insulators.

De Magnete is well illustrated with ninety woodcuts of diagrams and pictures of loadstones and apparatuses used in Gilbert's experiments. An unusual feature of the text is the use of stars along the margins to indicate the importance of the discoveries described. Twenty-one large stars and nearly two hundred small ones show Gilbert's estimation of the relative value of his experiments.

Also included in the original edition is a glossary of new scientific terms invented by Gilbert, another significant contribution. It was he who introduced the word *electricity* into the language (from the Greek word meaning amber), and the words *axis* and *equator* (of a magnet), *magnetic meridians* (of the earth), and *armature*.

Among Gilbert's warmest contemporary admirers were Kepler and Galileo. No better estimate of his career has been expressed than by Galileo, who, after reading *De Magnete,* wrote:

> I think him worthy of the greatest praise for the many new and true observations which he has made, to the disgrace of so many vain and fabling authors, who write not from their own knowledge only, but repeat everything they hear from the foolish and vulgar, without attempting to satisfy themselves of the same by experiment.

De Magnete demonstrated not merely the value and importance of experiment, but also established magnetism and electricity as sciences, paving the way for further investigations down to the time of Michael Faraday.

12. THE GREAT ENIGMA

William Shakespeare's *Hamlet*

1603

Shakespeare's works have had so profound and pervasive an influence on the modern mind that it would be impossible to discuss here even the broad outlines of his contributions. It has been said that we think and communicate with the language of Shakespeare, and it is certainly true that the cohesive intellectual and cultural bonds among English-speaking peoples owe much to the genius of this master craftsman of poetry and drama. Great men in all the Western nations have acclaimed him as the universal literary artist whose creations have, directly or indirectly, molded the thought patterns, moral values, and human relationships of the modern world.

Shakespeare wrote 37 plays (tragedies, comedies, and histories) as well as magnificent poetry—the superb sonnets called the most perfect specimens of literature in history. *Hamlet,* perhaps the most influential drama of all time, has been chosen to represent his genius.

Hamlet illustrates excellently the most important of Shakespeare's basic contributions to the development of the modern mind: his sharp departures from the emphasis of ancient literature upon Fate and also from the emphasis of medieval literature upon morality, church, and state—authority, faith, and power. Hamlet in *Hamlet* is an individual, depicted in a terrible moral and psychological dilemma, who must, yet feels he cannot, make his own decisions. He is a perfect example of how Shakespeare turned the attention of people toward individual psychology and activity, that is, toward the motives, capacities, and behavior of the individual human being torn by inner conflicts and by outer circumstances. The individual, not the idea or tradition or institution, becomes the center of man's world. This view of the individual is at the root of modern ways of thinking, and nowhere has it been more eloquently set forth than in *Hamlet.*

Among students of literature agreement would be virtually universal in ranking *Hamlet* as the world's greatest play, and its central figure as the most fascinating character in dramatic literature. "It is difficult," André Gide once remarked, "to imagine a text more supersubtle and crafty, more full of ambiguities, snares, and pitfalls than *Hamlet.*" A phrase used by Winston Churchill in another connection fits: "It is a riddle wrapped in a mystery inside an enigma." Since the early seventeenth century, innumerable actors, critics, scholars, philosophers, psychologists, and theologians have attempted to interpret what one writer described as "Hamlet's endless labyrinth of meaning."

Aside from the enigmatic character of Hamlet, Prince of Denmark, perhaps the greatest part ever written for the stage, the play itself is rich theatrical fare, including superb speeches, violent action, royal pageantry, a midnight ghost, a play within a play, a duel, a poisoned cup, and eight tragic deaths.

As the play begins, Hamlet meets the ghost of his royal father on

THE

Tragicall Hiftorie of

HAMLET

Prince of Denmarke

By William Shake-fpeare.

As it hath beene diuerfe times actedby his Highneffe fer-
uants in the Cittie of London : as alfo in the two V-
niuerfities of Cambridge and Oxford, and elfe-where

At London printed for N.L. and Iohn Trundell.
1603.

the battlements of Elsinore Castle. The ghost tells Hamlet that he
was the victim of a "murder most foul," that he was killed by his
brother Claudius, who then usurped the throne and hastily married
Hamlet's widowed mother. Hamlet is commanded by the ghost to
seek revenge, and he swears to obey. But, seized by a fit of melancholy, fearing that the ghost may have been a demon trying to mis

lead him, Hamlet feigns madness, during which he mistreats his sweetheart Ophelia. Brooding and despondent, unsure of his uncle's guilt, and contemplating suicide, Hamlet speaks the most eloquent and moving passage in all literature, beginning:

> To be, or not to be: that is the question:
> Whether 'tis nobler in the mind to suffer
> The slings and arrows of outrageous fortune,
> Or to take arms against a sea of troubles,
> And by opposing end them? To die: to sleep;
> No more; and by a sleep to say we end
> The heart-ache, and the thousand natural shocks
> That flesh is heir to, 'tis a consummation
> Devoutly to be wish'd.

Racked by indecision, forced into action foreign to his nature, Hamlet laments: "The time is out of joint. O cursed spite, that ever I was born to set it right." A visiting troupe of actors presents Hamlet with an opportunity to determine whether Claudius is innocent or guilty. Under Hamlet's direction, the actors give a play in the palace re-enacting the ghost's story of the murder. "The play's the thing," says Hamlet, "wherein I'll catch the conscience of the king." Claudius, watching the play and keenly observed by Hamlet, leaves the play hurriedly, obviously angry, upset, and suspicious—full proof of his guilt. Hamlet follows, but finds the murderer at prayer and is prevented from killing him then by the realization that, were he to do so, the king would go to heaven.

The queen sends for Hamlet and reproves him for offending Claudius. His emotions out of control, Hamlet berates the queen with such scorn and violence that she calls for help. The chancellor, Ophelia's father Polonius, spying on the prince from behind a curtain, answers. Hamlet, mistaking him for Claudius, stabs him to death. Unrepentant, Hamlet continues scathingly to condemn his mother's behavior until the ghost reappears, reminds him that he has failed thus far to avenge his father's murder, and admonishes him, so far as the queen is concerned, to "leave her to heaven."

In an atmosphere of madness, suicide, treachery, and murder the play builds up to its climax. Ophelia, deeply disturbed by her father's death and Hamlet's brutal treatment, goes insane and drowns herself. Her brother, Laertes, tormented by grief for his sister and hatred for Hamlet, conspires with Claudius to challenge him to a fencing match, in which Laertes would kill him with a secretly poisoned sword. For double measure, the king also prepares a poisoned cup for Hamlet. As the duel begins, the queen, ignorant of the plan, toasts her son with the poisoned drink and dies. Laertes wounds Hamlet. There is a scuffle, swords are exchanged, and Hamlet kills Laertes. He then turns and stabs the king. Standing for a moment triumphant, he mutters, "The rest is silence," and dies. His friend Horatio pronounces Hamlet's epitaph, "Now cracks a noble heart. Good night, sweet prince, and flights of angels sing thee to thy rest."

The character of Hamlet himself has intrigued countless commentators. According to some appraisals, Hamlet is a neurotic, a weakling, a hopeless procrastinator, a cynical eccentric, or a brooding introvert. By turns, he has been called weak-willed and headstrong, melancholy and violent, dreamy and brutal, superstitious and philosophical, sensible and mad. Goethe imagined him to be a sensitive plant too tender for this world. Nineteenth-century actors interpreted him as a "philosopher of death, a scholar of the night," whose will was paralyzed and mind in endless debate with itself. That interpretation gains credibility from such lines as these:

> Thus conscience does make cowards of us all;
> And thus the native hue of resolution
> Is sicklied o'er with the pale cast of thought,
> And enterprises of great pith and moment
> With this regard their currents turn awry
> And lose the name of action.

Perhaps the least credible explanation is offered by Ernest Jones, Freud's biographer, who suggested that Hamlet is in part Oedipus, that he has long contemplated parricide and incest and is maddened and paralyzed by the fact that they were commited *for him.*

A noted Shakespearean, George Lyman Kittredge, called the belief that Hamlet was a weak-willed procrastinator "a complete misrepresentation of his mental and moral character." Another critic, Gustav Mueller, points out that "the man who dispatches Polonius and his fellows, the man who immediately seizes the opportunity of the players, the man who jumps at the throat of Laertes in the grave of Ophelia, the fighter who first boards the pirate ship, the cold-blooded and ruthless speaker of daggers, the idol of the people whose terrible strength and popularity the king fears—this man is neither a theorist nor an aesthete. He is a 'man of parts,' a universal man, a courtier in the sense of Castiglione's ideal of a courtier, an allsided man of the world."

When we are confronted by such paradoxical judgments of Hamlet's personality, its infinite complexity becomes apparent. The situation is reminiscent of Walt Whitman's defense: "Do I contradict myself?" asks Whitman, "Very well, then, I contradict myself. I am large, I contain everything." Hardin Craig, another leading Shakespearean, has perhaps come closest to a solution of the mystery when he says that "Hamlet is Everyman. His faults and his troubles, as well as his virtues, are merely those of all men. He is not typically a procrastinator or a pessimist; but his procrastination, his self-distrust, and his bitterness are merely those that attend the living of a human life." Harold Child, Shakespearean editor, is in substantial agreement, remarking that "when the mystery of Hamlet has been solved the mystery of human life will have been solved."

The quality above all else that makes *Hamlet* a work of genius is its incomparable poetry. Like the King James Bible, *Hamlet* has become so much a part of the English language that its lines are quoted by millions of people who have never seen or read the play.

13. PURSUIT OF KNOWLEDGE

Francis Bacon's *Of the Proficience and Advancement of Learning, Divine and Human*

1605

Hardly less controversial than the theory that Sir Francis Bacon wrote the Shakespearean plays is the question of the nature and extent of his contribution, if any, to modern scientific research methods. On one side his defenders, who call him "the Columbus of experimental science," claim that he "did much to usher into the world the present scientific age" and believe, along with Macaulay, that Bacon "moved the intellects which have moved the world." On the opposite side, his attackers voice their unanimity in arguing that "the result reached by Bacon's method is always zero" and that "the overthrow of scholasticism by Bacon was the warfare of the famous knight with windmills." As is usually the case in such debates, there is a measure of truth in both arguments.

Whichever view we adopt, it will be worth noting the judgment of a leading historian of science, Florian Cajori, who asserts: ". . .

one thing is clear, Bacon ranks as the earliest prominent methodolo- gist of scientific inquiry. He represents an effort to proceed beyond the crude and slovenly inductive procedure of a simple enumeration of affirmative observations. Bacon insists that men should mark when they miss as well as when they hit; they should observe many cases—the more the better."

The Baconian doctrines were first set forth in detail in *Of the Proficience and Advancement of Learning, Divine and Human* and developed further in the author's *Novum Organum* (1620). The former was the only philosophical work published by Bacon in a language other than Latin, the universal scholarly language of the day.

Science in Bacon's time was in a rudimentary stage. The fundamental science of dynamics did not exist; in astronomy, despite Copernicus, it was still generally held that the earth is the fixed center of the universe, with the sun and planets revolving about it; the existence of electricity was unknown, not to mention its connection with magnetism; chemistry was to develop little beyond alchemy for another century and a half; and the Aristotelian theory that the earth is composed of four elements—earth, air, fire, and water—prevailed. Man had not yet harnessed nature. The only sources for mechanical energy, for example, were clockwork, water wheels, and windmills; land transport was either on foot or by horse, and rowing and sailing were the only ways to get across water. The population was frequently struck by catastrophic and uncontrollable epidemics of the plague. Since the days of antiquity, Bacon noted, scientific progress had been remarkably slow.

Bacon begins his work by attacking the sterile scholasticism inherited from the Middle Ages. Aristotelian logic served only to foster debates and controversy, while the empirical method led to general conclusions based on limited and emotionally biased experiments. Bacon insists that men ought to "throw aside all thought of philosophy, or at least to expect but little and poor fruit from it, until an approved and careful natural and experimental history be prepared and constructed." The medieval schoolmen and logicians are compared by Bacon to spiders which "bring forth indeed cobwebs of learning, admirable for the fineness of thread and work, but of no substance or profit." For what purpose, he asks, "are these brain-creations and idle displays of power?" Scientific investigation had been continually handicapped because of its entanglement with the philosophical search for final causes. Deploring the fact that there was virtually no practical application of such theory, observation, and experiment as had occurred, Bacon firmly asserts that the right method of scientific research, that is, the inductive method, could give mankind sovereignty over nature. The tendency to make general statements on the basis of preconceived ideas led him to regard "the present method of experiment," mainly in the hands of charlatans and misguided zealots, as "blind and stupid."

The *Advancement of Learning* is divided into two books. In the first Bacon undertakes a defense of knowledge, the pursuit of which is recommended as a vocation suitable for kings and statesmen. Of greater interest to modern readers is the second book. Here Bacon includes all branches of learning within his domain. Reviewing each major field of study, in an effort to reveal the limitations of existing knowledge, he then proceeds to show how men might make further progress. This section contains Bacon's famous classification of the sciences, the value of which was attested by Diderot, the encyclopedist, who wrote in his *Prospectus*:

> If we come out successful from this vast undertaking, we shall owe it mainly to Chancellor Bacon, who sketched the plan of a universal dictionary of sciences and arts at a time when there were not, so to speak, either arts or sciences. This extraordinary genius, when it was impossible to write a history of what men knew, wrote one of what they had to learn.

Learning is divided by Bacon into three categories: history, which corresponds to memory; poetry, which corresponds to imagination; and philosophy, which corresponds to reason. There follow divisions and subdivisions of each branch of knowledge.

Attempting to renovate and reorganize the sciences, Bacon sought for an entirely new system of scientific methodology; the necessity of experiment in determining fundamental phenomena in nature was his philosophical prerequisite. By accumulating a sufficient quantity of observations and facts, the basis for a new philosophy, not founded upon Aristotle or other ancient authorities, could be provided. In place of existing philosophical methods Bacon advocated "inductive" reasoning, a system which progresses from particular and observable facts to broad generalizations, testing each generalization at every step by seeking possible exceptions to it and rejecting or revising the generalization when such exceptions are found.

Bacon, impatient with the metaphysical search for final causes, believed that true knowledge must be materially applicable to practical life so that men might live as commodiously as possible. As he puts it, "men must know that in this theatre of man's life it is reserved only for God and the angels to be lookers-on."

Limitations in Bacon's scientific method have been cited by various critics. The weakness chiefly mentioned is his failure to provide for the use of preliminary hypotheses to be tested against known facts or to be demonstrated by special experiments—a method that has accelerated immensely the development of modern scientific theories. That Bacon neglected to recognize the vast importance of mathematics in the study of natural phenomena is another failure for which opponents seek to inculpate him. Nevertheless, the Baconian principles were predominant in the work of such later scientists as Linnaeus, Cuvier, Agassiz, Darwin, and Alexander von Humboldt. Their application to astronomy, physics, and other sciences making extensive use of mathematics is less noticeable.

Bacon has been criticized severely for his unsympathetic attitude toward such contemporary scientists as Copernicus, Galileo, Kepler, and Harvey. Because he rejected the theory of blood circulation, refused to accept the Copernican theory, and was contemptuous of the microscope and telescope, it has even been argued that Bacon obstructed scientific progress.

One Bacon biographer, Mary Sturt, comments, "It is hard to say what anyone ever learnt direct from Bacon. He was no scientist, he made no great discoveries, he lived and died an amateur, and yet his general ideas accord so exactly with the course that history has taken, that every laboratory might be decorated with his texts and every international society turn to him for a motto."

14. IDEALIST VS. REALIST

Miguel de Cervantes Saavedra's *Don Quixote de la Mancha*

1605–1615

In seventeenth-century Spain, *Don Quixote de la Mancha,* one of the world's great novels, was written by Miguel de Cervantes—a man whose biography is mainly a threading together of few facts and much conjecture. The book is a comic masterpiece, a demonstration of the common root of tears and laughter—two sides of the same coin. *Don Quixote's* immense popularity in all countries and all languages since its first appearance can be attributed in large measure to its uniquely tragicomic quality.

Cervantes' exact motives in writing his celebrated novel have been a matter of considerable debate among literary historians. His avowed object was to satirize the picaresque novel then in vogue in Spain. Critics agree that Cervantes used fiction to satirize scathingly contemporary Spanish culture (literature in particular), manners, and society. As his novel developed, the author progressed from the simple satire that may have been his intended object to the creation of a veritable microcosm—a work designed to show the frustration and defeat of lofty ideals in a materialistic world. Perhaps Cervantes was not even aware of the range and scope of the novel as a whole; this fact, however, only serves to demonstrate that there is no one right critical interpretation.

The theme of *Don Quixote* is familiar to millions of readers. A Spanish squire, Alonso Quijana ("Lantern Jaws"), "tall, lean, lanky, with cheeks that appeared to be kissing each other on the inside of his mouth, and a neck half a yard long and uncommonly brown," has become mentally deranged from reading so many novels about the age of chivalry, with their wealth of enchantments, battles, challenges, wooings, and agonies. He believes that he is the last knight left in Christendom, charged with leaving his village on a sacred quest to right wrongs, rescue maidens, and slay giants. He renames himself Don Quixote and issues forth in rusty armor, on a gaunt nag Rocinante ("formerly a hack"), which he thinks is a fiery charger. Everything the knight-errant sees takes on a romantic and unrealistic appearance: a local middle-aged farmer, Sancho Panza, is enlisted as his squire; a husky farm lass, Aldonza Lorenzo, renamed Dulcinea del Toboso, becomes in his mind a beauteous damsel; a country inn appears as a castle; a flock of sheep is a Saracen host.

Setting out in search of adventure, Don Quixote attacks a giant who turns out to be a windmill (the origin of the expression "to tilt at windmills") and is knocked flat on his back. A row of wineskins in an inn is again mistaken for a giant and, slashed by the brave Don, fills the inn with its blood. There follows a battle with a hostile army (the flock of sheep) in which Don Quixote is nearly stoned to death by the enraged shepherds. The ordinary travelers met along the highway are transformed by the knight's fevered mind into warriors, distressed maidens, giants, and monsters. On one occasion, he disrupts a funeral procession, having decided that the corpse has been unjustly killed. In attempting to avenge his death Don Quixote creates havoc, only to be informed by the clergyman that the deceased had died of a pestilential fever.

Don Quixote and Sancho Panza are led into one painful and ridiculous situation after another, always with the intention of fulfilling their quest. Finally, the knight is persuaded that he had been enchanted, and, at the end of Part 1, he is placed in a cage and returned home.

The second part of the novel, written by Cervantes ten years later, is even richer in invention and understanding than the first. Don Quixote and Sancho Panza continue to be constantly frustrated by the consequences which ensue from the knight's inability to differentiate between reality and illusions. "I perceive now that one must actually touch with one's hands what appears to the eye if he is to avoid being deceived," the Knight of the Lions, as Quixote now calls himself, mournfully admits; and in despair he exclaims, "This world is nothing but schemes and plots, all working at cross purposes." Crushed by a hostile world, Don Quixote finally renounces all books of chivalry and dies of a broken spirit.

Despite his follies and comic misfortunes, Don Quixote never loses a certain dignity, nobility, and pathetic idealism, and the reader soon comes to admire, respect, and sympathize with him at the expense of his constant and uncompromising opponents, the hard-headed realists who frustrate his idealistic efforts. The faithful peasant, Sancho Panza, though academically ignorant is full of natural shrewdness and humor, and presents a striking contrast to his comrade in adversity; he is as frankly materialistic and practical as Don Quixote is romantic and idealistic. Sancho believes in his master, with a blend of simplicity, loyalty, and common sense that makes him one of the most beloved creations in literature.

Cervantes filled *Don Quixote de la Mancha* with more than 600 characters: hidalgo, bourgeoise, picaresque, ducal, provincial, soldier, student, priest, innkeepers, criminals, players, peasants, lovers, highwaymen, barbers, carriers, judges, officials, doctors, menagerie-men, damsels, duennas—a rich cross-section of seventeenth-century Spain.

Commenting on *Don Quixote,* an American poet and essayist, John Peale Bishop, suggests somewhat pessimistically that the hero exhibits a dilemma and weakness typical of the reformer: "He sees certain things before him; he has a concept of justice, of generosity, of honor; he is particularly concerned with questions of injustice. But what does he do? He takes injustice at a particular point without seeing the surrounding circumstances, without understanding what is behind it. We get this again and again in Don Quixote, as we get it in all reformers."

A different view is represented by Richard L. Predmore, of the Romance Language faculty, Duke University: "Among the unforgettable characters of fiction there is none more real or more appealing than the Knight of the Mournful Countenance. If we should try to account for his hold on our affections, we would probably think not so much of his hilarious misadventures as of his noble and courageous spirit. The world must ultimately respect men who pay allegiance to something higher than the satisfaction of their own needs and pleasures, who willingly suffer ridicule and privation to serve their ideals. . . . We may or may not look with approval on Don Quixote's ideal of chivalry, but we must admire the fortitude with which he strives to live by it."

15. LAWMAKER FOR THE UNIVERSE

Johannes Kepler's *Astronomia Nova* and *Harmonices Mundi* (The New Astronomy and Harmony of the World)
1609 and 1619

Johannes Kepler was born a little more than a generation after the death of Copernicus. One of the great creative scientists, Kepler represents both the mysticism of the Middle Ages and the positive, reasoning spirit of the Renaissance. As H. Dingle, Secretary of the British Royal Astronomical Society, remarked, "There run through all Kepler's works, as inseparable threads of their texture, the search, familiar to the scientist of today, for rational co-ordination of observations, and the almost infinite remoteness of a mysticism with which we have lost touch."

The contributions of five great astronomers of the sixteenth and seventeenth centuries, from as many different nations, together solved a cosmic enigma: the motions of the heavenly bodies. Nicolaus Copernicus, a Pole, first established the theory of a heliocentric (sun-centered) universe, supplanting the accepted notion of a geocentric (earth-centered) system. With improved instruments and painstaking methods of observation, Tycho Brahe, a Dane, assembled remarkably accurate data on planetary positions. Johannes Kepler, a German, discovered the laws of planetary motion, and Galileo, an Italian, was the first to use the newly-invented telescope in astronomy; his laws of dynamics were of incalculable aid in establishing the correct principles of motion. The fifth and last, was an Englishman, Isaac Newton, whose law of gravitation based on Kepler's scientific discoveries, provided a rational explanation for the motions of the celestial bodies and thenceforth enabled scientists to view the universe as one great system.

Though German-born, Kepler's investigations in astronomy were carried on principally in Prague, where he had gone as a young man to serve as Tycho Brahe's assistant. When Brahe died, in 1601, Kepler became successor to his patron's post, with the imposing title of Imperial Mathematician to the Emperor of Bohemia. In fact, the position was that of court astrologer, with Kepler's professional duties limited to casting horoscopes and issuing prognostications, tasks he considered to be pure charlatanry but which he performed for the sake of expediency. Of immeasurable value to his scientific investigations was the fact that he inherited Tycho Brahe's voluminous unpublished collection of astronomical data. Brahe had, with utter exactness, made accurate observations of the positions of the stars and had also recorded the time of their appearance. His records covered a period of thirty-five years and were indispensable to Kepler in carrying forward his own studies. Writing of Brahe's accumulation of data, Kepler commented, "Tycho is loaded with riches which, like most of the rich, he makes no use of."

Throughout his researches in astronomy, Kepler was determined to discover the general plan of the solar system. Since the time of the ancient Greeks, it had been universally believed that the planets move in circular paths—a theory accepted unquestioningly even by Copernicus. Kepler soon came to realize, however, that there were striking discrepancies between the circular orbit theory of planetary motion and the observed facts. Six planets—Mercury, Venus, Earth, Mars, Jupiter, and Saturn—were then known. Observations had revealed that these planets move in their courses at variable speeds, their rate decreasing as their distance from the sun increases.

Convinced that the theory of circular orbits was in error, Kepler began testing a variety of other hypotheses. After arduous labors, much trial and error, and six years spent in making innumerable calculations, he finally developed his two epoch-making "laws." His discoveries, correcting and supplementing those of Copernicus, inaugurated modern astronomy, eliminating such survivals of the Ptolemaic system as epicycles, deferents, and equants.

The two laws were first published in Kepler's *Astronomia Nova,* "The New Astronomy." According to the first law, the planetary orbits are not circular, but elliptical, the sun occupying one focus of the ellipses. With this law, Kepler upset the old Aristotelian notion that the circle is a perfect figure and that therefore the planetary orbits must be circular. This departure from tradition resulted in the prompt suppression of his book by the College of Cardinals.

Kepler's second law is concerned with the fact that the speed of a planet varies as it approaches or recedes from the sun. As described by J. R. Mayer, in his *Seven Seals of Science:*

> Kepler finally discovered the curious fact that the observed variations in speed are such that planets sweep over equal areas in equal times—which is to say that, if an imaginary line is drawn from the sun to a planet moving in its elliptical path, and one end of the line is considered as fixed at the sun while the other end moves with the planet, the quasi-triangular areas swept over by the line in like periods of time are always the same.

A decade went by before Kepler was ready to publish the third and last of the famous laws bearing his name. This law, appearing in his *Harmonices Mundi,* "Harmony of the World," deals with the periods of the planets, i.e., the lengths of time they take to complete their orbital paths. It had been known for centuries that the period of time varies for each planet and that the farther removed a planet is from the sun, the longer the time required to complete its orbit. Kepler's goal was to determine the relationship between distance and time. As finally formulated after extensive observation and calculation, the third law reads, in mathematical terms: The squares of any two planets' periods of revolution about the sun are proportional to the cubes of their mean distances from the sun.

Having a deeply religious and even mystical nature, Kepler considered his findings to be incontrovertible evidence of the harmony of a perfect universe. Any scientific explanation of the planets' movements escaped him, although he suspected that the sun exercises some physical control over the planets. Kepler, his spiritual beliefs not to be confounded by his scientific observations, finally came to express the belief that each planet was being held in its course by the governing power of a guiding angel. It remained for Newton's law of universal gravitation to demonstrate the physical relationship between the sun and the planets and to give the reason for the elliptical orbits.

Kepler's belief in a divine ordering of the universe is illustrated by an anecdote he relates. A new star had appeared in 1604 and the group of philosophers known as Epicureans offered a theory that the star was a fortuitous concourse of atoms. Kepler replied:

> I will tell these disputants, my opponents, not my own opinion, but my wife's. Yesterday, when weary with writing, and my mind quite dusty with considering these atoms, I was called to supper, and a salad I had asked for was set before me. "It seems then," said I aloud, "that if pewter dishes, leaves of lettuce, grains of salt, drops of water, vinegar, and oil, and slices of egg, had been flying about in the air from all eternity, it might at last happen by chance that there would come a salad." "Yes," says my wife, "but not so nice and well dressed as this of mine."

16. CREATOR OF THE LAW OF NATIONS

Hugo Grotius' *De Jure Belli ac Pacis*
(On the Law of War and Peace)
1625

It is historically accurate to say that Europe possessed no system of international law until the Dutch jurist, Hugo Grotius, formulated it in his *De Jure Belli ac Pacis*. Writers and statesmen had previously dealt with limited aspects of this field, but none in such comprehensive fashion as did Grotius.

In producing this cornerstone of modern international law, Grotius' main aim was to restrain what seemed to him to be an ever increasing desire on the part of princes and people for waging arbitrary and capricious wars. In his own words:

> I have had many and grave reasons why I should write a book on this subject. For I saw prevailing throughout the Christian world a license in making war, recourse being had to arms for slight reasons or for no

reason, and when arms were taken up, all reverence for divine and human law was lost, just as if men were henceforth authorized to commit all crimes without restraint.

Grotius admits of no distinction between national and international law. To him, they are similar in purpose and equally essential. "For as he that violates the laws of his country for the sake of some present advantage to himself," declares Grotius, "destroys that which is made for the perpetual security of what himself or his posterity shall be able to acquire: so that people which violates the laws of nature and of nations, breaks down the bulwark of their future happiness and tranquillity."

At no period in history had there been a greater need for restraints on international lawlessness than in Grotius' time. It was the age of the Medicis, of the Inquisition, of the worst popes in the history of the church, and of rampant cruelty and treachery in international relations. Political and religious wars had spread until all of Europe was a battleground. Formerly, disputes between nations had been adjudicated by the papacy, but the Reformation eliminated all future prospects of an acceptable international religious tribunal. Grotius himself spent two years in prison and was in exile the last twenty-five years of his life because of the religious controversies then besetting his native Holland.

In his *On the Law of War and Peace,* however, Grotius was concerned primarily with permanent principles of law rather than with the current political and religious condition. "If any one thinks that I have had in view any controversies of our own times," he says, "either those that have arisen or those which can be foreseen as likely to arise, he will do me an injustice. With all truthfulness I aver that, just as mathematicians treat their figures as abstracted from bodies, so in treating law I have withdrawn my mind from every particular fact."

Grotius begins his work by stating his basic assumption that the world is divided into a number of separate and independent states, each supreme within its own territorial boundaries and each at least theoretically equal. Since no supernational government exists, the basic problem is how to regulate relations between the numerous individual nations. Grotius believed the only possible solution was to apply the ancient doctrine of natural law or the law of Nature. He submits that because man is a rational being and social by nature, all of mankind must accordingly adopt a system of national and international law in order to make social life possible. A society of nations, as well as local communities, must recognize the eternal moral rules of the law of Nature governing in times of peace and of war. Unlike man-made law, natural law is unalterable.

On the Law of War and Peace is divided by Grotius into three parts. The first part considers the question of the validity of war per se and lists the causes which lead to war; the second part attacks the unrestrained right of waging war; and the final section discusses the laws and customs of warfare in Grotius' era and suggests limitations to them.

Four major principles are developed in this work. Foremost, is Grotius' doctrine that the conduct of nations amongst each other should be judged by the same criteria as is the conduct of individuals. In accordance with this doctrine, lawlessness among nations is to be suppressed in the same way as it is between individual persons. Next, Grotius proposes that the law of nations should be extended to all the people of the earth—orientals and occidentals, white and colored, civilized and uncivilized, Christians and non-Christians, and Europeans and non-Europeans. Finally, he advocates altruism and charity between nations instead of the egotism, greed, selfish rivalry, and unchecked competition which are detrimental to peaceful coexistence.

Grotius devotes a large portion of his work to the rules which should regulate the conduct of war. Nowhere in his writings does he denounce war as intrinsically wrong. Until injustice can be permanently suppressed he regards war as the only means of preventing the criminal aggression of one nation upon another. To Grotius, the use of international defense to punish criminal acts is exactly the same thing as the municipal administration of justice and police. States may be considered as criminals and only when a war is waged in punishment of such malignant states is it considered to be justifiable.

Prior to Grotius, the conquered had had no recognized rights. Here Grotius blazed a new trail, condemning the killing of prisoners and civilians alike (except in cases of extreme emergency or personal guilt), the devastation of enemy territory, the destruction of property except for reasons of military necessity, and the use of poisons or poisoned missiles. Grotius' counsel of moderation was founded upon principles of humanity, religion, and his farsighted and idealistic policy.

As Grotius sees it, in time of war there can be no such thing as neutrality. Even a state which has not been directly injured must participate in the punishment of a guilty state; if its defenses are too weak to do so, it must, as a minimal gesture, favor the "avenger" and denounce the "criminal." Grotius intentionally avoids the terms "neutral" and "neutrality," referring to non-belligerent states merely as "outsiders."

A notable feature of *On the Law of War and Peace* is the author's frequent citation of classical references, Grotius having lived in an age when the wisdom of the ancients was less likely to be challenged than the learned offerings of his contemporaries. As Durward Sandifer, U. S. Department of State legal advisor, remarked, "Few, if any writers, secular or profane, legal or literary, historical or philosophical, have ever marshalled such a variegated galaxy of star performers to support their theses. Through the pages of *On the Law of War and Peace* parades the learning of all the ages." Grotius' work contains over 600 references, nearly 50 per cent of which date from before 500 A.D.

The name of Grotius has become a symbol of justice in the intricate and subtle art of international relations. The essence of his teachings has been incorporated into the practice of international law and into the conscience of the entire civilized world. Sandifer notes that "probably no one has ever seriously read Grotius without coming away deeply impressed with the intensity of his passion for justice and peace. . . . He gave voice to an eternal ideal at the same time that he charted the basic course of a law of nations."

17. BIRTH OF EXPERIMENTAL MEDICINE

William Harvey's *Exercitatio Anatomica de Motu Cordis et Sanguinis in Animalibus* (Anatomical Exercise on the Motion of the Heart and Blood in Animals)

1628

At the beginning of the seventeenth century biological science and research were little more advanced than had been the study of astronomy prior to Copernicus. Physicians and medical schools still practiced and taught the anatomical and physiological theories concerning the heart, arteries, veins, and blood handed down from the great Asiatic-Greek physician, Galen, in the second century. For more than a thousand years, no substantial discoveries had been made to add to man's knowledge of blood circulation and the functions of the heart.

By 1600, the Renaissance in Europe had brought about an intellectual awakening immediately affecting the natural sciences. In Italy, fifty years earlier, the founder of modern anatomy, Andreas Vesalius, disproved Galen's theory that there were pores in the septum of the heart which directly transmitted blood from the right to the left chamber. About the same time, Servetus, who was later burned at the stake for holding views considered heretical by the Calvinists, stated his belief that blood circulates through the lungs; he did not, however, recognize the heart as the pumping organ. Another important link was supplied by Fabricius of Padua in 1603, who discovered that veins have valves, though he misunderstood their purpose.

To the brilliant and incisive mind of the English physician, William Harvey, fell the task of discovering and formulating an orderly, systematic, and scientific set of principles which would finally unveil the mystery of blood circulation and of the various functions of the heart. As a young man Harvey had gone to Italy to study medicine at the renowned University of Padua, for generations the medical center of Europe. There, Harvey experimented on various kinds of animals and learned the art of dissection. Under the guidance and influence of the renowned teacher Fabricius, his lifetime interest in the process of blood circulation was evidently aroused.

Throughout his life, Harvey had a predilection for medical research and experimentation, rather than for the practice of medicine. In 1616 he began lecturing before the Royal College of Physicians on the circulation of the blood. Though by this date Harvey had become convinced of the validity of his theories on blood circulation, another twelve years of experimentation and observation passed before he was ready to publish his conclusions. Finally, in 1628, his small seventy-two page volume, considered by many authorities to be the most important medical book ever written, was published in Frankfurt, Germany. Written in Latin, the universal scholarly language, the work is most frequently referred to by its abbreviated title *De Motu Cordis*.

In an introduction and seventeen concise chapters, Harvey gives a clear and cohesive account of the action of the heart and of the circular movement of the blood around the body. In the first chapter the author relates some of the problems that had confronted him:

When I first gave my mind to vivisections as a means of discovering the motions and uses of the heart, and sought to discover these from actual inspection, and not from the writings of others, I found the task so truly arduous, so full of difficulties, that I was almost tempted to think that the motion of the heart was only to be comprehended by God.

Because the circulatory system of cold-blooded animals, such as toads, frogs, serpents, small fishes, and shellfish, is less intricate in both structure and function, Harvey found he was able to study the heart's functions with less difficulty in these animals than in man. The same phenomena were also easily observable in dying warm-blooded animals, because of the decreased speed of the heart's action.

On the basis of his experiments Harvey noted that the heart's contraction forces the blood out; further, that as the heart contracts, the arteries receive the blood and so dilate. The heart, actually a muscle serving as a kind of pump, forces continuous circulation of the blood. The blood, impelled into the arteries, in turn produces the pulse. Harvey further demonstrated that the movement is all in one direction, the blood passing from the left chamber of the heart through the arteries to the extremities and then back by way of the veins to the right chamber of the heart. The momentous discovery, in short, was that the same blood is carried out by arteries and returned by veins, performing a complete circulation. The single missing link, the capillaries, minute vessels through which the blood cells pass from the arteries to the veins, was discovered only a few years after Harvey's death by an anatomy professor at Bologna, Marcello Malpighi.

To convince the skeptics, Harvey used the quantitative method. If the blood sent out by the heart in a single day is measured, he reasoned, the quantity is much in excess of all the food taken in and digested. Harvey thus concluded that "the blood could be furnished in no other way than by making a circuit and returning."

Harvey's use of animals for experimental purposes was an innovation in scientific research. He may rightly be regarded as one of the founders of the science of comparative anatomy. To obtain evidence that would prove his theories he dissected a great variety of animals (dogs, fishes, frogs, oysters, pigs, as well as insects). The results are thus reported by Harvey:

I have observed that there is a heart in almost all animals, not only in the larger ones with blood, as Aristotle claimed, but in the smaller bloodless ones also, as snails, slugs, crabs, shrimps, and many others.

Even in wasps, hornets, and flies have I seen with a lens a beating heart at the upper part of what is called the tail. In these bloodless animals the heart beats slowly, contracting sluggishly as in moribund higher animals.

Aside from these remarkable discoveries, Harvey's greatest contribution to science and medical research was his introduction of experimental or laboratory methods. He laid the foundations upon which more than three centuries of physiology and medicine have been built. The essence of Harvey's method was, as he states, "to search and study out the secrets of Nature by way of experiment."

The history of medicine goes back several thousand years before the birth of Harvey. Physicians had already learned to recognize and to describe with a fair amount of accuracy the principal diseases afflicting mankind. Observation, however, while important, is not in itself enough and frequently leads to erroneous conclusions. Herein lies the major difference which distinguishes Harvey from his predecessors. Little handicapped by superstitions or by reverence for antiquated theories, Harvey went beyond superficial observation: he drew up hypotheses and tested them by experiments. He was the first scientist to adopt the scientific method of experiment for the solution of a biological problem, a method which all his successors of significance have since followed.

18. EXPLORER OF OUTER SPACE

Galileo Galilei's *Dialogo . . . sopra i Due Massimi Sistemi del Mondo Tolemaico, e Copernicano* (Dialogue on the Two Chief Systems of the World, the Ptolemaic and the Copernican)

1632

It has often been remarked that in the single year 1564 the world gained two of its greatest men, Shakespeare and Galileo Galilei, and lost another, Michelangelo, who died on Galileo's birthday. Another coincidence is the fact that Galileo died in the same year (1642) that Sir Isaac Newton, destined to be his successor in scientific discovery, was born.

Galileo, the son of a Pisan nobleman, was an early convert to Copernicus' theory of a sun-centered universe. Mathematics held a particular fascination for him, specifically in its application to the investigation of bodies in motion. His experiments and demonstrations dealing with the phenomena of movement proved to be of extraordinary significance in the study of mechanics and provided a basis for research on the vaster problems of the movement of celestial bodies.

Prior to Galileo, Copernican ideas had had little impact on European thought. The theories advanced by Copernicus some seventy-five years earlier were viewed as mere hypotheses, a fact that led the church authorities to regard the Copernican discoveries as too inconsequential to ban. Galileo, however, soon changed the attitude from indifference to one of intense concern.

The invention of the telescope gave Galileo his first opportunity to make a major contribution to astronomy. As he related:

> About ten months ago probably in 1609 a rumor came to our ears that an optical instrument had been elaborated by a Dutchman, Johannes Lippershey, by the aid of which visible objects, even though far distant from the eye of the observer, were distinctly seen as if near at hand. . . . I applied myself entirely to seeking out the theory and discovering the means by which I might arrive at the invention of a similar instrument, an end which I attained a little later, from considerations of the theory of refraction; and I first prepared a tube of lead, in the ends of which I fitted two glass lenses, both plane on one side, one being spherically convex, the other concave, on the other side.

Though Galileo did not invent the telescope, he was the first astronomer to use it in order to observe the heavenly bodies. Never before had anyone viewed the skies except with the naked eye. Naturally, startling new facts were discovered. The ancient astronomers had described the moon as a smooth, perfect sphere. Galileo's telescope revealed contradictory evidence: "It is full of inequalities, uneven, full of hollows and protuberances, just like the surface of the Earth itself, which is varied everywhere by lofty mountains and deep valleys."

Continuing his observations, Galileo discovered sunspots, and by watching their changing positions calculated that the sun revolves on its axis every twenty-four days. He found that the Milky Way was "nothing else but a mass of innumerable stars planted together in clusters." But in Galileo's own opinion, most amazing was his discovery that there were four moons revolving around the planet Jupiter. Further observations revealed the phases of Venus and the rings surrounding the planet Saturn. "We are absolutely compelled to say," asserted Galileo, "that Venus and Mercury also revolve around the sun, as do also all the rest of the planets—a truth believed indeed by the Pythagorean school, by Copernicus, and by Kepler, but never proved by the evidence of our senses as is now proved in the case of Venus and Mercury."

Here was irrefutable argument, Galileo was convinced, validating the truth of the Copernican theory. "I am filled with infinite astonishment and also infinite gratitude to God," he wrote, "that it has pleased Him to make me alone the first observer of such wonderful things, which have been hidden in all past centuries."

Galileo's descriptions of the discoveries that had been made possible by the telescope were printed in his *Siderius Nuncius*, "The Messenger of the Stars," in 1610, for the purpose, as he expressed it, of "acquainting all the philosophers and mathematicians with some observations which I have made on the celestial bodies by means of my spy-glass and which infinitely amaze me." Publication of this work, justifying and supporting Copernicus, led to Galileo's first clash with the theologians. The Inquisition still ruled with unlimited power, and church officials had begun to realize the danger to the *status quo* inherent in the Copernican theory of the sun-centered universe. The authority of the Church must not be questioned.

In 1616 Galileo was denounced to the Holy Office of the Inquisition and ordered to present himself before the Grand Inquisitor, Cardinal Bellarmine. He was there commanded to "abandon his heretical opinions about the earth and the sun and the stars." Furthermore, the *Siderius Nuncius* and "all books which affirm the motion of the earth" were placed upon the *Index of Prohibited Books*. After this first brush with the Inquisition, Galileo wrote in a letter to a friend: "I believe that there is no greater hatred in the whole world, than that of ignorance for knowledge."

For fifteen years Galileo remained relatively silent. During this time, however, the election of a more liberal Pope, Urban VIII, aroused hope for an enlightened and sympathetic attitude toward new scientific discoveries. In 1632, believing that circumstances were once again favorable, Galileo issued the epoch-making work upon which he had been engaged for a number of years: the *Dialogue on the Two Chief Systems of the World*. To meet the objections of the Papal censor, Galileo warily included a pious preface condemning the Copernican theory on the grounds that it was contrary to the Holy

Scriptures. That this was mere camouflage is obvious, for the contents of the book clearly state and support the case for the Copernican system against every variety of objection and question.

Adopting a literary usage then in vogue, Galileo's work is in the form of four dialogues between three speakers: Salviati, a convinced Copernican, obviously representing Galileo; Sagredo, an intelligent layman, who raises common-sense criticisms and injects occasional humor into the proceedings; and Simplicio, a simple-minded Ptolemaist and defender of tradition, who presents the usual Aristotelian objections to acceptance of the Copernican system. Invariably, Simplicio is on the losing side of the discussion.

The *Dialogue* is spread over a four-day period. In the beginning, of the discussion the old concept of a perfect and unchangeable heaven is challenged on the basis of evidence furnished by new stars and sunspots, and similarities are pointed out between the earth, moon, and planets. There follow propositions relating to the earth's rotation and to the revolution of the earth about the sun. In each argument the Copernican doctrine emerges triumphant as constituting the simplest and most logical explanation of astronomical phenomena.

Subsequent to publication of the *Dialogue* Galileo's enemies persuaded the Pope that Simplicio was meant to be a caricature of him, since some of the arguments raised by this protagonist resembled those suggested by Pope Urban himself.

A few months later, Galileo was again denounced to the Inquisition and summoned to Rome to stand trial. Then approaching his seventieth year and in poor health, Galileo was nevertheless compelled to appear before the ten cardinals of the Inquisition. Threatened with torture unless he recanted his scientific beliefs, Galileo yielded, confessed his error, and stated, "I now declare and swear that the earth does not move around the sun." There is an apocryphal story that, as Galileo was led away from the tribunal, he remarked under his breath, "And yet it moves."

The *Dialogue* was placed on the *Index of Prohibited Books,* where it remained until 1835. Galileo was sentenced to prison, but the sentence was never executed, and he presently was allowed to return to his home in Florence. There he lived in technical confinement and continued his scientific research during the remaining eight years of his life. Shortly before his death, one of his greatest books, *Discourses on Two New Sciences* (1638), was smuggled out of the country for publication in Holland. The book presents a summary of the basic principles of dynamics and ballistics, and it is considered by some to be his most important work.

Galileo's experiments in dynamics and his astronomic observations laid the foundation of modern mathematical physics. Concerning his over-all importance and influence in the history of science, a distinguished Swiss physicist, Friedrich Dessauer, commented:

> Of all Galileo's achievements this was his greatest gift to posterity: the inductive method, the core of all exact science; extended in the years that followed, it proved to be the key to the mysteries of being, opening up ever new strata, ever new depths. And it is through the inductive method that our knowledge of the world has grown to be a million times greater than that of the ancients.

19. BEGINNING OF MODERN SCIENTIFIC METHOD
René Descartes' *Discours de la Méthode pour Bien Conduire sa Raison et Chercher la Vérité dans les Sciences* (A Discourse on the Method of Rightly Conducting the Reason and Seeking Truth in the Sciences)
1637

Mathematics is at the heart of modern science and has molded much of the human mind. Descartes, the greatest mathematician of his time, in his *Discourse on Method* paved the way for the application of the mathematical method to the investigation of scientific problems.

In his *The Origins of Modern Science,* Butterfield evaluates René Descartes' *Discourse on Method* as being "one of the really important books in our intellectual history," a ranking to which more than three centuries of pervasive influence bears testimony.

Descartes was reared and educated in a Jesuit college, and there, he tells us, "in one of the most celebrated schools in Europe," studied languages, mathematics, history, philosophy, theology, rhetoric, jurisprudence, and the sciences. "I had, in addition, read all the books that had fallen into my hands." Descartes felt, however, that instead of giving him "a clear and certain knowledge of all that is useful in life," his educational experience was responsible for "many doubts and errors." Accordingly, "I entirely abandoned the study of letters, and resolved no longer to seek any other science than the knowledge of myself, or of the great books of the world."

Descartes was not alone in his skeptical attitude towards the sterile scholastic method handed down from the Middle Ages, a method whose remaining adherents absorbed themselves in endless hair-splitting in philosophy and theology, and who slavishly clung to the letter rather than the spirit of Aristotle's texts. Outside the schools, medieval scholasticism, with its sacred texts, its authorities, and its subtle definitions, was becoming increasingly discredited. The scientific revolution, beginning in the sixteenth century with Copernicus, hastened the process of disillusionment, and it was to this new world of science that Descartes naturally gravitated. The time had come, he was convinced, to attempt the construction of an entirely new philosophical system.

In the *Discourse on Method*, Descartes' basic assumption is that "Good sense is, of all things among men, the most equally distributed." He himself, did not claim to have a superior mental capacity. But "to be possessed of a vigorous mind is not enough," Descartes declares. "The prime requisite is rightly to apply it." By describing his own thinking processes, he attempted to demonstrate how the ordinary individual can, alone and unaided, discover the truth.

Descartes' first step was to reject all ancient opinions, all the teaching that had been transmitted from the ancient and medieval world and, with his mental slate wiped clean, to begin his thinking anew. The unreliable, the vague, and the imaginary could be eliminated only by what Descartes called "methodical doubt," a systematic skepticism, which took nothing for granted except the existence of the doubter himself. "I think, therefore I am." As a historian of science, E. W. F. Tomlin, points out in his *The Great Philosophers*, "according to Descartes's New Method, the test of a truth was not whether it had been enunciated by Holy Writ, or St. Augustine or St. Thomas, or stated *ex cathedra* by the Supreme Pontiff, but whether it was coherent with itself and above all whether it was 'clear and distinct.' " Descartes did not advocate skepticism for its own sake; he doubted in order to find a firm basis for belief. One should, he held, trust only what can be observed with one's own senses; tradition does not make a thing true; its validity can be established only by rigid examination.

For objective testing of any opinion or theory, Descartes proposes four rules:

The *first* was never to accept anything for true which I did not clearly know to be such; that is to say, carefully to avoid precipitancy and prejudice, and to comprise nothing more in my judgment than what was presented to my mind so clearly and distinctly as to exclude all ground of doubt. The *second*, to divide each of the difficulties under examination into as many parts as possible, and as might be necessary for its adequate solution. The *third*, to conduct my thoughts in such order that, by commencing with objects the simplest and easiest to know, I might ascend by little and little, and, as it were, step by step, to the knowledge of the more complex; assigning in thought a certain order even to those objects which in their own nature do not stand in a relation of antecedence and sequence. And the *last*, in every case to make enumerations so complete, and reviews so general, that I might be assured that nothing was omitted.

Commenting upon these four principles, the noted mathematician and philosopher, Bertrand Russell, says, "the second and third especially—divide difficulties into as many parts as possible and proceed from simple to complex—I personally have found it always necessary to insist upon with advanced students who were beginning research. Unless they were very able they tended to take vast problems far beyond their powers, and I find Descartes' rules exactly what one has to tell them."

Descartes was first and foremost a mathematician. One of the world's most original thinkers in this field, he created co-ordinate geometry, thereby uniting geometry with algebra. In his day mathematics was the chief instrument used for discovering facts about nature. Characteristically, therefore, Descartes concluded that the mathematical method was the ideal tool to apply in every sphere of knowledge and that it would yield results of equal definitiveness and dependability in metaphysics, logic, and ethics. Like Galileo and Newton, he saw the universe as a gigantic machine in which everything is measurable; that which cannot be translated into mathematical terms is therefore unreal. According to this premise, the entire universe can be explained by mechanical and mathematical laws. Descartes' "vision of a single universal science so unified, so ordered, so interlocked," states Herbert Butterfield, in his *The Origins of Modern Science,* "was perhaps one of his most remarkable contributions to the scientific revolution."

Ironically, experimentation played a subordinate part in Descartes' own methodology. His insufficiency in this area was probably the result of his early educational preparation. Despite his avowed skepticism and his completion of numerous experiments, many of his accepted "facts" were actually uncritically accepted opinions of earlier scholastic writers. Even in scientific fields, Rufus Suter, writing in *The Scientific Monthly,* remarks, "the technique of pure mathematics is not enough when the thinker seeks to decode the laws of physics, chemistry, physiology, or of any other science treating of things in the physical world and presumably independent of our personal reasoning habits. . . . The thinker must quit his armchair and go into the laboratory." On the other hand, mathematical physicists, such as Albert Einstein, exemplify Descartes' method, depending upon little else besides pencil and paper to carry on their research. In general, however, a combination of mathematical and experimental methods adopted by later scientists, particularly in England, has largely superseded the strictly mathematical approach.

Descartes' true scientific spirit is exemplified by his statement that "the little I have hitherto learned is almost nothing in comparison with that of which I am ignorant," and he concludes the *Discourse on Method* by declaring: "I have resolved to devote what time I may still have to live to no other occupation than that of endeavoring to acquire some knowledge of Nature."

20. LIBERTY WITHOUT LICENSE

John Milton's Areopagitica: a Speech of Mr. John Milton for the Liberty of Unlicenc'd Printing, in the Parlament of England

1644

During the Tudor and Stuart periods in England there was scarcely an institution more hated than the Court of the Star Chamber. One of the primary functions of the Court was the censorship of books—an important feature of ecclesiastical and state policy since the invention of printing, and harshly enforced during the Roman Catholic Counter Reformation. Prior to the outbreak of the Civil War in 1642, several flagrant cases had aroused strong popular resentment against the censors. Offenders were sentenced to long terms in prison, were heavily fined, had their ears cut off and their noses slit, and were branded on the cheeks, pilloried, and otherwise subjected to cruel and inhuman punishments.

In the struggle between King Charles and the famous Long Parliament, the detested Star Chamber was finally abolished by Parliamentary action in 1641. With its passing, the great poet John Milton anticipated the lifting of arbitrary restrictions on a free press. Parliament, composed overwhelmingly of English Presbyterians, was alarmed, however, by the flood of "scandalous, seditious and libellous" publications that began to appear as soon as the censorship was lifted. On June 14, 1643, the Parliament passed a new censorship act, modeled upon the old Star Chamber rules, but with the distinction that the censors were to be appointed by Parliament. Unlicensed printing was forbidden, and the Stationers' Company (the organized printers and publishers of the country) and the officers of Parliament were authorized to search out and destroy unlicensed presses, confiscate unlicensed books, and arrest all printers and authors who issued uncensored books.

Milton, who had been violently denounced for writing two treatises favorable to divorce, stepped into the censorship fight with a purposely unregistered and unlicensed pamphlet entitled *Areopagitica,* the most celebrated of all his prose works. The *Areopagus* was the supreme court of ancient Athens, before which great causes were pleaded in eloquent oratorical addresses. Milton's work was also in the form of an oration, though intended to be read rather than spoken.

The *Areopagitica* abounds in eloquent declarations on the transcendent importance of books, and in compelling arguments supporting an unfettered press:

> Books are not absolutely dead things, but do contain a potency of life in them to be as active as that soul was whose progeny they are. . . . As good almost kill a man as kill a good book. . . . He who destroys a good book, kills reason itself, kills the image of God. . . . A good book is the precious lifeblood of a master spirit, embalmed and treasured up on purpose to a life beyond life.

Reviewing the history of censorship, Milton concluded that in Greece's classical era the only writings banned were those of a blasphemous, atheistical, or libellous nature. Great leniency was shown toward works considered immoral or licentious. Rome, before becoming Christian, had also been tolerant of all writings except those of a sacrilegious or defamatory nature. Milton traced the growth of censorship under the first popes, leading finally to the *Index Librorum Prohibitorum.* He blamed as a papal invention the system whereby

AREOPAGITICA;

A

SPEECH

OF

M^r. JOHN MILTON

For the Liberty of V N L I C E N C'D
P R I N T I N G,

To the PARLAMENT of ENGLAND.

Τὺλδ'θεον δ' ἐκεῖνο, εἴ τις θίλφ πόλφ
Χρησόν τι βύλδμ' εἰς μέσον φέρφιν, ἔχων.
Καί ταῦθ' ὁ χρήζων, λαμπρός ἐσθ', ὁ μὴ θέλων,
Σιγᾷ, τί τύτων ἐστιν ἰσαίτερον πόλφ;
Euripid, Hicetid.

This is true Liberty when free born men
Having to advise the public may speak free,
Which he who can, and will, deserv's high praise,
Who neither can nor will, may hold his peace;
What can be juster in a State then this?
Euripid. Hicetid.

LONDON,
Printed in the Yeare, 1644.

"no book, pamphlet, or paper should be printed . . . unless it were approved and licensed under the hands of two or three glutton friars."

"To the pure, all things are pure," said Milton, quoting the Apostle to the Thessalonians, "not only meats and drinks, but all kinds of knowledge whether of good or evil; the knowledge cannot defile, nor consequently the books, if the will and conscience be not defiled."

Even bad books should not be prohibited, for truth cannot be known without untruth, nor good without evil. What is bad will be forgotten, "No book may safely be suppressed. . . . Bad books are a part of the entirety of experience." Pursuing this line of argument, Milton asked, "How can we more safely, and with less danger scout into the regions of sin and falsity than by reading all manner of tractates and hearing all manner of reason? And this is the benefit which may be had of books promiscuously read."

Furthermore, Milton maintained, the censorship of books alone would be ineffective in extinguishing scandalous, seditious, and libellous thoughts. Ideally, the censor would have to eliminate the innumerable other avenues open to the mind and soul: old books, foreign books, music, dancing, dress, gluttony, drunkenness, idle and evil company, mixed conversation between the sexes, and all recreations and pastimes. Restraints on such myriad activities were likened by Milton "to the exploit of that gallant man who thought to pound up the crows by shutting his park gate."

But even if censorship were socially desirable, where could competent censors be found? And who would censor the censors? By the very nature of their task, Milton believed, licensers are apt to be "illiterate and illiberal individuals . . . ignorant, imperious, and basely pecuniary," since men worthy to judge books would refuse to submit to such tedious, humiliating, and unpleasant drudgery.

Milton's document is, however, primarily a plea for freedom of the press; the inefficiency of censorship was only used as a supporting argument. He viewed licensing as "the greatest discouragement and affront that can be offered to learning and to learned men." Censorship, he asserted, is the worst possible indignity to a free and knowing spirit, an insult to the nation, and an act hostile and detrimental to the survival of truth. Above all other freedoms, Milton demanded "the liberty to know, to utter, and to argue freely according to conscience."

The *Areopagitica* has been criticized by some because of Milton's failure to advocate unmitigated freedom for everyone. As one commentator pointed out, the treatise "was essentially limited to those who were agreed on the fundamentals of the social order." Milton had reservations about "popery and open superstition, which, as it extirpates all religious and civil supremacies, so itself should be extirpate, provided first that all charitable and compassionate means be used to win and regain the weak and the misled. That also which is impious or evil absolutely either against faith or manners no law can possibly permit."

Milton's vigorous denunciation of censorship and licensing apparently had no perceptible impact on his own time. The Presbyterians were in an intolerant mood. Parliament was deaf to all suggestions for reform, and press control continued without moderation for the next fifty years. It was not until the accession of William and Mary to the throne in 1689 that a new spirit of tolerance allowed the press licensing act to die. In the succeeding centuries, the *Areopagitica* has had a powerful influence upon the growth of free thought everywhere, and its message is one which bears repeating today more than ever before.

21. ADVOCATE OF AUTHORITARIANISM

Thomas Hobbes' *Leviathan, or The Matter, Forme, & Power of a Common-Wealth Ecclesiasticall and Civill*

1651

A seventeenth-century Englishman could scarcely be censured for yearning for a stable government. Thomas Hobbes' life spanned the greater part of an era (1588–1679) marked by some of the most troubled and uncertain times in England's history. Born in the year of the Armada, he was witness to the turbulent period that followed the first Civil War between King and Parliament (1642–1645), the second Civil War (1648), the execution of Charles I (1649), the rule of the Rump Parliament (1649–1653), Cromwell's Protectorate (1654–1658), and the Restoration (1660). Thus it is scarcely suprising that Hobbes' *Leviathan,* the first general theory of politics in the English language, should lay great stress upon the advantages of strong government and the importance of submission to civil authority.

Hobbes begins his thesis with the basic philosophical assumption that man originally lived in a state of nature, which, without a central and unifying power, was tantamount to living in a state of war. This abstract picture is hardly like Jean Jacques Rousseau's highly romanticized version of the "noble savage," for Hobbes illustrates how man's "naturall passions," expressed in a multitude of single

"Wills," inevitably lead to discord and strife. In such a condition, there is "continual fear and danger of violent death; and the life of man, solitary, poor, nasty, brutish, and short." Every man is against every man, "man is to man a wolf"; and force, fraud, and fear flourish. There is no place for industry, agriculture, navigation, trade, or the arts—indeed, there is, properly speaking, no true society.

Hobbes' solution for this anarchic state is the creation of the Leviathan (variously interpreted in the Bible as a whale, a dragon, and a crocodile), a state in which men confer all their power and strength on one man or body of men (the Sovereign) by means of a mutually protecting Social Contract. Possessing absolute power and incorporating in a single "Will" the wills of all men, the sovereign is charged with preserving order and protecting life and property. Hobbes' assertion is that peace, the common goal of all men, can never be had unless this supreme power is firmly established and dutifully obeyed. He considered monarchy to be the best form of government because it is more permanent and its authority less divided than in a democracy or aristocracy. Before accepting the possibility of two, simultaneously active sovereign powers, it should be realized, he suggested, that "if two men ride on a horse, then one must ride in front."

Despite inevitable cases of conflicting wills, Hobbes held that the subject must, at all times, obey the civil sovereign. Furthermore, once instituted, Hobbes argued, no check or limitations can be imposed on the sovereign's power; otherwise, the restricting person or group, by virtue of its role, becomes dominant, and the actual sovereign is reduced to a subordinate and dependent position. "The sovereign power implies an universal immunity." The sovereign's subjects possess no legal right to rebel or revolt—with one exception. Since it is the state's primary duty to maintain order and security for its citizens, any failure to do so constitutes a breach of promise and therefore invalidates the Social Contract. As Hobbes put it:

> The obligation of subjects to the sovereign is understood to last as long, and no longer, than the power lasts by which he is able to protect them. For the right men have by nature to protect themselves, when none else can protect them, can by no covenant be relinquished.

Hobbes believed that sovereignty must be indivisible, and he strongly opposed any agency that weakened the power of the state. The division or separation of powers led, in his opinion, to the two Civil Wars in England, sovereignty having been divided between

King and Parliament. For the same reason, Hobbes regarded the various church powers as serious perils and as prime sources of civil disobedience and disunity. His attacks on the Catholic Church were particularly bitter, but he was also opposed to interference in governmental affairs by the Puritans and Presbyterians.

Though Hobbes defended absolute government and the pre-eminence of the state over the individual, he never held that "the king can do no wrong." Instead, he discoursed at length on the duties of rulers, who in his view were as fully subject to the laws of nature and reason as other men. In providing "good government of the people," it is the sovereign's responsibility to preserve peace at home, provide defense against foreign attack, and safeguard "the commodity of living," i.e., trade, labor, food, and other necessities.

Hobbes' doctrines have been viewed askance by democrats and liberals during the past three centuries. Political scientists, however, recognize that his contentions have a certain validity. A. R. M. Murray's *Introduction to Political Philosophy,* for example, points out that "all government *necessarily* involves the exercise of force by the government upon the governed. It is of the essence of government that a relatively large group of people should be controlled by a relatively small group, or even by a single individual, and this relationship is found even where self-government is said to exist."

Hobbes has also been accused of providing communist and fascist totalitarians with a verbal defense for their aggressions. William Ebenstein, in his *Great Political Thinkers,* refuted this charge, but was obliged to state: "The fact that Hobbes was not—intellectually or emotionally—of the totalitarian cast should not create the impression that he was a democrat in disguise. He was not. . . . Compared with an advanced democracy, the Hobbesian state may appear dismal enough. Compared with twentieth-century totalitarianism, it is a vision of refined political civilization."

Hobbes' remarks on relations among nations, though incidental to his main theme, have greatly influenced ideas of international law. In the area of international relations, Hobbes noted, independent sovereign states have never progressed beyond the state of nature. There is no security because there is no over-all sovereignty; nations "are in continual jealousies, and in the state and posture of gladiators; having their weapons pointing, and their eyes fixed, on one another; that is, their forts, garrisons, and guns upon the frontiers of their kingdoms, and continual spies upon their neighbors; which is a pos-

ture of war." Hobbes' solution might conceivably have been the creation of a super-Leviathan of world government.

Hobbes' doctrines are in many respects antagonistic to the traditions of Western political thought, and they have been rejected. Nevertheless, because of its coldly realistic dissection of human nature
and behavior and frequently brilliant insights into the problems of
government, the *Leviathan* continues, after more than three centuries, to be a primary source book for the political scientist.

22. FIRST MODERN CHEMIST

Robert Boyle's *The Sceptical Chymist: or Chymico-Physical Doubts & Paradoxes*

1661

With the scientific achievements of Robert Boyle, the ancient grip
of philosophy on science was further and irrevocably loosened. By
the time of his birth, in 1627, Copernicus had published his heliocentric theory of the solar system, Brahe had recorded the motions
of the planets, Kepler had proved that the planets revolve about the
sun in elliptical orbits, Magellan had sailed around the earth, and
Francis Bacon had published his influential discussion of inductive
scientific methodology. In the following year the publication of William Harvey's researches on blood circulation and his insistence upon
actual laboratory experimentation went far toward emancipating biological studies. Everywhere the rapidly expanding field of science was
affecting all branches of thought, and a revolt against scientific dogmatism was in progress.

But one area was scarcely touched by this ferment against dogmatism. Chemistry, riddled with fears, superstitions, and taboos,
was kept in its infant state. The medieval cult of alchemy, with its
attachment to mysticism and the occult, still swayed even the most
sophisticated minds of the age, and, though emphasis had become increasingly directed toward the study of substances and their medici-
nal effect on the human body, the alchemists refused to give up the
possibility of the transmutation of baser metals into gold and silver.
Even Boyle was, to some extent, a child of his time, and not above
recommending ineffectual nostrums and inept remedies for the ail-

ments of his patients. But his keen mind and inexhaustible zeal for scientific experimentation helped raise chemistry to a science instead of a mere appendage to alchemy. Because of these qualities, Boyle played an instrumental role in establishing science as an inseparable part of man's daily existence, rather than as something apart and remote.

Boyle's scientific interests were all-encompassing. During his life-time he conducted experiments in nearly every branch of science then known. His thirty published scientific treatises are principally concerned with physics, chemistry, physiology, and medicine, and his investigations led to discoveries concerning the effect of air in the propagation of sound, the thermometer, the barometer, freezing mixtures, the gas laws, phosphorus, phosphorescence, and electricity. Particularly significant is Boyle's law on gas, stating that the volume of gas varies inversely as the pressure.

Despite the range of his scientific talents, Boyle's first love was chemistry. His *The Sceptical Chymist* is the best-known chemical work of the seventeenth century and the most influential of his extensive writings. The book is characterized by the scientific historian, William Wightman, as occupying "the same place in the history of chemistry as does Copernicus' *De Revolutionibus* in the history of astronomy."

In *The Sceptical Chymist*, Boyle undertook a critical examination of the two most popularly accepted chemical theories of his day: the Aristotelian and the Paracelsan or Spagyric. The book is written in the form of a dialogue between an Aristotelian, who believes that all matter is composed of four "elements" (earth, water, air, and fire), a Spagyrist, who supports Paracelsus' three "principles" (sulphur, mercury, salt) favored by the alchemists, and the sceptical "chymist." Boyle presides as chairman of the imaginary gathering, and addresses the others with these words:

> I am not a little pleased to find that you are resolved on this occasion to insist rather on experiments than on syllogisms. For I, and no doubt you, have long observed that those dialectical subtleties, that the schoolmen too often employ about physiological mysteries are wont much more to declare the wit of him that uses them, than increase the knowledge or remove the doubts of sober lovers of truth.

Among the alchemists and early chemists there was great confusion about the constitution of matter. The ancient Aristotelian theory held that all substances are compounded, in varying proportions, of the four fundamental elements of earth, air, fire, and water. The physician and alchemist Paracelsus (1493–1541) increased difficulties by adding the three "principles," sulphur, salt, and mercury, to distinguish the separate qualities of the elements. As Boyle expressed the situation:

> Methinks the chymists, in their searches after truth, are not unlike the navigators of *Solomon's Tarshish* fleet, who brought home from their long and perilous voyages, not only gold, and silver, and ivory, but apes and peacocks too: for so the writings of several (for I say not all) of your hermetick alchemical philosophers present us, together with diverse substantial and noble experiments, theories, which either like a peacock's feathers make a great show, but are neither solid nor useful, or else like apes, if they have some appearance of being rational, are blemished with some absurdity or other, that, when they are attentively considered, make them appear ridiculous.

In *The Sceptical Chymist,* Boyle demonstrated the fallibility of the alchemistic theory that all mixed bodies could be analyzed into their elementary ingredients by reduction through fire. He further argued that no one had ever been able to divide gold into any four component parts, whereas blood could be reduced to more than four constituents. He concluded that many substances exist which are scientifically impervious to decomposition and that, until experimentation proved otherwise, these substances must be regarded as elements. In an effort to identify the elements, Boyle undertook extensive experiments (which he called "analysis") with every available substance; those that could be readily separated into simpler forms were designated compounds or mixtures; others, such as metals, remained unalterable, and they were classified as elements. Boyle's definition of a chemical element, as one which cannot be decomposed, still remains the accepted definition. One hundred and six elements are recognized by modern chemistry. Today, however, the element is no longer considered to be the ultimate constituent, and it is believed that Boyle felt similarly.

Other of Boyle's experiments provided further substantial advances in chemistry, among them being new data about the interaction of various substances. Demonstrations of the reciprocal effect of substances included, for example, the detection of hydrochloric acid by precipitation with silver solution, the isolation of iron by use of tincture of galls, and the exposure of various acids by means of paper dyed with vegetable coloring matter.

The value of Boyle's work to the science of chemistry is summarized by Wightman:

> His contributions to the progress of actual chemical discovery amounted to very little; but the progress of science depends not so much on the accumulation of facts as on the framing of clear and distinct general ideas which may serve as the framework for new facts. . . . In laying down guiding principles for the recognition by tests of distinct chemical individuals, Boyle made chemistry possible.

Boyle viewed chemistry as an independent and vital science, thus freeing it from the limitations of alchemy and medicine. He demonstrated vividly the fruitfulness of the experimental method and cleared away a jungle of inhibiting theories. Henceforth, scientists would realize that "occult qualities" are nothing but "the sanctuary of ignorance."

23. OBSERVER OF THE INVISIBLE

Robert Hooke's *Micrographia: or Some Physiological Description of Minute Bodies Made by Magnifying Glasses with Observations and Inquiries Thereupon*

1665

The Renaissance symbol of the universal man found a worthy exemplar of its ideal in Robert Hooke. His was one of the most inventive and farseeing minds in the history of physical science, and his contributions spanned the fields of physics, chemistry, meteorology, geology, biology, and astronomy. In addition, he was also a notable disciple of the arts, exhibiting skill as an architect, city planner, artist, and musician.

Hooke's astonishing versatility, however, was undoubtedly a source of weakness as well as of strength, for the fertility of his ideas was not always matched by the necessary determination and perseverance to carry them through to solid accomplishment in all the fields to which he devoted attention. Nevertheless, the range of his discoveries is amazing, and more credit belongs to him than to any other individual for the development of the modern scientific instrument.

One such instrument invented by Hooke was the first practical compound microscope, an apparatus responsible for his *Micrographia,* the first published work dealing almost exclusively with microscopical observations. The investigations described in this renowned work have earned Hooke a place beside such great founders of microscopic biological study as Anton van Leeuwenhoek in Holland, Marcello Malpighi in Italy, and Nehemiah Grew in England. Samuel Pepys' diary records how he sat up until two o'clock in the morning reading the *Micrographia,* "the most ingenious book that ever I read in my life."

Whereas Galileo, for the first time in history, was able to investigate the celestial world through the ground lenses of a telescope, Hooke and his contemporaries used the newly invented microscope to examine the hitherto unseen world of minute organisms. Their discoveries provided future scientists with an organized method of biological research.

In the *Micrographia,* Hooke predicted that, with the aid of lately perfected instruments, "the subtilty of the composition of Bodies, the structure of their parts, the various texture of their matter, the instruments and manner of their inward motions, and all the other possible appearances of things, may come to be more fully discovered." He required that the true scientist have "a *sincere* Hand, and a *faithful* Eye to examine, and to record, the things themselves as they appear."

The most celebrated and striking feature of the *Micrographia* is some sixty plates of microscopic objects, accurately and beautifully drawn by Hooke himself, with assistance perhaps from the famous English architect, Sir Christopher Wren. The drawings depict a number of fundamental discoveries, many related to insect life. Among them are the compound eye of a fly, the foot of a fly, the sting of a bee, enlarged views of the structures of a flea (drawn nearly sixteen inches long), silverfish, and louse, the metamorphosis of gnat larva, and the progessive development of a mosquito. In the botanical kingdom, there are faithful representations of fungi, mould, moss, the sting of the nettle, pollen, seeds, leaves, the awn of the wild oat, and the construction of wood and cork. The facts illustrated won lasting acceptance; thus, Hooke's description of the structure of feathers remained standard for two centuries.

Hooke also examined inanimate matter such as rocks, snow crystals, raindrops, and textiles. He was the first scientist to study metals under a microscope: the point of a needle, the edge of a razor, and the minute spheres of steel struck off by a flint.

The discovery that permanently established Hooke's scientific reputation was his theory of the cell. The *Micrographia* records the first observation of the cellular structure of living tissue. Inspecting an exceedingly thin slice of cork under the microscope, Hooke was amazed to find it was composed of tiny "little boxes or cells" much like the compartments of a honeycomb. His use of the word "cell" is responsible for its application to the protoplasmic units of modern biology. Hooke's method of thin-sectioning or slicing to obtain a specimen for microscopic study has become a standard laboratory technique.

A certain amount of controversy has centered around the origin of the cell theory. Some biology textbooks still attribute the discovery to the German scientists Theodor Schwann and Mattias Schleiden. The record was cleared by Edwin Grant Conklin, a noted American biologist, who stated that Schleiden and Schwann's "theory was a special and in important respects an erroneous one. There is no present biological interest in their theory. . . . Cells were first seen, named, described by Robert Hooke 170 years before the work of Schleiden and Schwann. Hooke described among many other things the little chambers or cells which he had seen with his simple microscope in sections of cork."

Another widely prevailing misconception was that the early microscopists, such as Hooke and Nehemiah Grew, saw only the cell's outer membrane, and not the inner mass. Edwin B. Matzke, writing in *Science*, refuted this error by citing evidence from the *Micrographia*, itself:

> From these quotations it is evident that Hooke and Grew fully realized that cells in living plants had contents. Of course they had no knowledge of the internal structure and organization of the cell, of its nucleus and other constituent parts, of the protoplast as we know it to-day. They apparently did not appreciate the importance of the cell as a unit in the organism. However, they thought of liquids or juices moving within the plant through the cells, foreshadowing, unconsciously, much more recent work on hormones, vitamins, viruses and the translocation of substances in plants.

The fact that Hooke was at all times a humble servant of science, is reflected in the closing words of the *Micrographia*: "Wherever the

Reader finds that I have ventured at any small conjectures, at the causes of things that I have observed, I beseech him to look upon them only as uncertain guesses and not as unquestionable conclusions, or matters of unconfutable science."

24. EPIC OF PURITANISM
John Bunyan's *The Pilgrim's Progress*
1678

Dr. Samuel Johnson once remarked to Boswell, that *Don Quixote, Robinson Crusoe,* and *The Pilgrim's Progress* were the only three books that a reader might wish longer. He was obviously expressing a universal opinion, for *The Pilgrim's Progress* has been outranked in popularity only by the Bible. It has been translated into virtually every literate language and has found its place among all classes of society. Chief among the reasons for such esteem is that it was written by a master storyteller who fervently believed in the spiritual content of the tale he told.

Bunyan's classic is in allegorical form, with the universal vices and virtues personified. All action occurs on a pilgrimage—a device already old when the *Odyssey* was written. The idea of man's life as a pilgrimage was particularly popular during the Middle Ages, for then pilgrimages were a popular expression of religious devotion. An early English example of the device is the fourteenth-century *Vision of Piers Plowman;* Dante utilized it in *The Divine Comedy,* as did Chaucer in *The Canterbury Tales,* and Edmund Spenser in *The Faerie Queene.* Allegorical figures were stock material of medieval sermon literature, and in the drama they were used until the Restoration.

Bunyan's pilgrim expresses the spiritual necessity for this journey in a dramatic opening paragraph: "As I walked through the wilderness of this world, I lighted on a certain place, where was a Den, and I laid me down in that place to sleep; and as I slept I dreamed a Dream. I Dreamed, and behold I saw a man clothed with Rags, standing in a certain place, with his face from his own House, a Book in his hand, and a great burden upon his back. I looked and saw him open the Book, and read therein; and as he read, he wept and trembled; and not being able any longer to contain, he broke out with a lamentable cry, saying, What shall I do?"

The man in rags is the hero, Christian; his pilgrimage represents the Christian life; and the road he travels, straight and narrow, leads him through mud, through green fields, over rocks and up and down hill—all indicative of the complicated moral life of man. Thus, the reader has a constantly renewed image of man's moments of peace and happiness, his times of despair and despondency, and the challenges and temptations which confront him.

Each major crisis befalling Christian in the course of his pilgrimage reflects a type of spiritual struggle. At the outset, his entanglement in the mire of the Slough of Despond corresponds to the temptation to despair. Successive obstacles are met and conquered at the Hill Difficulty, the Valley of Humiliation, and Vanity Fair— the last being a brilliant display of items and entertainments to catch the eye of lust or greed. In the Valley of Humiliation, battleground of the soul, Christian overcomes Apollyon, the "foul Fiend" who tries to persuade him to transfer his allegiance from God to Satan. His last ordeal is imprisonment in Doubting Castle and his escape is final proof of his ability to withstand temptation. Christian is at last spiritually prepared to view the Celestial City; and the final stage of his journey—over the Delectable Mountains and Enchanted Ground to the Country of Beulah and across the River of Death— ends with his entrance into the Holy City. Christian is Bunyan himself, wavering, timid, yet ultimately triumphant despite his human frailties.

Bunyan exhibits amazing skill in character delineation, largely because the characters are drawn from his personal experiences. Universal representations of good and evil, they are at the same time distinctly individual. Mr. Worldly Wiseman, of the town of Carnal Policy, illustrates the dangers of materialism and a life of good works without true faith. Obstinate is the man whose mind was made up before he had ever begun to think; Pliable can never reach a firm decision; Talkative is nimble at mouthing the clichés of evangelical religion; and By-ends is overprone to compromise and toleration, always with an eye to opportunity. His fellow townsmen in the County of Deceit include Lord Turnabout, Mr. Facing-both-ways, Parson Two-Tongues, and a brisk lad, Ignorance. At the trial in Vanity Fair, the presiding judge is Lord Hate-good; the jury is composed of Mr. Blindman, foreman, Mr. No-good, Mr. Malice,

Mr. Love-lust, Mr. Live-loose, Mr. Heady, Mr. High-mind, Mr. Enmity, Mr. Liar, Mr. Cruelty, Mr. Hate-light, and Mr. Implacable; and the witnesses are Envy, Superstition, and Pickthank. Minor characters include Simple, Sloth, and Presumption, three fettered sleepers who perish because they refuse to act to save themselves; Formalist and Hypocrisy, who get lost trying to find easy paths to salvation; Mistrust and Timorous, who turn back when they find obstacles in their path; and Pope and Pagan, giants too feeble to trouble the traveler.

Combats with the powers of darkness are most memorable among the incidents of Christian's ordeal: evil is always a source of inspiration to the artist. It is more difficult to make the forces of good appear attractive. That Bunyan succeeds is evidenced in his description of the good counselors who befriend Christian: Help, who pulls him out of the Slough of Despond; Evangelist, the Pilgrim's adviser in moments of peril; his companions Faithful and Hopeful; and the three maidens, Piety, Prudence, and Charity, whose virtues Christian emulates.

Bunyan's symbolic use of physical topography, drawn mainly from the countryside of the English East Midlands, adds realism and verisimilitude to the story. The hills and valleys traveled by Christian are vividly described by Bunyan, who knew at first hand the muddy Slough, the Hill Difficulty, the highways, the deep, dark valleys, and the entrancing mountains. Rutted roads, sloughs, and highwaymen were everyday facts of life for the seventeenth-century English traveler and well-known phenomena to contemporary readers.

Sir Sidney Lee called *The Pilgrim's Progress* the epic of Puritanism, and the spirit of the work can be fully appreciated only if Bunyan's intensely religious nature and theological beliefs are understood. His doctrine was that of Luther, of Knox, of Oliver Cromwell, and of the best minds of Protestant England and Europe. To them, and to Bunyan, Protestant Christianity represented truth, without which all mankind was doomed to perish. No one challenged the literal interpretation of the Bible, except for a few heretical thinkers. The people, states Froude, "not only believed that God had miraculously governed the Israelites but they believed that as directly and immediately He governed England in the seventeenth century."

Bunyan paid heavily for his uncompromising beliefs. Under

Cromwell he had been free to preach, but following the Restoration he was arrested and imprisoned for twelve years in Bedford Gaol for the crime of unlicensed preaching. Among alleviating circumstances of this period was his freedom to write. About two-thirds of *The Pilgrim's Progress* was written during his confinement. While in prison, Bunyan had two books constantly by his side, the King James Bible and Foxe's *Book of Martyrs;* their direct impact upon his thought and writing style is clearly reflected in *The Pilgrim's Progress.* The language of the book is by no means entirely Biblical, however, for Bunyan introduced color and variety by using the colloquial English of his own day.

Among *The Pilgrim's Progress'* claim to fame is its general recognition as a forerunner of the English novel. The persons in the book are men and women of flesh and blood, whose afflictions and sufferings are mirrored in the lives of its readers. It is small wonder then, that, as Sidney says, the tale "holdeth children from play, and old men from the chimney corner."

Various attempts have been made to explain why *The Pilgrim's Progress* has established itself as a classic of English literature. Dean Inge suggests that "The great moralists always see life in silhouette. Evil and good for them are black and white. It is this tremendous moral earnestness, this haunting conviction of the infinite importance of the choice, which makes Bunyan's allegory a very great book." A biographer, G. B. Harrison, credits the author's "very wide observation of men in every variety of emotional experience . . . the acutest perception, ever noting, comparing, understanding the workings of the human mind." But perhaps the book's profound significance is most clearly seen by Edward Wagenknecht, literary critic and historian:

> It lives because, fundamentally, after all allowances for Bunyan's unenlightened Calvinism have been made, it is true; it bores down to the rock-bottom of our lives. Every man, whatever his creed, must, in one form or another, answer the age-old question, "Wilt thou join with the dragons? wilt thou join with the gods?" Every man has wallowed in the Slough of Despond, and battled with Giant Apollyon in the Valley of Humiliation; every man has starved and thirsted in the dungeons of Despair. And every man knows, however he may try to forget it, that he must go through the River at last.

25. MECHANICS OF THE UNIVERSE

Isaac Newton's *Philosophiœ Naturalis Principia Mathematica*
(Mathematical Principles of Natural Philosophy)
1687

Albert Einstein's principal contributions to physics were made before the age of twenty-seven; the greatest of his predecessors, Sir Isaac Newton, is credited with three major scientific discoveries within two years after his graduation from Cambridge University.

Any one of Newton's early discoveries would have entitled him to a distinguished place in the history of science. First was the mathematical method known as the differential calculus, which forms the basis of modern mathematics and is the chief instrument by which problems in theoretical physical science are solved. The second was the law of composition of light, which led Newton on to the study of the nature of color, the character of white light, and an explanation of the rainbow. The third and most famous revelation was the law of universal gravitation, which stirred the imaginations of scientists more than any other theoretical discovery of modern times, with the possible exception of the Copernican system.

Twenty years later, utilizing the principles he had discovered as a young man, Newton's monumental treatise on physical science, *Philosophiœ Naturalis Principia Mathematica,* was issued. The three volumes of the *Principia,* in Latin, were produced in a period of about seventeen months. This incredible achievement required the most intense and prolonged concentration on the part of the author. Newton drew upon his extensive knowledge of astronomy, chemistry, physics, and mathematics in the preparation of the work.

As a whole, the *Principia* deals with the motion of bodies treated mathematically; more particularly, it deals with the application of dynamics and universal gravitation to the solar system. An explanation of the differential calculus, which is used for calculations throughout the work, is followed by definitions of space and time and by Newton's formulation of the laws of motion. This last is the fundamental proposition that every particle of matter is attracted by every other particle of matter with a force inversely proportional to the square of their distance apart. Newton also states the laws governing the problem of bodies colliding with each other. The whole is expressed in classical geometrical forms.

The first book of the *Principia* is concerned with the motion of bodies in free space, while the second treats of "motion in a resisting medium," such as water. In the latter section, the complex problems of fluids are considered and solved, methods to determine the velocity of sound are discussed, and wave motions are described mathematically. Newton lays the groundwork in the *Principia* for the entire sciences of mathematical physics, hydrostatics, and hydrodynamics, as they are known today.

In the third book, entitled "The System of the World," Newton makes his most powerful contribution when he deals with the astronomical consequences of the law of gravitation. At the outset, he makes a fundamental break with the past by insisting that there is no difference between earthly and celestial phenomena. "Like effects in nature are produced by like causes," Newton declared, "as breathing in man and beast, the fall of stones in Europe and in America, the light of the kitchen fire and of the sun, the reflections of light on the earth and on the planets." Herewith he discarded the ancient belief that of all existing worlds only the earth is imperfect. The same rational laws now governed the entire universe.

The important topics discussed in the third book include the motions of the planets and of the satellites around the planets, methods for measuring the masses of the sun and planets, the density of the earth, the precession of the equinoxes, a theory of tides, the orbits of the comets, and the moon's motions—an impressive list.

By his theory of "perturbations" Newton proved that the moon is attracted by both the earth and the sun and that therefore the moon's orbit is disturbed by the sun's pull, although the earth provides the stronger attraction. He also proved that the planets are similarly subject to perturbations. In later times, applications of the perturbations theory led to the discovery of the planets Neptune and Pluto.

Newton determined the masses of different planets and the mass of the sun by relating them to that of the earth. He estimated that the earth's density is between five and six times that of water and on this basis calculated the masses of the sun and of the planets with satellites—an achievement described by Adam Smith as "above the reach of human reason and experience."

Newton next proceeded to explain that the earth is not an exact sphere but is flattened at the poles because of rotation, calculating the amount of flattening mathematically. By studying the exact shape of a planet, the possibility of estimating the length of day and night on it was shown.

In his study of the fluctuation of the tides, Newton applied the law of universal gravitation. When the moon is fullest, he discovered, the earth's waters experience their maximum attraction, and high tide results; since the sun also affects the tides, the tide is highest when the sun and moon are in line.

Still another subject of popular interest on which Newton shed light was that of comets. His theory was that comets, moving under the sun's attraction, travel elliptical paths of incredible magnitude, thus requiring many years to complete their circuits. Thereafter, comets, which were formerly regarded by the superstitious as evil omens, took their place as beautiful and harmless celestial phenomena. Using Newton's theories of planets, Edmund Halley was able to predict the reappearance, approximately every seventy-five years, of the comet that bears his name.

Newton recognized that his "System of the World"—the mechanics of the universe—was built upon the work begun by Copernicus and so notably carried forward by Brahe, Kepler, and Galileo. "If I have seen farther than other men," Newton said, "it is by standing on the shoulders of giants."

Scientific discoveries in the twentieth century have modified some elements of Newton's work, especially in relation to astronomy. Einstein's theory of relativity, for example, maintains that space and time are not absolute, as Newton had believed. Nevertheless, the consensus of various authorities in science and technology is that the structure of a skyscraper, the safety of a railroad bridge, the motion of a motor car, the flight of an airplane, the navigation of a ship across the ocean, the measure of time, and other illustrations of contemporary civilization depend fundamentally upon Newton's laws.

26. APOLOGIST FOR REVOLUTION

John Locke's *Two Treatises of Government*

1690

The second half of the seventeenth century was a period of revolutionary change in England. The era began with the overthrow and execution of Charles I, followed by the establishment of Cromwell's regime, the restoration of Charles II, the deposition of James II, and the accession of William of Orange to the throne—all before 1690.

In such a feverish atmosphere, divided sentiments and sectarian opinions were expressed in an open literary market. The inevitable result was a challenging answer from the opposition, followed by refutations, rebuttals, and recantations. Political pamphleteering flourished. Of most enduring importance in the flood of controversial writings of the time, however, is John Locke's *Two Treatises of Government*. The noted American historian Charles A. Beard described Locke as "the forerunner of the American and French revolutions as well as the supreme apologist for the English revolution of 1688."

Two years before the *Two Treatises of Government* appeared, Parliament had succeeded in ousting the last Stuart, James II, and in achieving its supremacy over the Crown in the "Glorious Revolution" of 1688. Locke sided with the Parlimentary Party, the Whigs, for whom his *Second Treatise* became a political gospel and remained so for the next century. The principal purpose in writing the *Two Treatises of Government,* Locke stated, was "to establish the throne of our great restorer, our present King William; to make good his title in the consent of the people; which being the only one of lawful governments, he has more fully than any other prince in Christendom; and to justify to the world the people of England, whose love of their just and natural rights, with their resolution to preserve them, saved the nation when it was on the brink of slavery and ruin."

The *First Treatise* was a rejoinder to Sir Robert Filmer's *Patriarcha or the Natural Power of Kings* and refuted in detail Filmer's "divine right of kings" doctrine—a theory even then discredited (though defended by Hobbes) and of slight interest today, when royalty has only an ornamental function. In the *Second Treatise* Locke outlined his own political system. Though written as an apology for the English Revolution of 1688, the treatise has proven to be the bulwark of all future democracies.

Antecedent to and progenitor of all existing governments was the anarchical "state of nature," in which, according to Locke, mankind enjoyed the right to life, liberty, and property, and "peace, good will, mutual assistance and preservation" prevailed. A "law of nature," based on man's innate reason, determined what was right and wrong, but its enforcement was "put into every man's hands," and principles of ethics and morality were individually concluded. Locke's "state of nature" was not a state of hostility that Hobbes had envisioned.

Obviously, the lack of an organized and unified body politic brought about serious disadvantages and endangered peaceful coexistence. "Thus mankind," said Locke, "notwithstanding all the privileges of the state of nature, but being in an ill condition while they remain in it, are quickly driven into society." Government came into being by common consent, created by the people through a social contract for the purpose of protecting and preserving life, liberty, and property against internal and external dangers. Entering into such a pact with his fellow men, the individual forfeits none of the rights that he enjoyed in the natural state, for government is established not to take away rights but to preserve them more fully. Locke insisted that government has no duties except to protect property, broadly interpreted, and he vigorously opposed any other type of governmental activity.

To keep society intact and to ensure that power resides in the community and not in the government, Locke insisted upon the principle of majority rule. "When any number of men have so consented to make one community or government, they are thereby presently incorporated and make one body politic, wherein the majority have a right to act and conclude the rest." A government's authority, Locke emphasized repeatedly, rests solely upon the consent of the people.

Locke's theories of property have served to reinforce the arguments of both conservatives and radicals. Every man, he contended, has a property in his own person. Consequently, the "labor of his body and the work of his hands we may say are properly his." As a creation of man's own labor, Locke regarded property as a natural right. In addition to creating property, labor determines its value. "It is labor indeed," he said, "that puts the difference of value on everything. . . . Of the products of the earth useful to the life of man nine-tenths are the effects of labor."

The labor theory of value has been utilized in defense of capitalism, on the ground that property is created by individual effort and initiative. On the other hand, beginning with the nineteenth century, Karl Marx and other socialists used the theory to demand communal control or ownership of the means of production, on the premise that labor adds "surplus value."

Foreshadowing Montesquieu's principle of separation of powers in government, Locke argued for the supremacy of the legislative branch. In his view, the executive is designed merely to enforce the legislature's will and therefore should occupy a subordinate position. Judicial power was to be invested in a division of the executive branch. Even the power of the legislature was greatly restricted; laws were to apply equally to all members of the community; taxation could not be imposed without the consent of the people or their chosen representatives; and legislative power was held to be nontransferable.

In the case of a government exceeding or abusing its delegated powers, Locke holds that revolution is justifiable. The ruler who attempts "to take away and destroy the property of the people, or to reduce them to slavery," is guilty of entering "into a state of war with the people, who are thereupon absolved from any further obedience, and are left to the common refuge, which God hath provided for all men against force and violence." In short, since the ruler has broken his contract with the people and violated a mutual trust, it is their right and duty to rebel against him. The sacredness of individual rights is inviolable.

Locke's influence on American institutions has been profound. His arguments for the origin of government and the relations of man to the state were summarized by Thomas Jefferson in the *Declaration of Independence;* the *Declaration's* preamble is almost a paraphrase of the *Second Treatise.* That the leaders of the Revolution drew inspiration from Locke's defense of the right to rebellion, is exemplified by Jefferson's classic statement: "The tree of liberty must be refreshed from time to time with the blood of patriots and tyrants."

In France, too, all the great pre-Revolutionary critics from Voltaire to Condorcet were well acquainted with Locke's theories. His writings had been early translated into French and were widely circulated on the Continent. Locke's conception of democracy is, in essence, a spiritual condition—a way of life that can conceivably exist in almost any kind of political system in which the government is made to serve man, and not man the state.

PART TWO

ENLIGHTENMENT, REASON, AND REVOLUTION

The "Enlightenment," sometimes referred to as the "Age of Reason"—corresponding roughly to the eighteenth century in Europe—was a natural culmination of the Renaissance and of the scientific revolution. Opposition to theological modes of thought among the intellectual classes had become almost universal. Beginning about 1650, educated persons were dominated by two concepts: first, the remarkable advances in science had convinced them that all Nature could be reduced to a series of mathematical laws; and, second, they concluded that, since he now possessed an infallible method of acquiring truth, man could achieve infinite progress through reason.

Three intellectual currents merged to produce the Enlightenment. One was Cartesian rationalism, the principle that all knowledge not acquired at first hand should be doubted; its progenitor, René Descartes, held that the mathematical method provided an instrument for the re-evaluation and reconstruction of everything the human race assumed it knew. A second major factor was the humanism and skepticism of Renaissance thinkers. Men's interests shifted from preoccupation with otherworldly concerns to mundane matters. Happiness *now* was placed ahead of salvation *later*. As Saint-Evremond stated, "Man ought to apply himself to the quest after his happiness, since it is in his power to augment his pleasures and to diminish his pains." Finally, the Enlightenment was very profoundly influenced by the philosophy of Locke, the science of Isaac Newton, and the traditions of British constitutionalism. In England, the religious and political liberties achieved through the Revolution of 1688 established a model for those fighting for religious and political liberties elsewhere.

Among the first philosophers to apply the Cartesian spirit of doubt to accepted beliefs was Pierre Bayle, who has been characterized as "the father of modern incredulity." His great *Dictionnaire Historique et Critique* constituted a prime source of inspiration for the *philosophes*, chiefly in France, whose writings laid the groundwork for the French Revolution. The only valid test of truth, Bayle maintained, is reason, and because he was convinced that natural laws could not be altered, Bayle doubted the possibility of divine miracles. Further, even seemingly irrational and heretical beliefs should be tolerated; no truth is certain enough to justify the suppression of supposed error by force or persecution. In Bayle's view, force cannot make any man believe what his reason informs him is false, but can only make a hypocrite of him. "We have an inalienable right," he insisted, "to profess those doctrines which we believe conformable to the pure truth."

The necessity for tolerance was recognized also by John Locke. From his point of view, it is no part of a government's function to save men's souls. Instead, its purpose is secular only, to preserve men's rights. A church he considered "a free and voluntary society." The true faith is most likely to prevail wherever toleration of all beliefs is an accepted principle.

Influenced by Bayle and Locke, other thinkers of the Enlightenment joined in upholding the ideal of toleration, though not, by any means, always practicing it in specific situations. By the beginning of the eighteenth century, a considerable body of literature defended the notion that religious differences should be tolerated and church and state separated. France was still predominantly a Catholic country, but several hundred thousand Protestants, deists, atheists, and skeptics were reasonably free to follow their own beliefs or lack of beliefs. Voltaire's friend Frederick II proclaimed full religious liberty in Prussia, the first nation to take such action.

Scientific progress vastly increased the faith of the men of the Enlightenment in Nature and reason. Notably, Newton's perfection of the calculus and his mathematical formulation of a "system of the world," showing the relationship of the planets to the laws of gravity, appeared to his contemporaries to explain, or at least to point the way to an explanation of, all natural phenomena. Instead of a dark, malevolent power to be feared and placated, as in earlier eras, Nature to the Enlightenment became a benign concept. The working of the universe was seen to be orderly and simple. If the same principles operative in Nature could be applied to human affairs, mankind's happiness would be assured. Such "unnatural" social phenomena as class distinctions, special privileges of clergy and royalty, and the distressing contrast between the rich and the poor would disappear.

The understanding of Nature and of its bearing on human behavior, according to the Enlightenment, can be achieved through Reason, represented in its purest form by the science of mathematics. As aptly phrased by Crane Brinton, "Reason applied to human relations will show us that kings are not fathers of their people, that if meat is good to eat on Thursdays it is good to eat on Fridays, that if pork is nourishing to a Gentile it is nourishing to a Jew." Reason enables man to differentiate between "natural" and "unnatural" human institutions and thus to eliminate error, injustice, and superstitions. A dominant theme running throughout the Enlightenment, consequently, is the desire to extend to man and society the methods and laws of the natural scientists. Reason, if logically followed, it was believed, is opposed to tradition, authority, and revelation. Voltaire called it "the light of common sense."

Growing out of their unlimited confidence in the omnipotence of controlled Nature and science is the somewhat naive faith in progress universally held by the *philosophes* of the Enlightenment. One historian, Franklin Le Van Baumer, notes that "the Enlightenment represents European civilization at its cockiest." With no distrust of human nature or of machine technology, there was an almost mystical trust in the future, and solutions were believed imminent for all the great political and social problems inherited from the past. This view was typified by Condorcet, writing toward the end of the eighteenth century, when he asserted that "we are approaching one of the grand revolutions of the human race."

Inevitably the new concepts of science and reason began to be applied to theories of government. The medieval notion of the divine right of kings could not bear close scrutiny in the atmosphere created by science. Existing governments, therefore, could only be defended if they met the tests of Nature and Reason. Such enlightened despots as Frederick the Great of Prussia, the Empress Catherine of Russia, and the Emperor Joseph of Austria were sufficiently perceptive to recognize the trend. In those nations, the criterion of the natural and reasonable was applied to the legal, social, and economic affairs of the state, and their governments survived. The incredible difficulty of the task confronting the rulers is shown by the fact that, as one commentator described it, "in every country of Europe an inextricable confusion of feudal customs, ecclesiastical immunities, guild privileges, social and financial inequalities, . . . an impenetrable jungle of ancient and recent growths" had survived. Any comparison between these man-made institutions and the simplicity which Newton had demonstrated to be the rule of the physical universe was completely disillusioning.

The monarchs of two nations, England and France, failed to discern the wave of the future and made no attempt to bring to their people the benefits of enlightened government. The inflexibility, ineptitude, and unreasoning resistance to change exhibited by James I, Charles I, and James II in Britain, and by Louis XIV and his successors in France, virtually invited drastic direct reform measures by their subjects.

In England, a solution was found in constitutional reform, whereby, in the Bill of Rights of 1689, the Parliament assumed the powers of the monarch, though without abolishing the monarchy as an institution. The chief apologist and philosopher of the movement, John Locke, proclaimed in his second *Treatise on Civil Government,* published the next year, the "social contract" or natural rights theory of government. In essence, the theory held that governments are based on contract and that whenever a tyrannical ruler infringes upon the natural and inalienable rights of his people, revolution is the appropriate remedy.

Revolution, in its most violent form, was required to achieve reform in France, whose Bourbon kings, like the Hapsburgs, "never learned anything nor forgot anything." In addition to Pierre Bayle, of the previous century, four names stand out among the writers whose theories provided the philosophical foundation for one of the most far-reaching upheavals in the history of mankind: Montesquieu, Rousseau, Voltaire, and Diderot.

Montesquieu belongs to an early moderate phase of the Enlightenment. Never manifesting the emotional or doctrinaire spirit of other contemporaneous theorists on government, Montesquieu was the true political scientist. His great work, *The Spirit of the Laws,* represented years of scholarly historical research, a prerequisite, he was convinced, for the scientific study of society and for a real philosophy of politics. Succeeding generations of legislators have found the book to be an inexhaustible mine of information and practical suggestions. A warm admirer of the British Constitution, Montesquieu was especially impressed by the value of its system of checks and balances as a device to prevent both tyranny and mob rule.

A theorist who exerted far more direct and profound influence on the character of the French Revolution was Jean Jacques Rousseau. His *The Social Contract* preached two radically new doctrines: the sovereignty of the people and the sacredness of the General Will. A social and political structure built upon the will of a majority of the people, he held, would insure equality, freedom, and harmony for all. The concept of government based on majority decisions has, of course, enormous historical significance because of its subsequent adoption throughout the world, even though usually with constitutional restrictions.

A striking contrast to Rousseau, the idol of the masses, was Voltaire, the darling of the intellectuals. "To Voltaire," said the English historian John Morley, "reason and humanity were but a single word." Even in his own lifetime, Voltaire became a legend, a symbol of the struggle for freedom of thought. Three years in England, observing the British constitutional form of government in operation, strengthened his conviction of the importance of intellectual freedom and made him a propagandist for reason. A prolific output of plays, poems, satires, and articles won for Voltaire the spiritual leadership of the Enlightenment. By open attacks on religious superstition and political tyranny, he contributed immensely to undermining the old regime in France. From the eighteenth century to the present day, Voltaire has loomed as an heroic figure in the endless fight for civil liberty and toleration.

Denis Diderot, fourth of the renowned quartet, possessed abilities of a still different nature. Fascinated by science and technology, Diderot ranks as the foremost exponent of the experimental approach in the Age of Reason. His *Thoughts on the Interpretation of Nature* is a classic of scientific method. Greater fame came to Diderot, however, through editorship of the monumental *Encyclopédie* (1751–1777). As designed by the editor, the work attempted to bring together in one place a summary of human knowledge in the spirit of the Enlightenment, giving wide circulation to political theories, industrial developments, and scientific discoveries. Diderot hoped thereby to influence ideas of progress and reform. Despite repeated attempts at official censorship, the *Encyclopédie* published numerous articles stressing the political backwardness of France and became a prime force in spreading the new ideals of the Enlightenment.

While lacking the color and fire of their French contemporaries, eighteenth-century observers of the social scene elsewhere were also composing works destined to leave permanent impressions on the modern mind. In Italy, Giambattista Vico was propounding a philosophy of history and a theory of historical cycles in the lives of nations of deep significance in the scientific study of history; and Cesare Beccaria's *Treatise on Crimes and Punishment* was pioneering new concepts in the reform of criminal justice and capital punishment. William Blackstone's *Commentaries on the Laws of England* presented the first systematic and definitive compilation of British statutes and common law principles, a work which has remained for over two centuries one of the legal world's primary sources. A few years later, Adam Smith's *The Wealth of Nations* appeared, influencing generations of economists and laying the foundation for the faith in natural liberty and in a laissez-faire system of economics which became England's guiding creed. In America, Tom Paine's *Common Sense,* Thomas Jefferson's *A Summary View of the Rights of British America,* and the *Declaration of Independence* were igniting revolutionary fires.

Scientific achievement in the eighteenth fell below the spectacular advances of the seventeenth century. But progress was far from negligible. New fields were entered. Scientists were busy gathering, describing, and classifying the infinity of things to be found in the world. Diderot noted in his *Encyclopédie* that "Men's minds seem caught in a general movement towards natural history, anatomy, chemistry, and experimental physics." Amateurs like Voltaire collected specimens of plants, birds, fossils, and rocks. Buffon, author of the celebrated *Natural History, General and Particular;* Lamarck, pre-Darwinian evolutionist; Cuvier, founder of the science of paleontology; and Linnaeus, the great systematizer of botany, were all diligent in collecting, classifying, and preserving specimens. The foundations of experimental chemistry were being laid by Cavendish's discovery of hydrogen and of the synthetic production of water, Rutherford's isolation of nitrogen, Priestley's discovery of oxygen, and Lavoisier's establishment of the science of quantitative chemistry. James Hutton and William Smith opened up a new science of geology by insisting upon a vastly greater age for the earth than the five or six thousand years allowed by Biblical chronology, offering as incontrovertible evidence the stratification of rocks and the study of fossils.

On the literary scene, likewise, there were no towering figures in the eighteenth to match the giants of the preceding century. Yet the age could claim, in Britain, Swift, one of the greatest of satirists; the novelists Defoe, Fielding, Richardson, Smollett, and Sterne; the multi-faceted geniuses of Samuel Johnson and Horace Walpole; the essayists Addison and Steele; and the poets Pope and Burns. French literature was dominated by Voltaire, who was at home in virtually every literary form, and by Rousseau, who, with his faith in Nature and the individual human emotions, was the most important precursor of the Romantic movement. Rousseau's teachings influenced particularly the leading writers of the "Storm and Stress" period in Germany, between 1770 and 1790, notably Herder, Schiller, and Goethe. The political writings of the German philosopher Kant were at the same time lending powerful support to the cause of republicanism, at home and abroad.

In summary, the philosophers and thinkers of the Enlightenment hardly foresaw or wished for a revolution, but their caustic criticism of existing conditions and their urgent insistence upon social betterment were undoubtedly instrumental in creating revolutionary sentiment. Their hopes and dreams were only partially realized by reforms growing out of the French Revolution. Nevertheless, the ferment of the Enlightenment left a permanent imprint upon the Western world. Among peoples everywhere, the desire for national independence, for constitutional government, and for personal liberty had been firmly implanted. In the New World, especially, liberal ideas were free to develop with few restrictions. The Age of Reason may be justly said to have reawakened faith in the destiny of man.

27. THE COMPLETE SKEPTIC

Pierre Bayle's *Dictionnaire Historique et Critique*
(Historical and Critical Dictionary)
1697

René Descartes' first principle, in his *Discourse on Method,* was "never to accept anything for true which I did not clearly know to be such." Within a few years after Descartes' death, this basic rule was applied to the letter by Pierre Bayle in his *Historical and Critical Dictionary,* a work which became a primary source, inspiration, and repository of ideas for the eighteenth century, especially in France.

Bayle, a professor of philosophy at the Protestant University of Sedan left France after the university was suppressed and spent the remainder of his life, 1681–1706, at Rotterdam. Relatively speaking, a considerable degree of intellectual freedom prevailed in the Netherlands of his day. The country was a clearinghouse for European thought—probably the only spot on the Continent where conflicting religious and political theories were even grudgingly tolerated. Numerous forbidden books were printed by the Dutch and from there smuggled abroad. Among Holland's inhabitants were some of Europe's leading scholars—refugees and exiles from France, England, Germany, Switzerland, and other nations. In this congenial atmosphere, Bayle, who possessed one of the most remarkable minds of his age, flourished.

Though Bayle's *Dictionary* contains articles on history, geography, literature, philology, philosophy, theology, and mythology, it is essentially a biographical compilation. For the most part, the author was interested in people, particularly in characters of significance in history, philosophy, and religion, but not in natural science —a field he largely ignored. Bayle was highly subjective in his choice of topics, for he selected only those that furnished him an opportunity to comment on his favorite themes. Thus an excessive amount of space is given to Protestant ministers, professors, and theologians, while many eminent authors and philosophers are excluded. A possible explanation for the omission of certain personalities is that

Bayle "had nothing worth while or nothing scandalous or paradoxical to say about them." In any case, the *Dictionary* must be regarded, first and foremost, as a record of Bayle's notions, opinions, and knowledge on particular men and topics. Partiality and one-sidedness were therefore inevitable.

The textual arrangement of the Bayle *Dictionary* is striking: the commentaries accompanying the text are more extensive and more important than the text itself. Often a large folio page contains a few lines of text spread across the top, the rest being filled by *Notes* in double columns and fine print. The plan served two purposes. Firstly, it gave Bayle a chance to insert lengthy quotations drawn from his rich background of reading in various languages. Secondly, and perhaps more important from his point of view, as George R. Havens, in his *The Age of Ideas*, points out, "this system permitted him to hide away in these closely-printed notes amid the learned references his dangerous thoughts and queries, hoping that the censor would nod his head wearily and approve by default what otherwise was sure to be forbidden."

Bayle's aim was to destroy the residue of medieval superstition and archaic scholasticism that still cluttered European thought, applying reason and doubt to every matter under consideration. Nothing was taken for granted. The technique followed in the *Dictionary* is to range authorities against one another, citing their contradictions and weaknesses and comparing the reliability and value of their contributions. Frequently, the reader is left to draw his own conclusions where the exact truth is difficult to determine, or where it might have involved Bayle in theological controversy. The overall effect is to implant skepticism in the mind of the reader. For example, the Bayle method critically investigates Biblical stories by examining them in the light of historical accuracy and scientific knowledge. By the use of apparently innocent cross references, Bayle questions scriptural miracles and other supernatural manifestations.

A number of Bayle's articles recall the bitter doctrinal disputes of his time. Three in particular were singled out for attack by the orthodox critics. Perhaps the most shocking to the devout believers of the period was the chapter on David, King of Israel, whom Bayle held to have been guilty of cruel, barbarous, and immoral conduct, including adultery and murder. A second article, on the Manicheans, is concerned with evil in the world. Assuming that God is good and omnipotent, Bayle asks, why then does He permit evil in the universe? Why did He allow Eve to eat the apple? Because of the multiple evils afflicting mankind throughout history, Bayle found himself agreeing with the heretical Manicheans, who believed in the existence of two spirits, one the source of good, the other of evil. The third heretical article deals with an ancient Greek thinker, Pyrrho, famous for his skeptical approach to all subjects. Bayle argues that such skepticism is dangerous neither to the state nor to morality, but may weaken theology. Morality, he insists, is based on conscience, not on religious orthodoxy.

The spirit of rationalism and tolerance pervading Bayle's work naturally led to a ban on its publication in France. The displeasure of such monarchs as Louis XIV with the *Dictionary's* lack of orthodoxy was heightened by Bayle's indulgence in occasional scandalous references illustrating the foibles of the great. Nevertheless, numerous complete and abridged editions, both in French and in translation, soon appeared in Germany, England, and Switzerland, and a great number of copies flowed across the border for sale by Parisian bookdealers.

Frederick the Great, one of Bayle's warmest admirers, who edited and published selections from the *Dictionary,* once remarked to Voltaire, "It was Bayle who began it all." He was referring to the attitude of skepticism so typical of the eighteenth century. In his reaction against civil and religious absolutism and in his advocacy of political and religious toleration, Bayle was the spiritual father of such revolutionary thinkers as Voltaire, Diderot, and Rousseau. Voltaire declared him to be the "greatest dialectician who has ever written" and "the eternal honor of the human reason." *The Dictionary* was a most important predecessor of Diderot's great *Encyclopedia.* Through Voltaire and other eighteenth-century philosophers Bayle's ideas permeated the entire French nation, preparing its people for the French Revolution. By teaching critical standards and respect for factual accuracy, Bayle also helped pave the way for a new age of scientific discoveries.

Among the many English scholars and writers who have held Bayle in high esteem was Edward Gibbon, who noted that "his critical Dictionary is a vast repository of facts and opinions; and he balances the false religions in his sceptical scales, till the opposite qualities annihilate each other." In America, it has been revealed that Herman Melville owned an English translation of the *Dictionary* and drew heavily upon it for the philosophical contents of *Moby Dick.*

28. FIRST MICROBE HUNTER

Anton van Leeuwenhoek's *Epistolae ad Societatem Regiam Anglicam* (Letters to the Royal Society of England)

1719

There are few lines in English literature more frequently quoted than Jonathan Swift's jingle:

> So, naturalists observe, a flea
> Has smaller fleas that on him prey;
> And these have smaller still to bite 'em,
> And so proceed *ad infinitum*.

The inspiration for this bit of doggerel was the microscopic studies of a Dutch amateur scientist and lens grinder, Anton van Leeuwenhoek, to whom historians have accorded such laudatory titles as "father of bacteriology and protozoology," "founder of microscopy," and "first of the microbe hunters." Leeuwenhoek's duties as a minor municipal official in Delft do not appear to have interfered with his avocation—a passion for constructing microscopes and for using them to observe natural phenomena—in which he indulged for most of his ninety-one years.

Though he was not the actual inventor of the microscope, Leeuwenhoek ground his own lenses, of quartz glass and diamonds, and perfected magnifying glasses of then unheard-of power: as high as two hundred and seventy to one. As a result, he was the first human being to see protozoa, bacteria, and many features of the minute structure of living organisms.

Leeuwenhoek's first step toward fame came through the intercession of Reiner De Graff, a fellow townsman, already known in scientific circles. In a communication to Henry Oldenburg, secretary of the Royal Society of London, De Graff stated: "I am writing to tell you that a certain most ingenious person here, named *Leewenhoeck,* has devised microscopes which far surpass those which we have hitherto seen. . . . The enclosed letter from him, where he describes certain things which he has observed more accurately than previous authors, will afford you a sample of his work." The Leeuwenhoek letter describes the microscopic structure of a bee and of a louse. It was the first of several hundred communications, all in Dutch, the only language he knew, written to the Royal Society by Leeuwenhoek over a period of fifty years. The letters, dealing with diverse chemical, physical, botanical, zoological, physiological, and medical topics, were originally published in the Society's *Philosophical Transactions* and subsequently collected under the title *Epistolae ad Societatem Regiam Anglicam.* In 1680, the Royal Society unanimously elected Leeuwenhoek to membership.

Modern historians of science have said that Leeuwenhoek's investigations were scattered and unsystematic. Through his remarkable lenses he peered at everything, like a boy fascinated by a new toy. Nevertheless, despite his lack of scientific discrimination, the keen-sighted amateur naturalist was an indefatigable observer who faithfully recorded his microscopic adventures. Furthermore, every observation was verified with infinite care before being announced for publication.

Of the original discoveries credited to Leeuwenhoek, the most celebrated is that of the existence of bacteria and of protozoan life in the mouth and in water—his demonstration that the world is filled with a vast teeming universe of "little animals." Looking at a drop of rain water through one of his lenses, he found revealed an invisible horde of animal life, fast-moving creatures, infinitely too minute to be seen with the naked eye. Leeuwenhoek called them "wretched beasties," and writes, "They stop, they stand still as 'twere upon a point, and then turn themselves round with that swiftness as we see a top turn round, the circumference they make being no bigger than that of a fine grain of sand." From his detailed descriptions, it is certain that he saw the three great morphological types—rod, spiral, and round—now called bacilli, spirilla, and cocci.

In a letter written October 9, 1676, Leeuwenhoek clearly and unmistakably describes both protozoa and bacteria. After noting the presence of three more or less recognizable types of protozoa, the author reports:

> The fourth sort of little animals [bacteria], which drifted among the three sorts aforesaid, were incredibly small; nay, so small, in my sight, that I judged that even if 100 of these very wee animals lay stretched out one against another, they could not reach to the length of a grain of coarse sand; and if this be true, then ten hundred thousand of these living creatures could scarce equal the bulk of a coarse sandgrain. I discovered yet a fifth sort, which had about the thickness of the last-said animalcules, but which were nearly twice as long.

In another paragraph of the same letter, Leeuwenhoek describes spirilla, as well as bacteria and bacilli, discovered in pepper-water. A later report, written in 1683, is also of special interest to the bacteriologist; it concerns the "scum from the teeth." Leeuwenhoek explains his research method:

> 'Tis my wont of a morning to rub my teeth with salt, and then swill my mouth out with water; and often, after eating to clean my back teeth with a toothpick, as well as rubbing them hard with a cloth.

Despite the elaborate cleaning operation, Leeuwenhoek found tartar still present between his teeth. In this matter suspended in rain water, he observed cocci, short rods, long thread-forms (*Leptothrix*) and spirochetes, from which he concluded that "all the people living in our United Netherlands are not so many as the living animals that I carry in my own mouth this very day." The findings were confirmed by an examination of matter from the teeth of several other persons, including an old gentleman who confessed to never having been guilty of cleaning his teeth.

The first representation of bacteria is to be found in a drawing accompanying one of Leeuwenhoek's communications, published by the Royal Society in 1683.

Next to the observations on microbes, Leeuwenhoek's most significant claim to scientific renown is the first accurate description of the red blood corpuscles and observation of the capillary circulation. Harvey's *De Motu Cordis* in 1628 had speculated on the nature of the connection between arteries and veins that made blood circulation possible, and in 1661 Malpighi described the circulation of the blood in the capillaries of a frog's lungs. Twenty-five years later, Leeuwenhoek actually witnessed, with the aid of his microscope, the circulation of the blood in the capillaries of the tail of the tadpole and eel, the web of the frog's foot, the fins of fishes, the bat's wing, and the ears of young rabbits—all of which was duly recorded and passed on to the Royal Society. Thus he completed the proof of Harvey's theory of circulation developed a half-century earlier.

Almost everything that Leeuwenhoek saw under his microscopes was new to the world. In 1677 he described and illustrated the spermatozoa in dogs and other animals, although in this discovery Stephen Hamm had anticipated him by a few months. Disproving prevailing superstitions about spontaneous generation of low forms of animal life, Leeuwenhoek showed, for example, that the flea, "this

minute and despised creature," did not consist of mere dust or sand
but reproduced itself in the same manner as other winged insects and
was "endowed with as great perfection in its kind as any large animal." He also recognized that the aphid was developed by partho-
genesis, that is from unfertilized eggs; made accurate observations
on the development of the ant and on the spinning and poison apparatus of spiders; investigated the generation of eels (at that time
supposed to be produced from dew); discovered minute globular
particles in fermenting liquids (he was the first to describe the yeast
plant); and noted that reproduction of hydra, an aquatic animal, occurs by budding, without male intervention, and also that the hydra
is the unwilling host of parasites one thousandth of its size. These
were among the hundreds of marvels observed by Leeuwenhoek, all
previously invisible to man's eyes.

Publication of his scientific discoveries spread Leeuwenhoek's
reputation throughout Europe. As his biographer, Clifford Dobell,
writes, "Kings and princes, philosophers and physicians and men of
science, statesmen and clergymen and even common men went to see
him and to look through his wonderful glasses."

Although he did not have the method and system of a modern scientist, Leeuwenhoek possessed a truly scientific spirit. In one of his
letters he remarked:

> As I aim at nothing but Truth, and so far as in me lieth, to point out
> mistakes that may have crept into certain matters; I hope that in so
> doing those I chance to censure will not take it ill; and if they would
> expose any errors in my own discoveries, I'd esteem it a service; all
> the more, because 'twould thereby give me encouragement towards
> attaining of a nicer accuracy.

29. MAN ALONE

Daniel Defoe's *Robinson Crusoe*

1719

For the convenience of readers, or perhaps to intrigue prospective
buyers, a charming custom among eighteenth-century authors and
publishers was to offer synopses of books on the title pages: for example, Daniel Defoe's *The Life and Strange Surprizing Adventures*

*of Robinson Crusoe, of York, Mariner, Who Lived Eight and Twenty
Years All Alone in an Uninhabited Island on the Coast of America,
Near the Mouth of the Great River, Oroonoque: Having Been Cast
on Shore by Shipwreck Wherein All the Men Perished But Himself:
With an Account of How He Was at Last as Strangely Delivered by
Pyrates. Written by Himself.*

This immensely popular novel, familiarly known today simply as
Robinson Crusoe, was like a modern detective thriller in elaborating
upon the plot accurately outlined on the title page; it has become a
permanent part of the world's literary heritage. Before the beginning
of the twentieth century, there had appeared at least seven hundred
editions, translations, and imitations of the story, with the number
mounting steadily ever since.

Authentic evidence exists that Defoe's inspiration for the celebrated novel was based on the actual experience of Alexander Selkirk,
a Scottish sailor who quarreled with his captain and, at his own re-
quest, was put ashore on an uninhabited island three hundred miles
off the coast of Chile. For five years he managed to survive there
and then was brought back to England, where he was a nine-days
wonder. Whether or not Defoe ever met Selkirk personally is uncertain.

Relating the story in the first person, Robinson Crusoe speaks in
a simple direct style: "I was born in the year 1632 in the city of
York of a good family, though not of that country, my father being
a foreigner of Bremen, who settled first at Hull. . . . Being the
third son of the family, and not bred to any trade, my head began to
be filled very early with rambling thoughts." A wayward youth, full
of a spirit of wanderlust, he leaves home without his father's consent,
sailing on a ship bound for London. A series of adventures and misadventures ensue, including a period in slavery to the Barbary
pirates. Eventually, at the age of twenty-seven, Crusoe is shipwrecked on a solitary island near the Orinoco River; of the ship's
crew, he is the only member saved. Concerning his comrades he
writes, in a realistic touch, "I never saw them afterwards, or any
sign of them, except three of their hats, one cap, and two shoes that
were not fellows." For twenty-eight years, two months, and nineteen
days, Robinson Crusoe is destined to remain marooned on the island.
In the absorbing tale that follows the shipwreck, the reader shares
his experiences from day to day and year to year.

At the outset, Crusoe has the good fortune to salvage much essential equipment from the wreck before it disintegrates and disappears. Here again, the author provides realistic detail by enumerating the items that were saved—all of which later contribute to the hero's survival: three bags full of nails and spikes, a great screw jack, seven muskets, three barrels of rum, a pair of large scissors, axes, hatchets, a bagful of corn and rice later to be planted, and so on with a full inventory.

Though Crusoe says "I had never handled a tool in my life," he displays extraordinary ingenuity as a builder, farmer, tailor, carpenter, potter, and all-round handyman. Quickly adjusting himself to the primitive conditions he finds on the island, he builds a hut, fortifies a cave, plants corn, constructs a raft, surrounds himself with a small menagerie of pets, and, in his isolation, finds constant consolation in the Bible.

Numerous commentators have attempted to analyze the magic of *Robinson Crusoe.* Superficially, the account appears humdrum and Crusoe himself a dull fellow. The careful descriptions of how he makes his pottery jars, his baskets, chairs, his great hairy umbrella, and his clothing, for example, would seem tedious in the telling, but each enterprise becomes an adventure and holds us enthralled while we await the outcome. As he conquers one obstacle after another, Crusoe captures our imagination and becomes an heroic figure—a man dominating nature. Illustrative of his resourcefulness are his attempts to kill the wild goats on the island:

> I observed if they saw me in the valleys, though they were upon the rocks, they would run away as in a terrible fright; but if they were feeding in the valleys, and I was upon the rocks, they took no notice of me, from whence I concluded that by the position of their optics, their sight was so directed downward, that they did not readily see objects that were above them; so afterwards I took this method, I always climbed the rocks first to get above them, and then frequently had a fair mark.

A perceptive observation by Walter De La Mare may furnish the key to Defoe's success: "The spell of his enchanting masterpiece is not, of course, mere romance, but the dressing-up of romance to make it look like matter-of-fact." To which Virginia Woolf adds: "By means of this genius for fact Defoe achieves effects that are beyond any but the great masters of descriptive prose." By going into a wealth of specific detail, Defoe easily persuades the reader to believe in the facts he presents.

Of Crusoe himself, an extreme point of view is expressed by the English critic V. S. Pritchett: "He is the one universal character in fiction one would loath to meet, the man in the street raised to the nth power of monstrous efficiency, a monumental dullard who stops himself from thinking by drudgery." Certainly Robinson Crusoe is an unsentimental, hardheaded fellow, but he nevertheless has the faculty of gaining our sympathy and holding our undivided interest at every turn of his fortunes.

For twenty-four years, Crusoe lives in solitude. Then occurs the most dramatic moment in his chronicle. As told by Crusoe, "It happened one day about noon, going towards my boat, I was exceedingly surprised with the print of a man's naked foot on the shore, which was very plain to be seen in the sand." Shortly afterward, he rescues from cannibals the Negro Friday, who becomes his servant and companion. The island's population gradually expands, through the arrival of shipwrecked sailors and a mutinous ship's crew. Crusoe helps the captain and mate to recapture their ship from the mutineers and eventually returns with them to England.

Inspired by the immediate popularity of *Robinson Crusoe,* Defoe wrote a sequel, generally regarded as inferior and anticlimactic to the original work. Part II recounts Crusoe's marriage, the return to his beloved island, and the death of Friday.

Aside from its fascination as a stirring tale of adventure, a leading literary historian, Walter Allen, attaches a deeper meaning to *Robinson Crusoe,* conceiving of it as an allegory of every man's life: "In the last analysis, we are each of us alone, condemned to solitariness. . . . This condition Defoe symbolizes in the sharpest possible way when he sets Crusoe down on his island, alone, with himself and with God. *Robinson Crusoe,* then, is a dramatization of universal experience: we are all Crusoes, for to be Crusoe is the human fate."

Of the innumerable books influenced by *Robinson Crusoe,* the greatest was Jonathan Swift's *Gulliver's Travels,* whose effects are achieved in considerable part by a similar use of circumstantial detail. Foremost among the numerous imitations is Johann Rudolf Wyss' *The Swiss Family Robinson* (1841), a perennial juvenile favorite. Jean Jacques Rousseau, planning the education of *Émile,* recognized the pedagogic value of *Robinson Crusoe* and introduced his protégé to it at the age of fifteen. Thus the book became a landmark in the history of education, as well as a work which has been read purely for pleasure by millions, young and old.

30. SCIENTIFIC HISTORIAN

Giambattista Vico's *Principi di una Scienza Nuova* (The New Science)

1725

Giambattista Vico's *The New Science* has been described as "one of the world's greatest books," but throughout most of its existence it has remained in obscurity. "Yet Vico rather than the intelligensia of the eighteenth century [or theorists such as] Condorcet, Marx, and Engels," maintains the distinguished American scientist Waldemar Kaempffert, "must be regarded as the first to have thought of history in materialistic terms and to have created the modern philosophy of history." By interpreting history in relation to the social evolution of mankind, rather than as the rise and fall of individual nations, Vico blazed the trail for such twentieth-century works as H. G. Wells' *Outline of History*.

Prior to the eighteenth century, formal history was little more than a chaotic mass of facts and legends, lacking in logical explanation and interpretation. As the noted American writer Edmund Wilson phrased it, "Human history had hitherto always been written as a series of biographies of great men or as a chronicle of remarkable happenings or as a pageant directed by God."

The astronomical revolution led by Copernicus and Galileo removed the earth from its position as the center of the universe, and Newton demonstrated that the whole world of nature was regulated by fixed laws. To Vico, a poverty-stricken professor of rhetoric at the University of Naples, occurred the thought that the actions of men and of human societies might also be regulated by definitely established rules. He was convinced that a new interpretation of the story of mankind must be found. Vico set out in *The New Science* to explain the world of man as completely and convincingly as Newton and other scientists had explained the world of nature. "There has hitherto been lacking," he wrote, "a science which should be at the same time a history and a philosophy of humanity."

In *The New Science,* Vico attempted to discover the cause of historical change and came to the basic conclusion that societies have passed through regular phases of growth in the same way as have human beings. In his words, "The facts of known history are to be referred to their primitive origins, divorced from which they have seemed hitherto to possess neither a common basis, nor continuity nor coherence." Further, "It is of the nature of things that they come into being in certain circumstances and in certain ways. Wherever the same circumstances are present, the same phenomena arise and no others."

Vico, a good Catholic, accepted the Old Testament account of Adam and Eve and the Garden of Eden. He theorized that after the Flood the descendants of Ham and Japheth and those of Shem, except the Hebraic line, became scattered, forgot the speech and customs of their ancestors, and reverted to a nearly beastlike savage state. After several centuries, the beginnings of primitive religion, chiefly inspired by fear of unfathomable natural phenomena, produced a certain degree of morality. There ensued family life, the cultivation of the soil, the institution of property and ownership, and the development of language beyond signs and gestures. Eventually, organized society emerged through the coming together of independent families.

The central idea in Vico's doctrine is the theory that all human affairs pass through cycles during which mankind is led step by step from barbarism to civilization through the guidance of a benevolent Providence.

Three stages of social development are distinguished by Vico. As a nation slowly rises from its primitive state, it passes through the "Age of the Gods" in which men live in a state of "superstitious fanaticism." Every force of nature is imagined to be a manifestation of the gods, and a fantastic universe of both benevolent and malignant spirits is built up. It is the age of myths, superstitions, divinations, and idolatry. Government is in the hands of the priestly class.

By gradual transition, the "Age of the Gods" is succeeded by the "Age of the Heroes." In this era human nature is heroic in stature, law is based on force, and right is decided by armed might. The leaders of patriarchal clans become the rulers of communities, and communities combine to form larger units of government. The dominant elements are strong men, heads of families, and patriarchs, as was typified by the Roman Senate. Government is aristocratic. It is the age of the heroic poets, such as Homer, and religion, philosophy, and literature remain essentially mythological in form.

The Age of the Heroes ends as the masses gain full rights and powers as citizens, and it is followed by the "Age of Man." Events in human society and in physical nature are no longer regarded as evidences of divine will. Language is written as well as spoken. Governments become democratic or combinations of democracies and monarchies. Law is directed by intelligence and reason. Unfortunately, the Age of Man contains the seeds of its own destruction as decadence sets in. Popular states become corrupt, skepticism undermines religion, and conflicts develop between rich and poor. "The corruption of a nation may advance so far," says Vico, "that no remedy can be found within itself, but must come from without; and in such a case a nation is either subdued by a foreign enemy or sinks into barbarism." Ancient Rome is cited as an example of the decay of the Age of Man. Then the cycle begins all over again: after the fall of Rome, the Age of the Gods reappears in the Dark Ages; the Age of the Heroes emerges in the Middle Ages; and the Age of Man starts to revive in modern times, that is, the Renaissance. Vico views history as moving continually onward, and perhaps gradually upward, according to his law of cycles.

Vico deeply mistrusted recorded history, choosing instead to rediscover and reconstruct the past for himself through analyses of language, myth, and poetry. Through the study of Latin, for example, he traced the savage and rustic beginnings of the Romans. An instance is the word for law, *lex,* originally signifying a collection of acorns, later a group of vegetables, then a gathering of citizens, and, lastly, the law made by the assembled citizens. Myth, legend, and poetry, Vico believed, reflect the thought of a whole people, not single individuals; thus Homer represents not a person but "the ideal or heroic character of the Greek people." Poetry, of a simple, sensuous sort, he regarded as the first form of language, a more natural expression of a barbaric than of a highly civilized age.

Vico's theory of the unity of history and of the interdependence of all phases of history has been largely accepted by later historians. Many of his ideas on Homer and on Rome were adopted by eminent historians, such as Barthold G. Niebuhr and Theodor Mommsen. Comte's famous three stages of man's intellectual development—theological, metaphysical, and positive—were based on Vico's three ages. Savigny, Maine, and other legal historians have followed his theory of the organic growth of law. From Vico, also, Karl Marx borrowed his concept of the class struggle; and Nietzsche's Superman was modelled on Vico's heroes. Altogether, opinions which Giambattista Vico was the first to utter have played a dominant role in the evolution of modern thought.

31. THE DAMNED HUMAN RACE

Jonathan Swift's *Gulliver's Travels*

1726

One of the strange ironies of literature is that the bitterest satire in the English language has become a children's classic—though in drastically expurgated form. *Gulliver's Travels* is a merciless diatribe against the follies, vices, and indiscretions of mankind, and the world has perhaps thought it pleasanter to relegate the book to the nursery than to face up to its cruel impeachment of *homo sapiens*. Jonathan Swift's opinion of his own species is epitomized in Mark Twain's acid phrase, "the damned human race."

The book is an account of four imaginary voyages and was inspired by the immense popularity of travel narratives, real and fictitious, during Swift's age; *Robinson Crusoe*, for example, preceded *Gulliver's Travels* by only seven years. The narrator of the tale is Lemuel Gulliver, a ship's surgeon, whose travels are prompted by his insatiable desire to see foreign lands. So authentic and specific are his descriptions that contemporary readers are reported to have searched their maps and atlases for the islands of Lilliput, Brobdingnag, and Laputa, and the country of the Houyhnhnms.

Gulliver, eager for adventure, first sets sail on a ship bound for the South Sea. During the course of the voyage he is shipwrecked and swims ashore to the island of Lilliput, where the miniature inhabitants—a mere six inches tall—manage to take him prisoner. The Emperor of Lilliput soon arrives to inspect the curious "Man-Mountain" and is similarly, though discreetly, scrutinized by the prisoner. Gulliver immediately comprehends the reason for the Emperor's greatness: "He is taller *by the breadth of my nail* than any of his court, which alone is enough to strike an awe into beholders." Swift's irony is double-strength, for the description specifically refers to George I of England and Louis XIV of France, who sought to increase their stature with the aid of six-inch heels and tall wigs.

Gulliver eventually wins the favor of his captors and is set free. Given permission to travel through Milendo, the metropolis, he discovers that Lilliput is not unlike his own homeland. Indeed, the character of the Lilliputians is amazingly like that of the Europeans, for, despite their good qualities, they soon display the same vices and pettinesses and the same general patterns of behavior.

The parallels run close. In order to court the favor of the mighty miniature ruler, candidates for office leap over or creep under a stick held in the Emperor's hand. Lilliput is highly organized politically, its two chief parties being the Tramecksan or High Heels and the Slamecksan or Low Heels (Tories and Whigs). "The animosities between these two parties run so high, that they will neither eat nor drink, nor talk with each other." While the political controversies flourish, the Lilliputians are threatened with an invasion from the island of Blefuscu (France), "the other great empire of the Universe," with which Lilliput has been engaged in a long-drawn-out war. Their mutual animosity stems from the ancient quarrel between the Big Endians and the Small Endians (Roman Catholics and Protestants) concerning which end of an egg should be broken. "It is computed that 11,000 persons have at several times suffered death rather than submit to break their eggs at the smaller end."

Swift, a master of ironic understatement and exaggeration, at once exposes the utter folly of the Lilliputians. That he has but low regard for their behavior is evidenced by the continual references, both typical (general) and topical (specific), that mark the whole of Part I. He does not, however, depict the Lilliputians as being wholly evil in their ways, for, by so doing, he would be unreservedly condemning all of Europe as well. Instead, he draws a highly favorable picture of the laws, learning, customs, and educational methods of Lilliput— a country, it is shown, where good and evil exist on a multitude of levels.

At length, however, Swift deals the final blow. Gulliver, after preventing an invasion by Blefuscu and saving the Emperor's palace from total destruction by fire, discovers that he is to be charged with high treason; his good services have aroused the distrust of the Lilliputians, and he is forced to flee for his life.

On his second voyage, Gulliver goes to Brobdingnag, where the natives are as tall in proportion to himself as the Lilliputians were short. Swift reverses the procedure, and Guilliver is now the miniature representation of man. Swift further demonstrates his unusual satiric gift: the great size of Gulliver's new hosts clearly points up their virtues and defects. The giant ruler is a philosopher, kindly and magnanimous, in contrast to the Emperor of Lilliput. In several audiences with His Majesty, England and humanity are again subjected to critical analysis. Gulliver boasts to the king about "my own beloved country, of our trade, and wars by land and sea, of our schisms in religion, and parties in the state." The king is not impressed, for as Gulliver states:

> He was perfectly astonished with the historical account I gave him of our affairs during the last century, protesting that it was a heap of conspiracies, rebellions, murders, massacres, revolutions, banishments, the very worst effects that avarice, faction, hypocrisy, perfidiousness, cruelty, rage, madness, envy, lust, malice or ambition, could produce.

His Majesty is even more amazed and horrified when Gulliver tells him of the use of gunpowder and the cannon by European nations for the destruction of an enemy's army and for the annihilation of the enemy's villages and cities. The king decides that the men of Gulliver's country are "the most pernicious race of little odious vermin that Nature ever suffered to crawl upon the face of the earth." As for lawyers, it appears to the king "that laws are best explained, interpreted, and applied by those whose interest and abilities lie in perverting, confounding, and eluding them." "Whoever could make two ears of corn or two blades of grass to grow upon a spot of ground where only one grew before," says the king, "would deserve better of mankind and do more essential service to his country, than the whole race of politicians put together."

Gulliver's third voyage takes him to the flying island of Laputa, inhabited by scientists and philosophers who have lost all sense of perspective. Their complete absorption in speculative philosophy leads them to indulge in a variety of foolish pursuits. So lost in meditation are the philosophers that in order to speak to them one must first attract their attention by flapping them on the ear with a bladder. The scientists occupy their time by extracting sunbeams from cucumbers, softening marble for pincushions, and producing literature by mechanical operations—extravagant but profitless projects. Swift also satirizes their astronomical researches, which he evidently regards as being inconsequential. Gulliver departs after deciding that there is nothing in Laputa "that could invite me to a longer continuance. . . ."

Part III is reputed to be a long attack upon Sir Isaac Newton, whom Swift detested. It is described by Samuel H. Monk as "a macabre scherzo on science, politics, and economics as they are practised by madmen." The chronicle of the third voyage also contains what William Duncan Taylor characterizes as Swift's "terrible picture of the past—of the Pimps, Parasites and Buffoons who have made History: and his dark and still more terrible picture of the horrors of old age."

A "Voyage to the Houyhnhnms," Gulliver's fourth and last adventure, has been called "a curse hurled at humanity." It is, in fact, the most vicious of all of Swift's satires. Again, the world has been turned upside down; this time, however, man is not being weighed against man, but against beast, and it is Swift's devastating conclusion that man, in the chain of ascendancy, is of decidedly lower status. Natural man is represented as being below the beast; civilized man, a veritable fiend. The Houyhnhnms are a race of highly intelligent, civilized horses who are served by a despised, filthy, and degenerate human race known as Yahoos. In Monk's opinion, the Yahoos "do not represent Swift's view of man, but rather of the bestial element in man—the unenlightened, unregenerate, irrational element in human nature." Gulliver is at first naturally mistaken for a Yahoo himself, though he finds them exceedingly repulsive and vehemently denies any kinship: "Upon the whole, I never beheld in all my travels so disagreeable an animal, or one against which I naturally conceived so strong an antipathy." When Gulliver protests to the Houyhnhnms that his resemblance to the Yahoos is only in the body and that his mind is comparable to that of a Houyhnhnm, he is given an opportunity to describe the civilization and history of his own country. The exposition is humiliating to Gulliver, for the recounting is actually a confession of the inferiority of the human race.

The description of Gulliver's return to civilization is probably the most scathing indictment in the whole of the fourth voyage. Gulliver returns to his wife and family, but finds them unbearable after associating with the utopian Houyhnhnms:

> As soon as I entered the house, my wife took me in her arms, and kissed me; at which, not having been used to the touch of that odious animal for so many years, I fell into a swoon for almost an hour. At the time of this writing, it is five years since my last return to England: during the first year I could not endure my wife or children in my presence, the very smell of them was intolerable; much less could I suffer them to eat in the same room. To this hour they dare not presume to touch my bread, or drink out of the same cup; neither was I ever able to let one of them take me by the hand.

At the conclusion of his account of Gulliver's voyages, Swift remarked "they [the travels] are admirable things, and will wonderfully mend the world"—expressing perhaps a hope and an intention. Further qualifying the extremely negative and pessimistic theme of the book, Swift wrote in a letter to Alexander Pope:

> I have ever hated all nations, professions, and communities, and all my love is towards individuals: for instance, I hate the tribe of lawyers, but I love Counsellor Such-a-one, and Judge Such-a-one: so with physicians . . . soldiers, English, Scotch, French, and the rest. But principally I hate and detest that animal called man, although I heartily love John, Peter, Thomas, and so forth.

The acid touch in Swift's satire was a reflection, at least in part, of his own personal disappointments and frustrations—his lifelong battle with the hierarchy of the Anglican Church, his embitterment over being exiled to Dublin, and his unsatisfactory relations with the women in his life.

Swift hated the stupidity, the sinfulness, and the folly of mankind. But no matter how bitter his attack, the implication is always present that the world could become a fit place in which to live and man could become a noble, high-minded creature if he would strive to follow the dictates of his highest faculty, reason. If the Houyhnhnms seem to be almost perfect, it should be remembered that they are a species devoid of emotion and, therefore, untroubled by conflicts arising between the mind and the soul. Gulliver, when forced to leave their land, allows himself the liberty of making one seemingly minor criticism: "I thought it might consist with reason to have been less rigorous. . . ." How much higher the level of perfection if ever man could resolve the conflict of reason versus emotion—a conflict the Houyhnhnms are never faced with.

32. FATHER OF SYSTEMATIC BIOLOGY

Carolus Linnaeus' *Systema Naturae* (System of Nature) 1758–1759

"Nomenclature," wrote Carolus Linnaeus, eighteenth-century Swedish naturalist, "is one of the foundations of botany." He went on to lament, "How great a burden has been laid on the shoulders of botanists by disagreements in names, which is the first step toward barbarism." It was imperative, Linnaeus held, that "botanists come to an agreement among themselves about the fixed laws in accordance with which judgment can be pronounced on names, that is to say, good names can be absolutely distinguished from bad ones, the good ones maintained and the bad ones banished without any exception, so that botany firmly built on immovable principles may remain a fortress inviolable and unshaken."

To this cause, Linnaeus devoted most of an active career, striving to make order out of chaos by bringing systematic organization to an increasingly complex field badly handicapped by lack of logic and method.

Though Linnaeus is commonly accepted as one of the great figures in the history of science, his position is a peculiar one. It has been observed that his name is not associated with any epoch-making hypothesis, not with a single important discovery, and not with one fundamental law or generalization in any branch of science. Linnaeus' role was a different one. He is the only scientist of first rank whose work was almost entirely of a descriptive or classificatory nature. As Arthur O. Lovejoy pointed out on the occasion of the bicentenary of Linnaeus' birth, "He was an unsurpassed organizer, both of scientific material and of scientific research; he introduced form and order, clearness and precision, simple definitions and plain delimitations of boundaries, into sciences previously more or less chaotic or confused or impeded with cumbrous and inappropriate categories and terminology."

The lack of systematic terminology and nomenclature in the biological sciences early in the eighteenth century, when Linnaeus began his activities, paralleled the condition that Lavoisier later found in the field of chemistry. Plants and animals were called by long Latin names, containing as many as fifteen or twenty words, with no attempt made to show relationships among species. Rousseau characterized the prevailing scheme as "a tirade of Latin names which sounded like a conjuration of hobgoblins." The muddled situation was further confused by world travelers bringing back specimens of plants and animals that had never been seen before on the Continent. Schwartz and Bishop estimated that 6,000 plants had been recognized by the year 1600 and that in the century that followed some 12,000 more were discovered.

Attempts at classification were frequent but inadequate. In botany, schemes were developed to group plants by the colors of their flowers, by the shapes of their leaves, or by the presence or absence of thorns. More scientific was the work of several of Linnaeus' predecessors, on whose discoveries he drew, notably that of John Ray (1627–1705), the "father of English natural history," Joseph Tournefort (1658–1708), Professor at the Jardin des Plantes in Paris, scene of many botanical researches in the eighteenth century, and August Quirinus Rivinus (1652–1723), noted German botanist. These three had made definite progress toward classifying the subjects of natural history.

It remained for Linnaeus, however, to conceive of the system of nomenclature which, with later corrections and modifications, has remained in use to the present day. This is the two-name or binomial method of naming organisms. Every plant or animal is given two scientific names in Latin, one for the species and the other for the group or genus within the species. To illustrate: man, standing at the top of the biological ladder, was termed *Homo sapiens* by Linnaeus—reasoning man—and the orangutan was called *Homo troglodytes*, anthropoid man (reportedly to the disgust of many of Linnaeus' contemporaries). Primroses, *Primula*, were subdivided as *Primula vulgaris*, common primrose, *Primula farinosa*, *Primula veris*, etc. All roses are *Rosa*, with such sub-groups as *Rosa gallica*, French rose, *Rosa odorata*, fragrant tea rose, and so on.

Linnaeus first applied his system of binomial nomenclature to zoology in the tenth edition of his *Systema Naturae* (1758), having applied it to plants in his *Species Plantarum* (1753). The first edition of the *Systema Naturae* (1735) was only a dozen pages in length; the twelfth edition in 1766, the last issued during Linnaeus' lifetime, had grown to three volumes, totaling 2,400 pages.

More complicated was the matter of classification. Linnaeus' plan was to assign a plant's or animal's position in nature by class, order, genus, and species. Plants were identified by the number and position of their male stamens and female pistils, the class being based on the number of stamens and the order depending on the number of pistils. The arrangement by genera and species was determined by natural distinctions, providing a basis for the two-name scheme of identification.

Linnaeus recognized that his system of classification was an artificial one, and he regarded it simply as a temporary convenience to be supplanted by a natural system whenever the fundamental relationships of plants and animals should become better known. Darwin's theory of evolution in the nineteenth century provided some of the principles needed for a natural system, but the broad outlines of the Linnaean scheme were retained.

Despite the generally acknowledged value of his contributions, historians of science have been inclined to criticize certain aspects of Linnaeus' work. Typical is the American educator Andrew D. White's comment: "In the second half of the eighteenth century a great barrier was thrown across this current scientific progress—the authority of Linnaeus. . . . The atmosphere in which he lived and moved and had his being was saturated with biblical theology, and this permeated all his thinking." Reference here is to Linnaeus' contention that each species of animal originated from a single pair and to his citing as incontrovertible proof the Mosaic account of the creation. The possibility of evolution did not occur to him; species could not change, new species could not be created, and none could disappear. In holding this view, a century before Darwin, Linnaeus was merely reflecting the persuasions of his own age.

Linnaeus has also been censured for limiting his work to naming and classifying, for his lack of interest in the physiology of plants and animals, for neglecting to make use of the microscope, and for failing to carry on laboratory experiments.

But perhaps the critics expect too much. Linnaeus was preeminently a classifier and believed that the groundwork of science required first of all the arrangement and naming of species. The study of natural history is indebted to him for three significant advances in science: the development of the principle of binomial nomenclature; the introduction of clear, terse descriptions; and the focusing of attention upon species, this last leading to increased interest in the question of their origin and paving the way for the theories of Darwin, Wallace, and others.

33. PIONEER POLITICAL PHILOSOPHER

Charles Louis de Secondat, Baron de Montesquieu's *De L'Esprit des Lois* (Spirit of the Laws)

1748

"Who was this man," asks Franz Neumann, "whose name appears in all textbooks of history, economic history, politics and social theory, who is still invoked by politicians and scholars, and whose formula of the 'separation of powers' as the device for securing liberty enjoys more reverence today than perhaps ever before in history?"

The man in question was Charles Louis de Secondat, Baron de la Brède et de Montesquieu (1689–1755), a French provincial lawyer and nobleman, whose reputation is founded mainly on his authorship of a large, unsystematic, and complex work of political philosophy, *Esprit des Lois, Spirit of the Laws.* Written over a period of some twenty years in pre-Revolutionary France, the book had an enormous influence on both the American and the French Revolutions, on the English system of government, and, less directly, on political developments all over the world during the past two centuries.

Montesquieu's definition of "laws" is broad, liberal, and visionary:

> Laws in their widest signification, are the necessary relationships which derive from the nature of things. . . . They should be relative to the climate of each country, to the quality of its soil, to its situation and extent, to the principal occupation of the natives, whether husbandmen, huntsmen, or shepherds: they should have a relation to the degree of liberty which the constitution will bear; to the religion of the inhabitants, to their inclinations, riches, numbers, commerce, manners, and customs.

Starting with this already comprehensive approach, Montesquieu discusses morals, customs, religion, education, economics, political institutions, soil cultivation, slavery, taxation, standing armies, relations between the sexes, etc. Indeed, as Jacques Barzun has remarked, "There is hardly a subject that one can think of which isn't referred to somewhere in this book."

In the beginning, said Montesquieu, "before the establishment of society," there existed a state of nature governed by natural law. With the advent of organized society and government, three kinds of law developed: the law of nations, pertaining to their reciprocal relations; political law, dealing with relations between a government and its people; and civil law, governing the relations of citizens among themselves.

Proceeding to analyze the various forms of government within which laws must operate, Montesquieu concluded that there are three main types: the republican, the monarchical, and the despotic. He defines a republic as a government in which the supreme power resides in the community, its success being completely dependent upon the civic virtue of its citizens. He was convinced, however, that the republic, a highly moral and intellectual state, belonged to the idealized period of the classical world, such as the Greek city-state, and he despaired of ever seeing it resurrected.

Montesquieu therefore took what he considered to be the realist's position: he concluded that an enlightened monarchy was best suited to the needs of those who inhabited a world where compromise spelled progress. Monarchy appealed to him largely because of its conservatism; he was aware however, that it could degenerate into despotism, as had been amply demonstrated in mid-eighteenth-century France. Thus, the kind of monarchy Montesquieu admired and proposed was one with established constitutional safeguards.

Montesquieu poured all of his scorn and hatred into his discussion of despotism—a type of government whose foundations rested on the fear of its people. Metaphorically expressing the idea of despotism, he wrote: "When the savages of Louisiana want fruit, they cut the tree at the root and gather the fruit. This is despotic government."

Revealing a somewhat cynical view of human nature, Montesquieu asserted, "It is an eternal experience that anyone who possesses power tends to abuse it." He therefore affixed to this premise the following proposal: "In order that power should not be abused it is necessary so to arrange matters that power should be checked by power." Here Montesquieu advanced the principle for which he is most noted—the separation of powers into legislative, administrative, and judicial categories. "If the legislative power," he stated, "is united with the executive power in the hands of one person or of one body of officials there can be no liberty; nor can there be any liberty if the power to judge is not separated from the legislative and executive powers."

In 1789 this doctrine was a dominant theme in the French Revolution's *Declaration of the Rights of Man:* "Any society in which the guaranty of rights is not assured or the separation of powers is not determined does not have a constitution." Its influence upon the Founding Fathers of the American Constitution was even more profound. In *The Federalist,* James Madison referred to Montesquieu as "the oracle who is always consulted on this invaluable precept in the science of politics." In George Washington's words, "The spirit of encroachment tends to consolidate the powers of all departments in one and thus to create, whatever the form of government, a real despotism."

Further to assure complete separation of powers, the American constitution makers excluded cabinet members from Congress (contrary to English practice) and, to enforce the system of checks and balances, divided the legislature into two houses. "The doctrine of the separation of powers," Justice Brandeis once stated, "was adopted by the Convention of 1787 not to promote efficiency, but to preclude the exercise of arbitrary power."

Perhaps if the peoples of the world during the past half-century had fully appreciated this basic principle expounded in *Spirit of the Laws*, the rise of totalitarianism might have been averted. Nor is it yet too late to emphasize Montesquieu's antidote against despotism as a powerful weapon in the contemporary struggle between dictatorship and democracy.

34. SPIRIT OF ENLIGHTENMENT

Denis Diderot's *Encyclopédie ou Dictionnaire Raisonné des Sciences, des Arts et des Métiers* (Encyclopedia, or Systematic Dictionary of the Sciences, Arts, and Crafts)

1751–1772

Denis Diderot has been called "the most typical, yet the least known, of the leading thinkers of the French Enlightenment." Of the four Major Prophets who prepared the way for the French Revolution—Voltaire, Rousseau, Montesquieu, and Diderot—the last, though the least brilliant writer, was the ablest organizer and the most effective journalist. His "role was greater than his work."

Though a prolific author on a variety of subjects, Diderot never created what may be termed a masterpiece. Of all his literary endeavors, his greatest contribution, unquestionably, was the editorship of the French Encyclopedia, the great rationalist compendium of the period of Enlightenment. To Diderot alone belongs the honor of conceiving, carrying on in the face of almost insurmountable difficulties, and finally completing this huge undertaking. "In accomplishing this extraordinary feat," remarked the American historian J. Salwyn Schapiro, "Diderot raised editorship from a critical function to a creative art of the first order." There had, of course, been encyclopedias prior to Diderot's work, but his striking innovations—making the *Encyclopédie* the collective work of famous specialists, and including articles dealing with science, agriculture, commerce, and industry—provided a model on which later encyclopedias of merit were patterned.

Diderot first became associated with the enterprise about 1745. The original plan had been for him merely to translate into French the two-volume English Chambers' *Cyclopaedia, or Universal Dictionary of the Arts and Sciences,* but he persuaded the publisher, Le Breton, to produce a work more original and ambitious in scope and more distinctly French in outlook. Under his expert guidance, the *Encyclopédie* became the first large-scale synthesis of all knowledge.

In an article appearing in the *Encyclopédie,* Diderot described the aim of his work: "to assemble the knowledge scattered over the face of the earth; to explain its general plan to the men with whom we live, and to transmit it to those who will come after us, so that the labors of past centuries may not be useless to future times; so that our descendants, by becoming better informed, may in consequence be happier and more virtuous; and so that we may not die without having deserved well of the human race." In these lines was epitomized the spirit of the "Age of Enlightenment."

In his brilliant list of contributors, Diderot had to vie with sensitive and often conflicting temperaments. His colleagues included D'Alembert on mathematics, Turgot on economics, Quesnay on agriculture, Buffon on nature, Rousseau on music, Montesquieu on taste, and Voltaire on a variety of topics. Diderot himself dealt with philosophy, the arts, and industry. For diverse reasons, usually controversial, Rousseau, D'Alembert, and several others dropped out before the project was finished.

No other encyclopedia ever had such a stormy career. Embodying, as it did, the essential spirit of the democratic and scientific movement in France immediately before the Revolution, bitter reaction from the entrenched forces of conservatism was inevitable. The powerful ecclesiastics and the despotic French court recognized instinctively that the work challenged blanket acceptance of the traditional explanations of natural phenomena and severely threatened autocratic authority. Directly or indirectly, numerous articles condemned religious intolerance, despotic government, arbitrary restrictions on the growth of commerce and industry, unfair taxation, and infringements on personal liberty. "Around the Encyclopedia," commented Lester Crocker, a Diderot biographer, "the greatest and most crucial fight of the century was waged," and Diderot was its hero.

The first volume of the *Encyclopédie* appeared in 1751, and the second followed early the next year. Then the Jesuits and absolutist critics bore down heavily. The King's Council forbade printing, reprinting, or sale of the *Encyclopédie*, on the grounds that it tended "to destroy royal authority, establish the spirit of independence and revolt, and, under obscure and equivocal terms, lay a foundation for error, corruption, irreligion, and incredulity." The ruling applied, however, only to the first two volumes and further publication was not specifically banned. Thereafter, a volume was issued each year until a second major crisis developed in 1759, caused by a new wave of repression. Publication was ordered suspended, and several of Diderot's collaborators, tired of suffering continual indignities, withdrew; the enterprise appeared doomed.

To circumvent the ban, Diderot and his publisher decided to print the remaining volumes in secret; the names of the editors and authors were omitted, and a false imprint of Neuchâtel, Switzerland, was inscribed. Not until 1772 was the complete series, consisting of seventeen volumes of text and eleven volumes of plates, off the press. It had occupied Diderot for more than a generation.

At the moment of apparent triumph, however, Diderot suffered the crowning blow when he discovered that Le Breton, apprehending government disapproval, had been systematically censoring copy for the encyclopedia after Diderot had returned corrected page proofs to him; though retaining its essential spirit, the work was irreparably damaged.

The *Encyclopédie* devotes much space to technical articles on different trades and manufactures of the period, to medicine, mathematics, physics, chemistry, biology, grammar, cookery, gardening, and numerous other subjects. Of primary interest today are the articles dealing with religion, philosophy, and political and social ideas. A small sampling of quotations follows:

On *Political Authority:* "No man has received from nature the right of commanding others. Liberty is a present from Heaven, and every individual of the human species has the right to enjoy it as soon as he enjoys reason." In condemning the cruelty of treatment of criminals in eighteenth-century France, the article on *Torture* states that this method is "a sure means of convicting an innocent man who is physically weak and of acquitting a guilty person born with great endurance." On *Sovereigns:* "Men have entered into society in order to be free, but experience always teaches us that the greater the power of men is, the more their passions lead them to its abuse." On *Consecrated Bread:* "Religion does not consist in adorning temples, in delighting the eyes or the ears, but in paying sincere reverence to the Creator, in following Jesus Christ." On *Almshouses:* "It would be far more important to work at the prevention of misery than to multiply places of refuge for the miserable." On *Man:* "The net profit of a society, if equally distributed, may be preferable to a larger profit, if it be distributed unequally, and have the effect of dividing the people into two classes, one gorged with riches, the other perishing in misery."

The influence of the *Encyclopédie* was by no means limited to France, but extended over the whole of Europe and to America. The English biographer Francis Gribble aptly said of Diderot that he was "the first great editor; and it is unlikely—in view of the extraordinarily difficult circumstances surrounding his work—that there has ever been a greater one."

35. THE GREAT LEXICOGRAPHER

Samuel Johnson's *A Dictionary of the English Language*

1755

One of the delusions under which some academicians have suffered is that living languages can be fixed, purified, and so standardized that they will thereafter remain unchanged. Thus to fix language was a prime purpose of the French and Italian learned academies in the seventeenth century, when their foremost savants labored for years to produce monumental definitive dictionaries of their national languages.

England was relatively slow to embark upon such an enterprise. The poet John Dryden, in 1693, complained that his countrymen "have yet no English *prosodia*, not so much as a tolerable dictionary, or a grammar; so that our language is in a manner barbarous." So rapidly had English changed that Chaucer was as difficult to read as a foreign language, and even Shakespeare was becoming progressively less intelligible. It was time, such literary men as Swift, Addison, and Pope felt, to try to "fix" the English language.

The King Canute chosen for the impossible task of holding back the tides of language was Samuel Johnson, Boswell's hero and the "Great Cham" of eighteenth-century English literature. Johnson undertook the assignment at the suggestion of a group of London booksellers, agreeing to complete the work in three years, though it was pointed out to him that forty members of the French Academy had needed forty years for a French equivalent. Actually, the task required eight years.

In a preliminary publication, *Plan of an English Dictionary,* addressed to Lord Chesterfield, his potential patron, Johnson states his objective: "This, my Lord, is my idea of an English Dictionary; a dictionary by which the pronunciation of our language may be fixed, and its attainment facilitated; by which its purity may be preserved, its use ascertained and its duration lengthened." It was further proposed to add a history and grammar of the English language. Also, the work was to be somewhat encyclopedic in character "since without some attention to such demands the Dictionary cannot become generally valuable."

Johnson expected that many purchasers of his *Dictionary* would read it for pleasure and profit. Accordingly, he "extracted from philosophers, principles of science; from historians, remarkable facts; from chymists, complete processes; from divines, striking exhortations; and from poets, beautiful figures."

A distinguishing characteristic of the *Dictionary* was the inclusion, apparently for the first time in an English work, of quotations from great literary figures to illustrate the uses of words. The opinion was once expressed that Johnson incorporated "every word that Shakespeare ever wrote, led by his reverence for genius to represent Shakespeare's divine verbal jugglings as authentic English idiom." The name of Dryden is said to occur on every page, and Pope, too, was often cited. In general, quotations were selected from the time of Philip Sidney (1554–1586) through Johnson's own period, though the lexicographer wished "to admit no testimony of living authors," for fear that he would be "misled by partiality."

Johnson's methods of work are described by one of his contemporaries, Sir John Hawkins:

An interleaved copy of Bailey's dictionary [*Universal Etymological English Dictionary* by Nathaniel Bailey, 1721] in folio he made the repository of the several articles, and these he collected by incessant reading the best authors in our language, in the practice whereof, his method was to score with a black-lead pencil the words by him selected, and give them over to his assistants to insert in their places. The books he used for this purpose were what he had in his own collection, a copious but miserably ragged one, and all such as he could borrow; which latter, if ever they came back to those that lent them, were so defaced as to be scarce worth owning, and yet some of his friends were glad to receive and entertain them as curiosities.

The system followed led Johnson to omit many technical words, "terms of art and manufacture." By way of excuse, he explained that he was unable "to visit caverns to learn the miner's language, nor take a voyage to perfect my skill in the dialect of navigation, nor visit the warehouses of merchants, and shops of artificers, to gain the names of wares, tools and operations, of which no mention is found in the books."

On February 20, 1755, after years of arduous labor, the *Dictionary* appeared in two large folio volumes, listing a total of 40,000 words. Its appearance caused an immediate literary sensation, but left Johnson exhausted, bankrupt, and depressed. His hopes of inducing Lord Chesterfield to become his patron had been disappointed, and he spurned Chesterfield's last-minute gesture of support. In the *Dictionary,* Johnson bitterly defines a *patron* as "one who countenances, supports or protects. Commonly a wretch who supports with insolence, and is paid with flattery."

Many other Johnsonian definitions have become classics. A *lexicographer* is "a writer of dictionaries; a harmless drudge, that busies himself in tracing the original, and detailing the significance of words"; a *poetess* is a "she-poet"; *oats:* "a grain which in England is generally given to horses, but in Scotland supports the people" (to which Lord Elibank replied: "Very true, and where will you find such men and such horses?"); *compliment:* "an act or expression of civility, usually understood to include some hypocrisy or to mean less than it discloses"; *tawdry:* "splendid without cost; fine without grace, shewy without elegance."

On occasion, Johnson loved to define ordinary words in grandiloquent terms—for example, *network:* "any thing reticulated or descussated, at equal distances, with interstices between the intersections"; *blister:* "a pustule formed by raising the cuticle from the cutis, and filled with serous blood"; *cough:* "a convulsion of the lungs, vellicated by some sharp serosity."

Such extravagant and tortuous definitions led the American literary critic John T. Winterich to remark "that there has grown up a rather commonly-held assumption that the work is a vast compendium of unconscious humor. On the contrary it is, of course, a landmark in the science of lexicography no less than a noble monument to the industry and genius of its compiler." All English dictionaries since 1755 have been obviously indebted to Johnson's work.

Inevitably, as Johnson himself soon recognized, the original aim "to fix the English language" was doomed to failure, but the *Dictionary* fixed English spelling so firmly that it has changed little since. The Johnsonian etymology, however, is inaccurate and incomplete, since little scientific research in philology was done until the following century.

An appreciation of Johnson penned by Thomas Carlyle is famous:

> Had Johnson left nothing but his Dictionary, one might have traced there a great intellect, a genuine man. Looking to its clearness of definition, its genuine solidity, honesty, insight, and successful method, it may be called the best of all Dictionaries. There is in it a kind of architectural nobleness: it stands like a great solid square-built edifice, finished: symmetrically complete; you judge that the Builder did it.

Years after publication of the Dictionary, Johnson, prompted by a spirit of candor, rather than egotism, told Boswell: "I knew very well what I was undertaking, and very well how to do it—and have done it very well."

36. APOSTLE OF REVOLT

Jean Jacques Rousseau's *Du Contrat Social, ou, Principes du Droit Politique* (The Social Contract, or Principles of Political Right)

1762

Mid-eighteenth-century France was boiling with discontent, ripe for revolt. A despotic king ruled by "divine right," while the glaring inefficiency of royalist government steadily became more manifest. Of the nation's land, a corrupt church owned one-fifth, virtually all free of taxation. About one-seventh of the remaining territory was held by princes of the blood, and a like amount belonged to a few thousand nobles—these also mainly exempt from the land tax. The heavy burden of supporting a decadent court, a numerous parasitic class, and a series of disastrous wars fell upon millions of peasants and commoners. Revolution needed only a voice for explosion, and eventually that voice was provided by such spokesmen as Voltaire, Diderot, and Rousseau.

Jean Jacques Rousseau, a native of Geneva, son of an impecunious watchmaker, was one of the most controversial, perplexing, and fascinating figures of the "Age of Reason." His operas, plays, novels, essays, political tracts, social discourses, and autobiography fill forty-seven volumes. As a political theorist, however, Rousseau's fame rests primarily upon one small book, *The Social Contract, or Principles of Political Right.*

In *The Social Contract,* Rousseau argues with conviction and passion that all government must rest upon the consent of the governed. His first sentence furnishes the setting: "Man is born free, and everywhere he is in chains." How did this happen and what can be done about it? asked Rousseau. He believed that he held the answers.

Under a primitive society, suggested Rousseau, man lived in a "state of nature," without law or control. While this condition carried with it certain natural rights for the individual, in time he found it necessary for self-preservation to associate himself with his fellows. But, "the problem is to find a form of association which will defend and protect with the whole common force the person and goods of each associate, and in which each, while uniting himself with all, may still obey himself alone, and remain as free as before." The solution is the social contract. Under such a political compact, man loses his natural liberty, but gains civil and moral liberty. Because each man gives himself to all, "there is no associate over whom he does not acquire the same right as he yields others over himself, he gains an equivalent for everything he loses and an increase of force for the preservation of what he has."

The ideal system of government, in Rousseau's view, is complete popular sovereignty. The people, he asserted, cannot give away or transfer to any person or body their inherent right of self-government. Sovereignty always depends upon the General Will of the community, and government is simply a temporary agent of the sovereign people. The General Will is the source of law and justice, determining what is right or wrong, i.e., "The voice of the people is the voice of God." It follows, therefore, that rulers are nothing more than public servants; if they become arbitrary and defy the General

Will, it is society's duty to rebel against them to restore its freedom and rights.

By making the people collectively supreme, Rousseau subordinated the individual will to what he considered the common good. "Whoever refuses to obey the General Will shall be compelled to do so by the whole body." The apparent assumption here is that a man who disagrees with the majority is really disagreeing with his better self. "The popular will," stated Rousseau, "is always right; if I find that I do not agree with it, then I have been in error." There is no provision for personal freedom, for the rugged individualist.

Totalitarian dictators have claimed that Rousseau's ideas support unlimited collectivism. "Yet," as William Ebenstein, a political scientist at Princeton, pointed out, "the master conception of *The Social Contract* is a community of free men living in a small state in which democracy can be practiced directly by the people, a community of men who see in freedom not only an invitation to personal enjoyment and advantage but also shared responsibility for the welfare of the whole."

Three forms of government were compared by Rousseau: a monarchy, an aristocracy, and a democracy. The monarchical form was rejected because it is to the despot's personal advantage "that the people be weak, wretched, that they be unable to resist him." Further, the monarch's ministers are usually "petty cheats, burglars, intriguers, whose base talents procure high posts for them." Rousseau's preference is for an elective aristocracy, chosen for experience and age. "It is the best and most natural order," he asserted, "when the wisest men govern the multitude, provided that we are sure that they govern for the good of the many and not for their own profit."

Rousseau's attitude toward religion was curious. While contending, on one hand, that "tolerance should be given to all religions that tolerate others, so long as their dogmas contain nothing contrary to the duties of citizenship," Rousseau thought, on the other hand, that there should be a civil religion, which every one must accept on pain of banishment—doubtless a mirror of opinion of the period in which he was writing.

Rousseau's ideas were part of the lives of the men who made the French Revolution. The Revolution's declaration of the rights of man was based upon *The Social Contract,* as were its watchwords: Liberty, Equality, Fraternity. The book was used as justification as well as inspiration for the Reign of Terror. Rousseau was read in chorus at Jacobin meetings; he was quoted time and again in the National Assembly and in the revolutionary press; Marat was seen in public reading *The Social Contract* aloud to enthusiastic audiences; and Robespierre was an equally fervent disciple. The whole social system of the old regime had been undermined and the way paved for a new democratic order with Rousseau's philosophy of liberty, equality, and fraternity for mankind.

The Founding Fathers in America also drew inspiration from *The Social Contract*. Rousseau's doctrine that life, liberty, and the pursuit of happiness are man's inalienable rights profoundly influenced Thomas Jefferson in the writing of the *Declaration of Independence*.

37. GENIUS OF MOCKERY

François Marie Arouet de Voltaire's *Dictionnaire Philosophique Portatif* (Philosophical Dictionary)
1764

Echoing the verdict of a multitude of contemporary and later critics, Edward Gibbon, the historian, declared Voltaire the most extraordinary man of the eighteenth century. Certainly none exceeded him in prolificness—approximately one hundred volumes in fields as diverse as history, biography, poetry, drama, fiction, science, theology, metaphysics, and literary criticism.

Born during the regime of the Sun King, Louis XIV, Voltaire lived until near the outbreak of the French Revolution, a cataclysmic event for which he helped to pave the way. His entire career was motivated, as one commentator pointed out, by "a passionate desire to refashion the world according to the dictates of enlightened reason." As the foremost exponent of the gospel of reason, Voltaire found himself in constant conflict with church and state—the vested interests of France—and on frequent occasions paid for his temerity in opposing them by imprisonment, exile, physical mistreatment, and the destruction of his writings.

Of all the extensive output of Voltaire's pen, none of his works is more characteristic of the author or more devastating in its attacks on social injustice, superstition, religious persecution, oppressive laws, war, and other objects of his detestation than the *Philosophical Dic-*

tionary. This book is reputed to have been conceived by Voltaire in 1752 while he was a guest at Frederick the Great's supper parties in Potsdam, "when every subject in heaven and earth came up for review." The first edition was issued anonymously in 1764, a small octavo containing seventy-three articles. Until near the end of his life, Voltaire continued to add to the *Dictionary,* eventually filling nine volumes—the largest single title in his collected works.

The form of the *Philosophical Dictionary* was ideal for Voltaire's purpose, an alphabetical medley covering a vast range of topics, on each of which the author could exercise his sharp wit. Beginning with Abraham, Abuse, Academy, Adoration, Adultery, Allegories, Altars, Amazons, Ambiguity, Anecdotes, Angels, Apocalypse, Apostate, Appearance, Ass, Atheism, Austerities, and Avarice, Voltaire proceeds through the alphabetical sequence, combining wit and wisdom, learning and prejudice, history and philosophy. Occasionally he varies from the conventional essay with dialogue or verse.

A few brief excerpts will indicate the flavor of the *Dictionary.* The key subject of religion is the concern of numerous articles. He questions the existence of Moses, and he is critical of the morals of Abraham, Isaac, Jacob, and other Biblical figures. Biting satire is aimed at man's numerous religious wars, with their myriad victims. In reply to the question, What religion would be the least objectionable? Voltaire replied:

> Would it not be that which should be the simplest; that which should teach morality and very few dogmas; that which should tend to make men just, without making them absurd; that which should not ordain the belief of things impossible, contradictory, injurious to the Divinity, and pernicious to mankind; nor dare to threaten with eternal pains whomsoever should possess common sense? Would it not be that . . . which should teach only the adoration of one God, justice, tolerance, and humanity?

"Theological religion," maintained Voltaire, "is the source of all imaginable follies and disturbances; it is the parent of fanaticism and civil discord; it is the enemy of mankind." In discussing "Laws, Civil and Ecclesiastical," he advocated complete separation of church and state, insisting that the state must assume all secular functions.

Another basic article in the *Philosophical Dictionary* relates to "Government." An ardent admirer of the English government, Voltaire asks rhetorically: "Has not the love of liberty become the dominant characteristic of the English as they have grown more enlightened and more prosperous? . . . To be free is to be dependent only on the laws." The English constitution, he concluded, "has restored each man to all the rights of Nature of which he has been deprived in most monarchies. These rights are: full liberty of his person, of his goods; freedom to speak to the nation by pen; freedom not to be tried in any case except according to the precise terms of the law; freedom to profess peacefully any religion he wishes." The essential rules of free government, in Voltaire's view, were:

> that no ecclesiastical law should be valid without the express sanction of the government; that all ecclesiastics should always be subject to the government, since they are subjects of the state; that there should be but one weight, one measure, one tax; that all law should be clear, uniform, and precise; that all imposts should be proportional.

These principles were among the demands stated by the French Revolutionists in 1789.

A target for some of Voltaire's most scathing remarks is war, "the malady which tears us into a thousand pieces. . . . The marvelous part of this infernal enterprise is that each chief of the murderers causes his flags to be blessed and invokes God solemnly before going out to exterminate his neighbors."

French government circles and the church hierarchy reacted instantly and violently to the *Philosophical Dictionary*. In 1765 the Parliament of Paris had the book burned by the hangman, and in the same year it was placed on the Catholic *Index Librorum Prohibitorum*. A short time later possession of the book was cited in the evidence against a young man, La Barre, charged with sacrilege and blasphemy—the trial ending with the two being burned together. The Calvinists at Geneva declared the work "impious, scandalous, audacious, and destructive of religion."

Voltaire's influence over the nobility and the cultivated bourgeoisie of his time was immense. From him they imbibed a liberalism that opened their eyes to the horrors of bigotry and persecution, the corrupt alliance between church and state, the waste of war, and the absurdities of superstition. His impact on the French Revolution, of whose excesses he would undoubtedly have disapproved, was equally strong. Thirteen years after Voltaire's death, during the Revolution, his remains were exhumed and, with one hundred thousand men marching in solemn procession, transferred to the Pantheon at Paris —evidence of the elevated place held by Voltaire in revolutionary thought.

One of the most famous of Voltaire's contemporaries, Condorcet, declared that "Voltaire felt himself called upon to destroy every kind of prejudice which enslaved his country." Lord Macaulay added: "Of all the intellectual weapons that have ever been wielded by man, the most terrible was the mockery of Voltaire. Bigots and tyrants who had never been moved by the wailings and cursings of millions turned pale at his name." The key word in Voltaire's credo was toleration. Intolerance, he argued, begets cruelty, and cruelty leads to persecution and war. At the end of his life, he is quoted as saying: "I die worshipping God, loving my friends, without hatred of my enemies, and detesting superstition."

38. PROTECTOR AND DEFENDER OF HUMANITY

Cesare Bonesana Beccaria's *Dei Delitti e delle Pene* (Of Crimes and Punishments)
1764

Man's inhumanity to man was never exhibited in more horrible fashion than in European penal practices of the mid-eighteenth century. The incredible conditions that inspired the young Italian Marchese de Beccaria to write his famous book, *Of Crimes and Punishments,* seem relics of the Dark Ages, a veritable reign of terror.

The prevailing penal law of the period was characterized by secret accusations, virtually no provision for the defense of accused persons, savage types of torture, the use of capital punishment for innumerable minor crimes, and such other barbarous punishments as whipping, branding, and mutilation. In England, for example, Parliamentary action had made no less than a hundred and sixty different offenses punishable by death. In France, a prisoner might have his hands cut off, his tongue torn out, and his body burned alive. Sentences imposed by the corrupt judiciary everywhere were arbitrary, capricious, and dependent upon the status and power of the convicted. Persons could be deprived of their freedom, property, and life without any "due process of law." Under the dreadful prison system, old and young, men and women, innocent and guilty, first offenders and hardened criminals, bankrupts and murderers were thrown together promiscuously.

Beccaria, member of a noble Milanese family, was an intimate friend of the governor of the prison in Milan. On frequent visits to the prison he witnessed revolting scenes that provided him with primary facts concerning the existing penal system and stimulated his moral indignation to the point of writing *Of Crimes and Punishments,* a work which in his own day gained for him the title of "protector and defender of humanity." Therein, Beccaria proposed sweeping reforms of the entire code of criminal law and legal practice.

Accepting at the outset the social contract theory of the state's origin, Beccaria writes, "Laws are the conditions whereby free and independent men unite to form society." To prevent men from disrupting orderly social existence, laws are required and "punishments were established to deal with those who transgress against the laws." The only purpose of punishment is to defend the liberty and rights of all the people. Legitimately, penal laws can be enacted only by legislators, after which it is the duty of judges to inflict the prescribed penalties. Futhermore, before the law all members of society should be treated as equals, regardless of wealth or influence.

Beccaria treats at length the question of the severity of punishment. Since, in his view, "the end of punishment . . . is no other than to prevent the criminal from doing further injury to society, and to prevent others from committing the like offense," crimes would be measured solely by the extent of the harm they caused society. For each crime there would be a definite penalty of an appropriate nature. "To make the punishment fit the crime," for example, violence would bring a sentence of corporal punishment and robbery would be penalized with a fine. According to Beccaria's classification, the most serious crimes are high treason or other acts against the state, inasmuch as these threaten the existence of all members of society. Second in importance are crimes that injure the security and property of individuals. In a third category he places crimes that disrupt public peace and tranquility, such as riots and rabble-rousing.

If punishment is to serve its essential purpose of deterring crime, contends Beccaria, it must be prompt and certain. The inevitability of punishment, rather than its cruelty or severity, is the most powerful restraining influence on the potential criminal. Punishments that are too severe, cruel, and inhuman not only fail to prevent crime, but may actually produce the opposite effect. As Beccaria states his case:

The certainty of punishment, even though it be moderate, will always make a stronger impression, than the fear of one more severe if it is accompanied by the hope that one may escape that punishment, because men are more frightened by an evil which is inevitable even though minor in nature. Further, if the punishment be too severe for a crime men will be led to commit further crimes in order to escape punishment for the crime.

Following this logic, Beccaria expresses strong opposition to the death penalty. It seemed to him the height of absurdity "that laws, which are an expression of the public will, which abhor and punish murder, should themselves commit murder." Capital punishment, in essence, is an act of ferocity intended to curb ferocity, and in Beccaria's opinion it is not legitimate, necessary, or effective. "The greatest effect that any punishment has upon the human mind," he says, "is not measured by its intensity but by its duration." Perpetual loss of liberty is therefore more of a deterrent than death.

Vigorously attacking two of the most flagrant abuses in the administration of justice, Beccaria condemns the use of torture to extract confessions from accused persons and dependence upon secret informers. All accusations and trials, he insists, should be public, and every man should be tried by his peers. To avoid misunderstandings and miscarriages of justice, laws must be clear and simple, written in a language completely understandable to the people—an ideal not yet fully realized.

Believing that "it is better to prevent crimes, than to punish them," Beccaria suggested that the most certain method of preventing crimes is to perfect the system of education. With the increase and extension of knowledge, public enlightenment will grow and the citizenry will become more law-abiding.

In a final paragraph, Beccaria sums up his penal doctrine: "In order that every punishment may not be an act of violence committed by one man or many against a single individual, it ought to be above all things public, speedy, necessary, of least possible severity under the circumstances, proportional to the crime, and prescribed by the laws."

Beccaria's ideas were bitterly attacked by judicial and theological conservatives, but they made a tremendous impact upon the enlightened minds of his day. *Of Crimes and Punishments* became an immediate best seller, passed through numerous editions, and has been translated into twenty-two European languages. Its immense influence may be gauged by the many practical reforms of criminal jurisprudence that have grown out of the book in the past two centuries.

39. SYSTEMATIZER OF LAWS

William Blackstone's *Commentaries on the Laws of England*

1765–1769

Jonathan Swift, an older contemporary of Sir William Blackstone, once remarked that the law was a maze of unintelligible pedantry, while another famous eighteenth-century figure, Edward Gibbon, described law as "a mysterious science and a profitable trade." The leading legal textbook down to the middle of the eighteenth century was a work entitled *A Dialogue Between a Doctor of Divinity and a Student of the Laws of England,* first published in Latin in 1523.

William Seagle summed up the situation before Blackstone's advent on the stage: "It [the common law] was now absolutely beyond the comprehension of the layman, and had become the most highly prized and exclusive possession of a professional class." Another critic characterized eighteenth-century English law as "a disordered agglomeration of traditions, statutes, local customs, feudal vestiges, judicial interpretations, miscellaneous principles derived from the civil, canon, and other non-indigenous systems, and gradually emerging precepts of an unwritten constitution."

William Blackstone, author of *Commentaries on the Laws of England,* was the first English legal light to bring order out of this chaos, to systematize an extremely heterogeneous mass of material. A versatile personality—architect, poet, literary critic, businessman, printer, teacher, legislator, writer, prison reformer, lawyer, and judge—Blackstone came into prominence initially as the first professor of English law at Oxford University, an institution which had previously taught only the civil law of Rome.

Blackstone's *Commentaries,* which grew out of his series of lectures at Oxford, was written in a readable literary style. It comprises the most complete survey of the English legal system ever composed by a single individual. The four-volume treatise covers the entire field of common law as it existed in the eighteenth century, plus innumerable definitions and a vast amount of legal history. It brought its author fame and fortune. No gentleman's library in England or America was considered complete without a set, and royalties paid the author during his lifetime exceeded £14,000, the equivalent of a half-million dollars today. Eight editions were published in England before 1780, when Blackstone died, while numerous reprints were issued in America, and translations came out in France, Italy, Germany, Russia, and even China.

In preparing the *Commentaries,* Blackstone borrowed freely from preceding English and European legal and social writers back to the medieval period. His introduction begins with a discussion of the study of law, the nature of laws in general, the laws of England, and the countries subject to the laws of England. Therein, commenting on "the supreme power in a state," or sovereignty, Blackstone asserted that the sovereign or the government must have "supreme, irresistible, absolute, uncontrolled authority" (echoes of Thomas Hobbes' *Leviathan!*), a statement for which he was severely criticized and that would have been better suited to the Tudor or Stuart regimes insofar as England was concerned.

The common law was divided by Blackstone into four books: The Rights of Persons, the Rights of Things, Private Wrongs, Public Wrongs. Laws are of four kinds, according to the author: declaratory, directory, remedial, and vindicatory. The declaratory defined what was right and what was wrong; the directory included laws commanding what was right and prohibiting what was wrong; remedial laws were concerned with the enforcement of private rights and correcting private wrongs; the vindicatory prescribed the punishment for public wrongs. By way of further definition, Blackstone noted that the laws of England were of two classes: the unwritten or common law, a product of custom and immemorial tradition; and the written or statute law, enacted by the legislative agency to remedy defects in the unwritten law.

Blackstone's first book, on *The Rights of Persons,* is of special interest and much of it is pertinent to the twentieth century. Persons are divided into "natural persons" and "bodies politic, or corporations." The first were evidently regarded as of greater importance, since Blackstone devoted seventeen chapters to them and only one to corporate bodies. The rights of "natural persons" were again divided: first, absolute rights, i.e., enjoyment of personal security, personal liberty, and private property (translated later by Thomas Jefferson in the United States *Declaration of Independence* as "life, liberty, and the pursuit of happiness"); second, relative rights, such as master in relation to servant, husband to wife, parent to child, and guardian to ward.

Of the approximately two thousand pages of the *Commentaries,* about five hundred deal with the law of property, some four hundred are on criminal law, and three hundred are concerned with the law of procedure. It is obvious, on the basis of space allotted, that real property and maintenance of the social order of the landowners were the law's most vital concern in Blackstone's era. To corporation law, a field which has since vastly expanded, Blackstone devoted only twenty pages.

In another respect Blackstone represented the conservatism of eighteenth-century English legal thought. He viewed with pride and awe the superb structure of English law, seeing the constitution "so wisely contrived, so strongly raised, and so highly finished" that it approached perfection. Such overly laudatory opinions incurred the wrath of Jeremy Bentham, John Austin, Joseph Priestley, and other reformers of the time.

Nevertheless, Blackstone was not a reactionary. In a number of respects, he actively supported law reform, criticizing, for example, the severity of English criminal law and deploring the frequency of capital punishment. The death sentence, he declared, was "inflicted, perhaps, inattentively, by a multitude of successive independent statutes upon crimes very different in their natures. So dreadful a list," he insisted, echoing Beccaria, whom he had read, "instead of diminishing, increases the number of offenders." Indirectly, also, Blackstone contributed to legal reform, because, for the first time, the whole body of existing law was brought together in one place.

From the time of its publication in the Colonial period through the nineteenth century, Blackstone's *Commentaries* was the basic legal work in America. It exercised a profound influence on the formation of the Federal Constitution and of American institutions generally. Such terms as "crimes and misdemeanors," "ex post facto laws," "judicial power," "legislative power," "due process," and "levying war" were derived from Blackstone. Subsequently, most of the state constitutions were influenced by the *Commentaries.* Both in America and in England, the work helped to shape the course of legal education and to encourage the university teaching of law. Before the present century, knowledge of the *Commentaries* was enough to gain admission to the bar in many states of the Union. Among those who learned law in this fashion were John Marshall, Thomas Jefferson, James Madison, James Monroe, and Abraham Lincoln. The immense popularity of the *Commentaries* in America established a link of common legal principles between England and the United States. Although many of the specific laws are today obsolete, the historic importance of the work is clearly evident.

40. PRELUDE TO REBELLION

Thomas Jefferson's *A Summary View of the Rights of British America*

1774

When Thomas Jefferson, then only thirty-three years of age, was selected by the Continental Congress, meeting at Philadelphia in 1776, to draft the *Declaration of Independence*, he was relatively unknown to the world at large. But he had already attained fame among his fellow delegates for his "peculiar felicity of expression" and for the originality and forcefulness of his political views.

Jefferson's unique qualifications for the important new assignment had been demonstrated two years earlier in his authorship of *A Summary View of the Rights of British America*, reflecting a political philosophy substantially identical with that subsequently contained in the *Declaration*. It was therefore entirely logical and natural that Jefferson should be chosen to draft the *Declaration of Independence* when that famous manifesto came to be written.

The *Summary View* was prepared by Jefferson as a proposed draft of instructions to the Virginia delegates in the Continental Congress. Because of illness, he was unable to present the statement in person to the Virginia representatives meeting at Williamsburg, but copies were forwarded by messenger to Patrick Henry and Peyton Randolph. The document was raw meat, highly iconoclastic, and the leaders rejected it as too extreme for acceptance. John Dos Passos has accurately characterized the work as "saturated with the doctrines of the Long Parliament and of the Glorious Revolution." Nevertheless, Jefferson's enthusiastic friends arranged for publication without his knowledge, prefacing the pamphlet with the explanation: "In it the sources of our present unhappy differences are traced with such faithful accuracy, and the opinions entertained by every free American expressed with such a manly firmness, that it must be pleasing to the present, and may be useful to future ages."

Jefferson begins *A Summary View* in the usual form of a "humble and dutiful address" from Congress to His Majesty as Chief Magistrate of the British Empire, petitioning for relief against the "many unwarrantable encroachments and usurpations, attempted to be made by the Legislature of one part of the empire, upon those rights which God and the laws have given equally and independently to all." Citing "natural rights," Jefferson took the position that the British Americans were entitled to emigrate and establish laws and regulations of their own, exactly as their remote Saxon forefathers had done in earlier centuries. The conquest and settlement of the American wilds had been accomplished entirely at the expense of individual colonists: "for themselves they fought, for themselves they conquered, and for themselves alone they have right to hold." Not until the colonies were solidly established and had become "valuable to Great Britain for her commercial purposes" did Parliament offer "to lend them assistance against the enemy."

Boldly attacking the king himself, Jefferson reminds George III of the numerous petitions from the colonies that he had neglected to answer, objects to the practice of parceling out lands to royal favorites, accuses the king of rejecting desirable laws enacted by the colonial assemblies, states that attempts of the colonies to rid themselves of the institution of slavery had been frustrated, and condemns stationing armed forces in the colonies on the ground that the king had "no right to land a single armed man on our shores." To make the monarchical status clear, Jefferson points out to the king "that he is no more than the chief officer of the people, appointed by the laws, and circumscribed with definite powers, to assist in working the great machine of government, erected for their use, and consequently subject to their superintendence." The fate of tyrannical rulers is exemplified, Jefferson recalls, by the Stuarts "whose treasonable crimes against their people brought on them afterwards the exertion of those sacred and sovereign rights of punishment reserved in the hands of the people for cases of extreme necessity."

Jefferson directed some of his most scathing criticism at Parliament's arbitrary and selfish actions:

Not only the principles of common sense, but the common feelings of human nature, must be surrendered up before his majesty's subjects here can be persuaded to believe that they hold their political existence at the will of a British Parliament. Shall these governments be dissolved, their property annihilated, and their people reduced to a state of nature, at the imperious breath of a body of men, whom they never saw, in whom they never confided, and over whom they have no power of punishment or removal, let their crimes against the American public be ever so great? Can any reason be assigned why 160,000 electors in the island of Great Britain [a reference to the rotten borough system] should give law to four millions in the states [note the reference to *states*, not colonies] of America, every individual of whom is equal to every individual of *them,* in virtue, in understanding, and in bodily strength.

Jefferson's view was that the British Parliament was the legislature of *one* portion of the king's dominions; the various legislatures in the empire, according to his interpretation, were equally independent and equally sovereign. The authority of Parliament over the colonies was completely denied. Further, the exercise of free trade with all parts of the world was held to be a natural right of the colonists, despite parliamentary attempts to restrict and hamstring such commerce.

Throughout his life, Jefferson sought to limit or end the slave system. In *A Summary View*, therefore, he denounces the king for vetoing legislation aimed at the abolition of domestic slavery. "It is necessary," Jefferson declares, "to exclude all further importations from Africa. Yet our repeated attempts to effect this by prohibitions, and by imposing taxes which amount to a prohibition, have been hitherto defeated by His Majesty's negative; thus preferring the advantages of a few British corsairs to the lasting interest of the American States, and to the rights of human nature, deeply wounded by this infamous practice."

The threat of revolution is always in the background of *A Summary View*. If their elected legislatures are arbitrarily dissolved by royal fiat, "the power reverts to the people, who may use it to unlimited extent. . . . We forebear to trace consequences further; the dangers are conspicuous."

Jefferson's pamphlet met with immediate and widespread response. The Williamsburg publication was extensively distributed through the colonies, where it was read with eager interest. Within a short time, a Philadelphia edition appeared, and, more extraordinary, a

London version was printed in the same year, apparently at the instigation of Arthur Lee, a colonial agent.

A Summary View was a seminal document, clearly foreshadowing the Jeffersonian principles subsequntly incorporated in the *Declaration of Independence*. Here were boldly expressed Jefferson's challenge to and contempt for a stubborn, unyielding ruler, a weak Ministry, and a corrupt Parliament. The essay strips royalty of all mystic qualities; it compels political authority to justify itself by its usefulness to the governed and makes it dependent upon their consent. It asserts the right of the people to the land which they had wrested from the wilderness, as opposed to the claims of royal favorites who had never left England. With the appearance of *A Summary View*, Jefferson established himself as one of the great pamphleteers of the Revolution, a man to whom the rebellious colonists would naturally turn for leadership.

The concept of government advocated by Jefferson for the British Empire, but rejected during his time, was ultimately adopted and prevails today in the British Commonwealth of Nations, composed of self-governing states, with the monarch serving as the connecting link. The organization of the United States itself is of course a lasting monument to Jefferson's dream of a federation of states or nations.

41. PROPHET OF MODERN CAPITALISM

Adam Smith's An Inquiry Into the Nature and Causes of the Wealth of Nations

1776

When Adam Smith was writing his celebrated *The Wealth of Nations* in the third quarter of the eighteenth century, economic theories prevailing in England were the reverse of every principle for which the author stood. Reigning supreme was the mercantilist notion that the nation's wealth consisted of gold and silver, rather than of consumable goods. The powerful new class of merchants and industrialists contended that money should flow in, but not out; exports were highly desirable, but imports were to be avoided, in order to maintain a "favorable balance of trade." Home industries, they insisted, must be protected by high tariffs, and a strong merchant marine must be developed to carry industrial products abroad. Wages should be kept low and hours of labor long; otherwise, England would be handicapped in economic competition with other countries.

Under pressure from vested interests, nearly all phases of English economic life of the period were under strict governmental control. Prices were stabilized, wages, and hours of labor were fixed, production was regulated, and exports and imports were completely dominated by the state. The equitable distribution of wealth, as a concept, was vigorously opposed by the ruling classes; education was restricted to a privileged few; criminal laws—especially in their application to the poor—were extremely severe; and political rights for the masses existed in theory rather than in practice.

Adam Smith's monumental, two-volume *The Wealth of Nations,* to the writing of which the Scottish-born economist devoted some twenty-five years of his life, was essentially a rebellion against the established economic order. Smith's sympathies were with workers and farmers. He maintained that a nation's real wealth is in consumers' goods, instead of gold and silver. He opposed tariffs, export subsidies, and "favorable balances of trade," favoring, on the contrary, free competition and a free market, as little governmental interference with business as possible, and high wages for workers—all of which might be classified today as "enlightened capitalism."

In its breadth of scope, *The Wealth of Nations* is almost encyclopedic. It was described by one commentator as "a history and criticism of all European civilization." Beginning with a discussion of the division of labor, Smith branches out into reviews of the origin and use of money, prices of commodities, wages of labor, profits of stock, land rent, value of silver, and differences between productive and unproductive labor. Next follow an account of the economic development of Europe since the fall of the Roman Empire, criticisms of the commercial and colonial policies of European nations, the revenue of the sovereign, various methods of defense and administration of justice in primitive societies, the origin and growth of standing armies in Europe, a history of education in the Middle Ages and a criticism of contemporary universities, a history of the temporal power of the church, the growth of public debts, and an examination of principles of taxation and systems of public revenue.

Every human being, Smith was convinced, is chiefly motivated by self-interest, of which the desire for wealth is only one indication. Rather than being distressed by this aspect of human nature, Smith argues that it actually promotes society's welfare. A nation's prosperity depends upon allowing the "uniform, constant, and uninterrupted effort of every man to better his condition." In working for his own gain, man is contributing to the good of the whole. A natural corollary, therefore, is a laissez-faire policy: a minimum of government interference with the economic organization.

Smith's deep feeling for the laboring classes is revealed in numerous passages. He points out that workers were forbidden by law to organize for the betterment of their situation, while nothing prevented employers from combining to exploit labor. He continues:

> Servants, labourers and workmen of different kinds, make up the far greater part of every great political society. . . . No society can surely be flourishing and happy, of which the far greater part of the members are poor and miserable. . . . The liberal reward of labour increases the industry of the common people. . . . Where wages are high, accordingly, we shall always find the workmen more active, diligent and expeditious, than where they are low.

The emancipation of labor, at least in the free world, during recent decades makes the restrictive practices of Smith's day appear incredible. For example, apprentices to various trades were in a virtual state of bondage for not less than seven years, during which they received only subsistence; and the law of settlements placed almost insuperable barriers in the way of a workman who wished to move from one locality to another. Such regulations were condemned by Smith in the strongest terms; to him they were further evidences of the iniquities of government interference with the rights of man and with the natural workings of the economic system.

Somewhat analogous was the system of slave labor, then flourishing in the American colonies. In Smith's judgment, "The experience of all ages and nations . . . demonstrates that the work done by slaves, though it appears to cost only their maintenance, is in the end the dearest of any."

In the perspective of history, Smith's statement on colonial policy is one of the soundest ever written. Smith viewed restrictions placed on colonies by the mother country, in order to maintain monopolies of their trade, as violations of their "natural rights." He was able, therefore, to be more objective about the rebellious American colonies than were most of his fellow countrymen. The difficulties could be solved, he believed, by representation of the colonists in the British

Parliament. Failing peaceable reconciliation, Smith recommended independence for the colonies.

The key division of *The Wealth of Nations* is "Book IV," treating "Of Systems of Political Economy." Here Smith develops in detail his laissez-faire theories concerning labor, land, commodities, money, prices, agriculture, and stock. He pleads for unrestricted domestic and foreign commerce, and he asks for the abolition of trading monopolies and other pernicious practices that hampered the natural growth of industry and trade.

The proper functions of government, as Smith sees them, are relatively few, primarily those of warding off foreign attack and maintaining internal order. In addition, he urges participation by the government in the general education of the people, a proposal well in advance of his time.

The American journalist Max Lerner once remarked that *The Wealth of Nations* "has done as much perhaps as any modern book thus far to shape the whole landscape of life as we live it today." Through business executives, legislative leaders, and intellectual adherents in the universities, he noted, "it has had an enormous influence upon the underlying population of the world . . . and through them also it has had an enormous influence upon economic opinion and national policy."

Many radical and liberal thinkers have censured Smith, probably unfairly, for the excesses of laissez faire perpetrated by businessmen and industrialists, who have twisted Smith's doctrines to mean unbridled license for themselves, free of all government control or interference. Unquestionably, Adam Smith spoke for the new economic liberalism at a most propitious moment in history. The great economic transformation in Britain during the nineteenth century was effected by following his precepts, and his ideas have continued to exert a vital influence on world economic thought down to the present era.

42. MANIFESTO FOR REVOLUTION

Thomas Paine's *Common Sense, Addressed to the Inhabitants of America*

1776

When Tom Paine arrived in America at the age of thirty-seven, there was little in his previous career to indicate that he would soon become one of the greatest pamphleteers in the English language and one of the most controversial figures in American history. Benjamin Franklin had met Paine in London, perceived his genius, and persuaded him to try his luck in the New World.

In America, Paine took naturally to journalism, and his background of experience for that field proved invaluable. He had observed the primitive brutality with which justice was administered in England, he had known abject poverty, he had heard and read much about man's natural rights, he had seen the vast chasm separating millions of ordinary people from the few members of the royalty and nobility, and he had formed a low opinion of the honesty and intelligence of the royal family. Paine was possessed with a profound compassion for humanity, a love of democracy, and an urge for universal social and political reform.

A few months after Paine landed at Philadelphia came the battles of Concord, Lexington, and Bunker Hill. Leaders in the colonies—George Washington, Benjamin Franklin, Thomas Jefferson, Samuel Adams, John Hancock, and others—were badly divided over the question of separation and independence. Paine saw clearly the trend of events, and from the beginning viewed separation from England as inevitable. The fall of 1775 was spent setting down his ideas.

On January 10, 1776, Paine published an anonymous pamphlet of forty-seven pages, priced at two shillings, and entitled *Common Sense*. In three months, 120,000 copies had been bought, while estimates of total sales have ranged up to half a million, equivalent in terms of population to a sale of thirty million copies in the United States today. Virtually every literate person in the thirteen colonies is believed to have read the fiery pamphlet.

Probably nothing comparable to *Common Sense* in its immediate impact is to be found in the history of literature. It was a clarion call to the American colonists to fight for their independence—without compromise or vacillation. Revolution was pointed out to them as the only solution of their conflict with Great Britain and George III, "The Continental Belt is too loosely buckled," writes Paine. "Independence is the only bond that can tie and keep us together. . . . A continent could not remain tied to an island."

The first portion of the pamphlet relates to the origin and nature of government, with special application to the English constitution. The author's philosophy of government is contained in such sentences as: "Government, even in its best state, is but a necessary evil; in its worst state an intolerable one. Government, like dress, is the badge of lost innocence. The more perfect civilization is, the less occasion has it for government."

Paine draws a sharp distinction between society and government. Men are attracted into society, he declares, because certain wants can be satisfied through social co-operation. Upon society rather than government depend the security, progress, and comfort of the people.

For the institution of hereditary monarchy, Paine reserves his harshest words and most scathing contempt. He attacks the whole principle of monarchy and the English form in particular. "One of the strongest natural proofs of the folly of hereditary rights in kings," says Paine, "is that Nature disproves it, otherwise she would not so frequently turn it into ridicule by giving mankind an ass for a lion." George III is referred to as "the hardened, sullen-tempered Pharaoh of England" and "the royal brute of Britain."

Having exploded popular ideas of monarchical government, Paine proceeds to discuss American affairs. Economic arguments for separation from Britain are stressed. To the Tories' contention that America had flourished because of her connection with England, Paine retorts, "America would have flourished as much, and probably much more, had no European power had anything to do with her." Furthermore, there would be numerous disadvantages to continued connection with England. Such association, Paine emphasizes, would continually embroil the colonies in European wars and quarrels and interfere with peaceful trade and commerce.

Paine devotes the final chapter of *Common Sense* to some practical considerations designed to build up the self-confidence of the Americans and to convince them that they had the man power, manufacturing experience, and natural resources to wage a successful war for independence against Britain. He concludes by expressing his conviction that "nothing can settle our affairs so expeditiously as an open and determined declaration for independence."

This was the revolutionary message communicated to the American people by *Common Sense,* running the gamut from down-to-earth, realistic, practical arguments to emotion-charged, violently partisan, and biased appeals of the born agitator. The immediate and cataclysmic effects of the work are reflected in contemporary comments by George Washington, John Adams, Benjamin Rush, General Charles Lee, and Benjamin Franklin, among others.

Shortly after the appearance of *Common Sense,* most of the colonies instructed their delegates to vote for independence. On July 4, 1776, less than six months from the date when Paine's famous pamphlet came from the press, the Continental Congress, meeting in Philadelphia, proclaimed the independence of "The United States of America," a phrase first used by Tom Paine. Thomas Jefferson and Paine were closely associated while the *Declaration of Independence* was being composed, and except for the omission of an antislavery clause which Paine advocated, the principles for which he stood were incorporated in the celebrated manifesto.

After the Revolutionary War, in which Paine played an active role, he went to Europe, where he became an enthusiastic supporter of the French Revolution. In defense of the Revolution, he produced *The Rights of Man,* a reply to Edmund Burke's *Reflections on the French Revolution.* When Paine returned to America in 1802, he found himself not received as a Revolutionary hero, but virtually ostracized by political leaders and churchgoers because of his authorship of *The Age of Reason* and his radical political theories. After seven incredible years of abuse, hatred, neglect, poverty, and ill health, he died in 1809, at the age of seventy-two. The bitterness, falsehoods, and violent prejudices that plagued Paine's last years have persisted to recent times, represented, for example, by Theodore Roosevelt's description of him as "a filthy little atheist"—an epithet which did not fit him in any particular. But even in his own time the hymn of hate and misrepresentation was not universal; and in 1814 Cheetham's biography, *Life of Paine,* praised *Common Sense* "as speaking the language the American colonists had felt, but had not thought, its popularity terrible in its consequence to the Parent country . . . unexampled in the history of the press." A century after Paine's death, another biography (*Life of Thomas Paine,* by Moncare D. Conway) ended with the comment: "Here then close my labors on the history and writings of the Great Commoner of mankind, founder of the republic of the World, emancipator of the human mind and thought."

No better index to Paine's character can be found than in his reply to Franklin's remark, "Where liberty is, there is my country." "Where liberty is not," Paine said, "there is mine."

43. GREATEST ENGLISH HISTORIAN

Edward Gibbon's *The History of the Decline and Fall of the Roman Empire*

1776–1788

Works conceived on a grand scale were characteristic of the second half of the eighteenth century in England; witness, for example, Adam Smith's *Wealth of Nations,* Boswell's *Life of Johnson,* Hume's *History of England,* and Gibbon's *Decline and Fall of the Roman Empire.*

The most monumental of these ambitious undertakings was inspired by Edward Gibbon's visit to Rome. In his words, "It was at Rome, on the fifteenth of October 1764, as I sat musing amidst the ruins of the Capitol, while barefooted friars were singing Vespers in the Temple of Jupiter, that the idea of writing the decline and fall of the City first started to my mind." Then a young man of only twenty-seven, Gibbon already possessed a wide background of reading, excellent linguistic training, especially in French and Latin, and considerable travel experience. Twelve years passed, however, before the first volume of the *Decline and Fall of the Roman Empire* came from the press. The initial volume appeared during the same year in which the *Declaration of Independence* precipitated the American Revolution. A short time after the final volume appeared, the French Revolution erupted.

The *Decline and Fall* covers more than twelve centuries of time and the whole of the then known world. Receiving fullest treatment is the 460-year era starting about the time of the Antonines in 180 A.D. The next 800 years, to the fall of Constantinople in 1453, are dealt with in more summary fashion, emphasizing the impact of Byzantine civilization on Rome.

In Gibbon's view, the Roman Empire reached its acme during the regime of Marcus Aurelius, and a long, slow disintegration began after that emperor's death. At its best, according to Gibbon, "in the

second century of the Christian era, the empire of Rome comprehended the fairest part of the earth, and the most civilized portion
of mankind. The frontiers of that extensive monarchy were guarded
by ancient renown and disciplined valour. The gentle but powerful
influence of laws and manners had gradually cemented the union of
the provinces. Their peaceful inhabitants enjoyed and abused the
advantages of wealth and luxury. The image of a free constitution
was preserved with decent reverence."

How account for the gradual disappearance of this idyllic state?
Critics have asserted that Gibbon nowhere presents a clear analysis
of the causes of Rome's decline and fall. True, Gibbon is generally
content to let the record speak for itself; nevertheless, in the course
of the work, he puts forward several theories. His concluding phrase
is, "I have described the triumph of barbarism and religion," the two
principal reasons, he was convinced, for the ultimate ruin of the
Roman Empire. The progress of Christianity, in particular, dealt
the old Roman religion a deathblow and encouraged a spirit of revolt
against all existing political and social institutions.

But other forces were at work. The Empire was a despotism,
though disguised as a commonwealth, and its well-being depended
largely on the moral qualities of single rulers. A dreary succession of
despots, domestic or foreign, was broken only occasionally by the
emergence of a wise or vigorous leader. Gibbon also attributed the fall
of Rome to the disappearance of strength, vitality, and creative
power: the population had lost its vigor and public spirit; genius had
gone from art and literature; the legions had degenerated, first in discipline, then in courage and physical endurance; the balance of military strength had gradually shifted to the side of the barbarians. Another factor, suggested by Gibbon, was the enormous extent of the
Empire, for "the decline of Rome was the natural and inevitable
effect of immoderate greatness. Prosperity ripened the principle of
decay; the causes of destruction multiplied with the extent of conquest; and as soon as time or accident had removed the artificial supports, the stupendous fabric yielded to the pressure of its own
weight."

Most controversial of Gibbon's judgments on the decline and fall
of the Empire was the role of Christianity, highlighted in his famous
fifteenth and sixteenth chapters. Christianity, he held, corrupted and
eventually annihilated "the philosophic spirit," substituting for it
superstition, fanaticism, and intolerance—a transformation that

roused his contempt and derision. His ironic attitude comes out in such sentences as, "The various modes of worship which prevailed in the Roman world were all considered by the people as equally true; by the philosopher as equally false; and by the magistrate as equally useful."

Nevertheless, though Gibbon maintained that a great civilization had been undermined by the barbarians and by the new religion, his bias was not unrelieved. Concerning the medieval era, he wrote: "The authority of the priests operated in the darker ages as a salutary antidote: they prevented the total extinction of letters, mitigated the fierceness of the times, sheltered the poor and defenceless, and preserved or revived the peace and order of civil society." It should also be noted that Cardinal Newman characterized Gibbon as "the only Church historian worthy of the name who has written in English."

Gibbon, generally acknowledged to be the greatest of English historians, held strong opinions on the nature of history, views that are naturally reflected in his writings. History, he believed, "is, indeed, little more than the register of the crimes, follies and misfortunes of mankind." He pointed out further that "wars, and the administration of public affairs, are the principal subjects of history." Consequently, social and economic conditions, literature, and the arts occupy a minor place in the *Decline and Fall*. That Gibbon is not unaware of their significance, however, is evidenced by his comment, for example, on the invention of gunpowder: "If we contrast the rapid progress of this mischievous discovery with the slow and laborious advances of reason, science and the arts of peace, a philosopher, according to his temper, will laugh or weep at the folly of mankind."

A pessimistic spirit pervades Gibbon's great work as the author contemplates the constantly changing spectacle of human greatness and absurdities. He has observed the victory of the powers of darkness, men hating and fighting each other, and their minds being poisoned by fanaticism, superstition, and passions. Greatness and happiness are rare and of brief duration.

Historians and readers in the mid-twentieth century are more concerned with the possible decline and fall of their own world than with that of the Roman Empire. As Gibbon examined the dissolution of the Roman imperial order, he asked himself whether a like disaster might strike the Europe of his own time. His answer, in contrast with historian Arnold Toynbee's, is perhaps more optimistic than actual events have warranted. In any case, one of the reasons for the continued popularity of Gibbon's work is its almost prophetic relevance to modern history. As the English historian, E. J. Oliver, suggests, "Gibbon is read with more interest than ever before because he presents so lucid a picture of what happens in the disruption of civilization and the emergence of a new world."

44. FIGHT FOR FEDERATION

Alexander Hamilton, James Madison, and John Jay's *The Federalist: A Collection of Essays Written in Favour of the New Constitution*

1788

The acute troubles of the infant American republic were far from ended when a formal peace treaty was made with England in 1783. The loosely drawn Articles of Confederation, adopted by the Continental Congress in 1777 and approved by the states at the conclusion of the Revolution, were essentially nothing more than a league of friendship among the states, permitting each state to retain its sovereign powers.

As an inevitable consequence, near anarchy prevailed. Congress lacked power to levy taxes; the infant nation's weaknesses were ridiculed abroad; the states were seething with disputes among one another; riots, bloodshed, and even armed rebellion bedeviled the individual state governments; trade discriminations were growing up between states; and there was open talk of secession to form a southern confederacy.

With the young nation about to go on the rocks, emergency action was demanded. One of the most brilliant minds of the Revolutionary era, Alexander Hamilton, rose to the occasion with an address calling for a constitutional convention to meet in Philadelphia in May, 1787, for the purpose of establishing a federal government strong enough to maintain order and to preserve the Union.

Twelve of the thirteen states were persuaded to send delegates to the Philadelphia convention. For three months, the representatives worked in secret, tossing aside the Articles of Confederation and writing a wholly new constitution. The fruit of their labor, it was decided, would be submitted to specially elected state constitutional conventions, instead of to the separate legislatures. The constitution would become effective when ratified by nine states.

The Constitution of 1787 is, of course, a world-famous document, regarded with veneration by patriotic citizens of the United States. It is of interest to note, therefore, that the work might appropriately be entitled "The Great Compromise." Widely divergent views were held by the convention delegates, and the Constitution finally agreed upon represents a series of compromises, since all members of the convention realized that it was the only scheme of central government likely to be acceptable to the electorate. An example is the provision for two houses of Congress, one giving equal representation to all the states and the other elected on the basis of population—an attempt to satisfy both the large and the small states.

When the Philadelphia convention completed its deliberations, there remained the exceedingly difficult task of persuading the people of the country to adopt the new system. Formidable opposition materialized among those who distrusted a powerful national government, who objected to the Constitution because it failed to guarantee certain individual rights (later added in the Bill of Rights), or who had a selfish stake in the *status quo.*

New York was a key state in the ratification process. As Alpheus Thomas Mason commented, "It was recognized on all hands that any system omitting New York State would be analogous to *Hamlet* without Hamlet." Bitter opposition to ratification was being led by Governor George Clinton.

At this critical juncture, Alexander Hamilton, who had served as one of the New York delegates, was inspired to plan the now celebrated *Federalist* papers as ammunition for proponents of ratification. James Madison, sometimes referred to as the "Father of the Constitution," and John Jay, experienced diplomat and expert on foreign affairs, were induced by Hamilton to join him in the undertaking. During the winter and spring of 1787–1788, eighty-five letters were printed in four different New York newspapers. The letters reviewed the Constitution point by point in logical order, explaining and defending the actions of the convention and appealing to the citizens' public spirit. All the letters were signed "Publius," and the exact authorship of several is debatable. At least fifty were written by Hamilton, twenty-five or more by Madison, and five by Jay. Immediately, the papers were collected, and the first edition of *The Federalist* was published in New York in 1788.

The newspaper campaign in New York played a significant part in gaining support for the Constitution, not only in that state but in other states as well. After ten months of strenuous debate, New York endorsed the new scheme of government by a narrow majority of three votes in the state convention.

Though written for a particular time, place, and purpose, *The Federalist* remains of permanent interest and value as a commentary on the American form of government. The American political scientist William Bennett Munro called it "the first notable survey of the history of federalism and the first systematic review of the principles of federal government. But *The Federalist* is more than a general treatise on federal government. It is an exposition and defence of that scheme of political organization which the thirteen states adopted in the later years of the eighteenth century." Another distinguished authority, Charles A. Beard, concurred: "In my opinion it is the most instructive work on political science ever written in the United States; and, owing to its practical character, it ranks first in the world's literature of political science."

On May 30, 1790, after adoption of the Constitution, Thomas Jefferson, writing to his young son-in-law, recommended that for his political education he read Smith's *Wealth of Nations*, Montesquieu's *Spirit of Laws*, and "Locke's little book on government," and added, "Descending from theory to practice, there is no better book than the *Federalist*."

The concept of federal government is familiar to the world today —in the United States, Canada, Australia, Brazil, and elsewhere. When proposed in 1787, however, the idea was new, untried, and radical, at least as visualized by the Philadelphia convention. Actually, such a government was without precedent, a partial explanation, no doubt, of the strong opposition it stirred up, but the pressure of events forced the development of new principles, as John Quincy Adams put it, "from the grinding necessity of a reluctant nation." It has been suggested that the most important American invention, judged by its effect on world history, is not the skyscraper, mass production, nor the atom bomb, but the federal system of republican government created in 1787.

During the past 170 years the American Constitution has inevitably undergone substantial changes. A series of amendments has expanded its specific applications, and it has been continually modified by judicial interpretation, by federal statutes, and by political pressures. Nevertheless, *The Federalist* remains a primary source for interpreting the original content of the Constitution and understanding the intentions of its makers.

45. PIONEER OF MODERN GEOLOGY

James Hutton's *Theory of the Earth; or an Investigation of the Laws Observable in the Composition, Dissolution, and Restoration of Land upon the Globe*

1788

An odd aspect of the history of science is that man's study of the earth and its physical characteristics did not, until relatively recent times, keep pace with astronomy—the study of distant stars. The fascination of the remote and unattainable far exceeded interest in the commonplace world around us.

Theories were not lacking, however, on the origin of the earth. Among the bizarre hypotheses current in the eighteenth century, for example, was that, in the beginning, the earth was a solid mass of ice, becoming animated after being struck by a comet. Another held that the original globe was a mass of water, with vapors containing solid elements floating over it, and that eventually these elements precipitated to form a crust upon the water.

Great pains were taken, not only by theologians but even by most geologists, to reconcile any theory of physical geology with the Mosaic revelation, literally interpreted. If, as the theologians contended, the earth was created in 4004 B.C., its present state could be explained only by a series of cataclysmic events, perhaps an ocean which covered the highest mountains, devastating floods, earthquakes, and volcanic eruptions. Conceptions of natural phenomena were strongly influenced by the religious belief dating back to remote times, that destructive geological occurrences had been inflicted on an erring humanity.

The first important effort to establish a scientific view of the operations of natural forces in the earth's geological history was made by a Scotsman, James Hutton, late in the eighteenth century. Hutton, trained as a physician, occupied his early years as a gentleman farmer. At the age of forty-two, he moved from his farm in Berwickshire to Edinburgh, and for the remainder of his life he devoted himself entirely to scientific studies. He was a keen observer of natural phenomena, accustomed to going directly to nature to find the facts; his data were collected on extensive travels through Scotland, England, and the Continent.

A preliminary edition of Hutton's major contribution to geological literature, *Theory of the Earth,* appeared in 1788 in the *Transactions* of the Royal Society of Edinburgh, an organization of which Hutton was one of the founders. Seven years later an expanded version, in two volumes, appeared. Literary critics have characterized the book as "appallingly repetitive and leisurely in style," "abstruse," and "almost unreadable," but, as a trail-blazer exploring new frontiers in science, it has vital historical significance.

Hutton's announced purpose in the *Theory of the Earth* was "to examine the construction of the present earth, in order to understand the natural operations of time past; to acquire principles by which we may conclude with regard to the future course of things, or judge of those operations by which a world so wisely ordered, goes into decay; and to learn by what means such a decayed world may be renovated, or the waste of habitable land be repaired."

The scheme of the earth as outlined by Hutton is simple and convincing. His essential thesis was that the past should be interpreted, as far as possible, in the light of the present. The earth's features are constantly changing, he states in discussing erosion: "From the top of the decaying pyramids to the sea, throughout the whole of this long course, we may see some part of the mountain moving some part of the way." Rocks disintegrate, soil is carried away by rivers, coasts are worn down, and all loose material moves toward the sea. Through the action of wind, rain, and frost and by chemical decomposition, mountains, rock, and soil are steadily wearing away, and the debris ends up on the ocean floor, where it forms strata or layers of rock. In the process, mountains are carved out and valleys formed.

If the changes described by Hutton continued indefinitely, with the earth disintegrating and filling up the oceans, eventually the earth would be covered with water. But, Hutton theorized, over eons of time, the process is reversed. The sediment in the sea is continually building new continents. Subterranean heat solidifies the ocean beds, and at times that heat becomes so intense that it produces volcanic upheavals, lifting the overlying rock masses. Evidences of the gigantic convulsions are rugged mountains, broken and tilted rock strata, and folds. Hutton dismissed as nonsense the "convulsions of Nature," "sudden and great catastrophes," and "universal debacles," previously used to explain these phenomena.

Transformation of the earth's surface, continuing slowly but incessantly, in Hutton's view exhibited "no vestige of a beginning, no prospect of an end." None before Hutton had fully realized the immensity of geological time. In terms of geology, recorded history is only yesterday. "Time, which measures everything in our idea, and is often deficient to our schemes, is to Nature endless and as nothing," declared Hutton, for countless ages are required to form mountains, rocks, and soil.

Such radical doctrine was too strong for most of the author's contemporaries to stomach. Hutton was soon charged with heresy for expounding ideas contrary to the Scriptures and was condemned as an enemy of religion. One critic pronounced Hutton's theories "not only hostile to sacred history, but equally hostile to the principles of probability, to the results of the ablest observations on the mineral kingdom, and to the dictates of rational philosophy."

A useful service was performed for Hutton, a few years after his death, by his friend John Playfair, who brought out a work entitled *Illustrations of the Huttonian Theory of the Earth,* discussing, explaining, and illustrating Hutton's beliefs. Written in a clear, readable, and understandable style, Playfair's book aided substantially in popularizing the Hutton thesis. Even so, the theories did not win wide acceptance for another fifty years.

With the progress of science, some of Hutton's views have been modified and a few rejected, but the essential features, for the most part, have been confirmed by later investigators. Though ignored or attacked for many years, Hutton's theory marks the beginning of modern geological science.

46. ARCHITECT OF MODERN CHEMISTRY

Antoine Laurent Lavoisier's *Traité Élémentaire de Chimie*
(Elementary Treatise of Chemistry)

1789

On May 8, 1794, in the midst of the Revolutionary Reign of Terror in France, Antoine Laurent Lavoisier was guillotined because of his prior association with the deposed government. Hearing of his friend's death, the mathematical genius Lagrange exclaimed: "It took a moment to cut off that head, but it will take France a century to produce another like it." Lagrange underestimated, for it is nearly two hundred years later, and no figure comparable to Lavoisier has yet appeared.

Only fifty-one years of age at the time of his execution, Lavoisier had been active in scientific research and government service. Within his relatively brief life span, he had succeeded in revolutionizing the whole science of chemistry, the world in which he felt most at home.

Scientific chemistry did not originate with Lavoisier. Since the beginning of the seventeenth century, such men as Van Helmont, Boyle, Glauber, Lemery, and Stahl had been developing an important body of chemical knowledge. Lavoisier's own investigations were substantially aided by the discoveries of some of his contemporaries, notably Black, Priestley, and Cavendish. It has been remarked, in fact, that Lavoisier "discovered no new substances, devised no really novel apparatus, and worked out no improved methods of preparation." His major contribution consisted in establishing order among the experiments that had preceded him and in drawing from them meanings which were to place chemistry on a new foundation.

When Lavoisier began his work, the doctrine of phlogiston was the dominant theory in chemistry. The idea was an ancient one: that all things that burned contained an essence of fire called "phlogiston," which flowed out of inflammable substances as they burned. The more inflammable the substance, the more phlogiston was supposed to be present. Georg Ernst Stahl (1660–1734), the originator of the notion, argued that differing substances—wood, metal, coal, paper, cloth—can be burned and therefore must have phlogiston in common. In his view, the ash which remains when wood is burned, for example, is the original substance minus phlogiston.

It was Lavoisier who completely demolished the phlogiston theory and who first presented the true explanation of combustion. "Chemists have made phlogiston a vague principle," he objected, "which is not strictly defined and which consequently fits all the explanations required of it; sometimes the principle has weight, sometimes it has not. . . . It is a veritable Proteus that changes its form every instant. It is time to lead chemistry back to a stricter way of thinking." Burning, stated Lavoisier, is the union of the burning substance with oxygen, the name he gave to the "dephlogisticated air" discovered by Joseph Priestley. Using extremely delicate balances, he observed that the ashes of burned-out metals weighed more than the original metal because of the weight of the air which combined with the burning body. Combustion, whether it takes place inside the body, a furnace, or an engine, was thus seen as a chemical combination of other elements with oxygen. The process, known as oxidation, occurs at different rates of speed—slowly, as when iron rusts, or rapidly, as when gasoline explodes. Lavoisier also concluded that respiration in animals is a kind of slow combustion.

The explanation for the combustion of "inflammable air" (hydrogen) came to Lavoisier when he heard of Cavendish's discovery that the burning of inflammable air produced pure water. Lavoisier experimented and concluded that water is a compound of the two gases, oxygen and hydrogen.

From his various experiments, Lavoisier evolved the law of the conservation of matter, a cornerstone of modern chemistry—not a new concept, but one which had never before been so accurately demonstrated. The principle makes possible the expression of chemical changes in the form of equations in which the combined weight of materials used must be equal to the total weight of the products. Again, by resorting to his balance, Lavoisier showed that every chemical operation ends in an equation, and though matter may be altered by the chemical process, it does not change in amount. Briefly stated, matter can neither be created nor destroyed. Even life moves in a circle—dust to dust.

Lavoisier's success in establishing the composition of water and other compounds and formulating the law of the conservation of matter was immensely facilitated by his three delicate balances, the most sensitive of which could weigh the five-hundredth part of a grain. He insisted upon absolute exactness in measurements, the magic key to the new chemistry. With his balances, he weighed chemical elements and compounds, before and after reactions, and he designed equipment for weighing gases. Trattner, noted scientific historian, comments: "By introducing the balance into chemistry as an instrument of precision, Lavoisier placed the new science upon the definite quantitative basis of an exact discipline. It provided the *coup de grâce* to the whole system of outworn methods. . . . By the keen temper of his logic Lavoisier realized from the outset that there could be no progress without the ability to weigh and measure all things chemical."

Another essential reform was a revised nomenclature for chemistry. For the most part, chemical terms had come down from the ancient days of alchemy, a pseudo-science filled with barbarous and meaningless expressions. Lavoisier and a small group led by him set out to introduce a comprehensive revision of the language. "Butter of arsenic" became arsenic chloride, "flowers of zinc" was changed to zinc oxide, "dephlogisticated air" to oxygen, and "phlogisticated" or "inflammable air" to hydrogen. Terminations were invented to describe classes of substances, such as oxide, sulphide, and phosphide, corresponding to their chemical composition. Many of the terms invented by Lavoisier have become the international vocabulary of chemists.

The publication of his *Elementary Treatise of Chemistry* marked the culmination of Lavoisier's years of experimentation and investigation. This first modern textbook of chemistry is divided into three parts. The first deals with the formation and properties of gases, oxidation, fermentation, and putrefaction, and with the composition of air, water, acids, bases, and salts; the second relates to chemical elements, listing thirty-three substances then regarded as elements, and contains detailed tables of nomenclature of chemical compounds; the third part is concerned with apparatus and methods of chemical experimentation and includes many engraved plates drawn by Lavoisier's talented wife. The *Elementary Treatise* was immensely successful from the outset, and Lavoisier's ideas and terminology set down therein were almost universally adopted.

Lavoisier's philosophy of science is summed up in these words: "Thoroughly convinced of these truths, I have imposed upon myself as a law, never to advance but from what is known to what is unknown; never to form any conclusion which is not an immediate consequence necessarily flowing from observation and experiment."

PART THREE
THE BOURGEOIS CENTURY

The thinkers of the Enlightenment prepared the ground for the French Revolution. Absolute monarchy and the special privileges enjoyed by the clergy and the nobility were their prime targets. By action of the relatively moderate National Assembly from 1789 to 1791, the king's powers were strictly circumscribed and all privileges of an economic and political nature were abolished.

Moderate reforms, however, were not enough to satisfy the restless French masses. Within two years, the new constitution had been rejected and the king and queen sent to the guillotine. In all likelihood, if France had been left free to work out her own destiny, the people would have been content with a constitutional form of government patterned after England's. But the monarchs of Europe, fearing for their own heads, urged on by Edmund Burke's *Reflections on the Revolution in France,* and sympathizing with the plight of the French king, determined to suppress the democratic revolt before the infection could spread. Foreign invasion, aided and abetted by the French king himself, roused the masses in France to a declaration of war on monarchical Europe. Like an unfolding drama, step by step, there followed the formation of an invincible citizens' army, the terrible excesses of the Reign of Terror, and the rise of Napoleon Bonaparte.

Napoleon, one of the most remarkable characters in history, has been termed a child of the Enlightenment. In seizing power from the democratic, but ineffective, executive body known as the Directory, Napoleon was motivated, at least in part, by an ardent desire to inaugurate the reforms which thus far the Revolution had been unable to put into effect. Most important of the innovations which Napoleon proceeded to impose on the French people were an efficient centralized system of administration and a new legal code—the Code Napoleon. The latter wiped out the last remnants of the old regime and established the equality of all citizens before the law.

The lasting consequences of the French Revolution were many. Still under the spell of the Enlightenment, the whole fabric of law,

economics, politics, education, religion, and society in general underwent basic modification in France, with shock waves felt throughout
Europe and America. The results of the Revolution may be summarized under three headings: (1) *The ending of feudalism, accompanied by the rising dominance of the middle class.* Such vestiges
of the past had vanished as privileged groups, inequality before the
law, and oppressive religious intolerance. (2) *The principle of majority rule.* Solidly established now was Rousseau's doctrine of the
sovereignty of the people and the rule of the majority, leading logically as it developed to the concept of universal suffrage. (3) *Nationalism.* Originally, the Enlightenment had advocated an international
brotherhood of man. Opposition to the Revolution among other
European powers, however, brought an almost hysterical upsurge
of nationalism in France. The Napoleonic wars stimulated similar
sentiment among the nations opposing the French armies. Thus was
immensely strengthened one of the most powerful forces affecting
world history of the past two centuries.

The period following the French Revolution is sometimes referred
to as the bourgeois century. The middle class was riding the crest
of the wave, and the culture, economics, and government of the age
reflected the values of that class. Even Karl Marx, bitterly opposed
to bourgeois civilization, had to pay grudging tribute to its accomplishments. In the *Communist Manifesto* of 1848, he and Friedrich
Engels conceded that "the bourgeoisie, during its rule of scarce one
hundred years, has created more massive and more colossal productive forces than have all preceding generations together."

Aside from Marx, criticism of the prevailing social order was a
common phenomenon. A ferment of ideas, comparable to the first
half of the eighteenth century, marked the times. In his *History of
European Thought in the Nineteenth Century,* Merz comments:
"No age has been so rich in rival theories, so subversive of old ideas,
so destructive of principles which stood firm for many ages."

Various factors were responsible for the intellectual complexities
of the bourgeois age. Fundamental, of course, was the heritage of
theories and concepts from the Enlightenment and the French
Revolution. But society was also being rapidly and radically transformed by another major force: the Industrial Revolution. Labor
was on the move from the home to the factory and from the country
to the city. Social conditions in factory communities were inde-
scribably bad. Child labor, exploitation of women, long hours of

work, and slum conditions were characteristic features. Protests against the terrible plight of the workers came from such warm-hearted humanitarians as Charles Dickens, John Ruskin, and Thomas Carlyle, all demanding reforms.

The new middle-class capitalists and manufacturers took readily to Adam Smith's laissez-faire doctrines, determined to follow policies of extreme individualism and to resist governmental control or regulation. Their opposition to any form of labor organization was equally vigorous. The philosophy of individualism was supported by the English Utilitarians, headed by Jeremy Bentham. Free competition and the law of supply and demand, it was argued, would result in the highest wages industry could afford. Under this system, each person would struggle for what he wanted and receive as much as he merited. The end result would be "the greatest good for the greatest number." The state's sole functions should be to maintain peace, enforce contracts, and protect individuals in their property rights.

Further justification for their practices, in the eyes of the industrialists, was found in Thomas Malthus' population theories. Europe's population had doubled in a short term of years—a fact which led Malthus to conclude that human beings multiply at a geometrical rate, while the food supply could be increased only in arithmetical progression. Consequently, wage increases and charity were mistakes, and the constant threat of starvation was essential to keep the world's population in balance. The Malthusian theory has had a prolonged influence upon economic, political, and social thought, as lively today as when first set forth one hundred and sixty years ago.

More enlightened views of society's responsibility for the welfare of the people were not lacking. Robert Owen, of Scotland, successful factory manager and advocate of a "plan of amelioration and reform without revolution," for example, conducted his New Lanark experiment pointing toward a possible method of organizing industrial communities for an uprooted rural population. Proudhon, in France, offered a radical proposal to reorganize the whole of society upon the basis of voluntary association. To Proudhon, possession of property except for use was theft, and he considered the prevailing laissez-faire philosophy seriously at fault in failing to guarantee liberty for men—an opinion shared by William Godwin, author of *An Enquiry Concerning Political Justice.*

Other highly articulate critics deplored various aspects of the new era. Balzac expressed keen distaste for the materialism of bourgeois civilization. The esthetic sensibilities of the art critic John Ruskin were offended by the ugliness and over-standardization of contemporary culture. The inequality of man and the misery of the masses were favorite themes of other influential writers.

Nevertheless, it was in numerous respects an age of remarkable creativity. The outstanding artistic movement of modern times began with the rise of Romanticism in the eighteenth century. A revolt against classicism in all the arts was intimately tied to the prevailing attitude of reform and revolution. For a century the phenomenon of Romanticism dominated the literature, arts, and music of Europe. One phase was an attempt to restore links with the national past, shown by renewed interest in early ballads, folklore, and legends, the historical novels of Victor Hugo and Sir Walter Scott, and a revival of Gothic architecture. Lyric poetry reached its highest pinnacle in the work of Coleridge, Byron, Shelley, Keats, Hugo, Lamartine, Alfred de Musset, Goethe, Schiller, and Heine. The novel form culminated in the two great Victorians, Dickens and Thackeray, and three Russians, Turgenev, Dostoevski, and Tolstoy. Perhaps the peak of the Romantic movement was the development of modern music, represented by such towering figures as Beethoven, Wagner, Liszt, Brahms, Mendelssohn, Schubert, and Schumann.

A curious manifestation of the idealism and mysticism associated with Romanticism, especially in Germany, was the tendency to regard the folk of a particular nation, or the nation itself, as a spiritual entity and object of devotion. Under such circumstances, the sentiment of nationalism reached an extreme and irrational height. Examples are the writings of the philosophers Fichte and Hegel. In his *Addresses to the German Nation,* Fichte argued that the German people alone among Europeans were capable of creating a unified free culture for Europe, and he urged establishment of a national system of education to integrate and mold the character of the Germans. Fichte was careful to distinguish between a government and a nation or people. Hegel likewise idealized the nation-state, particularly the Prussian, seeing in it what he conceived to be the consummation of the World Spirit, for "The State is the Divine Idea as it exists on earth." The state is the medium, Hegel held, through which political freedom could be achieved, and only by obedience to the state could man attain freedom. The impact of the Fichte-Hegel doctrines upon German thought in the past century and a half has been profound.

Shortly prior to the appearance of Fichte's *Addresses* and Hegel's

Philosophy of Right, another and greater German philosopher, Immanuel Kant, published his essay on *Eternal Peace.* Seeing beyond national borders, Kant took a world view and concluded that effective international law must be supported by a federation of free states. Furthermore, ownership in foreign lands ought not to be permitted, and no state should have a right to interfere violently with the government of another. Napoleon, on the other hand, visualized a single European or world government ruling over equal subjects.

Less spectacular than the spirit of Romanticism and the issue of nationalism versus internationalism, but of comparable significance, were the beginnings of reforms in education and in the treatment of women, exemplified in the writings of Johann Heinrich Pestalozzi and Mary Wollstonecraft. Taking his cue from Rousseau's doctrine that every individual should be aided and encouraged to develop to the fullest his unique potentialities, Pestalozzi built an educational program about such an ideal and thereby precipitated a revolution in European and American educational practices. Among his influential followers were Johann Friedrich Froebel, Friedrich Herbart, and Horace Mann. The long fight for the emancipation of women from medieval servitude was measurably advanced by Mary Wollstonecraft's polemic, *Vindication of the Rights of Women.*

Political and social experimentation likewise proceeded apace in America. The great lexicographer Noah Webster was even trying to establish a new American language. A spirit of confidence and optimism suffused the New World, reflected, for example, in one of the most celebrated American success stories, Benjamin Franklin's *Autobiography,* and later by such works as Ralph Waldo Emerson's *Essays* and Walt Whitman's *Leaves of Grass.* The process of hammering out a national constitution, described by Hamilton, Madison, and Jay in *The Federalist,* had been successfully completed. Forty-seven years later, its operation and that of the American political system were brilliantly analyzed by a young and perceptive Frenchman, Alexis de Tocqueville, in his *Democracy in America.*

But there was a cancer at the heart of the new republic—the institution of human slavery. Attempts to abolish slavery in drafting the United States Constitution had failed. Controversy over the issue mounted steadily in the first half of the nineteenth century. In his *Resistance to Civil Government,* Henry David Thoreau offered a drastic proposal—civil disobedience and refusal to pay taxes—as a means of forcing an end to the evil. Shortly afterward, Harriet

Beecher Stowe's *Uncle Tom's Cabin* ignited an explosion that could have but one outcome: civil war. Finally, immediately prior to the tragic era, 1861–1865, Abraham Lincoln and Stephen A. Douglas' *Political Debates* performed an essential function in educating the nation as to the principles at stake. The debates had the further effect of placing Lincoln in the national limelight and assuring his nomination for the Presidency.

Revolutionary movements and national uprisings in the Western world were stimulated rather than terminated by the American and French Revolutions. In Europe, the post-Napoleonic period was an age of revolution. Despite the attempts at repression by conservative forces, revolutionary outbreaks occurred in each decade from 1820 to 1850. None was comparable in scope to the great upheaval of 1789, and in the main they were abortive affairs, but all contributed to a general atmosphere of unrest and dissatisfaction with the status quo. Scarcely had the peacemakers at Vienna in 1815 finished setting up a neat European balance before the first revolutionary outburst erupted in the Iberian states of Spain and Portugal and in the Kingdom of the Two Sicilies. The Greek War of Independence, 1821–1829, to win emancipation from the Ottoman Empire, gained international sympathy and support. Nearly a century before the successful Russian Revolution of 1917, a brief and futile uprising took place in Russia. There followed the Revolution of 1830 in France and in the same year outbreaks in Belgium and Poland. More widespread and formidable were the revolutions which swept Europe in 1848.

The factors motivating these revolutionary currents were complex. In large part, they were designed to preserve, regain, or establish the principles of liberty, equality, and fraternity inherited from the French Revolution. Liberals everywhere were demanding civil rights, representative assemblies, and the granting of constitutions. In Italy and Germany, nationalism was a major force, with revolutionary leaders seeking to bring about national unification. Foreshadowing the future was the beginning of class warfare, as demands for far-reaching social and economic reforms began to accompany the earlier insistence upon political reform. These basic conflicts of interest were destined to continue into the twentieth century, and their satisfactory resolution in many areas of the world is yet to be achieved.

The march of scientific progress continued uninterrupted throughout the period. Astronomy had dominated the thinking of scientists in the sixteenth and seventeenth centuries, and the eighteenth was outstanding for pioneer investigations in chemistry. Important beginnings had also been made earlier in biological research, notably by Vesalius, Harvey, Leeuwenhoek, Linnaeus, Buffon, Cuvier, Lamarck, and others. But it is the nineteenth century that may properly be entitled the Age of Biology, especially if the term is interpreted broadly to include medicine. A field closely related in many of its aspects, geology, also came of age and firmly established itself as a major science.

By 1800 a foundation had been laid for the biological sciences in the classification of plants and animals (taxonomy) and their form and structure (morphology). Biology, however, rated below older branches of science, as is evidenced, for example, by Auguste Comte's priority listing of the sciences. Mathematics and astronomy were held to be most perfect and complete, followed in descending order by physics, chemistry, biology, and psychology. The life sciences, according to Comte, had yet to prove themselves.

Among the distinguished biologists of the nineteenth century, Charles Darwin unquestionably ranks first. For several generations a long line of workers had been developing the idea for which Darwin is most celebrated—the theory of organic evolution. Charles Lyell and his predecessors in geological research found incontrovertible evidence that life on the earth had existed for millions of years. Furthermore, fossil remains indicated a progression from simple to complex forms of life. It was Darwin's masterly achievement to bring the mass of facts and theories derived from studies by himself and others into a coherent whole. Darwin acknowledged particular indebtedness to Lyell for his conclusions on ancient life forms and to Malthus' view that population tended to increase faster than food supply. Seeking an explanation of why some species survive and others perish, Darwin formulated the principle of natural selection, theorizing that those individuals would survive and perpetuate the species which were best adapted to live in their particular natural environment. Evolution occurred chiefly, it was held, through minute variations among individuals.

Though Darwin conceded that man is evolution's major triumph, the theory still made man a descendant from lower forms and a member of the animal kingdom. Inevitably, therefore, the Darwinian hypothesis was an object of bitter theological attack, on the grounds that it contradicted the Bible and degraded man. Nevertheless, with the enthusiastic support of such aggressive and able advocates as

Huxley and Spencer, the general concept of evolutionary progress rapidly invaded all fields of thought. Medical science was also making phenomenal advances. After the work of William Harvey in the seventeenth century, the next great landmarks were Edward Jenner's discovery, in 1796, of vaccination as a preventive of smallpox, and Louis Pasteur's development of the germ theory in the mid-nineteenth century. Subsequently, the British surgeon Joseph Lister applied Pasteur's bacterial discoveries to antiseptic surgery, with remarkable success, and Robert Koch in Germany used them as a basis for pioneer researches in preventive medicine.

Great names in other divisions of science dot the period. Pierre Simon Laplace carried forward Newton's work, with his *Treatise on Celestial Mechanics,* exploring the origin and development of the solar system into its present form and proposing the nebular hypothesis. John Dalton placed the atomic theory upon a definite mathematical basis, setting the stage for modern chemical investigation. Michael Faraday ushered in the electrical age by discovering and formulating the laws of electrostatics and electromagnetism and with brilliant insight conceived the idea of an electromagnetic field—later developed mathematically by Clerk Maxwell. Successive editions of Charles Lyell's *Principles of Geology* presented a comprehensive synthesis of the field, and a special aspect was given almost definitive treatment in Louis Agassiz's studies on glaciers.

Numerous forces and movements have reshaped the world since 1750, and any attempt to summarize them necessarily tends toward oversimplification. There would be general agreement, however, on several factors as most characteristic and influential for the period here under consideration. First, the Industrial Revolution transformed the economic and social system. Second, liberal ideas spread, accompanied by a trend toward greater democracy and universal education. Third, a spirit of nationalism pervaded the Western world, with almost incalculable consequences, good and bad. Fourth, there occurred a reaction from the extreme individualism of the Enlightenment and of the revolutionary era and a growth of social consciousness. Finally, continued faith in the idea of progress led to constant stress on scientific research and on the practical applications of science to human affairs. By the end of the era, virtually all the elements that were to mold the twentieth century were present, at least in embryo form.

47. THE GREAT REFORMER

Jeremy Bentham's *An Introduction to the Principles of Morals and Legislation*
1789

In approximately the middle of the eighteenth century, when Jeremy Bentham was born, England was beginning to experience a technological and industrial transformation: the Industrial Revolution. Cities were expanding, the population was rapidly increasing, and the long-time dominance of the landed aristocracy was being overturned by the new manufacturers, merchants, and financiers. The year 1776, the date of Bentham's first book, has been called the beginning of our modern world, marked by the onset of the American Revolution, which in turn inspired the world-shaking French Revolution. Everywhere, men were disposed to question, criticize, and reject legacies of the past.

The temper of the time was most opportune for Jeremy Bentham, "Founder of Utilitarianism," and other reformers of law and politics. Since he was never a seeker of wealth or political power, Bentham's influence was exerted entirely through his writings and his disciples. His interests were extremely diverse—economics, logic, psychology, penology, theology, ethics—but his most abiding concern was with the common law and its reform. In the latter field, as John Stuart Mill says, "He found an incondite mass of barbarian conceits, obsolete technicalities and contrivances which had lost their meaning, bound together by sophistical ingenuity into a semblance of legal science, and held up triumphantly to the admiration and applause of mankind."

The most readable and best general statement of the Benthamite gospel is *An Introduction to the Principles of Morals and Legislation.* The opening words present the theory universally associated with the author's name:

Nature has placed mankind under the governance of two sovereign masters, *pain* and *pleasure*. It is for them alone to point out what we ought to do, as well as to determine what we shall do. On the one hand the standard of right and wrong, on the other the chain of causes and effects, are fastened to their throne.

All man's actions, Bentham held, are determined by the desire for pleasure or happiness (defined as synonymous) or the wish to avoid pain. From that assumption, he derived "the principle of utility" or, expressed in a more popular phrase, the concept of "the greatest happiness of the greatest number." The primary duty of both individuals and governments, as Bentham sees it, is to increase pleasure and, insofar as possible, to eliminate pain. The rightfulness of an act is measured by its *usefulness* in promoting pleasure, the basic idea of Utilitarianism. As Murray states the case, "A Utilitarian believes that it is wrong to tell a lie if doing so is likely to diminish pleasure; but that it is right to tell a lie if this is likely to increase pleasure. . . . A right action is one which increases or does not diminish happiness while a wrong action is one which diminishes happiness." In order to promote happiness, all human institutions should be so organized that pleasure results from social and pain from unsocial conduct.

Bentham intended that his doctrine should apply not only to morals, but also to legislation; in fact, his chief aim was to apply the principles to constitutional and legislative reforms. He was thinking of the good of the community and not simply of the welfare of the individual, though never losing sight of the fact that the community is composed of individuals. When the justice of a given law is in dispute, Bentham maintained, application of the criterion of the greatest happiness for the greatest number will test its rightness or wrongness.

The laws of a community, according to Bentham, are upheld by a force called "sanctions," i.e., by the pain or the pleasure attached to obedience or disobedience of the law. Four sanctions are described: physical, political, moral, and religious. Pain or pleasure (reward or punishment) in the case of physical sanctions comes from the operation of natural causes, such as good health in temperate and poor health in intemperate people; political or legal sanctions from judicial action; moral or popular sanctions from the pressure of public opinion; and religious sanctions from fear of supernatural forces. In brief, people are likely to behave properly if they believe they are apt to suffer pain or if they will be rewarded with pleasure from any of these four sources.

Discussing one of his favorite subjects, penal law, Bentham worked out a classification of crimes and punishments based on the principle of utility. Punishment, since it is an infliction of pain, can be justified only if it prevents a greater pain, as "all punishment in itself is evil." Further, punishment ought not to be motivated by hatred or desire for revenge—the mere desire to make the criminal suffer for his crime. The evil of the punishment must not be greater than the service to the community, which requires that criminals be incapacitated or deterred. In applying this principle, Bentham drew up an elaborate analysis to calculate the quantity of pleasure or pain that will result from any specific act. The value of a pleasure or a pain can be measured by "its intensity, its duration, its certainty or uncertainty, its propinquity or remoteness." Great stress is laid upon certainty. Finally, punishment should aim at the reformation of the individual transgressor.

Sir Henry Maine, is quoted as saying, "I do not know of a single law reform effected since Bentham's day which cannot be traced to his influence." How did Bentham achieve these miracles? In the first place, the chaotic condition of English law in his day invited drastic reforms. Bentham had been indefatigable in codifying the law, an essential prerequisite, he believed, for any general overhauling of the system. Equally important was the band of devoted disciples whom Bentham gathered around him. In Parliament and elsewhere, under Bentham's leadership, these loyal followers opened up attacks, which soon bore fruit, on the antiquated structure of English criminal and civil law.

In addition to penal reforms, Bentham was a moving spirit in parliamentary reform, municipal reform, poor law reform, abolition of imprisonment for debt, repeal of religious tests for office, establishment of a public health service, creation of a system of national education, the setting up of a permanent civil service, old-age pensions, the gathering of census statistics, reform of land laws, colonial self-government, and the introduction of cheap postage, and also advocated free trade, women's suffrage, the secret ballot, international peace, and a world court.

Bentham began as a strong Tory. Because of the opposition to reform on the part of vested interests, however, he gradually became a radical in politics. Since the politicians and ruling classes apparently did not desire the greatest happiness of the greatest number, Bentham was converted to the principle of absolute equalitarian democracy. Only by putting government into the hands of all the people and establishing majority rule, he decided, could the greatest happiness for the greatest number be guaranteed.

48. APOSTLE OF MODERN CONSERVATISM

Edmund Burke's *Reflections on the French Revolution*
1790

For his *Speech on Conciliation with the Colonies,* Americans will always have a warm place in their hearts for Edmund Burke. Pleading for moderation on the part of the Crown in settling the rankling disputes that were shortly to erupt in the *Declaration of Independence,* Burke's voice echoed throughout the New World.

Strikingly different, however, was the great orator's attitude toward another major upheaval of his time—the French Revolution—inspired in part by the events in America. In the first instance, he had appeared sympathetic and understanding; now he was violently antagonistic. Why the complete reversal of feeling?

In the beginning, English sentiment outside the ruling classes strongly favored the revolutionary cause in France. The leader of the English Whigs, Charles James Fox, termed the storming of the Bastille in 1789 the "greatest event" that ever happened, and later he spoke of the 1791 constitution as "the most stupendous and glorious edifice of liberty which has been erected on the foundation of human integrity, in any time or country." English sympathizers claimed that the French Revolution was accomplishing for France what the Glorious Revolution of 1688 had done for England.

The Irish-born Burke entered an emphatic dissent. His *Reflections on the French Revolution* bitterly denounced elements of French society who emerged as the Revolution progressed. To him they were "armed fanatics" resembling

> a den of outlaws upon a doubtful frontier; of a lewd tavern of revels and debauches, of banditti, assassins, bravos, smugglers and their more desperate paramours, mixed with bombastic players, the refuse and rejected offal of strolling theatres, puffing out ill-sorted verses about virtue, mixed with the licentious and blasphemous songs proper to the brutal and hardened course of lives belonging to that sort of wretches.

To Burke, the Jacobins in France were motivated by "determined hostility to the human race," the Revolution was "a hideous phantom . . . one of the greatest calamities that has ever fallen upon mankind," and its leaders were characterized as "the revolution harpies of France, sprung from night and hell."

The nightmare that haunted Burke, accounting in large part for his uncompromising enmity toward the French Revolution, was the fear that the radical theories fermenting there would jump the English Channel. He foresaw the danger of Britain's being influenced "through an admiration of successful fraud and violence, to an imitation of the excesses of an irrational, unprincipled, proscribing, wasting, plundering, ferocious, bloody and tyrannical democracy. . . . It is with an armed doctrine," he declared, "that we are at war." Burke realized that the Revolution must have serious repercussions on every country in Europe. He was impatient with his fellow countrymen who failed to share his view that the kind of liberty advocated by the revolutionists was a caricature of real freedom, for Burke saw the state of affairs in France as anarchy leading inevitably to tyranny.

The basic reason for Burke's hatred of the French Revolution and its partisans was his conviction that change should never be sudden or arbitrary. The future must be built securely and legally upon the customs and beliefs of preceding generations. In Burke's eyes, the British method—gradual modifications in the constitution and other institutions over centuries of time—represented perfection. The complete destruction of much that he regarded as precious and irreplaceable in France left no foundation, he felt, upon which to begin building anew. Throughout the *Reflections* there is evident a strong sense of history. The leisurely pace of history, to Burke, was an ideal antidote to radical ideas and revolutionary haste.

In contrast to what he regarded as the catastrophe in France, the American uprising a few years earlier, in Burke's opinion, had been a horse of an entirely different color. At the time of the American Revolution, Burke had held that the conflict, in principle, was a constitutional quarrel among Englishmen. As he saw it, the Americans were fighting for English liberties and had no intention of destroying long-established institutions. Likewise, the English Revolution of 1688, which Burke greatly admired, was designed to preserve institutions, rather than to subvert or destroy them, though Burke conveniently overlooked the fact that in the Puritan Revolution a half century earlier a king had lost his head. In any event, to Burke the

French Revolution of 1789 stood for nothing except destruction, anarchy, and terror. His conservative point of view is reflected in the statement, "People will not look forward to posterity, who never look backward to their ancestors."

Actually, Burke was uninformed about the intolerable conditions in France that had caused the people to revolt against their government. The oppressive abuses, feudal exactions, and generally terrible plight of the French common people under the monarchy were largely ignored by Burke, who glorified the old order and apparently believed that opposition to the French king and the beautiful Marie Antoinette was heretical and criminal.

Under the impact of Burke's ominous warnings against the perils of the tremendous changes in France, English national sentiment underwent a complete turnabout. Panic succeeded reason. Speaking of the effect of the *Reflections,* one commentator said that "a voice like the Apocalypse sounded over England, and even echoed in all the courts of Europe." Armed intervention was demanded by Burke to suppress the threat to English institutions posed by the French revolutionary movement. The violent passions that he and his adherents were instrumental in whipping up culminated in the European coalition determined to crush the revolutionary spirit by force of arms.

William Ebenstein, in his *Great Political Thinkers,* offers a fascinating speculation:

> Had there been no military coalition of Europe (for which Burke himself labored with utmost frenzy) against revolutionary France, no invasion of her soil by the Prussians and their allies, it is at least conceivable that France might have worked her passage from royal autocracy to popular government without so much violence and bloodshed. . . . The civil strife that developed in France after the outbreak of the Revolution was largely the result of foreign interference, in which the King himself was treacherously implicated.

It is doubtless an oversimplification, but nevertheless a logical deduction, that if there had been no Burke there would have been no Napoleon.

For its championship of the traditional ways of society, its support for gradual and moderate change, its defense of property rights, and its thorough distaste for radical political theory, Burke's *Reflections* has been described as "the bible of modern conservatism."

49. THE GREAT AMERICAN SUCCESS STORY

Benjamin Franklin's *Autobiography*

1791

Summing up Benjamin Franklin's extraordinary career, it may be fairly stated that he was the most versatile American of his century, if not of all time. His influence was felt deeply both at home and abroad. When Franklin died at Philadelphia in April, 1790, he was reputed to be the most famous private citizen in the world. Jefferson called him "the greatest man and ornament of the age and country in which he lived." As a scientist, inventor, printer, diplomat, politician, journalist, educator, administrator, and philosopher, among other accomplishments, Franklin ranks as a universal genius.

His *Autobiography* was intended by Franklin to be a kind of philosophical legacy to young men. The first third, written in 1771, was addressed to his natural son, William, then Governor of New Jersey, and carried the story from his birth, in 1706, to his marriage in 1730. With the Revolutionary War approaching, Franklin's mind was so preoccupied with public affairs that he was unable to resume the narrative until 1784, when he was serving as Minister to France. Other fragments were composed in 1788–1789, shortly before the author's death. The account ends with the year 1757. For unknown reasons, the first edition of the *Autobiography* was an incomplete, badly garbled translation in French, printed in Paris. The complete English text was not published until 1868.

Franklin's book established the great American tradition of the self-made man. The author's aim, as stated in a letter to a friend, was

> to omit all facts and transactions, that may not have a tendency to benefit the young reader, by showing him from my example, and my success in emerging from poverty, and acquiring some degree of wealth, power, and reputation, the advantages of certain modes of conduct which I observed, and of avoiding the errors which were prejudicial to me.

In one sense, the *Autobiography* is another success story, an earlier version of Samuel Smiles, Horatio Alger, and Dale Carnegie. Franklin reveals the difficulties of his career, describes his struggles as an apprentice, journeyman, and, finally, master printer—how he sat up late to study, how he became a vegetarian to save money for books, how he eventually made his way through trade to prosperity and high standing in the community. There is no evidence of self-consciousness or false modesty in the chronicle of the hero's progress. His associates in business, science, politics, and public welfare are unfailingly accorded whatever credit he thinks is due them, but he just as unhesitatingly claims credit due to himself. Franklin recognizes, with some amusement, this trait in his own character, for he remarks, "It would not be altogether absurd if a man were to thank God for his vanity among the other comforts of life."

The *Autobiography* is rich in the type of homely aphorisms and worldly wisdom that brought fame to Franklin's *Poor Richard's Almanac*. After gaining the friendship of a cold, distant gentleman by borrowing a book from him, Franklin draws the moral, "He that has done you a kindness will be more ready to do you another, than he whom you yourself have obliged." As his business prospered, he "experienced, too, the truth of the observation, 'that after getting the first hundred pounds, it is more easy to get the second,' money itself being of a prolific nature." Explaining his success in avoiding disagreements with business partners, Franklin suggests that it was "owing, I think, a good deal to the precaution of having very explicitly settled, in our articles, every thing to be done by or expected from each partner, so that there was nothing to dispute, which precaution I would therefore recommend to all who enter into partnerships."

Constant industry is praised and practiced in the *Autobiography*. "In order to secure my credit and character as a tradesman," the author recalls, "I took care not only to be in reality industrious and frugal, but to avoid all appearances to the contrary." Supervising the building of forts for protection against the Indians, Franklin observes that "when men are employed, they are best contented." This reminds him of the story of the "sea-captain, whose rule it was to keep his men constantly at work; and when his mate told him that they had done everything, and there was nothing further to employ them about 'Oh,' said he, 'make them scour the anchor.' "

In Franklin's search for moral perfection, he lists, and discusses at length, thirteen useful virtues and guiding precepts, which he himself conscientiously attempted to follow:

1. Temperance. Eat not to dullness; drink not to elevation. 2. Silence. Speak not but what may benefit others or yourself; avoid trifling conversation. 3. Order. Let all your things have their places; let each part

of your business have its time. 4. Resolution. Resolve to perform what you ought; perform without fail what you resolve. 5. Make no expense but to do good to others or yourself; i.e., waste nothing. 6. Industry. Lose no time; be always employed in something useful; cut off all unnecessary actions. 7. Sincerity. Use no hurtful deceit; think innocently and justly, and, if you speak, speak accordingly. 8. Justice. Wrong none by doing injuries, or omitting the benefits that are your duty. 9. Moderation. Avoid extremes; forbear resenting injuries so much as you think they deserve. 10. Cleanliness. Tolerate no uncleanliness in body, clothes, or habitation. 11. Tranquillity. Be not disturbed at trifles, or at accidents common or unavoidable. 12. Chastity. 13. Humility. Imitate Jesus and Socrates.

Observing the precept of *Order,* Franklin outlines a "scheme of employment for the twenty-four hours of a natural day." Each morning begins with the question, "What good shall I do this day?" and each evening he asks himself, "What good have I done to-day?"

Some critics, for example D. H. Lawrence, have been repelled by what they conceive of as Franklin's emphasis upon material success. "It is in the *Autobiography,*" writes William Cabell Bruce, noted Franklin biographer, "that the story of Franklin's struggle, first for the naked means of subsistence, and then for pecuniary competency, is told; and the harsh self-restraint, the keen eye to every opportunity for self-promotion, and the grossly mechanical theory of morals disclosed by it readily give color to the notion that Franklin was nothing more than a sordid materialist." This impression is strengthened by Franklin's perfect candor in describing the means and methods by which he rose in the world; there are no apologies, no attempts at concealment of facts. Realism and worldliness, rather than utopian idealism, are the *Autobiography's* predominant features. Nevertheless, Franklin maintains that he had always "endeavoured to convince young persons that no qualities were so likely to make a poor man's fortune as those of probity and integrity."

50. FIRST OF A NEW GENUS

Mary Wollstonecraft's *Vindication of the Rights of Woman*
1792

Striking proof of how far in advance Mary Wollstonecraft was of her own time, when in 1792 she advocated woman suffrage, is the fact that the Nineteenth Amendment to the Constitution, giving women the right to vote in the United States, was not approved until 1920, and all restrictions were not removed in Great Britain until 1928. Progress has since been rapid, but the battle still rages in many areas of the world.

It is difficult nowadays to conceive of the degrading position and the popular attitude toward women in eighteenth-century society—the conditions that inspired Mary Wollstonecraft's famous polemic, *Vindication of the Rights of Woman*. Not only did women possess no political power, but, under prevailing laws, a wife was regarded as her husband's chattel; she could not dispose of her own property, her husband was permitted to punish her physically, and she had no parental rights. Her legal status was in accord with general social opinion, which held that women were placed in the world for the comfort and pleasure of men. This concept was reflected in Rousseau's argument for keeping women in a state of sex subjection:

> The education of women should always be relative to that of men. To please, to be useful to us, to make us love and esteem them, to educate us when young, to take care of us when grown up, to advise, to console us, to render our lives easy and agreeable; these are the duties of women at all times, and what they should be taught in their infancy.

Earlier, Milton had viewed a husband as a kind of priest standing between a woman and God: "He for God only, she for God in him." An even more forthright statement came from a Wollstonecraft contemporary, Lord Chesterfield. "Women," he asserted, "are only children of a larger growth. . . . A man of sense only trifles with them, plays with them, humors and flatters them, as he does with a sprightly, forward child; but he neither consults them about, nor trusts them with serious matters."

The one career open to women was marriage, and all their training was directed toward that end. Young girls learned a few accomplishments, were taught a smattering of ornamental knowledge and such virtues as would appeal to a husband in a subject wife—chiefly submission, chastity, and the art of pleasing.

In this strictly man's world, Mary Wollstonecraft threw her bombshell, upsetting the complacency both of the masculine world and of her own sex. It was a period ripe for revolt, the era of the American and French Revolutions (Mary Wollstonecraft, in fact, subsequently wrote a history of the French Revolution), when new thoughts about the rights of man were fermenting. To Mary Wollstonecraft, it appeared to be a propitious time to overthrow another despotism—that of men over women. She was, in her own words, "the first of a new genus."

The author based her crusade to win freedom and self-respect for women on the principle that they would thereby become more capable wives and mothers. She opens the book with a picture of the contemporary state of women:

> Women are still reckoned a frivolous sex. . . . It is acknowledged that they spend many of the first years of their lives in acquiring a smattering of accomplishments; meanwhile strength of body and mind are sacrificed to libertine notions of beauty, to the desire of establishing themselves—the only way women can rise in the world—by marriage. And this desire making mere animals of them, when they marry they act as such children may be expected to act—they dress, they paint, and nickname God's creatures. Surely these weak beings are only fit for a seraglio! Can they be expected to govern a family with judgement, or take care of the poor babes whom they bring into the world?

The reforms in this pernicious system proposed by Mary Wollstonecraft were momentous and revolutionary for their own time but would scarcely be viewed as anything except moderate today. She urged that women should be educated, for "ignorance is a frail base for virtue." Women, she believed, should have an equal opportunity with men to develop their mental and moral capacities and become the companions, rather than the playthings, of men. To this end, a drastic shake-up in educational practices was recommended. Boarding schools should be abolished, and national day schools should be established and supported by the government. In the new public schools, boys and girls would be taught together, to avoid premature sex-consciousness. Further, there would be no distinction based on rank or wealth.

The author suggested that, beginning at age nine, the students should receive more specialized training. The boys would learn mechanical trades and the girls the domestic arts. New careers would open up for women: medicine, agriculture, shopkeeping, and every kind of business. This was written only a few years after Boswell records Dr. Samuel Johnson as saying that even portrait painting and writing were "improper employment for a woman." Mary Wollstonecraft, who had observed frequent instances of hardship and tragedy caused by the complete economic dependence of women on men, expanded her ideas further:

Though I consider that women in the common walks of life are called
to fulfill the duties of wives and mothers by religion and reason, I
cannot help lamenting that women of a superior cast have not a road
open by which they can pursue more extensive plans of usefulness and
independence. . . . I really think that women ought to have representatives instead of being arbitrarily governed, without having any
direct share allowed them in the deliberations of government.

Thus did the *Vindication* plead for equal educational and economic
opportunities for women and a voice for them in government. In the
past, the author declared, men "have been more anxious to make
women alluring mistresses than affectionate wives and mothers";
future progress depended upon a changed attitude of men toward
women and of women toward themselves.

The *Vindication of the Rights of Woman* created a great sensation
immediately upon publication. Translations were issued in French
and German. The book both shocked and scandalized the conservative and puritanical, who considered it a gross offense against decency
and womanly reserve. Horace Walpole called the author "a hyena in
petticoats" and a "philosophizing serpent." Mary Wollstonecraft
was made more vulnerable to attack by her own unconventional personal life. Her lack of orthodoxy was encouraged by association with
such individuals as William Godwin, whom she married shortly before her death, Thomas Paine, and other radical thinkers of the period.

As the feminist cause has advanced, however, Mary Wollstonecraft's contentions have become commonplace. Nevertheless, her contributions to the principle of education for citizenship instead of sex
subordination, to civil rights, and to similar equal prerogatives for
women have been of immeasurable importance.

51. PHILOSOPHICAL ANARCHIST

William Godwin's *An Enquiry Concerning the Principles of Political Justice, and Its Influence on General Virtue and Happiness*

1793

William Godwin is remembered today chiefly through having been
the husband of Mary Wollstonecraft, pioneer champion of women's
rights, and the father of Mary Shelley, wife of the noted English

poet. In his own time, as prophet of a new utopia, however, Godwin was a celebrated, or, as conservatives viewed him, a notorious character. His fame derives almost entirely from authorship of the longest and most systematic defense of anarchism ever produced by an Englishman: *An Enquiry Concerning the Principles of Political Justice.* Unfortunately for Godwin and his book, violent reaction in England against the French Revolution turned the people away from radical thought of all varieties and led to the virtual suppression of his *Political Justice.*

Godwin begins his *Enquiry* upon the assumption "that the happiness of the human species is the most desirable object for human science to promote, and that intellectual and moral happiness or pleasure is extremely to be preferred to those which are precarious and transitory." Endeavoring to discover how this grand purpose can be achieved, Godwin concludes that "erroneous and corrupt government was the most formidable adversary to the improvement of the species," and therefore political enquiry is "the first and most important subject of human investigation." By politics is meant not simply the machinery of government but the general science of human virtue and happiness.

Godwin's indictment of government and its deficiencies is unrestrained. "The history of mankind," he declares, "is little else than the history of crimes," with war, inequality, and despotism the predominant characteristics. Since ancient times, governments have bred disastrous wars, usually for trivial reasons, in which millions of men have died for causes of no personal concern to them. "May it not happen," asks Godwin, "that the grand moral evils that exist in the world, the calamities by which we are so grievously oppressed, are to be traced to political institutions as their source and that their removal is only to be expected by their correction?"

The failings of government internally are as catastrophic as the external evidences, such as war. Even within civilized nations, "hundreds of victims are annually sacrificed at the shrine of positive law and political institutions." Among despotic governments, in power over most of the world, "dungeons, chains, and racks are the most approved and established methods of persuading men to obedience, and impressing upon their minds the lessons of reason." Because of social injustice and maldistribution of property, "a large family has in the lower orders of life become a proverbial expression for an uncommon degree of poverty and wretchedness." In England, one person in seven has received aid from the poor rates. Law is primarily for the protection of the rich and oppression of the poor. Consequently, the poor have come "to regard the state of society as a state of war, an unjust combination, not for protecting every man in his rights and securing to him the means of existence, but for engrossing all its advantages to a few favoured individuals, and reserving for the portion of the rest want, dependence and misery."

These conditions, maintains Godwin, are both undesirable and unnecessary. Society could be transformed by changing its institutions, especially government. Environment and not heredity, it is held, is the most important factor in shaping character. "Our virtues and vices may be traced to the incidents which make the history of our lives, and if these incidents could be divested of every improper tendency, vice would be extirpated from the world." To determine the most favorable environment for the development of individual personality, Godwin analyzes forms of government. Monarchy and aristocracy are utterly condemned. Democracy, the least objectionable, has serious drawbacks; the principle of majority rule means that the minority will is always overridden, there are evils in the party system, and reason is perverted by oratory, disputes, and the victory of ignorance.

For the foregoing reasons, Godwin decides that even the best government is evil. It interferes with the activity of reason, maintains the existing order by propaganda and force, and obstructs intellectual and moral progress. Discussing numerous types of governmental activity, Godwin condemns in particular any restrictions upon the expression of political and religious opinion, and the maintenance of established churches. He likewise opposes any system of national education, on the theory that only orthodox opinions and prejudices favorable to the government would be taught. A fixed body of laws is objected to, for such reasons as their vast and unmanageable bulk, their contradictory character, and the obstacles they place in the path of progress.

The enforcement of laws, in Godwin's judgment, leads to some of government's worst abuses. Evidently under the influence of Beccaria's writings, he argues against the prevailing system of criminal punishment. In an ideal society, he suggests, wrongdoers would be censured rather than punished. Imprisonment is justified only to restrain violent criminals from doing further mischief. "Man is not originally vicious."

Next among existing social institutions to be denounced by Godwin is property:

> And here with grief it must be confessed that, however great and extensive are the evils that are produced by monarchies and courts, by the imposture of priests and the iniquity of criminal laws, all these are imbecile and impotent compared with the evils that arise out of the established system of property.

The grounds for condemning private property and for demanding its abolition, as Godwin sees them, may be summarized thus: the system damages human personalities by forcing the poor to behave obsequiously toward the rich; it promotes class war, causes moral and intellectual degradation, and encourages crime; and the private ownership of land causes underpopulation, "strangling a considerable portion of our children in their cradle." The institution of marriage is regarded by Godwin as simply a branch of the property system and therefore is rejected on the basis that it retards individual development, is adverse to happiness, and places woman in a degrading economic position.

Godwin's remedy for the sad state of society is essentially anarchistic. Man could be regenerated by reason. Man is perfectible and is capable of indefinitely improving. As a first step, priestcraft, aristocracy, and coercive legislation—the main forces poisoning the mind —would be eliminated. Afterward, there would be established a loose federation of small self-governing, self-sufficient communities. Each community would elect a governing body or jury to restrain evildoers and to settle local disputes. A parliament elected by the villages or parishes would meet one day each year to consider any controversies between communities and matters of defense against foreign invasion.

In the future utopia visualized by Godwin, political government will have disappeared, along with war, crime, punishment, and poverty, property will be fairly distributed, the working day will be short, and, finally, man will have vanquished even sleep and death. Reason, virtue, and happiness will have prevailed.

Godwin's marked impression upon the English Romantic poets is generally acknowledged. Three-fourths of Shelley's poetry, it is estimated, is based on ideas in *Political Justice*. For a time, Wordsworth, Southey, and Coleridge, among others, were also strongly influenced by Godwin's doctrines. In the realm of political science, Godwin has been called "the first scientific socialist," and unquestionably his theories carried weight with the leading nineteenth-century and early twentieth-century socialists. More aptly, however, he should be regarded as the founder of the anarchist movement, the reverse of socialism in most respects. By no stretch of the imagination could he be called a Communist, for he disliked co-operation as much as he detested government.

52. VISION OF PERPETUAL PROGRESS

Antoine-Nicolas de Condorcet's *L'Esquisse d'un Tableau Historique des Progrès de l'Esprit Humain* (Sketch for a Historical Picture of the Progress of the Human Mind)
1795

Few scenes in history are more inspiring or more moving than that of Antoine-Nicolas de Condorcet, a fugitive from the Reign of Terror's guillotine, hiding in a Parisian attic and seeing the revolutionary ideals for which he had fought collapsing around him, devoting the last few months of his life to the composition of a testament of faith in the inevitability of human progress.

Of all the philosophers—Montesquieu, Voltaire, Rousseau, Diderot, Helvetius, Turgot, and others—whose writings and influence paved the way for the French Revolution, only Condorcet survived to become an active participant in the great drama. The passive role of spectator was not one Condorcet was content to play. For a time he served as President of the Legislative Assembly, presented a famous report on education, and drafted a liberal constitution. The Jacobins' seizure of power in 1793, followed by the violent excesses of the Reign of Terror, however, forced him and other moderates to flee for their lives.

Condorcet's *Sketch for a Historical Picture of the Progress of the Human Mind* was described by the renowned Italian philosopher Benedetto Croce as "the last will and testament of the eighteenth century," intended by its author to be a comprehensive history in brief of the human spirit from primitive times to the French Revolution. The book's running thesis is that the evils of life have resulted from bad institutions and that from these mankind will eventually free itself. Throughout the *Sketch* the idea of progress is presented as a common factor pervading all history. Unlike most eighteenth-century social critics and reformers, Condorcet does not see the record of the past as simply "a mass of crimes, of follies, and of misfortunes." On the contrary, he comes to the optimistic conclusion that progress has been continuous, gradually surmounting every obstacle.

The study of history, asserts Condorcet, has two principal uses: to discover "what man has been and what he is today" and "to instruct us about the means we should employ to make certain and rapid the further progress that his nature allows him still to hope for." As visualized by Condorcet: "Nature has set no term to the perfection of human faculties . . . the perfectibility of man is truly indefinite, and the progress of this perfectibility . . . has no other limit than the duration of the globe upon which nature has cast us."

The chief impediments to progress, says Condorcet, are prejudices, mostly inherited from past ages. Among the errors from which evil consequences have flowed are the hereditary transmission of governmental power—to blame for enslaving a large portion of mankind—and the social inequality of women, a major deterrent to the general happiness. Also disastrous in retarding the progress of the human race, Condorcet believes, is religion; he is firmly convinced that belief in the supernatural has inflicted countless calamities on a suffering humanity.

Having stated his philosophy of history, Condorcet proceeds to consider the various stages by which man has risen from the brute simplicity of primitive life to the enlightenment of a scientific civilization and to political liberty. The same idea is found, for example, in Voltaire and Turgot, but Condorcet was original in extending the doctrine of progress to every phase of human activity: intellectual, political, economic, social, and artistic.

Nine epochs in history are recognized by Condorcet, and he foresees a tenth, to begin with the conclusion of the French Revolution, representing "the future progress of the human mind." In outline, the nine epochs begin with prehistoric man, who originated a belief in supernatural forces. There ensued, in order, the second phase, during which arts and sciences advanced, and primitive institutions were created for the maintenance of order; the third, the agricultural stage, ending with the invention of the alphabet; the fourth, the period of the ascendancy of the Greeks, a people "whose genius opened all the avenues to truth, and whom nature had prepared and whom fate had destined to be the benefactors and guides of all nations and of all ages"; the fifth, down to the beginning of the medieval era, marked by advances in mathematics and medicine, the Alexandrian period of Greek civilization, and the rise of the Romans, whose only contribution, according to Condorcet, was a system of jurisprudence; the sixth and seventh, dealing with the Middle Ages, a "disastrous period," characterized by religious intolerance and persecutions; the eighth, highlighted by the invention of printing, vastly facilitating the advancement of knowledge, the discovery of America, the scientific revolution of the sixteenth and seventeenth centuries, and the Protestant Reformation; and the ninth, extending from Descartes to the Revolution, made notable by the coming of the Age of Reason.

Modern historians have criticized Condorcet's treatment of history as too mechanical, rigid, and schematic, with "shocking omissions." It should be remembered, however, that the author worked under extreme physical difficulties, a refugee from the Terror, cut off from sources of information. In any case, the *Esquisse* was intended only as a prospectus for a universal history, not as the definitive work itself.

In his final and most celebrated chapter, Condorcet is concerned with the future of mankind. He is convinced that the advance of medicine and of sanitary science will abolish disease and prolong life; the equality of nations and of individuals will be universally accepted; war will come to be regarded "as the greatest of plagues and as the greatest of crimes"; a permanent league of nations will be established; free trade will accompany freedom of commerce and industry; a universal language will be invented; economic opportunities for all the people will be equalized; there will be "complete destruction of those prejudices which establish between the sexes the inequalities of rights that are bad even for the favored male sex"; and a system of universal education will be instituted.

The *Sketch* was completed in 1794 and published posthumously the following year, when the Terror was reaching an end. The story of Condorcet's undying faith achieved immediate and widespread popularity. Thousands of copies poured from the presses in France, and translations appeared in England, Germany, and elsewhere.

The influence of the *Sketch* was so great that it materially modified the social philosophy of the nineteenth century. Malthus' classic work on population was written partly in answer to it, and Condorcet's ideas inspired James Mill, John Stuart Mill, and other Utilitarians in England. Auguste Comte, it may be noted also, expressed the opinion that the *Sketch* laid the basis of all subsequent developments in sociology.

53. MAGNA CHARTA FOR A UNITED NATIONS

Immanuel Kant's *Zum Ewigen Frieden; ein Philosophischer Entwurf* (Eternal Peace; a Philosophical Proposal)

1795

Immanuel Kant, whose influence has probably been more profound than that of any other philosopher of modern times, is most celebrated for his three philosophical treatises: *Critique of Pure Reason, Critique of Practical Reason,* and *Critique of Judgment,* issued between 1781 and 1790. With his deep interest in the field, Kant could also have achieved a distinguished career as a physical scientist; in his early years, for example, he published a correct theory on the slowing effect of the tides on the earth's rotation, put forward a form of the nebular hypothesis forty years before Laplace, and suggested the evolution of man from some lower animal form a century prior to Darwin's *Origin of Species.*

It was Kant's intention to follow his three great works of critical philosophy with a comprehensive treatise on the philosophical aspects of politics, but his health and advancing age compelled him to abandon the plan. He did, however, publish several essays indicative of the spirit of his political ideas. Best known of these is *Eternal Peace,* one of the last writings of his memorable life.

The era in which Kant was discussing international peace was far from peaceful. The government of the United States had just been established by revolution; the smoke of the French Revolution had not yet cleared away; and Great Britain was moving toward governmental reform and greater democracy, after prolonged controversy. Absolute monarchies remained the prevailing pattern of government in Europe. Disregard of moral rules in international relations, especially on the parts of the most powerful nations, was generally accepted and justified by cynical statesmen. A significant instance of the slight regard for international obligations was the dropping of a project for the publication, in 1780, of a collection of European treaties concluded since 1740, because of the opposition of the rulers of the states concerned.

Primitive society, said Kant, was dominated by the "unsocial sociability" of mankind. The state of nature, in effect, was a chronic state of war. This condition was corrected by the creation of a strong state, able to repress lawless and immoral acts. Thus the state marked an essential step forward in man's progress from savagery to civilization. But another advance, Kant insisted, was important and necessary. The large number of separate states must establish a powerful league of nations, capable of maintaining eternal peace. Until this further step was taken, the individual nations would continue in a "state of nature," as individuals had done previously. Eternal, universal peace is not only desirable, but feasible and inevitable, declared Kant:

> Through the wars, through the excessive and never realized preparation for them, through the want which hence every state even in the midst of peace must feel, Nature drives man to make attempts, at first quite inadequate, to leave the lawless state of savages, and to enter a league of nations; where each state, even the smallest, may expect his security and his rights—not from its own power or its own legal views, but alone from this great league of nations, from a united power, and from the decision according to laws adopted by the united will.

In the preliminary section of *Eternal Peace,* Kant enumerates six conditions required for the establishment of peace among states.

First, "No treaty of peace is to be regarded as such, which has been made with the secret reservation of matter which would lead to a future war." Most peace treaties, the author points out, are really nothing more than armistices—breathing spells preparatory to the next war.

Second, "No state having an independent existence, whether it be small or great, may be acquired by another state, through inheritance, exchange, purchase or gift," since a state is a society of men over whom that state alone has a right to command and to dispose.

Third, "Standing armies shall gradually disappear," because such armies are constant threats to peace, stimulate armament races between states, and are economically burdensome.

Fourth, "No debts shall be contracted in connection with the foreign affairs of the state," particularly if money so obtained is to be used for waging war.

Kant's fifth condition is that, "No state shall interfere by force in the constitution and government of another state"—essentially the principle of the Monroe Doctrine.

Finally, "No state at war with another shall permit such acts of warfare as must make mutual confidence impossible in time of future peace: such as the employment of assassins, of poisoners, the violation of articles of surrender, the instigation of treason in the state against which it is making war, etc."

Following his listing and discussion of the six negative factors, Kant reviews three "definitive articles for eternal peace among states." First, "the civil constitution in each state should be republican." Peace could never be safe and stable, he believed, until the mass of the people had the deciding vote whether war should be declared or not. Monarchs and legislative bodies are untrustworthy in wielding such power, motivated, as they frequently are, by emotion, passion, or ambition. Kant's second "definitive article" holds that "the law of nations should be based upon a federation of free states." The third, a natural corollary, declares that "the rights of men as citizens of the world in a cosmopolitical system shall be restricted to conditions of universal hospitality," i.e., as members of the world order they should be able to travel freely from place to place, assuming the privilege is not abused.

The question of whether a federation or a union of nations would be more effective in maintaining peace was considered at some length by Kant. A federation of states, he felt, must depend for its success upon the willingness of each member to enter freely into certain obligations and, even more important, to abide by its undertakings. By its nature, each state is sovereign and can acknowledge no power above itself. The ultimate goal should be a government of nations, a comprehensive world state, although, because of difficulties in obtaining agreement on this concept, Kant suggests that the league "need not be a world government." Elsewhere, in his *Theory and Practice,* Kant suggests that a universal cosmopolitan constitution might end up in a terrible despotism and therefore be even more dangerous to freedom than war.

Many of the principles urged by Kant in *Eternal Peace* were incorporated into the League of Nations Covenant, following World

War I, and subsequently into the United Nations Charter. Edwin D.
Mead, a noted political commentator, has pointed out: "Woodrow
Wilson, himself more a philosopher than a politician, and a Kantian
at that, was undoubtedly profoundly influenced by Kant's international thought, and his whole work at Paris was, whether consciously
or not, an heroic effort to realize that thought in the practical organization of the world."

54. DISCOVERER OF VACCINATION

Edward Jenner's *An Inquiry into the Causes and Effects of the
Variolæ Vaccinæ, a Disease Discovered in Some of the
Western Counties of England, Particularly
Gloucestershire, and Known by the Name
of the Cow Pox*

1798

Of all the ancient scourges of mankind, the most deadly and
devastating was smallpox, a disease which can be traced back at
least to Egyptian mummies more than 3,000 years ago. Only leprosy,
influenza, cholera, typhus fever, and bubonic plague were as dreaded,
and over the centuries none of these had rivaled smallpox in its dire
consequences. In Europe alone, sixty million people died of smallpox in the eighteenth century. One out of every fourteen persons
born in England during these years succumbed to the disease, which
attacked the high and the low, the young and the old, alike. Many
occupants of the French throne, among them Louis XV, died of the
affliction, as did Mary II, Queen of England and consort of William II (at age thirty-two). A favorite theme of novelists was the
pathetic disfigurement of beautiful women by smallpox. Victims of
the disease who survived were usually marred for life and frequently
blinded.

Credit for relieving the human race of this awful pestilence belongs to an English country physician, Edward Jenner. The idea of
preventive inoculation for smallpox was not original with Jenner.
Long before his time, the practice of injecting small doses of matter,
from a smallpox sore on a patient with a mild case, under the skin

AN

INQUIRY

INTO

THE CAUSES AND EFFECTS

OF

THE VARIOLÆ VACCINÆ,

A DISEASE

DISCOVERED IN SOME OF THE WESTERN COUNTIES OF ENGLAND,

PARTICULARLY

GLOUCESTERSHIRE,

AND KNOWN BY THE NAME OF

THE COW POX.

BY EDWARD JENNER, M. D. F. R. S. &c.

———— QUID NOBIS CERTIUS IPSIS

SENSIBUS ESSE POTEST, QUO VERA AC FALSA NOTEMUS.

LUCRETIUS.

London:

PRINTED, FOR THE AUTHOR,

—

BY SAMPSON LOW, Nº. 7, BERWICK STREET, SOHO:

AND SOLD BY LAW, AVE-MARIA LANE; AND MURRAY AND HIGHLEY, FLEET STREET.

—

1798.

of a well person, to cause the latter to build up an immunity, had been known in the East. An English traveler, Lady Mary Wortley Montague, had brought the idea from Turkey as early as 1721. The method, however, had serious faults; the resulting disease was often not mild, and sometimes it proved fatal. Furthermore, each inoculated person was a source of infection to other people.

A tradition among the dairy folk of the Gloucestershire countryside led to Jenner's epochal discovery. Dairy maids who had contracted cowpox when milking were believed by the farmers to be ever afterward immune from smallpox. Jenner noted also that persons who had had smallpox in a mild form thereby acquired immunity against a second attack. He determined to undertake a series of experiments to test the prevailing folklore. His first operation was performed in 1796 upon an eight-year-old country boy, James Phipps, using matter from the hand of a milkmaid, Sarah Nelmes, who was suffering from a typical case of cowpox. About eight weeks later, the boy was inoculated with smallpox virus. In a letter to a friend Jenner described the results:

> A boy named Phipps was inoculated in the arm from a pustule on the hand of a young woman who was infected by her master's cows. Having never seen the disease but in its casual way before, that is, when communicated from the cow to the hand of the milker, I was astonished at the close resemblance of the pustules in some of their stages to the variolous [smallpox] pustules. But now listen to the most delightful part of my story. The boy has since been inoculated for the small-pox which, as I ventured to predict, produced no effect. I shall now pursue my experiments with redoubled ardour.

Thus was marked the first successful vaccination for smallpox in history. Over the next two years Jenner continued his experiments, by the end of which period he had demonstrated in twenty-two cases that vaccination with cowpox matter gave complete protection against smallpox. Sixteen of the cases had occurred accidentally among people working with cows and horses; the others were contrived under Jenner's direction.

The evidence was beyond question. To announce the great medical triumph, Jenner published in 1798 one of the masterpieces of scientific literature, *An Inquiry into the Causes and Effects of the Variolæ Vaccinæ*, a thin quarto of seventy-five pages with four colored plates. Full descriptions were included of the cases personally directed or observed by Jenner. In somewhat florid opening paragraphs the author began:

The deviation of Man from the state in which he was originally placed by Nature seems to have proved to him a prolific source of diseases. From the love of splendour, from the indulgencies of luxury, and from his fondness for amusement, he has familiarized himself with a great number of animals, which may not originally have been intended for his associates.

The Wolf, disarmed of ferocity, is now pillowed in the lady's lap. The Cat, the little Tyger of our island, whose natural home is the forest, is equally domesticated and caressed. The Cow, the Hog, the Sheep, and the Horse, are all, for a variety of purposes, brought under his care and dominion.

The Inquiry went through several editions and within a few years had been translated into a number of other languages, spreading knowledge of Jenner's discovery around the world. Soon the results of vaccination began to be felt in the declining death rate from smallpox. Napoleon Bonaparte, for example, had all of his soldiers vaccinated, and his armies were thereafter free of the disease.

Nevertheless, conservative opposition in medical and lay circles was vociferous. Ministers denounced vaccination from their pulpits as man's interference with the ways of God. Antivaccinationist societies, some of which are still in existence, were formed. The fantastic idea was circulated that vaccination would cause the human subject to sprout horns, grow a tail, low like a cow, bellow like a bull, and acquire other bovine characteristics. Overzealous advocates of vaccination harmed its reputation by using contaminated vaccine matter producing serious illnesses.

Such obstacles, however, were gradually surmounted. A grateful Parliament recognized Jenner's work by two grants, totaling 30,000 pounds, to cover his expenses, and in his later years he was accorded numerous honors.

In succeeding generations, Jenner's original discovery has been vastly expanded by other research workers in the development of a formidable battery of toxins and antitoxins and various forms of inoculation to protect the individual against many contagious diseases.

Jenner's successful solution to the smallpox problem has probably saved more lives and suffering than any other single accomplishment in the history of medicine. As Thomas Jefferson stated in a letter to Jenner, May 14, 1806: "You have erased from the calendar of human afflictions one of the greatest. Yours is the comfortable reflection that mankind can never forget that you have lived; future nations will know by history only that the loathsome small-pox has existed, and by you has been extirpated."

55. OVERCROWDED WORLD

Thomas Malthus' An Essay on the Principle of Population

1798

A major concern of twentieth-century political leaders, economists, sociologists, and other social scientists is the world's "exploding" population. The vast literature on this problem of steadily growing proportions began, at least for modern purposes, with Thomas Malthus' *An Essay on the Principle of Population.*

The basic principle stated by Malthus, a young English cleric, is that population increases far faster than food. In his words:

> Population, when unchecked, increases in a geometrical ratio. Subsistence increases only in an arithmetical ratio. A slight acquaintance with numbers will show the immensity of the first power in comparison to the second. . . . Through the animal and vegetable kingdoms, Nature has scattered the seeds of life abroad with the most profuse and liberal hand. She has been comparatively sparing in the room and the nourishment necessary to rear them.

A logical sequence of the Malthus line of reasoning is that there must be constant checks upon the growth of population. The most drastic check of all is the scarcity of food. Other checks include unwholesome occupations, severe labor, extreme poverty, diseases, bad nursing of children, great cities, plagues, famine, and vice, to which Malthus later added "moral restraint."

Malthus concluded that, if human beings were to enjoy the greatest possible happiness, they should not assume family obligations unless they could afford them. Those without adequate means to support a family should remain celibate. Furthermore, public policy, such as the poor laws, should avoid encouraging the laboring class and others to bring into the world children whom they could not support. Charity, private or governmental, was undesirable because it gave money to the poor without increasing the amount of food available, thereby raising prices and creating shortages. Also objectionable were public housing schemes, for they had the effect of stimulating early marriages and consequently of causing a rapid increase in population. Higher wages had similar effects. In Malthus' view, the solution lay in later marriages and "moral restraint," that is, continence.

In essence, according to Malthus, any project to better society and alleviate want was likely to end by merely aggravating the evils it sought to cure. This tough-minded, apparently antisocial attitude of the young clergyman alienated humanitarians of his own and succeeding generations. The Malthus doctrines were received enthusiastically, however, by the wealthy and power-holding classes of his time. Mass poverty and other social maladjustments could now be blamed on early marriages and too many children—rather than on maldistribution of wealth.

Malthus expressed his strong disapproval of government relief programs in the following statement:

> The poor-laws of England tend to depress the general condition of the poor in these two ways. This first obvious tendency is to increase population without increasing the food for its support. A poor man may marry with little or no prospect of being able to support a family in independence. They may be said therefore in some measure to create the poor which they maintain. . . . Secondly, the quantity of provisions consumed in workhouses upon a part of the society, that cannot in general be considered the most valuable part, diminishes the shares that would otherwise belong to more worthy members; and thus in the same manner forces more to become dependent.

Malthus believed that the prevention of a rapid birth rate was practiced increasingly by nations as they became more civilized and better educated and as they acquired higher living standards. His views were summarized in these words:

> Other circumstances being the same, it may be affirmed that countries are populous according to the quantity of human food which they produce or can acquire, and happy according to the liberality with which this food is divided, or the quantity which a day's labour will purchase. Corn countries are more populous than pasture countries, and rice countries more populous than corn countries. But their happiness does not depend upon their being thinly or fully inhabited, upon their poverty or their richness, their youth or their age, but on the proportion which the population and the food bear to each other.

The appearance of the *Essay on Population* loosed a storm of criticism, protest, and vituperation, chiefly from theological conservatives and social radicals. Malthus' chief biographer, Bonar, writes that he was the most abused man of the age, damned as "a man who defended smallpox, slavery and child murder, who denounced soup kitchens, early marriage and parish allowances; who had the impudence to marry after preaching against the evils of a family; who thought the world so badly governed that the best actions do the most harm; who, in short, took all romance out of life."

An objection also frequently brought against the Malthusian thesis when it was first published was that it was inconsistent with the benevolence of the Creator. Against these and other accusations Bonar defended the author, insisting that his "heart's desire for the human race" was a lower death rate for all, a higher standard of life and livelihood for the poor, and an end of the waste of young human lives.

Controversies, pro and con, continue to rage around Malthus and his theories. At the end of the eighteenth century, when the *Essay* was written, the world's population was estimated at one billion. One hundred and sixty years later it has increased to three billion and by the end of the twentieth century is expected to double the present figure. Critical areas of the globe serve as perfect illustrations of Malthusian principles. Despite tremendous increases in food production since Malthus' time, there remain hundreds of millions of people in Asia, Africa, and elsewhere who exist on a near-starvation or bare subsistence level. Thus the spectacle of perhaps two-thirds of the world's population enduring malnutrition, famine, ill health, and disease makes the issues raised by Malthus as real and vital today as they were in the eighteenth century.

56. MATHEMATICAL ASTRONOMER

Pierre Simon Laplace's *Traité de Mécanique Céleste* (Celestial Mechanics)

1799–1825

Sir Isaac Newton's investigations of astronomic phenomena led him seriously to question the stability of the universe. Believing that the movements of the planets were affected not only by the sun but also by other planets, he feared that eventually the whole system would become deranged. When or if this occurred, only divine intervention could restore equilibrium and order.

Pierre Simon Laplace, often referred to as "the Newton of France," one of the greatest intellects in the history of science, devoted his masterpiece *Mécanique Céleste,* to proving the essential stability of the solar system. Laplace's life work was a detailed application of the Newtonian hypothesis of universal gravitation to the universe. The *Mécanique Céleste* may be rightly regarded as the mathematical masterpiece of the nineteenth century, comparable in many respects to Newton's *Principia*.

Living in a deeply troubled era and being a political opportunist of the first water, Laplace had a most complex personality. As Eric T. Bell remarked, "On the human side he is perhaps the most conspicuous refutation of the pedagogical superstition that noble pursuits necessarily ennoble a man's character." Coming from poor parents in Normandy, he transferred his allegiance in succession from Louis XVI to the Revolution, to Napoleon Bonaparte, and, finally, to the restored monarchy, ending as a Marquis of the Restoration—a decided contrast to, for example, his contemporary and one-time collaborator, Lavoisier, who died on the guillotine during the Revolution, at the height of his career.

Laplace's *magnum opus,* the *Mécanique Céleste,* appeared in five volumes over a period of twenty-six years. The work is a highly technical treatise on mathematical astronomy; Laplace declared its purpose to be the treatment of astronomy "as a great problem of mechanics, from which it is important to banish as much as possible all empiricism," that is, largely to omit observation and experiment, while reducing all known phenomena of the universe to strict mathematical principles. By carrying forward and completing Newton's investigations of the motions of the planets, satellites, and comets, Laplace proposed "to present a connected view of these theories."

Beginning with the discoveries previously made by Galileo, Huygens, and Newton, the *Mécanique Céleste* gives an exposition of all existing knowledge of physical astronomy. The solar system is exhibited as a vast and complex machine, every movement of which is a mere working out of the laws of mechanics and gravitation. Valuable mathematical methods are developed for studying the motion of the planets, the moon, and ocean tides, including formulas for calculating the disturbances of planets and moons by their mutual gravitational forces. Applying mathematical theories of probability to celestial bodies, Laplace concluded that the apparent changes in the motion of planets and their satellites are changes over tremendously long periods, and that, consequently, the solar system is in all probability very stable.

Laplace's conception of the universe was purely mechanistic, for he was unwilling to concede any divine hand in its creation or control. According to a favorite story, the author presented a copy of his work to Napoleon, who remarked, "You have written this huge book on the system of the world without once mentioning the author of the universe." Laplace replied, "Sir, I had no need of that hypothesis."

Closely associated with Laplace's name is the nebular hypothesis, though the famous German philosopher Immanuel Kant had suggested the same idea about a half-century earlier. The theory was first advanced by Laplace in his *Exposition of the System of the World* (1796), an earlier and simpler version of *Mécanique Céleste*, with most of the mathematics omitted. The nebular hypothesis attempts to explain the origin of the planets by assuming that the sun began as a vast heated nebula, composed of gas. As the gas gradually cooled, it shrank and, traveling in rotary fashion, whirled faster and faster. The sun threw off the hot, rotating gases, and these contracted and solidified to form planets, meanwhile continuing their rotation around the sun. According to Laplace, the speed of rotation caused the sun to break up and produce planets. In common with the other planets, the earth began in a hot, gaseous state, finally cooling and contracting until it could support life.

The nebular hypothesis captured the imagination of the scientific world and held sway for more than a century. Various technical objections to it, as new facts accumulated, however, caused this Laplacian conception to be superseded in recent decades by the planetesimal theory developed by T. C. Chamberlin.

Laplace's rank as a mathematician is on a par with his fame as an astronomer. His *Analytic Theory of Probabilities* (1812), for example, is a classic in its field. But Laplace is reported to have had no interest in mathematics except as a tool for solving technical problems. His work in the theory of probabilities was inspired by the need for it in mathematical astronomy.

One connection between Laplace's work and the American scene is worthy of note. Nathaniel Bowditch translated *Mécanique Céleste* into English. Issued in Boston, 1829–1839, in four volumes, this was the first work of such major scientific significance to be published in America.

57. EDUCATIONAL INNOVATOR

Johann Heinrich Pestalozzi's *Wie Gertrud Ihre Kinder Lehrt* (How Gertrude Teaches Her Children)

1801

As the eighteenth century drew to a close, teaching methods were scarcely distinguishable from those that prevailed in Ptolemy's day. At ancient Alexandria, in the third century B.C., the principle had been established that the school's purpose is to teach the written word, and this dogmatic belief remained fixed for the next two thousand years. The modern era in education dates from the advent of a young Swiss teacher, Johann Heinrich Pestalozzi (1746–1827), whose theories were to produce a major revolution in educational practices.

Prior to Pestalozzi's appearance on the scene, the process of teaching, essentially, was to require pupils to memorize words—a process invariably accompanied by unmerciful punishments. The children quickly came to associate learning with nothing except constant floggings and hatred of their teachers. On their part, the teachers were simply accepting the popular convictions that children are innately bad and antagonistic to learning and that the rod is the only device for reforming their erroneous attitudes. In the most complete exposition of his pedagogical theories, *How Gertrude Teaches Her Children,* Pestalozzi described the existing system:

> We leave children up to their fifth year in the full enjoyment of nature. . . . And after they have enjoyed this happiness of sensuous life for five whole years, we make all nature round them vanish from before their eyes; tyrannically stop the delightful course of their unrestrained freedom; pen them up like sheep, whole flocks huddled together, in stinking rooms; pitilessly chain them for hours, days, weeks, months, years, to the contemplation of unattractive and monotonous letters.

From Pestalozzi's point of view, the most deplorable aspects of the system were the practical exclusion of the poorest children from education; the "superficial verbosity," as he termed it, of pupil recitation; and the cruel custom of corporal punishment of children who failed. In *How Gertrude Teaches Her Children,* Pestalozzi demonstrates that there are other and better ways of teaching, methods that would interest and stimulate both teachers and students. As his principles developed, they were based upon the education of the common people as well as the rich, the kindly treatment of children, and his own concepts of the psychology of children and of learning. All these doctrines were in opposition to the evils, as Pestalozzi saw them, in the current educational pattern.

The first Pestalozzi experiment in education occurred in 1774, when, at the age of twenty-eight, he opened a farmhouse, in which he was living, as a school for the children of poor farmers and various and sundry waifs and strays. Pestalozzi thought that a country life, in which the cultivation of the land was combined with some sort of handicraft, would provide the best means of teaching the poorest children. Instruction included practical farm work, household chores, and spinning and weaving, along with elementary lessons in reading, writing, and arithmetic. For the firsthand study of nature, the children were taken on long walks through the neighboring valleys. There were no memorizing and no flogging. Educationally, the enterprise was highly successful, but after a few years the school was forced to close because of financial difficulties.

A second experiment was carried on over a five-year term, at Burgdorf, Switzerland (1799–1804), where Pestalozzi established an institute for the training of teachers. An important project during this period was designing objects to use in teaching language, geography, arithmetic, and science. It was at Burgdorf, also, that Pestalozzi published *How Gertrude Teaches Her Children*, presenting his educational principles.

Pestalozzi's last educational venture of any consequence was at Yverdun, 1805–1825, an extension of the program begun at Burgdorf. The school at Yverdun comprised elementary and classical courses, industrial training for boys and girls, and the preparation of teachers. A number of nationalities were represented among the pupils, and distinguished visitors came from all over Europe and America to become acquainted with the now celebrated Swiss institution. Textbooks were written and the Pestalozzian methods were spread further by teachers who had gone through the preparatory program.

A primary principle of Pestalozzi's thought was that the individual personality is sacred. Each child was seen as a person with a nature of his own, and it was the teacher's job to develop the personality to the fullest extent. According to Pestalozzi, teaching should be done through experience, observation, and the handling of actual objects, rather than by precept, books, or blind memorization. "Either we go from words to things," he writes, "or from things to words." He insisted upon starting with things. Geography and geology could best be learned by observing natural phenomena, numbers by counting objects, letters by manipulating alphabet blocks, and fractions by calculating from squares cut up into halves, thirds, and quarters.

One of the consequences of the Pestalozzi ideas was a considerable expansion in the curriculum. In addition to the customary reading, writing, and arithmetic, the children in his schools were taught singing, drawing, pasteboard modeling, gardening, natural history, the study of rocks, "mental" arithmetic, and geography. Lessons were presented orally—but not for memorization; reading was taught by the word method instead of by use of the alphabet; and definite efforts were made to stir student interest. The child was viewed as "a little seed" containing "the design of the tree . . . the educator only takes care that no untoward influence shall disturb nature's march of developments."

The doctrines which Pestalozzi represented were new and he was a pioneer in their development. The study of psychology in its modern sense had scarcely begun in his era. He was forced to depend, therefore, on intuition, controlled by logic and judgment. Despite such handicaps, Pestalozzi's contributions to educational philosophy and progress are of extraordinary significance. His accomplishments included a fresh approach to the learning process in children, leading such pioneering thinkers as Johann Friedrich Herbart and Friedrich Froebel to further investigation; an individual approach to pupils' needs; and the substitution of humane, kindly guidance for the harsh disciplinary methods then prevailing.

The Swiss reformer's influence outside his own country was widespread throughout the nineteenth century. Historically, the greatest single effect of Pestalozzi's teachings was on the German educational system. Horace Mann and other American educators visiting Europe prior to the Civil War returned home vastly impressed by their observations of the Swiss and German schools. The great reform of American education during the period 1830–1860 was inspired directly or indirectly by Pestalozzi.

58. MASTER RACE AND NATIONALISM

Johann Gottlieb Fichte's *Reden an die Deutsche Nation*
(Addresses to the German Nation)
1807–1808

Three German philosophers are generally charged with inspiring the National Socialist ideologies of state despotism and of the innate superiority of the German people: Hegel, Nietzsche, and Fichte. Of these, Johann Gottlieb Fichte was the pioneer, widely celebrated as the first major prophet of German nationalism.

In Fichte's day, Germany was merely a geographical expression. There was no nation, in a true sense, but only a host of separated and autonomous states, kingdoms, and principalities. Kept apart by the jealousies, ambitions, and rivalries of their rulers, these states lacked any real feeling of national unity. Conditions were not unlike those prevailing in Italy when Machiavelli, one of Fichte's heroes, wrote *The Prince* for the purpose of unifying the Italian people against foreign aggression.

Fichte's political and social ideals went through a curious evolution. Of humble origin, he was at first full of enthusiasm for the French Revolution and thoroughly disliked monarchs, privileged classes, soldiers, and economic inequality. But out of the French Revolution emerged Napoleon, and at his hands Prussia and her German allies suffered disastrous defeat. In 1806–1807, Napoleon took possession of most of Prussia and entered Berlin in triumph. By the French-dominated Treaty of Versailles, Germany was demoted to the status of a third-rate power, suffered a prolonged military occupation, and was forced to pay heavy indemnities.

It was in this political framework that Fichte delivered his famous series of fourteen lectures, *Addresses to the German Nation*. These addresses left a permanent imprint upon German political thought.

In the *Addresses,* delivered to small audiences in Berlin during the time of the occupation of the city by French troops, Fichte seeks an explanation of the terrible catastrophe which had struck his country. The basic cause of the calamity, he was convinced, was the degeneration of the German character. It had been shortsighted and sinful for the separate states not to have presented a united front, the higher classes were egoistic, and the older people unprogressive. The first address declares the old political system doomed because:

> It has been educated in a false philosophy; it was wholly individualistic and selfish. It had a wrong conception of society and the state. Ideals like Humanity, Liberalism, and Popular Rights were dominant, and these had really become synonymous with laziness and a behavior without dignity. Government was weak and ineffective and tried to insure its stability and continuation by leaning on foreign powers.

Not only the German nation but the whole world, Fichte felt, was urgently in need of rehabilitation. The German people had a great spiritual and moral mission to fulfill for the benefit of mankind. These people, he believed, were uniquely qualified for the task. "The German spirit is an eagle whose mighty body thrusts itself on high and soars on strong and well-practiced wing into the empyrean," he declared. "You will see in spirit the German name rising by means of this generation to be the most glorious among all peoples. . . . You of all modern peoples are the one in whom the seed of human perfection most unmistakably lies. . . . If you go under, all humanity goes under with you." The first aim, therefore, was to bring about the union of all Germany, but the long-range objective must be to Germanize the world.

Starting the myth of racial purity, Fichte calls the Germans the most unmixed of all peoples and the closest to the mystic powers of Nature. To achieve their destiny, Fichte recognizes the necessity for physical might: "Between states, there is neither law nor right save the law of the strongest." The German folk, he argues, "has the moral right to fulfill its destiny by *every* means of cunning and force."

Fichte based his theory of German superiority in large part upon the German language, for "men are formed by language far more than language is by men." Reviewing the backgrounds of various European peoples, he concludes that the Germans alone had preserved their original language, while the others had taken over alien tongues and gradually changed them to meet their requirements. The German language remained alive because it was rooted in nature, unlike French, Italian, English, or Spanish whose roots were dead.

Fichte's further contention that political boundaries should coincide with linguistic boundaries was used by Hitler to justify Germany's forcible seizure of Austria and Czechoslovakia's Sudeten areas. Mussolini's Fascists adopted the same doctrine in demanding the annexation of Corsica, Nice, and other Italian-speaking areas of France.

One exception was made by Fichte in identifying language and nationality. He disliked Jews, even those whose ancestors had lived in Germany for centuries and whose native tongue was German. The Jews, he maintained, could never be true Germans, and they should be deprived of all rights and deported to Palestine. Apparently, Fichte's hatred was based on the fact that Napoleon had freed the German Jews from their medieval ghetto restrictions, and as a consequence many Jews were more loyal to Napoleon than to their native Germany.

The salvation of the German nation and of mankind at large, according to Fichte's program, was to be accomplished through universal education, making use of Pestalozzi's pedagogical ideas, strictly controlled by the state. The schools would be organized as self-supporting, autonomous communities, and the students' characters would be formed in the direction of unselfishness and self-sacrifice for humanity. The individual must be made to realize that the community is more important than himself. The importance of physical education is stressed, and manual work is praised for its physical, social, and moral effects upon the growing child. The educational value of family life is questioned by Fichte, who advocates the complete abolition of family education.

The American writer Peter Viereck suggests that "Fichte is the first influential German who consciously and systematically combined nationalism with socialism and with a totalitarian system of education." In the *Addresses,* Fichte held that the German contribution was the one thing which gave meaning, purpose, and permanence to Western civilization and that without the Germans mankind would be backward and degenerate.

Fichte's biographer, H. C. Engelbrecht, states that "beginning in 1840, and especially through the centenary of 1862, Fichte was treated more and more as a national hero and prophet. Of all his works the *Reden* [Addresses] were chiefly remembered, and these were interpreted in any way that happened to suit the immediate needs of the nationalists."

59. BIRTH OF THE ATOMIC THEORY

John Dalton's A New System of Chemical Philosophy
1808–1827

A century and a half ago it was possible for relatively uneducated and untrained experimenters, such as John Dalton and Michael Faraday, to make scientific discoveries of immense significance. Today, when scientists are customarily required to go through long periods of formal preparation, when a tremendous body of complex knowledge has accumulated for the major branches of science, and research is carried on in expensive and elaborately equipped laboratories, important scientific advances are likely to result from team rather than individual effort.

John Dalton, son of a poor Quaker hand-loom weaver, born in Cumberland, and largely self-taught, earned a living throughout his life as a private tutor of children. His acquaintance with John Gough, the blind philosopher, was of material assistance to him. With Gough as teacher, he learned some Latin, French, and Greek, mastered differential calculus, and studied the works of English mathematicians. From Gough, too, he learned to keep a meteorological journal.

In his Cumberland days, Dalton began to study the weather systematically. Over a period of fifty-seven years, he recorded two hundred thousand weather observations and laid the foundations of meteorology as a science. His *Meteorological Observations and Essays* (1793) offered the now accepted hypothesis that the aurora borealis is purely electrical in origin. The investigation of weather phenomena led Dalton to "speculate upon the nature and the constitution of the atmosphere," a study that set in motion his subsequent ideas on the atomic theory.

Dalton was not, and never claimed to be, the first to propose an atomic theory of matter. As early as 1200 B.C., Hindu literature shows the existence of a theory that regarded matter as a union of tiny, separate particles, separated by empty space, but naturally attracted to one another. Later, the Greeks held similar views, adding, however, the notion that the particles are indestructible and always in motion. One of the first exponents of these ideas was Democritus (460–360 B.C.). During the medieval era, atomic speculations lingered among the Arabs, though they were generally rejected by

Christian theologians. A revival of interest among seventeenth-century and eighteenth-century scientists caused Newton, for example, to conceive of atoms as "solid, massy, hard, impenetrable, movable particles."

But, despite such pioneer attempts at explanation, atomic theories prior to Dalton were chiefly in the realm of philosophy for lack of quantitative evidence. Dalton's distinctive contribution was in specific measurement. "Are all atoms," he asked himself, "alike in size and weight?" He suggested the hypothesis that the atoms of the same element are uniform and always fixed and never vary, but that the atoms of different elements are unlike in both form and weight. Every element, according to this postulate, is composed of atoms, and an atom of carbon or sulphur is identical with every other carbon or sulphur atom, but is distinct from the atoms of other elements.

From his investigations and deductions, Dalton came to the conclusion that chemical combination takes place in the simplest possible way: an atom of one element combines with an atom of another element. Combining atoms of oxygen and hydrogen, to illustrate, produces water, erroneously assumed by Dalton at first to contain an equal number of atoms of each element. Later he discovered that water contains twice as many atoms of hydrogen as of oxygen.

On the basis of experiments with a variety of compounds, Dalton formulated the principle for which he is most famous, the "law of multiple proportions." As stated by him: "If two elements combine in more than one proportion, then the volumes of one of those elements combined with a fixed volume of the other are in simple numerical proportion." More simply put, many pairs of elements combine to form more than one compound. The same elements combined in different proportions by weight produce different results.

Concerning the mechanism of chemical combination, Dalton writes:

> Chemical analysis and synthesis go no further than the separation of particles one from another, and to their reunion. No new creation or destruction of matter is within the reach of chemical agency. We might as well attempt to introduce a new planet into the solar system, or to annihilate one already in existence, as to create or destroy a particle of hydrogen.

Observing the proportions by weight by which elements combine, Dalton reasoned that it was possible to determine the *relative* weights of the atoms of which an element is composed. Atoms are much too small to see or weigh singly, he conceded, but the weights could be obtained through measures of chemical composition. Accordingly, through his own experiments and those of fellow scientists, Dalton prepared the first table of atomic weights. Starting with the lightest element known, hydrogen gas, as a standard, all other elements were assigned weights in ratio to hydrogen. Dalton's original table of relative atomic weights contained twenty-one elements. The table was necessarily crude and inaccurate, since the available laboratory equipment was too primitive for exact experimentation.

In 1808 Dalton presented a brief account of his atomic theory in the first volume of his *New System of Chemical Philosophy*, with the table of atomic weights and plates of chemical symbols.

Though an awkward, cumbersome scheme, Dalton originated the first system of atomic notation or chemical shorthand. In his formulas for the various elements, he introduced a complicated series of circles with markings within the circles to denote the atoms of each element. The oxygen atom was represented, for example, by a simple circle, the hydrogen atom by a circle with a dot in the center, and the nitrogen atom by a vertical line bisecting a circle. Compounds were indicated by joining one circle to another. Ultimately the elaborate scheme was discarded, and notations designed by Berzelius, a Swedish chemist, in use to the present day, were adopted, indicating elements by letters and compounds by letters and arabic numerals.

Dalton's atomic theory differs in important respects from modern theory, but it laid a solid foundation for future progress. Since his day, an overwhelming mass of experimental verification has accumulated to support the atomic concept. As early as 1811, Avogadro made a distinction between the atoms of a chemical element and its molecules, and an army of scientific investigators is currently concerned with such aspects of atomic research as analysis of the electron, proton, neutron, and positron.

Every scientific advance must have a beginning, and contemporary advanced research in atomic theory can be traced back directly to its foundations in Dalton's work. In the words of the science historian J. Newton Friend, "just as a crystal dropped into a solution may yield a vast crop of crystals entirely unrelated in quantity to the size of the original crystal, so Dalton's theory has been a nucleus around which have collected, and are still collecting, new laws, hypotheses and theories."

60. TRAIL BLAZER FOR BRITISH SOCIALISM

Robert Owen's *A New View of Society, or, Essays on the Formation of the Human Character*

1813–1814

Leslie Stephen, editor of the *Dictionary of National Biography*, characterizes Robert Owen, perhaps not unfairly, as "one of those intolerable bores who are the salt of the earth." In fact, Owen was amazingly versatile in his activities and interests. He was a successful manufacturer, a factory reformer, an educational experimenter, a trade-union leader, a creator of ideal communities, a pioneer in socialism and co-operation, and the founder of the "Rationalist" movement—during a career spread over eighty-seven years. His personality was somewhat inscrutable even to his own contemporaries.

Except in the eyes of the most benighted industrialists and reactionary politicians, there existed a crying need for social reform in England at the beginning of the nineteenth century. Factory laborers were crowded into miserable houses and tenements, surrounded by filth and disease, and working in overheated, poorly ventilated mills for long hours at low wages. Women and children were mercilessly exploited, the children entering the mills at age seven or younger and required to work twelve hours a day.

Owen was convinced that such evil conditions were not the necessary price of progress. The nation would become and remain prosperous, he contended, without leaving the vast majority of its people helpless victims of ignorance and destitution. Governments were confronted by a choice between two alternatives, Owen held: either the laboring classes would have to be brutally suppressed, raising the constant specters of revolution and unemployment, or efforts must be made to educate the masses and to raise the economic level.

At the age of twenty-three, Owen became a factory manager and immediately demonstrated his genius for business. Some of his social theories were tried in a limited way in his first position, but he wished to experiment with an entire community. In 1799, the cotton mill at New Lanark, Scotland, near Glasgow, was offered for sale. The mill was the sole industry in a village of 2,500 inhabitants, and, with a group of associates, Owen purchased both the mill and the town.

Near East—where Western civilization began. Succeeding stages of major significance were the Greek states and the Roman Empire. The fourth stage, in Hegel's view, was the rise of the Germanic world. "Soon Prussia will dominate the entire Continent." The World Spirit does not manifest itself in every state. Only one nation is the bearer of the World Spirit at any given time; accordingly, all the others must be subservient to the nation which has inherited the burden of carrying progress onward. "In contrast with the absolute right of this nation to be the bearer of the current phase in the development of the World Spirit, the spirits of other existing nations are void of right." Hegel asserted that Germany, as the embodiment of the World Spirit must be supreme over less favored nations. Bloody sacrifices, cruel exploitations, and broken treaties were moderate prices to pay for the evolution of the World Spirit.

The Nazi conception of the totalitarian state, which dominated German political thought during the interval between the two World Wars, had Hegel as its direct ancestor. Earlier, such dictatorial rulers as the Austrian Metternich and the Russian czars had adopted the Hegelian philosophy as a justification for tyranny.

The influence of Hegel on Marxian theory and the Soviet state has been equally striking. Karl Marx claimed to have put the Hegelian system "on its feet rather than on its head," by which the father of modern socialism meant that he interpreted Hegel's World Spirit to mean the dialectic movement of society; this, according to the laws of economic determinism, must inevitably lead to communism. Marx's class struggle theory grew directly out of the Hegelian doctrine. The new World Spirit was fully as ruthless, however, as the old one. Speaking in the spirit of Hegelian philosophy, Lenin asserted that, if necessary, two-thirds of mankind should be exterminated in order to assure communism's final glorious world triumph.

62. CHAMPION OF THE AMERICAN LANGUAGE

Noah Webster's *An American Dictionary of the English Language*

1828

In 1789, seventeen years before he published his first dictionary of the American language, Noah Webster wrote:

> As an independent nation, our honor requires us to have a system of our own in language as well as in government. Great Britain, whose children we are and whose language we speak, should no longer be *our* standard, for the taste of her writers is already corrupted and her language on the decline. But if it were not so, she is at too great a distance to be our model and to instruct us in the principles of our tongue.

Thus early in his variegated career did Webster begin dreaming of a national language for the United States. His lectures on the necessity for an American language and for an American system of education won for him the friendship of Benjamin Franklin, who twenty years earlier had devised a scheme for a simplified alphabet. "A national language," Webster proclaimed, "is a bond of national union." He saw that as the new nation expanded over a vast territory and absorbed a people of diverse cultural elements, unity of language (both in written form and in speech) was a prime essential.

Webster's interest in lexicography and words began early. At twenty-five, he completed and published his grandiloquently titled *The Grammatical Institute of the English Language,* Part One of which is better known as the *Blue-Backed Speller.* H. L. Mencken, a latter-day Webster in his researches into and belief in the existence of a distinctive American language, pointed out that "the influence of Webster's Spelling Book was really stupendous." At least 70,000,000 copies of the Speller were sold in the years following. Subsequently, as Parts Two and Three, there were added *A Plain and Comprehensive Grammar,* and a reader, titled *An American Selection of Lessons in Reading and Speaking.* Historians are generally agreed that only the McGuffey Readers (published some fifty years later) can compare with the Webster textbooks in the impression made on the youth of the country. Like the McGuffey works, the Webster volumes exhibited a high moral and patriotic tone which contributed to their wide acceptance.

Increasingly, Webster became aware of the need for an American dictionary. He was irked by the inclination of the English dictionaries to ignore the United States and the thousands of new words being added to the language. His exceptional qualifications for writing a new dictionary were well summarized by his chief biographer Harry R. Warfel, who noted that Webster had literally universal interests and had written on a variety of subjects. In law, he had practiced in courts and served as judge and legislator; in medicine, he had studied the history of epidemic diseases and carried on scientific experiments; he was a student of economics and a theologian of some standing; and he was an experienced lecturer, schoolmaster, and editor.

In addition, Webster possessed an innate talent for defining words. He enjoyed research into the history of words, and he was a man of infinite patience, with a passion for perfection. As an indication of his systematic methods, his son-in-law, Chauncey A. Goodrich, stated that Webster had "a particular mark by which he denoted, in every work he read, all the new words, or new senses of words, which came under his observation."

Webster's first venture into lexicography, begun in 1800, resulted in 1806 in publication of his *Compendious Dictionary of the English Language,* a work listing 5,000 words which had not appeared in any other dictionary. An abridged edition for schools was issued the following year.

All this, however, was mere prologue to the *magnum opus* on which Webster was to spend the next twenty years. In preparation for his monumental enterprise, by 1813 he had learned twenty languages, seven of which were Asiatic or dialects of the Assyrian. To these he later added Portuguese, Welsh, Gothic, and the early dialects of English and German. Extensive investigations into etymology, then practically a virgin field, were carried on by Webster as he studied and compared all languages of which dictionaries were available, attempting to trace the origins of English words. Finally, to perfect the work and because of the inadequacies of American libraries, he spent a year in France and England, working in the Bibliothèque du Roi, Paris, and the Cambridge University Library.

In Webster's seventieth year, 1828, his *An American Dictionary of the English Language,* in two volumes, came off the press. There were included 70,000 words—12,000 more than were to be found in any previous dictionary. Altogether, it was a remarkable one-man performance. The word "American" in the title was fully justified; the work was based throughout on American usage in spelling and pronunciation, and it relied heavily upon prominent American authors and statesmen in citing authorities.

In historical perspective, certain aspects of Webster's contribution rank high in importance, while others have fallen by the wayside. Most significant, unquestionably, is the vocabulary. Spelling reforms which Webster attempted to introduce have been accepted in part, while certain oversimplified and eccentric forms have been rejected. The same holds for pronunciation; some practices then current and recommended by Webster have changed with time. His definitions were generally excellent; furthermore, in range the *American Dictionary* far surpassed anything before its day. The weakest feature was the etymologies, for, in the light of later scholarship, many of his theories and concepts on the origins of words were proved to be invalid.

An abridged edition of the large dictionary, edited by Joseph Worcester, was published in 1829, and shortly before his death Webster carried through to completion a second edition of the major work, issued in 1841. Subsequently, George and Charles Merriam purchased the copyright from the Webster family, and their firm's Merriam-Webster dictionaries have continued to flourish to the present day.

No more fitting tribute to Webster has been paid than appeared in the London *Times Literary Supplement* on May 29, 1943:

All the English-speaking nations can join this week in commemorating the centenary of the death on May 28, 1843, of that partriarchal dictionary-maker, Noah Webster. His actual dictionary, it is true, may now be out of date, just as Johnson's is; but it lives on eponymously —"a Webster" having become almost a synonym for a dictionary— and spiritually in the American language itself, which, though English, is no longer that of England or of colonial New England, but of a great and independent nation. Webster, in fact, was in his own sphere as much a founder of his nation as Washington, and consciously so; for he had the vision to perceive that his country, which ceased to be a colony when he was a young man, must henceforward grow its own culture, look no more to London and Europe for its sanctions, and speak and write no more as a provincial. In his own way Webster was the Pericles of his country, who presented it with an enduring temple in which to enshrine its words; or as its Augustus, who found its spelling to be of rough-cast and left it of polished marble.

63. INTERPRETER AND SYNTHESIZER

Charles Lyell's *Principles of Geology, Being an Attempt to Explain the Former Changes of the Earth's Surface, by Reference to Causes Now in Operation*

1830–1833

It has been remarked that James Hutton, on whose theories a large share of the superstructure of modern geology now rests, was born fifty years too soon. Neither scientists nor the lay public found his radical beliefs acceptable, and he died virtually unhonored and unsung.

By coincidence, in the year of Hutton's death, 1797, there was born another Scotsman, Charles Lyell, who was to champion and expand the Huttonian teachings and play an instrumental part in obtaining their adoption by the world of science. This was accomplished by Lyell through his *Principles of Geology*, a work which for more than a century has exercised an immeasurable influence on the development of geological science.

While other sciences were moving ahead in the eighteenth and early nineteenth centuries, the progress of geology was seriously retarded. During these years, the biblical story of the Creation and the Flood remained the fundamental textbook of geology. Fossils were believed to be the remains of animals lost in Noah's Flood. Geologists in general held the view that the whole history of the earth consisted of a series of sudden and violent catastrophes, by which the bed of the ocean was suddenly raised and its waters precipitated onto the land, carrying with it universal ruin and extermination of all life. Following such catastrophes, there would be periods of quiet, during which the new earth was repopulated, by direct act of creation, with new forms of life adapted to the new conditions. Species of life were unchanged until another universal cataclysm exterminated them.

Still raging in Lyell's youth was the controversy between the Neptunists, who argued that the earth's crust was formed by layers deposited or precipitated by an ocean that once covered the entire surface of the globe, and the Vulcanists, who maintained that the earth's present contours are accounted for by volcanic action.

Into this murky atmosphere came Charles Lyell, with extraordinary talent for synthesizing the findings of other scientists and for interpreting the most varied natural phenomena. Coupled with this ability were powers for keen observation and a clear logical writing style. It was said of Lyell by Sir Andrew Ramsay, "We collect the data and Lyell teaches us to comprehend the meaning of them." While still in his early thirties, Lyell produced the first edition of the *Principles of Geology,* a work that was to go through a dozen editions during his lifetime.

The dominant idea in Lyell's writings is that geological causes and processes, i.e., past events, can be discovered only by studying the forces at work on the earth today. Fully convinced that the present is the key to the past, he amassed overwhelming data to support his theory. His observations were that mountains and continents are being built, strata are being folded and broken, igneous and sedimentary rocks are being formed, and fossils are being buried in the same manner now as in past ages. There have been no vast cataclysms or devastating floods. All processes have been orderly and uniform.

Thus arose the uniformitarian doctrine to oppose the theories of the apostles of catastrophism. According to Lyell, given eons of time, all the phenomena in geological history can be accounted for by natural forces in daily operation. Catastrophic changes in either the organic or inorganic world were ruled out.

Strong support for the uniformitarian approach came from the researches on fossil remains of plants and animals, especially in relation to strata formation, carried on by such scientists as William Smith in England and Cuvier in France. This branch of geology, paleontology, was almost unknown in James Hutton's time. Year by year it became evident that the earth's crust contained materials for a history of organic nature from early geological periods to the present. Fossils also provided evidence on the nature and order of physical changes, such as alternations of sea and land and revolutions in climate. The scattered observations of numerous individuals concerned with paleontology were assembled by Lyell and generalized upon in his *Principles of Geology.* Lyell's work served as a trail blazer for the later acceptance of Darwin's theory of evolution.

Lyell's *Principles* was, in effect, a rewriting of the whole of the existing science of physical and historical geology, a systematic synthesis and interpretation of all prevailing knowledge of the subject. Lyell was not content, however, to depend entirely upon investigations by others. To verify facts, to clarify doubtful points, and to reinforce his own conclusions, he traveled widely through Great Britain, the Continent, and North America, examining peaks, precipices, snow fields, glaciers, and lakes in the Alps and Pyrenees; the cones, craters, and lava streams of the Vesuvius and Etna volcanoes; and similar natural phenomena of geological interest. Traveling he considered "as the first, second and third requisite for a modern geologist in the present adolescent state of the science."

Lyell and Charles Darwin were close personal friends, and Darwin was encouraged by Lyell to publish the *Origin of Species.* In his journals, Darwin has recorded the deep impression made on his mind by the first reading of the *Principles of Geology.* The book had been taken with him by Darwin on the celebrated *Beagle* expedition around the world. On the occasion of Lyell's death, he wrote, "How completely he revolutionized geology; for I can remember something of Pre-Lyellian days—I never forget that almost everything which I have done in science I owe to the study of his great works."

64. RELIGION OF HUMANITY

Auguste Comte's *Cours de Philosophie Positive* (Course of Positive Philosophy) 1830–1842

The turmoil and popular unrest in Europe growing out of the French Revolution and the Napoleonic Wars produced a veritable flood of prescriptions for social reform. Liberal ideas were rampant, and the concept of continuous progress had been firmly implanted by Condorcet. Salvation for the world and an exceedingly bright future for mankind, according to various reformers, merely awaited acceptance of their patricular gospels or nostrums.

Perhaps the most fully developed program designed to bring order and progress to society was the handiwork of Auguste Comte in France, sometimes referred to as the "father of sociology." Early in his career, Comte became associated as secretary, disciple, and friend with Saint-Simon, the famous socialist, and was deeply influenced by the latter's doctrines. Specifically, Saint-Simon advocated the reorganization of society on an industrial basis, to be controlled by scientific law, and a scientific classification of the sciences, with a major spot reserved for political science. These ideas are readily apparent in Comte's own writings.

In several pamphlets published in his early twenties, Comte had shown an interest in social reorganization. One of these, *A Plan of the Scientific Operations Necessary for Reorganizing Society,* issued in 1822, states the principal features of Comte's philosophy. Preliminary to presenting a comprehensive statement of his views on social policy, however, Comte decided to undertake a systematic examination of all scientific knowledge. This vast project resulted in the six-volume *Course of Positive Philosophy,* generally regarded as Comte's most significant work, the writing of which occupied him for sixteen years.

Positivism as defined by Comte is the "religion of humanity," which he conceived of as the "substitution of the permanent government of humanity for the provisional government of God." In Comte's scheme of an advanced society, there was to be no place for the supernatural. History, he contends, has passed through three successive periods in the course of its development. The "law of the three states," as he calls it, is thus described: "The race, like the individual, necessarily passes through three intellectual stages—the theological, the metaphysical, and the positive."

Theology dominated mankind, states Comte, until the thirteenth century, leading to a military and monarchical social organization, the era of the divine right of kings. At this primitive level of mental development, the world was full of imaginary spirits, assumed to be the cause of all unexplained phenomena. In the second or metaphysical stage, the concept of God is destroyed, and the best minds are reaching out beyond mythology and theology. Now governments are built on theories of natural rights—to Comte an anarchic principle, since it tends, he believes, to destroy authority, order, and discipline and establishes the pernicious doctrine of individual liberty of judgment. Finally, at the highest level, says Comte, man finds the ideal answer in positivism, with the application of scientific methods to the study of society. Reasoning and observation replace divinities and abstract thinking, natural forces are utilized to maximum advantage, industrial enterprises flourish, and the earth's material resources are fully exploited—all for man's benefit and happiness.

The foundation of Comte's scheme is a classification of the sciences. His superstructure is built upon mathematics, the most precise of the sciences and possessing a solid body of laws. Astronomy, next in order, depends upon mathematics and adds other laws peculiar to its own complex phenomena. Then come physics, chemistry, biology, and, finally, sociology, a term invented by Comte. The procession is from the simple to the complex, with each field supplying basic elements for the science that follows it. Furthermore, Comte states, each branch of knowledge has passed through the three historical stages: the theological, the metaphysical or abstract, and the scientific or positive. Concerning his arrangement of the sciences, he explains that:

> This classification marks, with precision, the relative perfection of the different sciences, which consists in the degree of precision of knowledge and in the relation of its different branches. It is easy to see that the more general, simple, and abstract any phenomena are, the less they depend on others, and the more precise they are in themselves, and the more clear in their relations with each other. Thus, organic phenomena are less exact and systematic than inorganic; and of these again terrestrial are less exact and systematic than those of astronomy.

Of the six disciplines classed by Comte as sciences, sociology is regarded as the most inclusive and the least precise. Sociology draws from biological, chemical, physical, and astronomical knowledge and uses mathematics as a tool. A general understanding of all the sciences, Comte insists, is essential to the sociologist, if he is to apply scientific methods to the study of society.

Though Comte laid the foundation for sociology, he produced no general treatise on the subject. His contribution was rather to insist on the proper place for the new field among the sciences and to emphasize the significance of sociological study as an aid to man in controlling his environment.

Having laid the philosophical basis for a new social order, Comte proceeded to the preparation of his second major work, the four-volume *System of Positive Polity* (1851–1854). Therein he develops his doctrine of the religion of humanity, visualizing a society founded upon an all-powerful state ruled by a scientific priesthood. Inspired by the organization of the Catholic Church, Comte proposes a hierarchy, ritual, and other forms analogous to those of the Church, but substituting scientific concepts and scientists for the theological models. Science would take the place of religion as the organizing principle of the world. Humanity, "the Great Being who manifests to the fullest extent all the highest attributes of life," would be worshiped.

Fervent admirers of the earlier *Positive Philosophy,* such as John Stuart Mill and Herbert Spencer, were repelled and alienated by the fantastic proposals elaborated in the *Positive Polity.* Comte's error, commented Noel Annan, is that "he fell into a trap which Marx was to avoid. The Communist Utopia, when the State withers away, is never described—Marx merely hints at its joys. But Comte unveiled the whole of his design."

In spite of his idiosyncrasies, Comte's influence on the social sciences has been far-reaching. The sociological methods developed by him were relatively primitive. More basic was his effort to integrate sociology with mathematics, physics, and biology. Comte was convinced that similar research procedures could be applied both to the natural and the social sciences. The history of the social studies since his day, in essence, is the story of attempts to prove the validity of this theory.

65. MASTER MILITARY STRATEGIST

Karl von Clausewitz's *Vom Kriege* (On War)

1832–1834

General Karl von Clausewitz as a military strategist has been compared to Adam Smith as an economist and Isaac Newton as a physicist. The history of modern warfare can scarcely be understood without knowledge of Clausewitz's military principles, stated in his *On War.* Therein, for the first time, was formulated the modern concept of total war.

Clausewitz lived in a world at war—the Napoleonic epoch. Virtually his entire life was spent in the camps, barracks, and military schools of Prussia, where he rose through the hierarchy to the rank of major general. His views on military strategy and tactics, set forth in *On War* and other writings, were therefore based on firsthand experience and observation.

Prior to the advent of Napoleon, war had become a kind of chessboard operation, carried on by small armies of mercenaries. A high percentage of these professional soldiers were foreigners or were drawn from the dregs of the population. They were held together by rigid discipline and fought in strict formations. Orthodox methods of warfare had been elaborately formalized in a number of military treatises.

This neat pattern was upset with devastating effect by Napoleon Bonaparte. Instead of using a standing army of limited size, Napoleon had the genius, based on French Revolutionary experience, to recognize the far greater potential strength of a nation in arms. The French people rose to his call to protect their borders. War ceased to be a matter of careful maneuvering for positions with small, expensive armies, trying to reach a decision by interrupting the enemy's lines of supplies. War now became a contest of mass armies, emphasizing speed and concentrated superior force. In swift movements, Napoleon's loosely grouped divisions fell like lightning upon the weakest point in the enemy's front or turned the flank and cut off the opponent's lines of retreat. These tactics were invariably successful against the old-fashioned armies, and not until the forces opposing Napoleon emulated his methods were they able to defeat him.

Clausewitz was profoundly impressed by the Napoleonic strategy, and his efforts to understand the fundamentals of warfare were vastly aided by his analysis and study of the great French general's contributions to military science.

From a purely military point of view, Clausewitz concluded, the first aim of war is the destruction of the enemy's armed forces. "War is an act of force to compel our adversary to do our will." In stating that "the military forces must be destroyed," Clausewitz meant that they should be "put into such a condition that they can no longer continue to fight." In theory, he said, in discussing the "Plan of War," war is an unceasing act of "utmost violence" raging in a series of desperate encounters until the enemy is annihilated. In practice, however, an army on the battlefield has to contend with "friction"— a term used by Clausewitz to describe rain, snow, mud, fatigue, timidity, false intelligence, or anything else that may go wrong. "It is such friction which makes that which looks so easy so very difficult in reality." Simplify in every possible fashion, urged Clausewitz, for the more complex the plan of campaign, the greater the friction.

Sentimentality and humanitarian principles were ruled out by Clausewitz as having no place in principles of warfare. A stricken foe should "shed the maximum of blood," and terrorism must be employed "to break the spirit of a civilian population." War is not something to be fought by Christian gentlemen. "We do not like," declared Clausewitz, "to hear of generals who are victorious without the shedding of blood. If bloody battling is a dreadful spectacle, that should merely be the reason to appreciate war more and not to allow our swords to grow blunt by and by, through humanitarianism, until someone steps in with a sharp sword and cuts our arms off our body."

Clausewitz stressed the superior strength of the defense as against the offense, stating that "the defense is the stronger form of making war." He had in mind, however, not a passive but a highly active form of defense, such as the Russians used against Napoleon in the 1812 campaign: retreating into the interior of the country, using a scorched-earth policy, constantly harassing the pursuing enemy, attacking his lengthening supply lines, and, when he is exhausted and his forces depleted, destroying him. The identical strategy was of course adopted by the Russians again in defeating Hitler's German armies in 1941–43.

For the first time, the principles of psychological warfare were developed by Clausewitz's *On War*. Military morale and the pressure of public opinion, he showed, are extremely important in war. Good or bad morale is held to be almost everywhere decisive. Such intangible qualities as courage, audacity, and self-sacrifice are essential to victory. Therefore, the military leader must aim for the complete demoralization of his enemy, breaking his will, destroying his morale, humiliating and crushing his spirit. The more generally frightful war can be made, the sooner will military objectives be achieved.

War was not regarded by Clausewitz as an end in itself, but only as "a continuation of policy by other means." Political considerations came first, in his view, and a state's military leadership should be subordinated to its political leadership. The nature of war is therefore determined by political objects. On the assumption that war is a normal activity of a nation, Clausewitz pointed out that the state has two weapons with which to accomplish its purposes:

diplomacy and war, and these should be closely co-ordinated. Nowhere has this lesson been learned more thoroughly than in the Soviet Union, with its "cold war" tactics.

The tremendous technical developments since Clausewitz's time have naturally outdated some of his conclusions. Nevertheless, since *On War* is more important as a philosophical and psychological treatment of its subject than as a military manual, the book possesses a timeless quality. Every great German general from von Moltke to Ludendorff and von Blomberg has been a Clausewitz disciple, lauding him as "the High Priest of Strategy," though frequently distorting his views. It is reported that Hitler was often observed with a volume of *On War* open in front of him; if he had understood its content, however, he would doubtless have avoided duplication of Napoleon's tragic blunder in invading Russia in midwinter. The Russian Marxists have studied Clausewitz with care and have appropriated his ideas freely. For example, the Soviet Government published Lenin's notebook on Clausewitz in 1933, and Stalin was known to have modeled his military ideas on Clausewitz's principles.

66. ARISTOCRAT DEFENDING DEMOCRACY

Alexis de Tocqueville's *De la Démocratie en Amérique* (Democracy in America) 1835–1840

It is a curious fact that perhaps the two most perceptive and searching inquiries into the nature of American institutions have been made by observers from other countries: a Frenchman, Alexis de Tocqueville, in *Democracy in America;* and an Englishman, James Bryce, in *The American Commonwealth* (1888).

Strange, also, in the case of *Democracy in America,* is the fact that Tocqueville was not primarily interested in America at all. His subject is democracy. A young nobleman, whose sympathies by birth and training were basically with the old regime and the aristocratic traditions of France, he had become convinced that democracy was the wave of the future. His purpose in coming to the United States in 1831 was to study the world of tomorrow, believing that here he would find the most highly developed form then existing of a political system destined to spread over the world. He proposed to answer the questions: Was democracy, as some of the intellectuals of Europe saw it, a beautiful dream, or did it represent anarchy and ruin?

Tocqueville's aim was to portray "the very image of democracy itself, with its inclinations, its character, its prejudices and its passions." He wanted to discover what a democratic regime had to offer to his beloved France and to the cause of liberty.

In Tocqueville's interpretation of America, one grand theme predominates. This is equality. The concept of a new society founded upon equality among its members fascinated him. He saw the movement toward equality as a universal historical trend. In his introductory chapter, he comments:

> The more I studied the social conditions of America the more I saw that this equality of conditions was the vital fact round which every individual circumstance seemed to revolve, and I found it again and again as the one central point to which all my observations tended to return.

The first part of *Democracy in America* relates chiefly to government and politics. In that realm, Tocqueville was struck by the power of public opinion in the United States. Every party struggle or political discussion was an effort to influence this supreme force. Furthermore, the people willingly submitted to the judgment of their own majority when clearly pronounced; there was no thought of resistance or revolt.

Tocqueville viewed with some foreboding, however, the possible "tyranny of the majority," exercising a hateful despotism over minority rights and individual human judgment. Under the old monarchies of England and France, he pointed out, the king could do no wrong; similarly, under American democracy, the same notion was applied to the will of the majority. A count of heads, in Tocqueville's opinion, was no sure index of political wisdom.

Offsetting this danger were two powerful forces: law and religion. Both law and religion, Tocqueville noted, had an immense and far-reaching influence on Americans. The existence of the Supreme Court, with power to interpret the Constitution and all law, amazed the French visitor and inspired in him hope for the democratic form of government. The judicial power, he felt, would serve to repress the excesses of democracy and protect the rights of minorities.

Religion, also, Tocqueville believed was "indispensable to the maintenance of republican institutions" because "despotism may govern without religion, but liberty cannot."

Likewise having a vital bearing on the success of democratic institutions was the problem of centralization versus decentralization. The American experiment in democracy gained its greatest strength, thought Tocqueville, from local government and individual participation in government, represented, for example, by the New England town meeting. He considered the combination of centralized and decentralized government found in the United States to be "one of the greatest inventions known to political science." On the other hand, he questioned the strength of the federal tie, expressing the belief that if any considerable number of states wanted to secede, the central power would be unable to resist. This judgment was, of course, proved completely erroneous in 1861.

A prophetic insight into the dangers of slavery was shown by Tocqueville. If America were to encounter serious future problems, the troubles, he remarked, would "be brought about by the presence of the black race on the soil of the United States." He foresaw that slavery must be abolished, but freedom would not end race prejudices or social troubles. "The prejudice of race appears to be stronger," he declared, "in the States which have abolished slavery than in those where it still exists; and nowhere is it so intolerant as in those States where servitude has never been known."

The true prophet's voice is heard again in Tocqueville's observations on the future roles of America and Russia:

> There are at the present time two great nations in the world which seem to tend toward the same end, although they started from different points: I allude to the Russians and the Americans. Both of them have grown up unnoticed; and while the attention of mankind was directed elsewhere, they have suddenly assumed a most prominent place among the nations; and the world learned of their existence and their greatness at almost the same time. . . . The principal instrument of the Anglo-American is freedom; of the Russian servitude. Their starting point is different, and their courses are not the same; yet each of them seems to be marked out by the will of Heaven to sway the destinies of half the globe.

A brief sketch can do little except touch the high points of what Harold Laski described as "the greatest work ever written on one country by the citizen of another." Worthy of special mention are Tocqueville's discussion of the advantages and disadvantages of democracy, the influence of democracy upon intellectual development, the difficulties in recruiting men of superior ability for public office, the need for some measure of government control over large industries, and the importance of the press as "the chiefest democratic instrument of freedom."

Though unsympathetic to democratic government in some of its less attractive aspects, Tocqueville concluded that, "the progress of democracy seems irresistible, because it is the most uniform, the most ancient, and the most permanent tendency which is to be found in history."

67. THE JOLLY OLD PEDAGOGUE

William Holmes McGuffey's *Eclectic Readers*

1836–1837

The final lesson in the last volume of the celebrated McGuffey *Readers,* which covered nineteenth-century America like the dew, contained this much-quoted poem:

> 'Twas a jolly old pedagogue, long ago,
>   Tall and slender and sallow and dry;
> His form was bent and his gait was slow,
> And his long thin hair was as white as snow.
>   But a wonderful twinkle shone in his eye,
> And he sang every night as he went to bed:
> "Let us be happy down here below;
> The living should live, though the dead be dead,"
>   Said the jolly old pedagogue long ago.

In that burst of verse, William Holmes McGuffey drew a thumbnail sketch of himself and epitomized his own philosophy of education.

When McGuffey pioneered a revolutionary new series of elementary readers in the eighteen thirties, the field had long been dominated by the doleful *New England Primer.* For the preceding two centuries, children had been sternly exhorted to admit their sins and prepare themselves to escape hell. In characteristic vein, the *New England Primer* had warned:

In Adam's Fall
We sinned all . . .
There is a dreadful fiery Hell
Where wicked ones must always dwell . . .

Puritanical sermons of this nature on death, the future life, gloom, and terror were rejected by McGuffey, who chose instead such light-hearted selections as:

Hear the children gayly shout,
"Half past four, and school is out!"
See them, as they quickly go,
Tripping homeward o'er the snow . . .

The man whose name and fame were perpetuated in the *Readers,* William Holmes McGuffey, born in 1800 of Scotch-Irish Presbyterian ancestry, grew up under pioneer conditions in Ohio. His sketchy education at a local academy and college was supplemented by omnivorous reading. Subsequently, he held the presidency of three Ohio universities, before rounding off his career as Professor of Moral Philosophy at the University of Virginia for twenty-eight years.

A new western book trade had grown up by 1830 in Cincinnati, Lexington, and Louisville. Movable printing presses brought from the East were pouring out a varied assortment of books to meet an almost insatiable demand from an education-conscious people. Cincinnati, "the Queen City," took the lead, and it was a small Cincinnati publishing firm, Truman and Smith, that asked McGuffey in 1836 to prepare several school readers.

The publishing record established by the McGuffey *Readers* is phenomenal: an estimated 122,000,000 copies issued over a period of seventy years by eight publishers in 160 editions. They were the basic textbooks in thirty-seven states and even had a considerable sale abroad, in translation and through missionaries. During the Civil War, when the *Readers* could not be sold in the South, the Methodist Book Concern, in Nashville, Tennessee, reprinted "McGuffeys" for Confederate children.

The *First* and *Second* McGuffey *Readers* were published in 1836; the *Primer* and the *Third* and *Fourth Readers* came along the following year. An anthology of English and American literature, *Mc-Guffey's Rhetorical Guide,* compiled by William's brother, Alexander, was added later as the *Fifth Reader.*

A strict ethical code permeated the McGuffey books. They were expressly designed to inspire such virtues as truth, honesty, fair dealing, initiative, invention, and self-reliance. A foretaste of Horatio Alger is found in the story of a poor but honest bootblack who returns a lost purse and is rewarded by being set up in business; Ragged Davy, scorned by his schoolmates, who, on his teacher's advice, gathers and sells violets and becomes a prosperous florist; and Truthful George, who offers his new silver watch to recompense a wealthy merchant whose window he had broken with a snowball and is rewarded with a lucrative position and later a business partnership. Always, virtue pays in tangible rewards. As a corollary, drinking, gambling, and laziness are inevitably severely punished. In keeping with the conservative traditions handed down by the makers of the Constitution, respect for the property rights of others is constantly stressed, as are emotional appeals for national patriotism. Orthodox religious doctrines are inculcated by a liberal sprinkling of biblical stories.

The immense popularity gained by the *Readers* has been analyzed by McGuffey's chief biographer, Harvey C. Minnich, who concluded that the McGuffey *Readers* won out over all western and southern competition for these reasons: The *Readers* taught the child to read from the start, while other systems often kept him at spelling alone for months on end; McGuffey had far more illustrations than other readers; his texts taught the fine art of speaking and pronouncing correctly—very important in an area with so many foreign immigrants; the *Readers* adapted material for the minds of children, avoiding the theological mysticism of New England, presenting stories about nature and experiences familiar to rural and small-town children; and, finally, the McGuffey moral and social code fitted in well with the religious background of the Presbyterians, Methodists, Baptists, and Lutherans in the western states and with their Scottish and German thrift. To these explanations, other commentators have added the intellectual hunger of the West, the rapid spread of free public education, the enterprising salesmanship of McGuffey's publishers, thorough testing of the lessons in actual class practice before publication, careful grading to the age and mind of the child, and the vigorous and excellent literature contained in the *Readers*.

Considerable supporting evidence exists for one social historian's remark that the McGuffey *Readers* "probably did more to mold American thinking than any other single influence except the Bible."

As Mark Sullivan pointed out, "McGuffey's was the source of America's taste in reading—for many average Americans, the only reading of poetry or classic prose they ever had. Along with that, McGuffey's was the source of that stock of points of view and tastes held in common, which constituted much of America's culture, its codes of morals and conduct, its standards of propriety, its homely aphorisms, its 'horse-sense' axioms." Hamlin Garland's testimonial is typical of many: "From the pages of his [McGuffey's] readers I learned to know and love the poems of Scott, Byron, Southey, Wordsworth, and a long line of the English masters. I got my first taste of Shakespeare from the selected scenes which I read in these books."

A most perceptive comment came also from D. A. Saunders: "The ultimate measure of McGuffey's influence is, however, the wide dispersion of his poems, stories, and proverbs among generations who have all but forgotten his name. In that respect, indeed, he has fared better than many Americans: instead of being canonized as a historical saint, he lives in the everyday speech of the people."

68. ELECTRICAL WIZARD

Michael Faraday's *Experimental Researches in Electricity*

1839–1855

Michael Faraday's career fulfills all the specifications for a Horatio Alger hero: son of a poor blacksmith, industrious, persevering, honest, and unselfish, having almost no formal education, winning the good will and support of highly placed persons, and rising at last to become one of the most eminent scientists of all time, offered a knighthood and the presidency of the Royal Society, and loaded with other honors.

Modern civilization, based so largely upon electricity, owes more to Michael Faraday and his discoveries than to any other individual. Out of his extraordinary researches grew the principles of the generator and the electric motor, which provided a method of producing electrical energy by mechanical rather than chemical action. Faraday's experiments also revealed the principle of the transformer, making it possible to transmit electric current over long distances.

At the beginning of the nineteenth century, in Faraday's youth, electricity was nothing more than a laboratory toy. To fascinated scientists, it represented one of nature's most elusive secrets, but it could not be said to have any practical significance. The first great breakthrough was achieved by Alessandro Volta, an Italian physicist, when, in 1800, he invented a chemical source of electricity, the voltaic cell or pile, generating a steady flow of electric current. Volta's process was to place copper and zinc plates alternately, insert cloths soaked in a dilute acid between them, and then connect the end plates. Voltaic piles containing as many as two thousand plates were put together. The method was costly and produced only low-power current. It led, however, to the construction of the electromagnet, important for further research efforts.

Faraday's scientific career started with his appointment as assistant to Sir Humphry Davy, Director of the Royal Institution's laboratory and a notable teacher. From the outset, Faraday demonstrated genius in chemical experimentation, discovering the fundamental laws of electrolysis (chemical decomposition by the action of electric current), liquefying various gases, and isolating benzene for the first time.

But, increasingly, electrical researches claimed Faraday's interest and attention, and it is in this area that he was destined to gain his greatest fame.

The finding of a relation between magnetism and electricity had been announced in 1820 by a Danish physicist, Hans Christian Oersted. By running a current through a wire, he found that he could induce a movement in a nearby magnet. Oersted suggested that a magnetic field surrounded the wire conductor. Davy and Faraday promptly became interested in the new electromagnetic discovery and repeated experiments made by Oersted, Ampère, and other scientists of the time.

After repeated failures, Faraday, in September, 1821, working alone, demonstrated electromagnetic rotation. He found that the flow of electric current caused a magnet to revolve around a wire carrying current or a wire carrying current to revolve around a fixed magnet. Such motions continued as long as the current continued to flow. Here was the principle of the electric motor.

For the next ten years, Faraday was preoccupied with the problem of converting magnetic force into some form of electrical force. In his mind, the central question was: If an electric current could yield magnetism, could not a magnet produce electricity? Among other experiments, he tried to induce current in a wire by placing a magnet near it, but the attempt failed. Later he realized that it was the motion of the electric current in the wire that produced magnetism.

In the summer of 1831, Faraday began another experiment to solve the problem, an effort that culminated in his most epoch-making discovery. The experiment that succeeded now appears extremely simple: a coil of insulated wire, connected to a galvanometer (an instrument for measuring a small electric current by movement of a magnetic needle), was wound on a hollow paper cylinder. As a magnet was thrust in and pulled out of the cylinder or the cylinder was moved over the magnet, the galvanometer registered the passage of an electric current in the coil of wire.

A short while later, in October 1831, Faraday built the world's first generator, consisting of a copper disk rotating between the poles of a large magnet, mounted on an axle and operated by turning a crank. Thus was electricity finally generated from magnetism—the principle of the dynamo. It is upon this basic principle that all commercial electricity is produced today, for a modern electric generator is essentially a coil of wire (an armature) rotated between the poles of a set of magnets.

Faraday reported his results to the Royal Society within a month and formulated the discovery into a paper for publication, the first of a series of twenty-nine papers, eventually brought together in three volumes under the title *Experimental Researches in Electricity.*

The solution to the mystery of electromagnetic induction was not enough to satisfy Faraday's insatiable curiosity about natural phenomena. He wanted to know *why* a moving magnet induced an electric current in a conductor. The answer he proposed was that the space surrounding the magnet was filled with lines of force. In fact, Faraday concluded that all space is filled with various kinds of force: magnetic, electric, radiant, heat, and gravitational.

In direct contrast to Newton, who had conceived of space as rigid absolute emptiness, Faraday imagined space as being alive with moving, flexible, ever-changing electromagnetic forces. Here is the historic origin of the theory of the electromagnetic field, considered by many scientists to be Faraday's greatest contribution.

A younger contemporary of Faraday's, James Clerk Maxwell, was profoundly impressed by the field theory. By mathematical analysis, he proved that electromagnetic disturbances and waves of light are transmitted by the same medium and at the same speed. Consequently, Maxwell was able, in 1873, to announce the electromagnetic theory of light. In the hands of later scientists—Hertz, Marconi, and others—there developed out of these highly theoretical investigations such practical applications as wireless telegraphy, radio, and television.

Faraday himself had no interest in inventing devices to use electricity. Commercially feasible generators, electric lights, electric motors, and all the remaining paraphernalia of the age of electricity awaited the inventive genius of later generations of engineers and scientists.

Faraday's philosophy of scientific research is revealed in these comments:

> Let the imagination go, guarding it by judgement and principle, but holding it in and directing it by experiment. . . . In the most successful instances [of scientific investigation] not a tenth of the suggestions, the hopes, the wishes, the preliminary conclusions have been realized. . . . Nature is our best friend and best critic in experimental science if we only allow her intimations to fall unbiased on our minds. Nothing is so good as an experiment which, while it sets an error right, gives as a reward for our humility an absolute advance in knowledge.

69. THE CASE OF THE WANDERING BOULDERS

Jean Louis Rodolphe Agassiz's *Études sur les Glaciers* (Studies on Glaciers)

1840

A lone boulder seventy feet high stands on the shore of Lake Geneva in Switzerland, and in the western part of the country, in Neuchâtel, is a huge rock sixty-two feet high and forty feet across. Other massive boulders are scattered for many miles around but are most numerous in the region of the mountains.

Peasant folk tales variously account for the wandering boulders by reference to supernatural forces or credit them to prehistoric giants. Among early nineteenth-century scientists, several theories were in vogue. A famous geologist, Leopold von Buch, held that the rocks had reached their present sites as the result of great upheavals which had hurled huge stones from mountain to mountain and into the lowlands. Others regarded them as a residue of Noah's Flood. The most generally accepted hypothesis was Charles Lyell's: land surfaces had often been submerged beneath the sea, and, while so covered, icebergs had deposited the boulders over the land.

The true explanation had occurred to James Hutton, in Scotland, toward the end of the eighteenth century. Though Hutton never saw the boulders himself, he speculated that they were ice-carried, and his disciple, John Playfair, concluded that "a glacier is the only agent we now see capable of transporting them to such a distance, without destroying that sharpness of the angles so distinctive of these masses." Hutton and Playfair were not alone. During the first quarter of the nineteenth century, Jean de Charpentier, director of the mines at Bex, and M. Venetz, a civil engineer, had become converted to the glacial theory. The Alps, they were convinced, had once been embedded in a mass of ice.

In 1836, Charpentier brought these ideas to his friend, Louis Agassiz, a brilliant young Swiss biologist. Skeptical at first, Agassiz began an investigation on his own and soon became an enthusiastic advocate of the theory of glacial action. Furthermore, the imaginative Agassiz immediately perceived far greater implications in the theory than had Charpentier. Not only the Alps but also many other regions of the northern hemisphere, he decided, had once been covered with an ice sheet. Everywhere he saw evidence of the work of glaciers: transported boulders, scratched and polished outcropping rocks, moraine-like deposits, and glacial drift, as soil left by glaciers is called. In travels through Scotland and Wales, Agassiz observed similar signs of the work of long-vanished glaciers.

Agassiz's theory was introduced to the world in 1837 in a paper read to the Helvetic Association at Neuchâtel. Three years later, his famous *Études sur les Glaciers*, "Studies on Glaciers," was published. In his address, he announced his belief that a great Ice Age, due to a temporary fluctuation of the globe's temperature, had covered the surface of the earth with an ice sheet extending at least from the North Pole to Central Europe and Asia. In Agassiz's words:

> Siberian winter established itself for a time over a world previously covered with a rich vegetation and peopled with large mammalia, similar to those now inhabiting the warm regions of India and Africa. Death enveloped all nature in a shroud, and the cold, having reached its highest degree, gave to this mass of ice, at the maximum of tension, the greatest possible hardness.

Agassiz *Études sur les Glaciers,* consisting of one large volume of text and an atlas, presented a historical résumé of all previous work on glaciers, followed by an account of observations made by Agassiz and his companions during several years' study of the Alpine glaciers. New facts were reported on the appearance and structure of these streams of slowly moving ice, their method of formation, their internal temperature, and their rock loads. From the local phenomena of the Alpine valleys, Agassiz restated in almost poetic terms the vast conclusions that he had reached earlier:

> The surface of Europe adorned before by a tropical vegetation and inhabited by troops of large elephants, enormous hippopotami, and gigantic carnivora, was suddenly buried under a vast mantle of ice, covering alike plains, lakes, seas, and plateaus. Upon the life and movement of a powerful creation fell the silence of death. Springs paused, rivers ceased to flow, the rays of the sun, rising upon this frozen shore (if, indeed, it was reached by them), were met only by the breath of the winter from the north and the thunders of the crevasses as they opened across the surface of this icy sea.

For the next half-dozen years Agassiz's researches on glaciers continued. He climbed the Jungfrau and other "unscalable" mountains, spent several summers camping upon the Aar glacier, measured the depth and forward movement of glaciers, braved their treacherous crevasses, and studied the flora and fauna of the ice fields. The results of the later investigations were described in Agassiz's *Système Glaciaire,* "Glacial System," published in 1846.

After his appointment to the Harvard University faculty, in the eighteen forties, Agassiz tested his glacial theories further by examining North and South American geology. He explored for evidences of ice action the area extending from the Atlantic Coast to the Rocky Mountains and from the Great Lakes to the Gulf of Mexico, everywhere north of the thirty-fifth parallel finding abundant proof of the Ice Age. The whole northern part of the North American continent, he asserted, was modeled by a moving ice sheet, a statement verified by all subsequent investigators.

Like all other revolutionary scientific conceptions, Agassiz's theories met with opposition and violent criticisms when first announced. His own countrymen scoffed at the Ice Age theory and the leading English geologists considered him insane. Before his death in 1873, however, Agassiz had the satisfaction of seeing the views which he had first advanced in 1837 gain world-wide acceptance.

Since Agassiz's time, research in glacial geology has immensely expanded in variety and complexity. Among fields of interest to present-day geologists are: the petrography of the drift; mountain summit and mountain valley sculpture by the snow field and the valley glacier; the involved history of the Great Lakes region during the retreat of the last ice sheet; the changes of land level associated with glaciers; the history of the Ice Age (possibly a million years in duration), including effects on plant and animal life and on man; the study of vastly older glacial Ice Ages; and theories concerning their causes. Scientists are now generally agreed that the last glacial stage, ending approximately 20,000 years ago, was one of a series reaching back into the remote geological past. Furthermore, it has been suggested that the present is merely an interglacial stage and that another glacial stage, with its almost incalculable consequences for the human race, is beginning to take shape.

70. ATTACK ON THE STATE

Pierre Joseph Proudhon's *Qu'est-ce que la Propriété? ou Recherches sur le Principe du Droit et du Gouvernement* (What Is Property? or an Inquiry into the Principle of Right and of Government)

1840

Pierre Joseph Proudhon occupies a unique position among nineteenth-century reformers. He was one of the early leaders of French socialism and a merciless critic of capitalism in practically all of its manifestations. Unlike socialists in general, however, Proudhon was a bitter enemy of government and of state control, preaching instead the doctrine of free development of the individual. Tolstoy called him "the Robinson Crusoe of Socialism"—without a party, without a class, without a creed. Yet his prolific pen wielded a powerful influence on the social thought of his time.

Unquestionably, the trend of history in the century since his death has run strongly against every principle represented by Proudhon. Totalitarian forms of government rule one-half the world's population. Even in democratic nations, bureaucracy has steadily expanded, and state control over finance, commerce, industry, education, health, and other aspects of modern civilization has become more stringent. These developments Proudhon would have violently opposed. The alternative to the all-powerful state, urged by him and by like-minded theorists of the nineteenth century, is a concept known variously as libertarianism, individualism, self-government, mutualism, federalism, syndicalism, and anarchy.

Proudhon, of French peasant origin and self-educated, wrote over forty books. One of the earliest and most widely known is his *What Is Property?* This publication created a sensation and won for the author the hatred of bourgeois society and the admiration of the young revolutionaries (including, temporarily, Karl Marx) then flocking to Paris. Replying to the question in his title, Proudhon stated dogmatically that "property is theft." Actually, this often quoted declaration represents a one-sided view of his philosophy. Proudhon is referring to large-scale capitalism—as a system for exacting rent, interest, and profit without performing manual labor. Income derived from labor on the farm or in the shop, Proudhon terms "possession" and considers morally just and socially valuable. Property which reaps without sowing, consumes without producing, and enjoys without exertion is "the worst usurer as well as the worst master and worst debtor." Good property, in contrast, is defined as *possession populaire*, that is, the ownership of one's own farm or shop, wherein a man produces his own wealth by his own labor.

Proudhon proposes that every man shall have private possession of such property as he needs for actual use in production, and he and his heirs shall be permitted to retain it as long as they actually use it —but no longer. Capitalism as a property system is condemned by Proudhon as "industrial feudalism." There can be no justification, he feels, for property ownership which creates and maintains social inequality—the prime source of all social ills. Not even the French Revolution, he points out, had abolished the rule of propertied classes; it had simply substituted the rule of the bourgeoisie for that of the aristocratic property owners. The revolution must continue, he insists, until that type of property is abolished altogether and mankind can enjoy equality. When every man is a property owner, property will no longer be wrongly used for exploitation, and the "satanic" institution will have been turned into a powerful tool for the establishment of a free and equal social order. Universal ownership will achieve the miracle of "changing this angel of darkness into an angel of light."

The new economic order advocated by Proudhon is called by him "mutualism." Each industry would be carried on by a voluntary association of producers, agrarian and industrial, bound together by free contracts. A council representing federations of economic associations, with power to regulate their common affairs, would be the nation's supreme authority. The transition from capitalism to mutualism is to be accomplished quickly and peacefully through the creation of a People's Bank, to furnish free credit to any enterpriser requiring it. Thus an economic revolution would occur, according to Proudhon, "without confiscation, without bankruptcy, without an agrarian law, without common ownership, without state intervention, and without the abolition of inheritance." Free credit would cause capitalism to disintegrate and to be displaced by mutualism.

The key position in Proudhon's theory of social organization is held by the family. To him, society is essentially a grouping of families. Each family, of course, is self-seeking, but such an incentive is desirable and natural, and it does not jeopardize the solidarity which binds all the families together into a common society. After the family comes the free union of co-operators, and after these mutualist groups, the federation. The movement must come from the bottom by contract, maintains Proudhon, not from the top by decree. "I begin by *anarchy*," he says, "the conclusion of my criticism of the idea of government, to end by *federation* as the necessary basis of European public law, and later on of the organization of all states."

Proudhon is convinced that, in order to realize his ideals of individual freedom and social justice, all forms of authoritative government and capitalism must be abolished. In the light of these radical proposals, he is frequently referred to as the founder of anarchism.

Few writers have been so misunderstood or given such varying interpretations as Proudhon—in considerable part because he expressed so many contradictory ideas. J. Salwyn Schapiro, a noted historian, describes him as the "Dr. Jekyll and Mr. Hyde" among social philosophers. In the first capacity, he praises justice, denounces exploitation of man by man, pleads for individual liberty, and asserts the supremacy of morality in human relations. But as Mr. Hyde, he despises, for example, political democracy, trade-unions, and democratic socialism and opposes the movement for women's rights.

Like other early-nineteenth-century reformers, such as Godwin and Cobbett, Proudhon never fully comprehended the problems of great industry. Nevertheless, he occupies an important place in the history of social and political theories—especially in France, where his influence has been permanent and far-reaching. Proudhon's doctrines were staunchly upheld by Parisian workers during the mid nineteenth century, and he controlled the French section of the First International during its initial years. From an international standpoint, his influence has been notable in the development of anarchist principles.

71. GREAT MAN THEORY OF HISTORY

Thomas Carlyle's *On Heroes, Hero-Worship, and the Heroic in History*

1841

Every author whose works survive to be read by later generations is subject to frequent reappraisal. Sometimes such re-evaluations result in promotions to higher rank in the literary hierarchy; this has happened to Herman Melville and Henry James. In other instances, reputations may suffer. Thomas Carlyle is a perfect example of a sharp decline from a lofty height. In early and mid-Victorian times, he was probably the most influential writer in England. A drastic revision in former estimates, however, began with the outbreak of World War I. Though recognizing that Carlyle himself might have been personally charming and blameless, his critics accused him of creating a philosophy which could easily be translated by such leaders as Robespierre, Napoleon, and Hitler into a code of blood, iron, fire, and sword. They asserted that the Nazi state was the logical aftermath of the theories propounded by Nietzsche, Gobineau, Houston Chamberlain, and Carlyle.

The basis for this bitter attack on Carlyle was his adoration of strong leaders (exemplified by Oliver Cromwell, Frederick the Great, and Napoleon), his excessive admiration for Germanic peoples, and his denunciations of democratic institutions. The Carlylean opinions are scattered throughout his voluminous writings, but one of his early books, *On Heroes, Hero-Worship, and the Heroic in History*, presents most effectively his concept of the great man's role in history. The author sets the scene thus:

Universal History, the history of what man has accomplished in this world, is at bottom the History of the Great Men who have worked here. They were the leaders of men, these great ones; the modellers, patterns, and in a wide sense creators, of whatsoever the general mass of men contrived to do or to attain; all things that we see standing accomplished in the world are properly the outer material result, the practical realisation and embodiment, of Thoughts that dwelt in the Great Men sent into the world: the soul of the whole world's history, it may justly be considered, were the history of these.

To Carlyle, history is "the biography of great men," Luther, Goethe, and Frederick the Great were more significant and more fascinating subjects for study than Germany, Cromwell more important than England. In *Sartor Resartus* the author declares, "Great Men are the inspired (speaking and acting) Texts of the Divine Book of Revelations, whereof a chapter is completed from epoch to epoch, and by some named History." Carlyle sees, in all periods of human history, certain great individuals standing out unique. Whenever the world is in travail, racked by troubles, salvation comes from a Hero, a divine personality, who seizes authority and solves the besetting woes.

Carlyle had no faith in the democratic theory of human equality. Pure democracy has never existed, he holds, for even in the so-called "republics" of ancient times the mass of the people were slaves and the citizens were really aristocrats. "There is," Carlyle believes, "in every Nation and Community a *fittest*, a wisest, bravest, best; whom could we find and make King over us, all were in truth very well." Great men should be approached with reverence. "No sadder proof can be given by a man of his own littleness than disbelief in great men." Majority rule lacks validity, according to Carlyle, because "the wise and noblest minded" are always a minority.

To demonstrate his thesis, Carlyle searches history for Heroes to serve as ideals for the future. In his book he chooses six categories of Heroes, widely distributed in time and space, but all possessing similar qualities of heroism. Heroes are recognized as existing in different spheres of human activity. Not all the leaders of men have been kings or captains; some have been prophets and poets. Eleven characters are selected by Carlyle to illustrate his view that the history of the world can best be told in the lives of its great men. The first, "The Hero as Divinity," is represented by Odin of Scandinavian mythology. There follow, in succession, "The Hero as Prophet" (Mohammed), "The Hero as Poet" (Dante and Shakespeare), "The Hero as Priest" (Luther and Knox), "The Hero as Man of Letters"

(Samuel Johnson, Rousseau, and Robert Burns), and "The Hero as King" (Cromwell and Napoleon).

Carlyle's choice of names has been considered capricious, but he aimed to be original and to attract attention. In achieving this purpose he was highly successful, for he stimulated the study of Norse literature, brought about a change of attitude toward Mohammed, and created or renewed general interest in such personalities as Dante, Knox, Boswell, Johnson, and Burns. The Carlylean interpretations have continued to the present day to influence the popular conceptions of the "Heroes."

It is Carlyle's contention that all the eleven persons whom he selected as illustrations of his doctrine were divinely inspired, were characterized by a sincerity which came from God, and had been sent into the world to enlighten and guide mankind. Since such leaders possess superior spiritual insight, being successive embodiments of divine revelation, the masses should be willing and contented to follow them.

In another work, *Chartism,* Carlyle says, "Surely of all rights of man the right of the ignorant man to be guided by the wiser, to be, gently or forcibly, held in the true course by him, is the indisputablest. If Freedom have any meaning it means enjoyment of that right." This twisted interpretation of freedom would coincide with the Communist and Fascist definition of democracy. Government is *for* the people, not *by* the people. The Hero—the wise, strong man— is divinely chosen to tell them what to do.

Most fervently admired by Carlyle is the last of his six forms of heroism, "The Hero as King," represented by Cromwell and Napoleon:

> The Commander over men; he to whose will our wills are to be subordinated, and loyally surrender themselves, and find their welfare in doing so, may be reckoned the most important of Great Men. He is practically the summary for us of *all* the various figures of Heroism.

As a consequence of events of the twentieth century, "we now pick up *Heroes and Hero Worship* gingerly," remarks the literary critic V. S. Pritchett, for "we have had to crush one or two dictator-heroes. Carlyle's ultimate contempt for the masses, his dream of an aristocracy of the wise, his call for a labour corps, take us back twenty years into Fascism." Nevertheless, Carlyle continues to hold a keen interest for historians of ideas and literature.

72. SPOKESMAN FOR THE NEW AMERICA

Ralph Waldo Emerson's *Essays*

1841–1844

Ralph Waldo Emerson is popularly regarded as one of the most inspiring writers in American literature, and Matthew Arnold pronounced his *Essays* "the most important work done in prose" during the nineteenth century. Critics are by no means unanimous in supporting such judgments, but agreement is general on Emerson's extensive and continuing influence on American and European thought.

Emerson began his career as a Unitarian minister in Boston. His iconoclastic ideas were out of conformity with church tenets, however, leading to his early retirement from the pulpit. For the next fifty years, until his death in 1882, Emerson traveled the length and breadth of the United States and abroad, establishing fame as a public lecturer. The *Essays*, "elegant table talks, full of ripe wisdom, German transcendentalism, and poetic mysticism," were originally delivered as lectures.

For the *Essays*, Emerson chose broad philosophical themes: Love, Friendship, Character, Manners, Intellect, Nature. Even to more tangible concerns, such as Politics, History, Self-Reliance, and Art, his approach is characterized by a spirit of idealistic detachment— essentially presentations of his own inner reactions to the world around him. The pervading tone is one of invincible optimism: complete confidence and faith in man's ability to control the universe and to develop beauty, freedom, friendship, and peace. Emerson's doctrine was admirably suited to the temperament and genius of mid-nineteenth-century America.

The master idea binding the essays together is the concept of "The Over-Soul," the title of one piece. It is the theory of a basic force animating all mankind, from which the race derives every revelation of truth, beauty, wisdom, and virtue. The Over-Soul may manifest itself in a variety of ways: "When it breathes through man's intellect, it is genius; when it breathes through his will, it is virtue; when it flows through his affection, it is love." All history, in Emerson's view, is the record of the general soul. Within man will be found "the Foreworld; in his childhood the Age of Gold, the Apples of Knowledge, the Argonautic Expedition, the call of Abraham, the building of the Temple, the Advent of Christ, Dark Ages, the Revival of Letters, the Reformation, the discovery of new lands, the opening of new sciences and new regions in man."

A corollary principle is expounded by Emerson in the essay on "Compensation": whatever good or ill befalls a man, there is an offset, a balance, a compensation; divine justice requires that any act reward or punish itself. In Nature, darkness and light, heat and cold, the systole and diastole of the heart, male and female, balance each other; every animal's strength is offset by a weakness. Emerson dissented from the prevailing theological doctrine "that judgement is not executed in this world; that the wicked are successful; that the good are miserable." He does not attempt to deny the fact of evil nor to expect perfection, but to assert that justice ultimately triumphs.

Most celebrated of all the essays is "Self-Reliance," separately printed in innumerable forms and distributed in millions of copies. Its essential argument is that man's creative power is derived through absolute self-reliance. The individual should have the courage to resist social pressure, tradition, and authority when they run counter to his own principles and reason. As the noted American critic Van Wyck Brooks summarizes the theme: "We have only to follow the clue that Nature gives us, follow the line of our talent; in one direction all space is open to us. We are like a ship in a river: we run against obstructions on every side but one, but on that side the obstruction is removed, and we sweep serenely over a deepening channel into an infinite sea." "Self-Reliance" is filled with memorable phrases:

> To be great is to be misunderstood. . . . A foolish consistency is the hobgoblin of little minds. . . . In every work of genius we recognize our own rejected thoughts. . . . Trust thyself: every heart vibrates to that iron string. . . . All history resolves itself into the biography of a few stout and earnest men. . . . Whoso would be a man, must be a nonconformist. . . . Nothing is at last sacred but the integrity of your own mind. . . . An institution is the lengthened shadow of one man. . . . Insist on yourself; never imitate.

Emerson's essay on "Politics" sounds a modern note. Like Thoreau, he maintains that "the State is not superior to the citizen." Laws may be good or bad. "Laws are all alterable. Young civilians believe that any measure may be imposed on a people, if only you can get sufficient voices to make it a law. But the wise know that foolish legislation is a rope of sand which perishes in the twisting." People should be regarded by government as more important than property. Emerson insists: "The only interest for the consideration of the State is persons; for the highest end of government is the culture of men." Though preferring democracy to any other form of government, Emerson perceives its weaknesses: "Ordinarily, our parties are parties of circumstance, and not of principle. . . . The vice of our leading parties in this country is, that they do not plant themselves on the deep and necessary grounds to which they are respectively entitled, but lash themselves to fury in the carrying of some local and momentary measure, nowise useful to the commonwealth." Echoing Jefferson, Emerson holds that "the less government we have, the better—the fewer laws, and the less confided power."

A high moral idealism is Emerson's guiding motif in advocating forward-looking democracy, self-reliance, toleration—his role that of an apostle of man's divine potentialities. His faith in the human race is boundless.

More than one caustic critic has condemned misinterpretations and misuse of Emerson's teachings. "Emersonianism," they charge, is too often a vulgar, optimistic superstition, concerned principally with maintaining things as they are. This, however, is not the real Emerson. An examination of his writings reveals his sense of continuous change in human affairs and impatience with those who stand for the *status quo*. Everywhere there stands out Emerson's conviction that development and movement are the essence of life.

Emerson's advocacy of reforms in education, religion, and politics and his views on life in general rank him as one of the great American liberals, whose influence is still felt more than a century after the appearance of the *Essays*.

73. UNIVERSAL MAN

Alexander von Humboldt's *Kosmos* (Cosmos)

1845–1862

Simón Bolívar once declared that "Baron Humboldt did more for the Americas than all the conquistadores." Without doubt, the Great Liberator's judgment is correct, for Humboldt's early-nineteenth-century expeditions revealed a new America. His voluminous publications, his varied influence on American growth and development, his encouragement to the Latin American liberators, and his aid to innumerable later explorers entitle Humboldt to a unique position in the annals of American history.

Alexander von Humboldt's extraordinary career ended in 1859 in his ninetieth year. Since the early years of the nineteenth century, he had been a world-famous figure, second in renown only to Napoleon. Evidence of the esteem in which he was held is furnished by the numerous geographical features named for him in the New World: Humboldt Current (off the Pacific coast of South America), Humboldt Glacier (Greenland), Humboldt Peak (Venezuela and Colorado), Humboldt Bay (California), Humboldt Range (Nevada), and perhaps a score of American cities and counties.

In the universality of his interests, Humboldt has been compared to Pericles and also to Leonardo da Vinci. Son of an aristocratic family in Prussia, he received the best education then available in Europe, studying under famous savants at the Universities of Frankfurt and Göttingen. Subsequently, he was to shine brilliantly as an explorer, cosmographer, biologist, diplomat, engineer, and citizen of the world. Among his friends and associates were Agassiz, Ampère, Bolívar, Chopin, Cuvier, Faraday, Franklin, Frederick the Great, Gauss, Goethe, Irving, Jefferson, Lavoisier, Liszt, Lyell, Morse, Pitt, Gilbert Stuart, and other public leaders of his time. His warm admirers included Charles Darwin, who called him "the greatest scientific traveler who ever lived." Yet, despite his contemporary fame and the near adulation in which he was held, Humboldt today is largely a forgotten personality, and his most celebrated book, *Cosmos,* little read.

Probably more than any other single factor, Humboldt's career was shaped by his travels in Latin America, during the five years from 1799 to 1804. Starting in Venezuela, he explored the Orinoco and upper Amazon valleys, climbed Chimborazo (then believed to be the world's highest mountain), studied the Inca civilization in Peru, corrected the figures for the latitudes of South America, calculated a route for the Panama Canal (approximately the present site), investigated changing vegetation from the steaming tropical jungles to the top of the Andes, collected, with the aid of his botanist companion, Aimé Bonpland, sixty thousand plant specimens, provided the first accurate data on cinchona (source of quinine) and rubber trees, and assembled a vast collection of animals, insects, and geological fragments. Before returning to Europe, Humboldt visited Mexico and Cuba and stopped over for a stay with Thomas Jefferson at Monticello.

Twenty-five years later, at the age of sixty, Humboldt undertook an extended tour, subsidized by the czar of Russia, into the interior of Asia. His scientific labors during the ensuing three decades of his career, however, were chiefly influenced by the impressions and observations gained from his American travels. No less than thirty published volumes were drawn from the extensive notes he made while on that Odyssey to South and Middle America—scientific studies relating to botany, geology, zoology, and geography, as well as narratives of popular travel and discussions of economic, social, and political conditions.

At the age of seventy-six, Humboldt resolved to undertake his most ambitious work: to co-ordinate and synthesize all the knowledge of his era into a harmonious whole. Everything that he had previously written or done he regarded as prologue, mere preparation for the gigantic project now begun. As the author outlines his plan in a letter:

> I have been seized with the mad idea of representing in a single work the whole material world, everything that we know today concerning the phenomena of the heavens and of the earth, from the nebulae to the geography of mosses on granite rocks. . . . Every great and important idea, which anywhere shines forth, must here be given together with the relevant facts. It must represent an epoch of the mental development of humanity as regards its knowledge of Nature.

The result of this audacious enterprise was *Cosmos*, subtitled *Sketch of a Physical Description of the Universe*, issued in five volumes over the period 1845 to 1862. Humboldt was pre-eminently qualified for the task to which he now set himself, because of his extensive knowledge of many fields of learning, varied experiences as a traveler, and the resources of the scientific and literary world at his disposal. Collaborators pledged to his assistance included the greatest scientists of his generation, leaders in chemistry, astronomy, anatomy, mathematics, mineralogy, botany, and other areas. Not since Aristotle had any writer attempted to deal with the universe in such comprehensive fashion.

In *Cosmos*, Humboldt combines the broad philosophical ideas of the eighteenth century with the more exact scientific knowledge of the nineteenth century. His basic purpose is stated in the Introduction to the first volume:

The most important aim of all physical science is this: to recognize unity in diversity, to comprehend all the single aspects as revealed by the discoveries of the last epochs, to judge single phenomena separately without surrendering to their bulk, and to grasp Nature's essence under the cover of outer appearances.

Beginning with a general "portrait of Nature," Humboldt examines outer space: the Milky Way, cosmic nebulae, and planets, and then proceeds to the earth and its physical geography; climate; volcanoes; relationships among plants, animals, and mankind; evolution; and the beauty of Nature. The second part, on the history of science, is concerned with "the difference of feeling excited by the contemplation of Nature at different epochs," that is, the attitudes toward natural phenomena among poets, painters, and students of Nature through the ages. The three final volumes are devoted to a more detailed account of scientific studies in astronomy, the earth's physical properties, and geological formations.

Cosmos was both a literary and scientific achievement, immensely popular among nineteenth-century readers. Humboldt's object, "to represent Nature as one great whole, moved and animated by internal forces," was successfully accomplished. Since his day, the natural sciences have, of course, made tremendous progress, and *Comos*, though still highly readable, has become outdated in important particulars.

In restrospect, Humboldt's work gave a strong impetus to scientific exploration throughout the nineteenth century, inspiring, for example, the voyage of the *Beagle,* with Darwin aboard as the ship's naturalist. It may rightfully be claimed also that he laid the foundations of physical geography and meteorology. But, without question, Humboldt's most enduring contribution to scientific progress is his conception of the unity of science, of Nature, and of mankind.

74. INDESTRUCTIBLE ENERGY

Hermann von Helmholtz's *Über die Erhaltung der Kraft*
(On the Conservation of Force)

1847

A recurring phenomenon in the history of scientific thought has been the almost simultaneous discovery by a number of scientists, working independently, frequently in different countries, of some great principle projecting forward the frontiers of knowledge. The essential thought appears to be in the air, and investigators converge upon it from various directions. The point is well illustrated by the case of surgical anesthesia, whose priority of discovery was disputed by several claimants. Even better known is the theory of evolution, with its long pre-Darwinian history.

A similar instance of coincidental development is that of the concept of the conservation of energy. Quite independently of one another, two German physicians, Julius Robert Mayer and Hermann von Helmholtz, and an English physicist, James Prescott Joule, began to meditate on a possible relationship between heat and force. Each, following a different line of reasoning, arrived at the idea of the mechanical equivalent of heat and the principle of the conservation of energy. The first paper containing a clear statement of the law of conservation of energy and attempting to determine the mechanical equivalent of heat was published by Mayer in 1842. Being neither a mathematician nor a physicist, Mayer offered no experimental proof to support his theory. The following year, Joule's paper, advancing the same theory but citing experimental justification, appeared in the *Philosophical Magazine*.

The broadest and most definitive formulation of the law of the conservation of energy and the one that was to have the greatest influence on scientific circles, however, was the work of the German physicist, physiologist, and philosopher Hermann von Helmholtz. His statement was supported by a wealth of illustrations from mechanics, electricity, heat, and biology, and it also presented mathematically the law's profound general implications. At the time Helmholtz published his account of energy conservation, in 1847, he was not a practicing scientist but a young doctor, only twenty-six years of age, in the Prussian army. Helmholtz has been ranked with

Willard Gibbs of Yale as one of the greatest thinkers of all time. His scientific accomplishments were extraordinarily wide in range, including major contributions to medicine, physiology, psychology, physics, and mathematics. In the course of his experimental work, he invented many instruments, among them the ophthalmoscope, ophthalmometer, and telestereoscope.

Helmholtz had long been preoccupied with thoughts on the conservation of energy, his interest first being aroused by research in biology. A lively issue among scientists of the period was the theory of vitalism. What was the source of the energy to be observed in living forms? Helmholtz was skeptical of the prevailing notion that living organisms are governed by an "indwelling vital force." He set out to answer the question propounded by the great German chemist Justus von Liebig: "Are the mechanical energy and heat produced by an organism entirely the product of its own metabolism?" Helmholtz's first investigations into the metabolism of muscle, that is, the chemical changes in living cells, showed that the heat of the body comes entirely from the foodstuff and oxygen supplied to it. For example, he found that the heat given off by an animal was equivalent to that produced by burning the animal's food in a calorimeter. No residue remained to indicate the operation of a vital force.

Late in the eighteenth century, the French chemist Lavoisier had established the principle of the indestructibility of matter. Now, a half-century later, Helmholtz stated a corollary law: the indestructibility of energy. "Nature as a whole," he concluded, "possesses a store of energy which cannot in any wise be added to or subtracted from." The quantity of energy is as eternal as the quantity of matter. Like matter, energy cannot be created or destroyed but only transformed.

This idea proved to be one of the most revolutionary in the history of physical science. As A. C. Crombie, a noted science historian, pointed out, "Its implications and the problems it posed dominated physics in the period between the electromagnetic researches of Faraday and Maxwell and the introduction of the quantum theory by Planck in 1900." On the foundation which Helmholtz had provided, Clausius, Boltzmann, Kelvin, and other physicists constructed the modern science of thermodynamics. With the acceptance by physiologists of the principle of energy conservation, the fantastic theory of vitalism disappeared, and the body came to be regarded as a machine which converts food and oxygen into heat and work.

As research continued, it became evident that the doctrine of the conservation of energy was applicable everywhere—in inanimate objects as well as in living things.

In his epoch-making paper of 1847, Helmholtz assumed that perpetual motion is impossible. What, then, are the relations among the various known forces of nature? Since these forces cannot arise out of nothing, mechanical energy can be generated naturally only through the expenditure of energy. Illustrating the principle that energy cannot be lost, Helmholtz noted that in a weight-powered clock a quantity of energy may disappear when the weight reaches the bottom, but the kinetic (motion) energy of the clock's mechanism has been transformed into an equivalent quantity of heat. In other applications, Helmholtz showed how to compare the kinetic energy of a moving body, the electrical energy produced by a thermocouple (a thermoelectric couple used to measure temperature differences), the energy of a magnet moved by electricity, and simple heat energy. Kinetic energy or energy in motion was the yardstick used to measure all other forces.

Helmholtz concluded with the statement: "I think in the foregoing I have proved that the above-mentioned law [conservation of energy] does not go against any hitherto known facts of natural science, but is supported by a large number of them in a striking manner. I have tried to enumerate as completely as possible what consequences result from the combination of other known laws of nature, and how they require to be confirmed by other experiments."

In a tribute to Helmholtz, James Clerk Maxwell, noted nineteenth-century physicist, commented: "To appreciate the scientific value of Helmholtz' little essay on the Conservation of Force, we should have to ask those to whom we owe the greatest discoveries in thermodynamics and other branches of modern physics, how many times they have read it over, and how often during their researches they felt the weighty statements of Helmholtz acting on their minds like an irresistible driving power."

Through the work of Albert Einstein and other twentieth-century physicists, concepts of energy and matter or mass now tend to merge. The law of the conservation of energy has therefore been interpreted in a new light. Energy cannot be created or destroyed, but it may be increased or decreased in proportion to mass. Thus a single embracing principle covers the two fundamental laws relating to the conservation of energy and the conservation of matter.

75. HIGH PRIESTS OF THE PROLETARIAT

Karl Marx and Friedrich Engels' *Das Kommunistische Manifest* (The Communist Manifesto)

1848

Though *Das Kapital* is far more comprehensive and profound, Karl Marx's most widely read work is beyond doubt *The Communist Manifesto*. Unquestionably, the latter is the most influential political pamphlet of all time, written in a vivid style, full of dogmatic judgments passionately expressed, and challenging most of the accepted ideas of economics, history, and government.

Friedrich Engels is recorded as coauthor of the *Manifesto*, but subsequently Engels himself wrote, "I consider myself bound to state that the fundamental proposition which forms its nucleus, belongs to Marx." The proposition, in brief, is that the whole history of mankind, since it rose above primitive tribal societies, has been a history of class struggles, contests between exploiting and exploited, ruling and oppressed classes. Further, the *Manifesto* holds that only the proletariat could free society from all exploitation, oppression, class distinctions, and class struggles.

Marx and Engels, then comparatively unknown young men of twenty-nine and twenty-seven, respectively, were commissioned in 1847 by the congress of a small, obscure Communist League in London to write the *Manifesto*. Their assignment was completed a few weeks before the February Revolution of 1848 and published in German and French. During the past century, *The Communist Manifesto* has gone through countless editions, has been translated into nearly all languages, and remains the first and best-known expression of communist theory.

The *Manifesto* opens dramatically: "A spectre is haunting Europe —the spectre of Communism. All the powers of old Europe have entered into a holy alliance to exorcise this spectre; Pope and Czar, Metternich and Guizot, Radicals and German police-spies." The fear of communism among its opponents is interpreted by the authors as an acknowledgement of its power. "It is high time," Marx and Engels declare, "that Communists should openly, in the face of the whole world, publish their views, their aims, their tendencies, and meet this nursery tale of the Spectre of Communism with a Manifesto of the party itself."

In a quotable, lively style, the *Manifesto* traces the evolution of class society down to the rise of modern capitalism—to the beginnings of the bourgeoisie and the industrial proletariat. In every historical era evidences of class struggles are found, as "freeman and slave, patrician and plebeian, lord and serf, guild-master and journeyman, in a word, oppressor and oppressed, stood in constant opposition to one another." Throughout history, the authors find, society has been organized by social ranks. Coming down to their own time, Marx and Engels contend that:

> The modern bourgeois society that has sprouted from the ruins of feudal society, has not done away with class antagonisms. It has but established new classes, new conditions of oppression, new forms of struggle in place of the old ones.

Despite their highly critical view of the evils of capitalism, the authors concede that bourgeois achievements have been phenomenal: "It has been the first to show what man's activities can bring about. It has accomplished wonders far surpassing Egyptian pyramids, Roman aqueducts and Gothic cathedrals, it has conducted expeditions that put in the shade all former exoduses of nations and crusades. . . . The bourgeoisie, during its reign of scarce one hundred years has created more powerful, more stupendous forces of production than all preceding generations rolled into one." Capitalism is also credited with the growth of democracy, the applications of science to industry, and the development of an international culture.

All praise, however, is in the nature of a funeral oration. Capitalism is held to be in a decadent state, and the prophecy is made that its end will be brought about by the same relentless laws of social change that destroyed previous systems. Bourgeois civilization is compared to "the sorcerer who is no longer able to control the powers of the nether world whom he has called up by his spells." The periodical cycles of economic booms and depressions place "the existence of the entire bourgeois society on trial, each time more threateningly." Characteristic of capitalist economy, claim Marx and Engels, is the "epidemic of overproduction," creating the paradox of famine amid plenty. "Society suddenly finds itself put back into a state of momentary barbarism," they assert, "and why? Because there is too much civilization, too much means of subsistence, too much industry, too much commerce. . . . What the bourgeoisie therefore produces, above all, are its own grave diggers. Its fall and the victory of the proletariat are equally inevitable."

The new urban proletariat now emerges to replace the bourgeoisie, but not peacefully. In keeping with his theory of the class struggle, Marx's Communists "openly declared that their ends can be attained only by the forcible overthrow of all existing social conditions." All the tactics and strategy of war are necessary and justifiable, it is held, to enable the proletariat to seize political power, abolish the rule of private capital, and establish a classless society.

Marx and Engels explain why they place their faith in the workers alone to achieve a new society. The proletariat is without property, has no strong family ties, lacks national patriotism, and is disillusioned with a civilization guilty of cheating and oppressing it. To the worker, law, morality, religion, are so many bourgeois prejudices." Furthermore, the workers represent "the self-conscious, independent movement of the immense majority, in the interest of the immense majority."

The *Manifesto* proposes ten measures to be put into immediate effect after the Communists' seizure of power. The objectives include: the abolition of landed property; imposition of a heavy graduated income tax; destruction of all rights of inheritance; confiscation of the property of all "emigrants and rebels"; nationalization of all banks and transportation; state control of all instruments of production; enforced obligation on the part of all citizens to work; establishment of "industrial armies"; and free education for all children in public schools. Various commentators have pointed out that a substantial portion of this program is now in operation in non-Communist countries.

In the new workers' paradise visualized by Marx and Engels, to be limited to a single class, class antagonisms would naturally vanish, the state would ultimately wither away because no longer needed, and an era of creative world brotherhood would be ushered in.

"The proletarians have nothing to lose but their chains. They have a world to win. Workingmen of all countries unite!" proclaims the *Manifesto's* stirring conclusion.

When the *Manifesto* was written, the authors anticipated the early collapse of the capitalist system. Actually, capitalism in the mid-nineteenth century was on the threshold of its greatest period of expansion. Certain other predictions—e.g., the concentration of capital, the growth of giant monopolies, the limiting of competition, and the recurrence of economic crises—have been fulfilled.

While recognizing the fallacies in Marx and Engels' theories, we can scarcely overestimate their impact on modern history. Marxism's conquest of Russia, China, and other vast areas, bringing hundreds of millions of people under its sway, has posed urgent problems for the twentieth century. Actually, present-day Communist governments fulfill few of Marx and Engels' ideas and ideals for communism. In the Soviet Union, for example, there is a dictatorship by a hierarchy within the Communist Party, rather than a true dictatorship of the proletariat. The political state which was to "wither away" becomes more powerful with the passage of time. Beginning with Lenin, the Communist leaders have found it easier to preach the doctrines of Marx and Engels than to practice them. Though continuing to pay lip service to Marxian philosophy, they have modified the inherited dogma as political circumstances and expediency seemed to require.

76. TERRIBLE POWER OF THE MEEK

Henry David Thoreau's *Resistance to Civil Government*

1849

Henry David Thoreau—New England observer of Nature, lover of solitude and the outdoors, exponent of the simple life, poet and mystic—bore none of the earmarks of a social agitator or a radical. Nevertheless, he was the author of one of the most revolutionary manifestoes in American history.

Most celebrated and influential of Thoreau's contributions to the literature of social criticism is his *Resistance to Civil Government,* later issued as *Civil Disobedience.*

While visiting in Concord, Massachusetts, in 1843, Thoreau was arrested and jailed for nonpayment of the poll tax and used his arrest to protest against that state's support of slavery. Several years later, Thoreau told the story, in *Civil Disobedience,* of his brush with the law over the poll tax violation. The immediate stimuli for his action were the Mexican War of 1846–47 and the Fugitive

Slave Law, both of which Thoreau viewed as means to extend and strengthen the hated institution of slavery.

Why, Thoreau asks, should he be required to provide financial support for a government guilty of such injustices and stupidity? Here was the birth of his doctrine of civil disobedience. Thoreau decided the time had come to examine the nature of the state and its government. What should be the relation of the individual to the state, and of the state to the individual? In Thoreau's opinion:

> Government is at best but an expedient; but most governments are sometimes inexpedient. The objections that have been brought against a standing army, and they are many and weighty, and deserve to prevail, may also at last be brought against a standing government.

While acknowledging that the American government was a relatively excellent one, Thoreau maintains that "the character inherent in the American people has done all that has been accomplished; and it would have done somewhat more, if the government had not sometimes got in its way." Furthermore, "I cannot for an instant recognize that political organization as *my* government which is the slave's government also." It is the duty of citizens, Thoreau asserts, to resist evil in the state even to the point of open and deliberate disobedience to its laws.

Thoreau debates the proper attitude of the citizen toward unjust laws. Is it better to wait for majority action to change the laws, or to refuse at once to obey the laws? The uncompromising answer is that, if the government "requires you to be the agent of injustice to another, then, I say, break the law. . . . What I have to do is to see, at any rate, that I do not lend myself to the wrong which I condemn."

It is of the very nature of government, Thoreau believes, to oppose changes and reforms and to mistreat its critics. "Why," he asks, "does it always crucify Christ, and excommunicate Copernicus and Luther, and pronounce Washington and Franklin rebels?"

Thoreau urges that all who opposed slavery "should at once effectually withdraw their support, both in person and property from the government." As a symbol of civil disobedience, a method open to every citizen, Thoreau advocates refusal to pay taxes. By paying taxes to an unjust government, the citizen condones wrongs committed by the state. For six years, adhering to his principles, Thoreau reports that he paid no poll tax. His short prison term left him unshaken in his convictions, but with less regard for the state:

I saw that the State was half-witted, that it was timid as a lone woman with her silver spoons, and that it did not know its friends from its foes, and I lost all my remaining respect for it, and pitied it. Thus the State never intentionally confronts a man's sense, intellectual or moral, but only his body, his senses. It is not armed with superior wit or honesty, but with superior physical strength. I was not born to be forced. I will breathe after my own fashion.

Thoreau differentiates between taxes. He states that he "never declined paying the highway tax," nor the school tax, "because I am as desirous of being a good neighbor as I am of being a bad subject." Where he draws the line is in paying general taxes to support war and slavery. In these matters, "I simply wish to refuse allegiance to the State, to withdraw and stand aloof from it effectually."

In essence, Thoreau's basic premise in *Civil Disobedience* is that the state exists for individuals, not individuals for the state. A minority should not yield to a majority if moral principles must be compromised in order to do so. Further, the state has no right to offend moral liberty by forcing the citizen to support injustices. Man's conscience should always be his supreme guiding spirit.

The impact of *Civil Disobedience* on Thoreau's own time was negligible. The work remained obscure and largely forgotten until the following century, when it was destined to acquire world-shaking significance. In 1907, a copy of *Civil Disobedience* fell into the hands of a Hindu lawyer in South Africa, Mohandas Karamchand Gandhi, who was already meditating upon the merits of passive resistance as a defense for his people. As Henry Polak, one of Gandhi's closest associates in South Africa, recounts the effect:

We [Gandhi and Polak] were . . . enormously impressed by the confirmation of the rightness of the principle of passive resistance and civil disobedience . . . contained in the essay "On the Duty of Civil Disobedience." After consultation with Mr. Gandhi, I reproduced the essay in the columns of *Indian Opinion*, and it was translated into the Gujarati language, in which, as well as in English, the paper was published, and the essay was subsequently circulated in pamphlet form.

Gandhi, who had been dissatisfied with the term "passive resistance," but had found no suitable substitute, at once adopted "civil disobedience" to describe his movement. Here was a statement of principle, he decided, that meant firmness without violence, and a devotion to truth and justice—a political policy completely in accord with Gandhi's philosophy. *Civil Disobedience* in the hands of Mahatma Gandhi became a bible of nonresistance. For his Hindu followers, Gandhi coined an equivalent, Satyagraha, translated as "soul force" or "the force which is born of truth and love of nonviolence."

Gandhi used South Africa as a laboratory for the development of his new weapon—the weapon of nonviolent resistance in the struggle of a handful of Hindus against the might of the British Empire and the government of South Africa. Later, the same weapon was used in India—a campaign which ended in 1947, when India and Pakistan gained their independence from Britain.

77. THE LITTLE WOMAN WHO STARTED THE BIG WAR
Harriet Beecher Stowe's *Uncle Tom's Cabin*
1852

On a single point only do the pro-and-con critics of *Uncle Tom's Cabin* agree. Without exception, all recognize the book's tremendous impact on its time—specifically, its immense influence in instigating the American Civil War. Abraham Lincoln concurred in that judgment when he greeted the author, Harriet Beecher Stowe, on a visit to the White House in 1862, as "the little lady who wrote the book that made this big war."

Never was a book more topical or better timed psychologically. The struggle over the slavery question had grown tense, aggravated by the passage of the Fugitive Slave Law and the agitation for abolition of slavery. The national Congress was split down the center by the increasing controversy, while the clergy, North and South, boomed arguments for and against the "peculiar institution" of slavery. The surcharged moral climate simply awaited a spark to set off a world-shaking explosion. *Uncle Tom's Cabin* furnished the spark.

Mrs. Stowe, a member of the celebrated Beecher clan, spent virtually her entire life in a strongly religious atmosphere. Throughout her prolific writings, including *Uncle Tom's Cabin,* the religious background was ever in evidence, inspiring her to evangelistic fervor and eloquence. Though New England born, Mrs. Stowe grew up in Cincinnati, where her father served as head of the Lane Theological Seminary. The Seminary was a hotbed of antislavery sentiment and a station on the Underground Railroad, but Harriet's only firsthand

contact with slavery was on a brief visit paid to a Kentucky planta-
tion, across the Ohio River from Cincinnati.

Not until her return to New England in 1850 did Mrs. Stowe's
antislavery feelings become intense. Her indignation was aroused
particularly by incidents connected with enforcement of the Fugitive Slave Law. Urged on by members of her family, she resolved to
write something that would expose the evils of the slave system.
Uncle Tom's Cabin was the result. Originally, the work appeared
serially in the *National Era,* an abolitionist paper published in Washington, D.C. Almost immediately thereafter, in 1852, it was brought
out in book form, and ten thousand copies were sold in less than a
week. Pirated editions in England sold considerably over a million
copies. Within a short period, translations were available in a score
of languages.

The essential plot of *Uncle Tom's Cabin* is not complex, though
involving many characters. A benevolent Kentucky slave owner, in
order to pay his debts, is compelled to sell some of his best slaves,
including Uncle Tom, to a New Orleans slave dealer. Tom is separated from his wife and children. On the trip down the river, Tom
saves the life of little Eva, and in gratitude her father, St. Clare,
buys him from the dealer. The next two years are pleasant ones for
Tom as a servant in St. Clare's elegant New Orleans home, with
the saintly child Eva and her impish little Negro companion Topsy.
Then Eva dies, St. Claire is killed in a tavern brawl, and Tom is
sent to the slave market. At a public auction, Tom is bought by a
brutal drunken Red River planter, Simon Legree. Despite efforts to
please his cruel master, Tom is grossly mistreated. After a series of
incidents, Tom is beaten so viciously by Legree that he succumbs,
just as his old Kentucky master arrives on the scene prepared to
rescue him.

From the phenomenal record of sales, it appears that *Uncle Tom's
Cabin* was read by every reasonably literate person in the country.
Furthermore, the novel was promptly dramatized, and it became one
of the most popular plays ever produced on the American stage. In
fictional, dramatic, poetical, and musical form, the essence of the
story became the property of millions, circulating around the globe.

Mrs. Stowe's son and grandson later described the reception of
Uncle Tom's Cabin as it seemed to them: "Like the kindling of a
mighty conflagration, the sky was all aglow with the resistless tide
of emotion that swept all before it and even crossed the broad ocean,

till it seemed as if the whole world scarcely thought or talked of anything else."

From the South, a storm of wrath, denials, and vituperation descended upon *Uncle Tom's* author. At first, the novel circulated freely in the southern states, but after the bitter reaction possession of a copy in that area became dangerous. Ironically, Mrs. Stowe had hoped that her book might be a means of resolving the prolonged slavery dispute. She had attempted to present fairly both sides of the slavery controversy—the picturesque and patriarchal on the one hand, the cruel and sinister on the other.

But these concessions were insufficient to appease southern resentment. Mrs. Stowe was accused of falsifying facts. For example, it was pointed out that southern laws against the murder of slaves were stringent, and statutes usually forbade the separation of children below the age of ten from their mothers. Also, slaves as property were too valuable to be seriously maltreated.

In the North, *Uncle Tom's Cabin* received a mixed reception. The book was condemned by some because of the fear that it would stir up civil strife. For the most part, however, the novel was accepted by northern readers as a just indictment of the slavery system. As nothing else had done, it aroused the national conscience and humanitarian instincts. Its pervading religious overtones drove home the argument that slavery dealt in human souls.

An immediate effect of *Uncle Tom's Cabin* was to make impossible enforcement of the Fugitive Slave Law. Outside the South, non-co-operation with the law was virtually unanimous. More ominous, the book whipped up an enormous volume of antislavery sentiment and perhaps made inevitable the outbreak of the Civil War. Certainly it was a major cause of that catastrophic conflict. Incidentally, Charles Sumner is quoted as saying, "If *Uncle Tom's Cabin* had not been written, Abraham Lincoln could not have been elected President of the United States."

Critics have frequently debated the literary merits of *Uncle Tom's Cabin*. In historical perspective, the significance of the novel is as a sociological document rather than as a literary classic or work of art. Estimating Harriet Beecher Stowe's place in history, Kirk Monroe asserted: "Of course, the abolition of slavery was not, and could not be, accomplished by any one person, but the greatest and most far-reaching of all these influences was that of *Uncle Tom's Cabin*."

78. BATTLER FOR THE UNDERDOG

Charles Dickens' *Hard Times*

1854

By the mid nineteenth century, industrialism in its most drab and sordid form dominated English society. The air, earth, and water were polluted by factory smoke and chemical waste. Cheap, shoddy tenements, crowded and unsanitary, covered square miles around the industrial areas. Workers' hours were long, wages at the bare subsistence level, women and children unmercifully exploited. Meanwhile, government efforts to improve conditions were bitterly fought by employers and factory owners.

In the British Museum, Karl Marx was busily reading documents prepared by official commissions, combing out facts with which to indict the capitalist system and to buttress his arguments for socialism. Before Marx, however, the evils of extreme laissez-faire industrialism had been condemned by Mrs. Gaskell (describing the slums of Manchester), Charles Kingsley, Thomas Carlyle, Benjamin Disraeli, Elizabeth Barrett, Charles Dickens, and scores of lesser known literary figures. The nation's conscience was being aroused also by scathing reports of various parliamentary committees of inquiry.

All Dickens' novels have been called social tracts, critical of the dehumanizing effects of the Industrial Revolution on Great Britain. The prison scenes in *Pickwick Papers*, the horrors of the workhouse in *Oliver Twist*, the dreadful custom of imprisonment for debt in *Little Dorrit*, the cruel exploitation of child labor in *David Copperfield*, and the slum districts powerfully portrayed in *Dombey and Son, Bleak House*, and *Our Mutual Friend* are all utilized to present some aspect of the author's protest against social injustice—"man's inhumanity to man."

The Dickens work most thoroughly permeated by the spirit of social reform is *Hard Times*, a novel which deals with conditions in an industrial center known as Coketown. The depressing setting is thus described:

It was a town of red brick, or of brick that would have been red if the smoke and ashes had allowed it; but as matters stood it was a town of unnatural red and black like the painted face of a savage.

It was a town of machinery and tall chimneys, out of which interminable serpents of smoke trailed themselves for ever and ever, and never got uncoiled. It had a black canal in it, and a river that ran purple with ill-smelling dye, and vast piles of building full of windows where there was a rattling and a trembling all day long, and where the piston of the steam-engine worked monotonously up and down, like the head of an elephant in a state of melancholy madness.

Equally monotonous and devoid of pleasure and satisfaction were the lives of the people who inhabited this world of smoke, soot, grime, and noise:

It [the town] contained several large streets all very like one another, and many small streets still more like one another, inhabited by people equally like one another, who all went in and out at the same hours, with the same sound upon the same pavements, to do the same work, and to whom every day was the same as yesterday and to-morrow, and every year the counterpart of the last and the next.

The chief villain of the piece is Josiah Bounderby, "a rich man: banker, merchant, manufacturer, and what not. A big, loud man, with a stare, and a metallic laugh. . . . A man who could never sufficiently vaunt himself a self-made man. . . . A man who was the Bully of humility." The hero is Stephen Blackpool, power-loom weaver. Supporting roles are played by Thomas Gradgrind, retired wholesale hardware dealer, "the embodiment of utilitarian economic theory and its endeavor to dry up life into statistical averages"; his children, Louisa and Thomas, who suffer from his materialistic teachings; James Harthouse, a heartless young politician; M'Choakumchild, exacting schoolmaster; Sissy Jupe, daughter of a circus performer, deserted by her father; Rachael, a mill hand and Stephen's friend; and Mrs. Sparsit, Bounderby's housekeeper.

Hard Times opens in a schoolroom. The children, designated by numbers rather than names, sit like so many "little vessels . . . ready to have imperial gallons of facts poured into them until they were full to the brim." On the first day of school, Mr. Gradgrind gives the schoolmaster his instructions: "Now, what I want is, Facts. Teach these boys and girls nothing but Facts. Facts alone are wanted in life. Plant nothing else and root out everything else." There was to be no room for imagination, fancy, or emotion, only facts—a reflection of the adult world around them.

Bounderby serves as the mill owners' voice in denouncing workers who desire to improve their state. In his view, the laborers wanted "to be set up in a coach and six and to be fed on turtle soup and venison, with a gold spoon." Further, they "lived upon the best, and bought fresh butter; and insisted upon Mocha coffee, and rejected all but prime parts of beef, and yet were eternally dissatisfied and unmanageable." The Coketown industrialists constantly complained of government interference:

> They were ruined, when they were required to send labouring children to school; they were ruined when inspectors were appointed to look into their works; they were ruined, when such inspectors considered it doubtful whether they were justified in chopping people up with their machinery; they were utterly undone when it was hinted that perhaps they need not always make quite so much smoke.

As for labor unions, Bounderby held that "the united masters" should not "allow of any such class combinations." Dickens caricatures the figure of the labor organizer, Slackbridge, depicting him as a demagogue, a professional agitator, and as greedy and selfish as the employers. Nevertheless, on other occasions Dickens stated his belief in the laborers' right to organize, and, in fact, urged them to combine to force reforms from the government.

The writings of Dickens and other social-minded novelists and poets of his day eventually brought about a change of feeling among their countrymen more revolutionary than was achieved by any political party. George Bernard Shaw was one of many critics to recognize the importance of *Hard Times*. According to Shaw:

> This is Karl Marx, Carlyle, Ruskin, Morris, Carpenter, rising up against civilization itself as a disease, and declaring that it is not our disorder but our order that is horrible; that it is not our criminals but our magnates that are robbing and murdering us . . . Here you will find no more villains and heroes, but only oppressors and victims, oppressing and suffering in spite of themselves, driven by a huge machinery which grinds to pieces the people it should nourish and ennoble, and having for its directors the basest and most foolish of us instead of the noblest and more farsighted.

79. EXPLORER OF UNSEEN WORLDS

Louis Pasteur's *Mémoire sur la Fermentation Appelée Lactique*
(Treatise on the Fermentation Known as Lactic)

1857

Two centuries before Louis Pasteur's researches in bacteriology, Robert Boyle, "the father of chemistry," made the prophetic statement, "He that thoroughly understands the nature of ferments and fermentations shall probably be much better able than he that ignores them to give a fair account of divers phenomena of certain diseases (as well fevers as others) which will perhaps be never properly understood without an insight into the doctrine of fermentation." Boyle's prediction came true with the first man to understand the nature of fermentation, Louis Pasteur.

Ever since the phenomenon had first been observed by man, fermentation had been surrounded by mystery and superstition. Most widely accepted by scientists was the theory of spontaneous generation of living creatures—a theory that goes back at least to Aristotle and was treated as an unquestionable fact by Ovid, Pliny, Lucretius, and Virgil. Living matter, it was believed, came from dead substances. Virgil tells of bees swarming to life from the body of a dead bull. As late as the seventeenth century, it was the popular belief that eels, salamanders, lizards, flies, bees, and other lower forms originated by spontaneous generation. An Italian scientist, Buonanni, taught that "a certain timberwood after rotting in the sea produced worms which engendered butterflies, and these butterflies became birds," and a noted chemist handed down an infallible recipe for making mice: "Place a piece of soiled linen in a vessel; add a few grains of corn; and in twenty-one days the mice will be there, fully adult, and of both sexes."

The greatest chemist of Pasteur's time, Justus Liebig, had a somewhat different explanation for ferments. "The changes designated by the terms fermentation, decay, and putrefaction," he maintained, "are chemical transformations," a process caused by the decomposing of dead yeast cells whose bursting molecules sped up the decomposition of the fermentable matter. Liebig and many other chemists continued to hold this view for years after Pasteur's famous experiments had destroyed the idea of spontaneous generation. So overwhelming, however, was Pasteur's evidence that scientists generally promptly subscribed to the thesis, stated in defending his position before the Sorbonne, that "there is no circumstance known in which it can be affirmed that microscopic beings come into the world without germs—without parents similar to themselves."

Pasteur's epoch-making investigations into fermentation began in 1854, with his appointment, at the age of thirty-two, as dean of the science faculty at the University of Lille. There, in a center for the manufacture of alcohol, Pasteur, a trained chemist, was called upon to study the problems of the beet-root alcohol industry. Spoilage and variation in quality of the product, Pasteur found, were caused by the lactic acid formed in a living ferment. Subsequent experiments with wine, vinegar, and milk demonstrated that fermentation and souring invariably resulted from the presence of microorganisms. Further, it was shown that such organisms are neither spontaneously nor chemically created. They are always introduced from the outside, that is, from the air or by infection. Consequently, fermentation could be prevented by protection from the atmosphere and from contamination. Through the simple procedure of heating wine, milk, and other liquids at a relatively low temperature, the method now know as *pasteurization*, harmful bacteria could be killed.

His early researches on fermentation were published by Pasteur in 1857 in his *Mémoire sur la Fermentation Appelée Lactique*, "Treatise on the Fermentation Known as Lactic." Thus began the experimentation and research in a field which was to occupy Pasteur for the remainder of his life and produce one revolutionary discovery after another. The fascination which this branch of science held for him and the importance he attached to it are revealed in a letter to a friend: "I am pursuing as best I can these studies on fermentation which are of great interest, connected as they are with the impenetrable mystery of life and death."

If bacteria caused wine and milk to sour, butter to become rancid, and meat to putrefy, might they not also be responsible for disease in men and animals? This was the startling question that occurred to Joseph Lister in Scotland, after reading Pasteur's paper, and that led him on to the discovery of the cause of wound infection.

Pasteur first applied his findings on microorganisms to silk worms. Disease among the caterpillars threatened to wreck the silk industry in the south of France and elsewhere. After three years of research,

Pasteur discovered two different diseases caused by bacteria, showed the silk growers how to breed healthy stock, and restored the prosperity of the industry. Next, at the urging of the distressed farmers of France, Pasteur undertook a study of anthrax, a disease which had reached epidemic proportions and appeared likely to wipe out the nation's sheep and cattle stocks. Following the principles established by Jenner some seventy years earlier for smallpox vaccination, Pasteur prepared a weak form of virus; when injected into an animal, the attenuated virus caused a mild attack and thereafter gave immunity. Another contagious disease, chicken cholera, was prevented by similar means.

Pasteur's most spectacular triumph came in the perfection of a vaccine for rabies or hydrophobia, a dreadful disease caused by the bite of a rabid animal, previously one hundred per cent fatal to its victims.

Like all other great innovators and trail blazers, Pasteur soon found that his career inevitably engendered controversy. Jealous colleagues called him a "circus performer, a charlatan, and a clown." On one occasion, when being attacked in a meeting of the Académie des Sciences, Pasteur turned to one of his critics and said, "You are incapable of observing!" and to another, "You are incapable of reasoning!" When members of the Academy protested, Pasteur replied, "My vivacity has carried me away. I present my apologies to my colleagues." Then he hesitated—"May I, now that I have admitted my faults and made amends, make a statement in extenuation? What I said was true, absolutely true!" Pasteur is also quoted as remarking, "A man of science should think of what will be said of him in the following century, not of the insults or the praise of one day."

In view of much current discussion on the merits of applied versus pure science, it is of interest to note that Pasteur's researches were directed nearly always toward the solution of practical problems, especially those of economic importance, such as were posed to him by brewers, dairymen, vintners, and silk growers. Pasteur's pragmatic approach is revealed in his comment that "nothing is more agreeable to a man who has made science his career than to increase the number of his discoveries, but his cup of joy is full when the result of his observations is put to immediate practical use."

The genius of Pasteur lay in his understanding of scientific method, acute powers of observation, imaginativeness, and limitless patience in producing experimental proof. These extraordinary qualities enabled him to establish bacteriology on a sound basis and to transform that science into an invaluable ally of the medical world.

80. SURVIVAL THROUGH NATURAL SELECTION

Charles Darwin's *On The Origin of Species by Means of Natural Selection, or the Preservation of Favoured Races in the Struggle for Life*

1859

The basic principles of Charles Darwin's theory of evolution, as set forth in *The Origin of Species,* are today almost universally accepted in the scientific world, though controversies have raged around them for the past century.

The most important event in Darwin's life, determining his whole career, was his five-year voyage as naturalist on HMS *Beagle,* 1831–1836. During this period, the *Beagle* touched on nearly every continent and major island as she circled the world. Darwin was called upon to serve as geologist, botanist, zoologist, and general man of science—superb preparation for his subsequent life of research and writing.

Everywhere Darwin went, he made extensive collections of plants and animals, fossil and living, earth-dwelling and marine forms. He investigated, with the eye of a naturalist, the pampas of Argentina, the dry slopes of the Andes, the salt lakes and deserts of Chile and Argentina, the dense forests of Brazil, Tierra del Fuego, and Tahiti, the deforested Cape de Verde Islands, geological formations of the South American coast and mountains, active and dead volcanoes on islands and mainland, coral reefs, fossil mammals of Patagonia, extinct races of man in Peru, and the aborigines of Tierra del Fuego and Patagonia.

Of all the regions visited, none impressed Darwin so forcibly as the Galapagos Islands, five hundred miles off the west coast of South America. There he saw giant tortoises, elsewhere found only as fossils, huge lizards long since extinct in other parts of the world, enormous crabs, and sea lions. The birds on the islands were similar to those on the neighboring continent, but not identical. The strange phenomena of the Galapagos Islands, added to certain facts previously noted in South America, reinforced the ideas on evolution beginning to take shape in Darwin's mind.

Immediately upon his return to England, Darwin began keeping a notebook on evolution and collecting facts on the variation of species, thus taking the first steps toward his *Origin of Species*. In the beginning, the great riddle was how to explain the appearance and disappearance of species. Why did species originate, become modified with the passage of time, diverge into numerous branches, and often vanish from the scene completely?

The key to the mystery for Darwin came through a chance reading of Malthus' *Essay on Population*. Malthus had shown that mankind's rate of increase was retarded by such checks as disease, accidents, war, and famine. It occurred to Darwin that similar factors might keep down the populations of animals and plants. Thus was born the famous Darwinian doctrine of natural selection, struggle for existence, or survival of the fittest—the foundation stone for *The Origin of Species*.

For twenty years, Darwin's notebooks expanded to substantiate his theories. He read a vast range of literature, talked with expert breeders of animals and plants, studied skeletons of wild and domesticated birds, made crossing experiments with pigeons, and investigated seed transport.

Strong support for the principle of natural selection, Darwin thought, came from a study of "artificial selection." In the case of domestic animals and plants, man has selected and bred the varieties most advantageous to his own need, causing radical modifications from their wild ancestors. If evolution could be brought about by artificial selection, Darwin reasoned, Nature might function in the same manner, except that natural selection would result from the struggle for existence. Among all forms of life, he observed, an enormous number of individuals must perish; only a fraction of those born can survive. Some species furnish food for other species. The battle goes on ceaselessly, and the fierce competition eliminates animals and plants unfitted to survive. Variations in species take place to meet the conditions necessary for survival.

The first announcement of the theory of evolution by natural selection came in 1858, shortly after Darwin learned that a fellow scientist, Alfred Russel Wallace, carrying on natural history observations in the Malay Archipelago, had reached the same conclusions. *The Origin of Species* was published the following year.

At the outset, Darwin describes the changes that have occurred in domesticated animals and plants as a result of human control, and these are compared with variations resulting from natural selection. Wherever there is life, it is concluded, change is constant. To variation there is added the struggle for existence, and Darwin offers dramatic illustrations of how far the ability of living organisms to reproduce outstrips their capacity to survive.

The Origin of Species demonstrates the operation of the principle of natural selection in checking population increases. Some individuals in a species are stronger, can run faster, are more intelligent, more immune to disease, sexually more aggressive, or better able to endure the rigors of climate than their fellows. These will survive and reproduce as the weaker members perish. In the course of many millenniums, variations lead to the creation of essentially new species.

As expressed by Darwin: "Natural selection is daily and hourly scrutinizing, throughout the world, the slightest variations; rejecting those that are bad, preserving and adding up all that are good." In this fashion is the theory of unending evolution presented in *The Origin of Species*.

The contemporary reception of Darwin's celebrated book has been compared to "a conflagration like lightning in a full barn." If the revolutionary new theory were valid, the biblical story of creation could no longer be accepted. Church authorities immediately viewed the Darwinian thesis as dangerous to religion and roused a storm of opposition. In *The Origin of Species,* Darwin intentionally soft-pedaled any discussion of man's beginning, because he thought that any emphasis on this phase of evolution would cause his entire theory to be rejected. In a later work, *The Descent of Man,* however, a massive amount of evidence is advanced to demonstrate that the human race is also a product of evolution from lower forms.

Viewed in retrospect, Darwin's impression on nearly all major fields of learning was, and continues to be, profound. The doctrine of organic evolution has been accepted by biologists, geologists, chemists, and physicists, by anthropologists, psychologists, educators, philosophers, and sociologists, and even by historians, political scientists, and philologists.

Because he was an extraordinarily acute observer and experimenter, Darwin's findings for the most part have stood up well against the test of time. Even though his theories have been modified by the discoveries of modern science, Darwin succeeded in foreshadowing in a remarkable fashion the ideas prevailing today in genetics, paleontology, and a variety of other fields.

81. HOUSE DIVIDED

Abraham Lincoln and Stephen A. Douglas' Political Debates . . . in the Celebrated Campaign of 1858, in Illinois

1860

An important element in Abraham Lincoln's election to the Presidency of the United States in 1860 was a small book entitled *Political Debates Between Hon. Abraham Lincoln and Hon. Stephen A. Douglas in the Celebrated Campaign of 1858, in Illinois*—the only book ever personally seen through the press by Lincoln. The *Debates* became a major campaign document and a best seller, read by innumerable voters beyond the thousands who heard them delivered from the platform.

The future of slavery in the United States was the momentous issue in the Lincoln-Douglas debates of 1858. When Lincoln emerged from the debates as the undisputed leader of the western Republicans, the Union's destiny was decided. James G. Blaine, in his *Twenty Years of Congress*, described the debates as "a discussion which at the time was so interesting as to enchain the attention of a nation, in its immediate effect so striking as to effect the organization of parties, in its subsequent effect so powerful as to change the fate of millions." Abraham Lincoln, previously obscure, within a few weeks became a national figure, while Stephen A. Douglas' excellent prospects for gaining the Presidency were destroyed—results that were among the immediate causes of the Civil War.

Throughout the period from the adoption of the Constitution in 1787 to the outbreak of the Civil War in 1861, the slavery question was uppermost in the minds of the American people. As early as 1820, the status of Negro slavery in the territories of the United States had been the source of controversy between the free states of the North and the slave states of the South. A temporary solution was found in the "Missouri Compromise" of 1820, admitting Missouri as a slave state and Maine as a free state, but (except for

Missouri) excluding slavery from the Louisiana Purchase north of the southern boundary of Missouri. That agreement was nullified, however, by the Kansas-Nebraska Act of 1854, sponsored by Senator Douglas; following the concept of "popular sovereignty," the new act provided that the people of a territory would decide for themselves whether or not to admit slavery. Further bitter controversy was generated by the Supreme Court's Dred Scott decision in 1857, accepting, in essence, the right of slavery to go into the territories without restriction—rejecting both popular sovereignty and congressional control.

Thus were the issues squarely joined when Douglas returned to Illinois to seek re-election to the Senate as a Democrat, and Lincoln gave up the practice of law to accept the newly formed Republican Party's nomination for the Senate. The campaign began on June 16, 1858, when Lincoln delivered his "House Divided" speech at Springfield. After pointing out that slavery agitation "has constantly augmented," he concluded:

> In *my* opinion, it *will* not cease, until a *crisis* shall have been reached, and passed. "A house divided against itself cannot stand." I believe this government cannot endure permanently half *slave* and half *free*. I do not expect the Union to be dissolved—I do not expect the house to *fall*—but I do expect it will cease to be divided. It will become *all* one thing, or *all* the other.

Lincoln warned that a succession of recent events amounted to a conspiracy to spread slavery over the entire nation. These events included repeal of the Missouri Compromise by Congress, passage of Douglas' Kansas-Nebraska Act of 1854, the Dred Scott case decided by the Supreme Court in 1857, and approval of the Court's decision by Presidents Pierce and Buchanan.

Douglas, who regarded slavery as an affair of climate and latitude and not as a great moral issue, countered with his popular sovereignty doctrine: the principle of local self-government applied to slavery. Attacking Lincoln's assertion that the nation was in the position of a "house divided against itself," Douglas charged his opponent with attempting to array section against section—inciting a war of extermination. Douglas stated further his own strong conviction that the Negro is not the equal of the white man and insisted that the government of the United States must be based upon white supremacy.

Speaking the next day in Chicago, Lincoln, put on the defensive by Douglas' tactics, insisted that he and his party were not preaching rebellion against the Supreme Court and its decisions but would try to force the court to reverse itself. Lincoln also clarified his own attitude toward the Negro. Though agreeing that the black man is not the equal of the white man in all respects, he urged "in relation to the principle that all men are created equal, let it be as nearly reached as we can. If we cannot give freedom to every creature, let us do nothing that will impose slavery upon any other creature."

The Douglas-Lincoln debates were thus informally begun. At this stage, in response to Lincoln's challenge, Douglas agreed to a series of seven formal joint meetings, to be held in the seven congressional districts in which neither candidate had yet spoken. From August 21 to October 15, the most celebrated debates in American history were heard by an estimated total of 70,000 Illinois citizens at Ottawa, Freeport, Jonesboro, Charleston, Galesburg, Quincy, and Alton.

For his part in the debates, Lincoln hammered on the growing split in the Democratic party over the slavery question, denounced Douglas' indifference as to the right or wrong of slavery, noted the inconsistency between the principle of popular sovereignty and the effects of the Dred Scott decision, and forced Douglas to compromise himself as a presidential candidate in 1860 by taking a position which offended the South. Lincoln did not advocate abolition or the unconditional repeal of fugitive slave laws, nor did he urge political or social equality for the races. He shared with Douglas a passion for the preservation of the Union; both deplored sectionalism, and both wanted to quiet the slavery agitation.

In the November election, Lincoln won a plurality of the popular vote, but under the system of legislative election of Senators then in vogue, Douglas was chosen to succeed himself by the Democratic majority in the Illinois Legislature.

Lincoln's defeat turned out to be, in his own words, "a slip and not a fall." By the time of the 1860 conventions, his name was so well known that he could be chosen for the Republican presidential nomination. Without the reputation he had made in the debates, it is highly unlikely that Lincoln would have been selected to head the Republican ticket.

PART FOUR
MAKING THE MODERN WORLD

The tempo of change in the past one hundred years has constantly accelerated. Unquestionably, the principal factor in the rate at which the modern world has been transformed is the growth of science and technology. It is startling to realize that since 1870 there have come into existence such commonplaces of contemporary life as the electric light, the telephone, the automobile, the airplane, wireless telegraphy, radio broadcasting, moving pictures, and television.

More ominously, man has perfected weapons potentially capable, within the space of a few hours, of wiping all human life from the earth. Supersonic planes, flying at several times the speed of sound and only recently regarded as the ultimate in military aircraft are already obsolete or obsolescent. The atomic bombs which in 1945 virtually erased two Japanese cities from the map have been replaced by infinitely more devastating intercontinental ballistic missiles armed with hydrogen warheads.

Accompanying the increasing mechanization and dependence of Western culture upon technology has been a growing skepticism about the inevitableness of human progress. A Frenchman, Auguste Javary, writing in 1851, echoed the prevailing thought of his era: "If there is any idea that properly belongs to our century, it is, as it seems to me, the idea of progress, conceived as a general law of history and the future of humanity." As this beautiful dream faded, it was succeeded by what some historians describe as "the age of anxiety"—perhaps the dominant mood of the past fifty years.

How account for the changing temper of our times? Many elements played a part. The great economic depressions of the eighteen seventies and eighties and the nineteen thirties shook the liberal faith in laissez faire. The growth of giant corporations and industries, following Frederick Winslow Taylor's principles of scientific management, reduced millions of workers to mere cogs in a huge machine. What Ortega y Gasset called "the revolt of the masses" was spreading, with revolutionary sentiment in the air wherever authoritarian regimes were entrenched. Vitally affecting the Western world also was the emergence of a powerful new state in central Europe, a unified Germany, whose leaders, contemptuous of liberal democracy, adopted "blood and iron" policies. Darwinian theories of evolution undermined traditional theological beliefs. Out of the turmoil there came into common parlance such phrases as "struggle for existence," "survival of the fittest," "class struggle," "warfare between science and religion," "inequality of races," and "the will to power."

The anxieties of the nineteenth century were as nothing contrasted to those of the twentieth. Two world wars, by far the most catastrophic in history, decimated populations and devastated immense areas. Half the world's peoples came under the absolute control of totalitarian governments—powerful, ruthless, and unscrupulous. Individualism, in which eighteenth- and early-nineteenth-century philosophers had placed unlimited faith, began to lose ground to collectivism, while idealism was abandoned for materialism. Even in democracies, big government, big business, and big labor reduced the individual to relative insignificance.

Another badly battered concept, cherished by liberals of the preceding age, was that of harmony between individuals and nations. An extraordinary diversity of thought militated against genuine unity. The situation is well illustrated by a comparison of the doctrines of the three most popular and influential social philosophers of the nineteenth century: Auguste Comte, Herbert Spencer, and Karl Marx. Each advocated a social program radically at variance with the others. Comte was dedicated to the enlightened despotism of the older order; Spencer preached a businessman's individualism, a return to laissez-faire notions; and Marx was fanatically convinced that salvation could be gained only through industrial socialism.

As industrialization spread to more countries, business crises and depressions became frequent, and industrial competition raised both internal and international problems. Conflicts between employers and labor, recurring poverty and unemployment, trade wars, and the world-wide scramble for the control of raw materials were some of the earmarks of the times. The key dilemma was distribution: modern science had made possible the production of sufficient material things to feed and clothe the earth's inhabitants, but how could the wealth be effectively disseminated?

Karl Marx's *Das Kapital* maintains that these economic problems could be solved only by the abolition of the capitalist system. While approving science and technology, Marx condemned private owner-ship of the means of production as unjust, wasteful, and inefficient. He saw all history as basically a struggle between economic groups. An era of bourgeois capitalistic domination over a proletariat of wage earners would be ended, according to Marx, by a workers' revolution and the establishment of a collective or communist state. In his judgment, the proletarian revolution would occur first in the most highly industrialized nations—England, Germany, and the United States—while Russia was least ripe for revolt, a prediction of course not borne out by subsequent events.

The consequences of Marxism's conquest of Russia, China, and other vast areas, bringing an estimated one billion people under its sway, have posed urgent problems for the modern world. Actually, the present-day Soviet Union fulfills few of Marx's ideas and ideals for communism, though its leaders continue to pay lip service to Marxian dogma. Since the successful Bolshevist Revolution of 1917, Russia has been shaped primarily by Lenin, Stalin, and most recently by Khrushchev. Of the three, Lenin easily rates first as party dia-lectician and theorist. In his *The State and Revolution* Lenin sets forth his views on the relationship of the proletarian revolution to the state, on the forthcoming Russian revolution, on the dictatorship of the proletariat, and on what would happen in communist society after the bourgeois states had been overthrown. *The State and Revo-lution* is one of the fundamental works in the body of Marxist ide-ology, but Lenin's greatest service to Marxism was as organizer of a successful revolution in a backward country.

A far more moderate path to political and economic reform was chosen by the Fabians in England. The members of the Fabian Society, one of the first English socialist organizations, were com-mitted to "gradualism" rather than to socialism by revolution. Draw-ing inspiration from Henry George's *Progress and Poverty*, with its analysis of the causes of economic depressions and poverty and pro-posals for the use of political methods to remove social ills, the Fabian movement laid the groundwork for the British Labor Party. *The Fabian Essays in Socialism*, by Sidney Webb, George Bernard Shaw, and other leaders, is a classic statement of the Society's pro-gram.

Another approach to socialism, but more idealistic and further re-moved from reality, was made by Edward Bellamy in *Looking Back-ward*. Bellamy's new utopia, as he imagined that it would appear in the year 2000, was based upon the principle of complete governmental social controls, directing full use of all resources and productive powers, especially those of a scientific and technological nature. No other utopian has dreamed of a world more fully equipped with mechanical gadgets and conveniences—doubtless one of the explanations of the book's phenomenal popularity.

But socialist doctrine was far from universal in its appeal. Almost exactly a century ago, John Stuart Mill wrote *On Liberty*, a work which ranks with Milton's *Areopagitica* as a classic defense of civil liberties and cultural freedom. Mill held that governmental power over individual activities should be strictly limited, the principle of diversity ought to be respected, and there must be strong safeguards against the tyranny of the majority.

An eloquent American voice was also being raised in defense of individual freedom. Walt Whitman's *Democratic Vistas,* appearing in perhaps the most corrupt period of American political history, immediately following the Civil War, exposed, in the author's words, "the weaknesses, liabilities, and infinite corruptions of democracy." Nevertheless, Whitman never lost faith in "the free man in a just society" and remained convinced that "the democratic formula is the only safe and preservative one for coming times."

Individual liberty in extreme form was demanded by Herbert Spencer in *The Man versus the State*. The ideal society, Spencer held, is one in which each individual will enjoy as perfect a degree of freedom as is compatible with the same privilege for others. Spencer would have left the state with greatly reduced functions. It should not, he insisted, regulate industry or commerce, institute sanitary measures or charity, coin money or regulate its use, or improve harbors and waterways. In fact, the sole responsibilities remaining to the state would be the enforcement of contracts and the protection of its citizens against physical assault and foreign aggression. Those who supported socialistic legislation and theories, contended Spencer, were foolish sentimentalists merely preparing the ground for a new slavery. A firm convert to Darwinism, Spencer advocated elimination of the unfit in society, letting the weak fall by the wayside, in order to make room for the well integrated individuals who survived.

A much different concept of government's role in relation to the individual citizen was held by Woodrow Wilson, and spelled out in some detail in his *The New Freedom* and other writings. "It is still intolerable," Wilson declared, "for the government to interfere with our individual activities except where it is necessary to interfere with them in order to free them." But life had become infinitely complex, he pointed out. Consequently, "without the watchful interference, the resolute interference, of the government, there can be no fair play between individuals and such powerful institutions as the trusts." Wilson's legislative program during his first presidential term was therefore dedicated to establishing the conditions necessary for the economic freedom of the individual.

Another prophet of democracy whose conceptions have contributed tremendously to the reshaping of democratic aims and methods was John Dewey. To Dewey, democracy reaches its most successful expression in voluntary associations among individuals—any co-operative attempt at achieving some common good—rather than in governmental action. Firmly devoted to experimental procedures, Dewey believed that a democracy should make full use of the scientific method in deciding upon its policies. As he stated his creed, "freedom of inquiry, toleration of diverse views, freedom of communication, the distribution of what is found out to every individual as the ultimate intellectual consumer, are involved in the democratic as in the scientific method."

Throughout the nineteenth and well into the twentieth century there was slowly developed a radically different philosophy of government, one which would, with the possible exception of communism, ultimately offer the most dangerous challenge to the continued existence of democracy. Known in later stages as Fascism, its dark antecedents can be traced far back in political thought. The absolutism preached by Thomas Hobbes in the *Leviathan* is believed by some political scientists to have provided inspiration for twentieth-century Fascist and communist totalitarians, and a number of dictators have boasted of their spiritual descent from Niccolò Machiavelli. More directly, especially in Germany, ideological bases for Fascism were laid by such nineteenth-century philosophers as Fichte, Hegel, and Nietzsche. Fichte's identification of the individual with the state, his support of national absolute sovereignty and self-sufficiency, and his inflated ideas of the importance of German culture justify including his name among the intellectual forebears of Nazism. Likewise, Hegel's political theory, as elaborated in *The Philosophy of Right,* contains all the essential ingredients of Fascism: racialism, nationalism, the leadership principle, government by authority rather than consent, and the worship of power.

Nietzsche's case is somewhat different, for he appears to have had only contempt for the breeders of race hatreds, scheming politicians, military bullies, and self-satisfied leaders of industry. There is abundant reason to believe that if Nietzsche had lived he would have found Hitler, Goering, Goebbels, and their kind most odious. Nevertheless, because he was a bitter enemy of democracy and called for a race of supermen and because his language is frequently mystical, contradictory, and easily misinterpreted, Nietzsche has been called an apologist for violence against "herdmen," for pan-Germanic nationalism, and for the permanent enslavement of the mass of humanity to the "blond beasts" who were to be the civilizers of mankind.

Another prominent nineteenth-century writer frequently damned nowadays as an original Fascist is Thomas Carlyle. In his *Heroes and Hero-Worship, Shooting Niagara,* and *Nigger Question,* Carlyle acclaims the leadership principle, insists that the stupid masses must be subservient to the wise few, and shows boundless admiration for the strong man of action.

Also adding their bits to the devil's brew were the race theorists, notably the Comte de Gobineau, author of *Essay on the Inequality of Human Races;* Houston Stewart Chamberlain, whose biased views on race were set forth in his *Foundations of the Nineteenth Century;* and Alfred Rosenberg, author of *The Myth of the Twentieth Century,* the authoritative Nazi racial interpretation of history.

The culmination of the Fascist dream—subsequently translated into a nightmare for the rest of the world—was Adolf Hitler's *Mein Kampf.* In this work, described by Hendrik Willem Van Loon as "one of the most extraordinary historical documents of all time," Hitler plainly revealed his intentions several years before he came to power in Germany and more than a decade prior to the beginning of World War II. The threats were ignored, partly because the book was available in unexpurgated form only in the German language and partly because of the prevailing atmosphere of appeasement, wishful thinking, and peace at any price. The will to resist may also have been undermined among the Western powers by a guilt complex arising from the Versailles Treaty following World War I, with its harsh reparations imposed upon Germany. In attacking the Versailles settlement, some of Hitler's most effective propaganda was supplied by an Englishman, John Maynard Keynes, in *The Economic Consequences of the Peace.*

Another Englishman also provided inspiration for Hitler's soaring ambitions. The writings of Sir Halford Mackinder, "father of geo-politics," as interpreted by Karl Haushofer, convinced Hitler that the vast expansion which he visualized for Germany should take place principally at the expense of Russia. Also appealing to Hitler was the idea of a widely spaced population, for "military-geographi-cal" reasons, because it would be less vulnerable to an enemy—a prime feature of Mackinder's thesis in *The Geographical Pivot of History*.

Like Napoleon, Hitler fancied himself a great military commander. Though reportedly an avid reader of Karl von Clausewitz's *On War*, he failed to heed Clausewitz's warning to avoid Napoleon's fatal error in attempting a midwinter invasion of Russia. Actually, Hitler's military braggadocio more closely resembles that of two later German generals, Treitschke and Bernhardi. His obsession with submarine warfare and maritime might was doubtless a carry-over from the theories of Admiral Mahan, whose *Influence of Sea Power Upon History* had convinced pre-World War I statesmen that "whoever rules the waves rules the world."

In the mid nineteenth century, Romanticism in literature began to be displaced by stark realism—the predominant trend for the past hundred years—though it has been pointed out that "the realists are quite obviously children of the Romanticists." Even in the work of a Romantic novelist like Victor Hugo, there is much realism. Dickens in England and Balzac in France belong to the Romantic era, yet the works of both are primarily concerned with their own world, unlike those of a typical Romanticist, and are full of realistic detail.

The realistic or naturalistic novel really came into its own, how-ever, with, for example, Émile Zola and Guy de Maupassant in France, Thomas Hardy in England, and Stephen Crane, William Dean Howells, Henry James, and Frank Norris in the United States. Twentieth-century American novelists, such as Theodore Dreiser, William Faulkner, Sinclair Lewis, and Erskine Caldwell, have fol-lowed in the same tradition. Mark Twain, greatest of American hu-morists and satirists, is also essentially a realist.

Previous reference has been made to the scientific and technological advances of the past one hundred years and their bearing upon contemporary events. Among the constructive workers was an ob-scure Austrian monk named Gregor Mendel, whose experiments led to the formulation of the laws of normal heredity. A noted American scientist, Josiah Willard Gibbs, working in similar obscurity, discovered general principles upon which physical chemistry, with all of its implications for modern industry, is based. And researches of four scientists, Roentgen, Becquerel, Pierre Curie, and Marie Curie, culminated in the epoch-making discovery of X rays and the new element, radium.

In the public mind, the name that best represents the scientific revolution of the first half of the twentieth century is that of Albert Einstein. The work of great physicists and mathematicians like Einstein, Max Planck, and Niels Bohr produced, in quantum mechanics, researches in atomic structure, and the theory of relativity, new master-theorems about the physical universe, leading directly to the atomic age.

Perhaps less spectacular, but of profound significance for the human race, were the investigations of certain psychologists—Havelock Ellis, Sigmund Freud, and Ivan Petrovitch Pavlov—all trained originally in medicine.

By helping to remove Puritan restrictions upon the scientific investigation of sexual phenomena, Ellis facilitated acceptance of Freud and Jung in psychological theory, encouraged further studies in sex by such scientists as Alfred Kinsey, and in literature inspired development of the psychological novel by Joyce, Proust, and other writers.

Pavlov's most noteworthy contribution was the idea of conditioned reflexes, demonstrated through years of experiments on canine subjects. Human symptoms of neurosis, or even psychosis, could be produced in the laboratory animals by certain kinds of frustrations and induced mental confusion. Social scientists are in general agreement that the concept of conditioned reflexes developed by Pavlov goes far toward explaining habit formation in human beings and apparently irrational behavior of people under given sets of conditions.

Sigmund Freud has been characterized as one of the most complex figures in the intellectual history of the West, the subject of innumerable controversies. Whether supported or rejected, however, Freud has continued to exert a powerful influence not only on psychology and psychiatry, but on twentieth-century art, literature, biographical writing, and religious thought. In the medical field, the impact of his teachings has been felt particularly in the treatment of psychoneurotic personality disorders and the co-ordination of information about psychological and bodily functions known as psychosomatic medicine. It is perhaps appropriate that the final choice of the 111 titles considered in the present work to have shaped the Western world should be *Civilization and Its Discontents,* a product of Freud's later years. In this searching analysis, Freud presents a general view of the nature of man and calculates his chances for happiness.

82. UPHOLDER OF INDIVIDUALISM

John Stuart Mill's On Liberty
1859

Faith in the inevitable progress of liberty and freedom was more widespread in the mid nineteenth century than it was a hundred years later. Nevertheless, when John Stuart Mill wrote his famous essay *On Liberty,* a wave of reaction had been sweeping Europe, following the failure of the 1848 revolutions. Nearly everywhere in western Europe liberals were being hounded by dictatorial forces, and the outlook was bleak. Mill himself had no doubt, however, about the ultimate triumph of liberalism, and in writing *On Liberty* he was more concerned with the illiberal elements he saw rising in modern industrial society than with the repressive activities of governments.

The son of James Mill, an ardent disciple of Jeremy Bentham, John Stuart Mill had been indoctrinated early in the principles of Utilitarianism, with its philosophy of the greatest happiness of the greatest number. Essentially, *On Liberty* is concerned with one phase of the theme; Mill was convinced that man could be happy only when free.

The keynote of *On Liberty,* repeated throughout the work, is individual liberty. As Mill views it, the rights and liberties of the individual should be unlimited, except as they may infringe upon the rights of others or may endanger the safety of the community. As stated by the author:

> The only freedom which deserves the name, is that of pursuing our own good in our own way, so long as we do not attempt to deprive others of theirs, or impede their efforts to obtain it. . . . Mankind are greater gainers by suffering each other to live as seems good to themselves, than by compelling each to live as seems good to the rest.

Mill is acutely concerned about what he terms "the tyranny of the majority." Democracy as such, he thought, contains no guarantee of individual liberty, though its restrictions may appear less obvious than those of an authoritarian regime. Mill's reference is to "the tyranny of the prevailing opinion and feeling," that is, the attempt by society to impose its widely accepted ideas and practices upon those who refuse to accept them. In his eyes, social tyranny is more difficult to resist than despotic laws, because its victims have "fewer means of escape, penetrating more deeply into the details of life, and enslaving the soul itself." While recognizing the trait of human nature that makes one person want to impose his views on another, Mill argues that man is not completely free unless there is absolute freedom of opinion in scientific, moral, and theological matters.

The size of the minority group is of no significance, large or small: "If all mankind minus one, were of one opinion, and only one person were of the contrary opinion, mankind would be no more justified in silencing that one person, than he, if he had the power, would be justified in silencing mankind."

Political and social progress are highly dependent, Mill holds, upon intellectual freedom. From the free competition of ideas and opinions will emerge something approaching "truth." Since the prevailing opinion on any subject is unlikely to be completely accurate, "it is only by the collision of adverse opinions that the remainder of the truth has any chance of being supplied." Even wrong opinions have social value, serving to clarify right opinions. Mill was convinced that new ideas are always supplied by minorities and individual geniuses; consequently, these should be permitted to flourish in an "atmosphere of freedom."

The popular belief "that truth always triumphs over persecution" is rejected by Mill as "one of those pleasant falsehoods which men repeat after one another . . . but which all experience refutes." History, he says, "teems with instances of truth put down by persecution." Numerous examples are cited of successful cases of religious persecution—to demonstrate that "persecution has always succeeded, save where the heretics were too strong a party to be effectually persecuted. . . . It is a piece of idle sentimentality that truth, merely as truth, has any inherent power denied to error of prevailing against dungeon or the stake."

The "Greek ideal of self-development" strongly appeals to Mill. This is the doctrine of the full development of the individual personality, with different persons allowed to lead different lives. Society's trend toward uniformity is almost irresistible, since people "now read the same things, listen to the same things, go to the same places, have their hopes and fears directed to the same objects, have the

same rights and liberties, and the same means of asserting them."
Yet variety is essential to a civilized society, as Mill sees it.

Are there reasonable restrictions on liberty? Mill places definite
limitations on freedom of speech when it is used to incite violence.
"No one pretends," he declares, "that actions should be as free as
opinions. . . . An opinion that corn dealers are starvers of the poor,
or that private property is robbery, ought to be unmolested when
simply circulated through the press, but may justly incur punishment when delivered orally to an excited mob assembled before the
house of a corn dealer." The important distinction is, according to
Mill, that "whenever there is a definite damage, or a definite risk of
damage, either to an individual or to the public, the case is taken out
of the province of liberty, and placed in that of morality or law."

Contrary to the authoritarian belief that suppression of dissent
strengthens a state, Mill asserts that the worth of a state is basically
the worth of the individuals composing it. He concludes:

> A State which dwarfs its men, in order that they may be more docile
> instruments in its hands even for beneficial purposes, will find that
> with small men no great thing can really be accomplished; and that
> the perfection of machinery to which it has sacrificed everything, will
> in the end avail it nothing, for want of the vital power which, in order
> that the machine might work more smoothly, it has preferred to
> banish.

Innumerable admirers attest to the high rank of Mill's great work
in the literature of liberal thought. William Ebenstein, for example,
comments: "*On Liberty* has long been held to be, together with
Milton's *Areopagitica,* the finest and most moving essay on liberty
in English, perhaps in any language. As time goes on, *On Liberty*
grows in stature and meaning because its predictions have come to
life more realistically, and more tragically, than seemed possible in
the middle of the nineteenth century."

Not since the medieval era has the individual's freedom been more
imperiled, or even totally suppressed, than in many areas of today's
world. Modern totalitarians recognize no distinction between public
and private life, intent as they are upon making the individual a mere
cog in a vast, impersonal machine with every thought and action controlled and regulated by the state. The implications of Mill, with his
faith in the progress of mankind through freedom of thought, are
therefore as great for the mid twentieth century as for any period of
recorded history.

83. ROMANTIC HUMANITARIAN

Victor Marie Hugo's *Les Misérables*

1862

Following the critical and popular acclaim that greeted his *Notre Dame de Paris,* Victor Hugo spent thirty years meditating upon and writing what was to become his most famous novel, *Les Misérables,* a work heavily interlarded with sociological problems. In this tremendous fictional feat—running to 2,800 pages in the original edition—the author has successfully combined an engrossing tale and a series of dissertations on history, sociology, and psychology.

Hugo himself concedes that the story is designed to prove a thesis, stating at the outset: "The book which the reader has under his eyes at this moment, is nothing, from one end to the other, in the whole and in the details, whatever may be the interruptions, the exceptions and the failures, but the march forward from evil to good, from the unjust to the just, the false to the true, from night to day, from appetite to conscience, from decay to life, from bestiality to the sense of duty, from hell to heaven, from nothingness to God. Point of departure: matter. Goal: the spirit. A hydra at the beginning, an angel at the end." On another occasion, asked about the nature of the novel, Hugo replied, "Dante once made a Hell out of poetry, I shall write of the Hell that is the real life of our age."

The action of *Les Misérables* is set in the period 1807 to 1833, and the novel tells of Jean Valjean, an escaped convict. Beginning as an honest, simple peasant, Jean Valjean steals a loaf of bread in order to feed his sister's starving children. Caught by the police, he is condemned to five years of hard labor. When he tries, unsuccessfully, to escape, he is forced to serve nineteen years in the galleys. After his release, he finds himself socially ostracized and persecuted by the police. The result is a brief relapse into crime before he is rescued by a Christ-like bishop, Monseigneur Bienvenu. Valjean is deeply moved by the bishop's true Christian spirit and is converted.

In a turn of good fortune, after assuming another name, Jean Valjean becomes a wealthy manufacturer, a friend of the poor, and mayor of a large community. As her employer and protector, he saves Fantine, a Paris working woman, from a life of prostitution and, following her death, cares for her illegitimate daughter, Cosette.

Another spin of the wheel of fortune brings tragedy: in order to save the life of a man charged with a minor crime who has been identified as the ex-convict Jean Valjean, the real Valjean decides to surrender himself to the police. Sentenced to the galleys again, he once more escapes and loses himself in Paris under the pseudonym of Monsieur Leblanc. Cosette, posing as his granddaughter, shares his life there. But his nemesis, a police officer named Javert, is on his trail, pursues him through the streets of Paris, and forces him to take refuge in a convent. There he is befriended by the convent gardener, who helps him to make his escape, disguised as a gardener.

A new character enters: Marius de Pontmercy, a law student and son of an army officer. Marius falls in love with Cosette, whom he sees by chance in the Luxembourg Gardens with the disguised Jean Valjean. In the end, Cosette marries Marius. Jean Valjean cannot bear to give up Cosette to her young lover and dies of a broken heart, but with deep religious convictions.

Extended digressions account in part for the extreme length of *Les Misérables*. One, of 116 pages, is an essay upon the convent as an institution and upon the Christian church. Also inserted were detailed descriptions of the Battle of Waterloo and of a street insurrection, a sociological study of the Paris street urchin, and a history and description of the sewers of Paris. While these background scenes are being filled in, the story simply waits.

In *Les Misérables,* Hugo's central interest, apparent always, is social and humanitarian. The title itself, roughly translated, is "The Wretched Poor," and the novel is clearly a vehicle for Hugo's social ideas. His preface asserts that "the three problems of the age—the degradation of man through poverty, the ruin of woman through hunger, the crippling of children through ignorance—are not solved" and condemns the existence, "by virtue of law and custom, of a social damnation artificially creating hells in the midst of civilization." Much of the wretchedness depicted in *Les Misérables,* in brief, is created by man himself through vicious laws and customs.

Hugo also professes faith in popular revolution, despite its inevitable accompaniment of violence and similar evils. What the social revolutionists were seeking, he declared, is "the end of oppression . . . the end of the sword, work for man, instruction for the child, social sweetness for woman, liberty, equality, fraternity, bread for all, ideas for all, the Edenizing of the world—in short, Progress." Pity for the poor no less than love of liberty made Hugo a revolutionary.

When *Les Misérables* was published, the author was sixty years of age, but he rebelled as indignantly against injustice, oppression, and the starving misery of the great city slums as would any idealistic, inexperienced youth. Long before the actual writing of the novel, Hugo had begun to assemble notes about prison conditions, the injustice of legal penalties, and the dire effects of poverty on society. He was not alone. André Maurois points out that "it was but one more expression of the spirit of the times. George Sand, Eugène Sue, and even Alexandre Dumas and Frédéric Soulié [and, of course, Charles Dickens in England] were all of them writing novels about the sufferings of the poor."

Les Misérables was characterized by George Meredith, English novelist, as "conceived in black and white," though he acknowledged that it had the "blood and bones" of great drama and was "the masterwork of fiction in this century." The black and white label is particularly apropos in describing the *dramatis personae* created by Hugo. Each of the characters is little more than a type, in the view of a majority of critics. Nevertheless, the great mass of readers would agree with André Maurois' statement that "Jean Valjean, Bishop Myriel, Javert, Fantine, la Thénardier, Marius, Cosette, have taken their places in the not very large group of fictional characters with a universal appeal." Another Hugo biographer, Matthew Josephson, adds, "The greatest study of a child waif, outside of Dickens' novels, was that of Gavroche, in *Les Misérables.*"

From the beginning, *Les Misérables* gained an immense reading public. It became a powerful factor in the nineteenth-century movement for legal and social reform, and it is still read with emotion by European workers. Some contemporary critics, on the other hand, received the book coldly: one called Hugo "the leading demagogue of France," and another reported in alarm that "this is a dangerous book. . . . The masses can be infected by no more murderous, no more terrible, passion than a passion for the impossible."

Literary historians regard *Les Misérables* as one of the important precursors of the new theatre and the new social novel. Among Hugo's adherents were leading members of the new generation of writers, such as Zola. *Les Misérables* was admired, too, by Tolstoy and Dostoevsky and strongly influenced Russian literature of the late nineteenth and early twentieth century.

84. RIDDLE OF HEREDITY

Gregor Johann Mendel's *Versuche über Pflanzen-Hybriden*
(Experiments in Plant Hybridization)

1866

Approximately three centuries after the passing of Nicolaus Copernicus, who had won pre-eminence as the father of modern astronomy, another Catholic churchman, Gregor Johann Mendel, entered the hall of fame by founding the modern science of genetics. Further, Mendel, an Austrian, was born and spent his active career only a short distance from Copernicus' native Poland.

Heredity has long been viewed as one of the fundamental biological problems. Investigators had been accumulating a mass of facts prior to Mendel's mid-nineteenth-century experiments, but interpretations of the data were hopelessly muddled. There was no agreement except on the observation that offspring resemble one or the other parent or are intermediate between them. It is now recognized that Mendel's predecessors failed in their heredity studies because they concerned themselves with species or races as a whole, instead of concentrating attention on a few clearly defined characteristics—an error avoided by Mendel. His solution of the strange riddle of heredity came through the investigation of individual, sharply contrasted characteristics.

Questions of heredity began to interest Mendel as early as 1855. While serving as an Augustinian monk in Brünn (now Brno in Czechoslovakia), he was assigned a garden plot for his experiments in plant hybridization. During the eight years from 1856 to 1864 he observed over 10,000 specimens. After careful consideration, Mendel chose the ordinary edible pea as a subject for his experiments. The pea met several essential requirements: there are many distinct varieties, differing in inherited characteristics; it is an annual, growing a new generation year after year; and the sex physiology of the pea flower is ideal, since it is self-fertilizing, containing both male and female sex elements, and well protected from pollen contamination by other plants.

Following the selection of peas for his experiments, Mendel obtained seeds of thirty-four varieties and spent two years testing them to make certain that they were pure-breeding types. From the total,

twenty-two were chosen for experimentation. There were then singled out for study seven different pairs of contrasting characteristics:
differences in the shape of ripe seeds, round or irregular; the color of
the leaves, yellow or green; the color of the seed coat, gray-brown
or white; the form of the ripe pods, inflated or constricted between
the seeds; the color of the unripe pods, green or yellow; the position
of the flower, along the main stem or bunched at the top of the stem;
and the length of the stem, tall or dwarf.

Among the pea varieties were a giant growing seven feet tall and
dwarfs of less than two feet. Using his careful cross-fertilization or
hybridization techniques, Mendel crossed the two. The seed were
saved and planted the following season, with the astonishing result
that all produced giants. In the next generation, 'however, there
were three giants to one dwarf. Even more surprising was the fourth
generation: the seed from the dwarfs produced only dwarfs, but
the seed from the tall plants produced both giants and dwarfs.
Records showed that out of six tall plants, two would grow only
tall plants, and never anything else, while the other four would produce tall and dwarf in the proportion of three giants to one dwarf.
These ratios held true through all succeeding generations.

Similar crosses were made by Mendel with each of his other six
pairs, producing identical results. Always the parents transmitted
characteristics to their offspring in definite numerical proportions.
Mendel concluded that somewhere in the plants' hereditary constitution there were "units," now called genes, which determine character. The stronger units he described as "dominant" and the
weaker as "recessive." For example, in the first generation raised
from his crossbreds or hybrids, Mendel discovered there were 75
per cent dominants and 25 per cent recessives—indicating that tall-
ness was the dominant quality. He concluded that the recessive
genes are not destroyed or lost, but simply latent or suppressed,
ready to produce their effects upon a definite proportion of the succeeding generations. The genes remain pure indefinitely, never fusing.

The first report of his pioneer work was presented by Mendel
before the Brünn Society for the Study of Natural Science in 1865.
The following year the paper, *Versuche über Pflanzen-Hybriden* (Experiments in Plant Hybridization), was published in the Society's
proceedings. Copies went to institutions at home and abroad—with
a complete lack of response. Not until 1900, sixteen years after
Mendel's death, did the world of science become aware of the extraor-

dinary importance of Mendel's discoveries. Then, by an odd coincidence, Hugo De Vries in Holland, Karl Correns in Germany, and Erich Tschermak in Austria almost simultaneously rediscovered Mendel's long-neglected report. The Mendelian experiments were repeated, the findings confirmed, and the study of genetics thereby given a tremendous impetus toward becoming, as it is today, one of the most dynamic of the biological sciences.

Various scientists and social scientists have pointed out that the basic laws of heredity discovered in the plant and animal world are also applicable to man. Certain human abnormalities represent dominant traits and are transmitted from generation to generation. A famous example is hemophilia, a tendency to bleed, long a curse of European royalty. Experiments following Mendelian principles have thrown light on other hereditary diseases and on certain forms of nervous disorders and feeble-mindedness.

In the introduction to his 1865 report, Mendel commented: "It requires indeed some courage to undertake a labor of such far-reaching extent; this appears, however, to be the only right way by which we can finally reach the solution of a question the importance of which cannot be overestimated in connection with the history of the evolution of organic forms."

After nearly a century, the essential accuracy of Mendel's laws has been confirmed by a host of research workers on sex, cytology, embryology, albinism, genetics, eugenics, and heredity. Mendel's demonstration that, by careful selection and observation, pure types can be produced has proven of immense significance to plant and animal breeders as well as to those who, whether for the betterment or destruction of their fellow men, attempted to apply his precepts to the human being. Thus, a half century after Mendel's death, his principles of genetics, combined with the Nietzschean ideal of the superman, were mutilated and misused to provide a pseudo-scientific basis for Hitler's attempts to exterminate an entire race.

85. VOYAGE EXTRAORDINAIRE

Jules Verne's *De la Terre à la Lune*
(From the Earth to the Moon)
1865

Science and technology began to make their greatest impact on the Western world in the latter half of the nineteenth century. Factories were springing up, railroads were connecting remote areas, fast passenger liners were plying the oceans. Electric lights had been invented and were being installed, a few primitive automobiles were appearing in Paris and Vienna, and gas-filled airships were making short, experimental hops. In the new age of amazing inventions and scientific progress no idea appeared too fantastic or impossible of accomplishment. As Jules Verne confidently asserted: "What one man can imagine, another man will some day be able to achieve."

Verne and the nineteenth century were made for each other. His scores of pseudo-scientific novels—sixty-five titles in "Les Voyages Extraordinaires" series—foretelling the life of the future, were in perfect harmony with the times. No wonder his books sold in millions of copies, were translated into almost every language, made their author wealthy, and continue to provide scenario plots for highly successful moving pictures.

More incredible than the fantasies dreamed up by Verne is the fact that practically everything he predicted nearly a century ago has become commonplace today. Few, if any, other prophets in history have a comparable batting average. With unbelievable accuracy, Verne anticipated scientific headlines by at least fifty years. He imagined the helicopter, rocket, long-range cannon, searchlight, hydroplane, dirigible, submarine, radio, television, and plastics decades before any of them were even a gleam in an inventor's eye. Verne's submarine "Nautilus" was approximately the same size as a modern United States Navy submarine and traveled beneath the polar sea in a manner reminding us of Admiral Rickover's atomic-powered "Nautilus'" recent trip under the North Pole. Seventy-five years before the great 200-inch telescope was installed atop Mt. Palomar, Verne's public was reading about a super-telescope of similar size, also mounted on a mountain top. Further, he visualized harnessing of the tides, polar icecaps melted by atomic power, man's control of weather (with climates regulated and deserts turned into millions of fertile acres), interplanetary travel, and a world government centered in the United States.

The most celebrated of Verne's tales involve protracted journeys: *From the Earth to the Moon, Around the World in Eighty Days, A Journey to the Center of the Earth, Twenty Thousand Leagues Under the Sea*, etc. Of particular interest in our own era of Sputniks, space satellites, intercontinental ballistic missiles, and projected interplanetary travel is Verne's conception of outer-space travel in *From the Earth to the Moon* (1865) and *Around the Moon* (1870). The Verne project involved construction of a giant cannon, a bullet-shaped rocket car, and a telescope sixteen feet in diameter, the world's largest, with which to follow the projectile's flight.

Technical details are carefully plotted. The projectile's muzzle velocity is 36,000 feet per second, considered sufficient to reach its goal. Time, distance, the earth's rotation, and gravitational pull are minutely calculated. Three men, fully provisioned, occupy the projectile, which is nine feet in diameter. The cannon to send the rocket car on its way is located in Florida, foretelling the modern launching platforms of Cape Canaveral, also in Florida. Verne's telescope, designed to track the projectile all the way to the moon, was installed on Long's Peak in the Rockies, believed then to be the highest point in the United States.

In the sequel, *Around the Moon*, after various adventures the three space travelers reach the vicinity of the moon but do not actually land upon it. For three days they circle the moon, setting off rockets in a vain attempt to force a landing. Their momentum is too great, however, and their descent toward the earth commences. Fortunately for them they come down into the sea, and the ocean absorbs the shock of their fall, which is at the rate of 56,000 feet per second. The projectile floats, and their marvelous voyage is brought to a successful termination when they are rescued by a naval vessel.

To give his moon tale the appearance of truth and reality, Verne somewhat overloads the narrative with discourses on physics, mathematics, and astronomy and with detailed descriptions of the moon's topography as seen through the eyes of the three voyagers. For the mathematical formulas, Verne depended upon his cousin, Professor Henri Garcet, a teacher of mathematics.

Despite the meticulous attempts at scientific accuracy, modern astronomers point out numerous errors in *From the Earth to the Moon* that would have doomed the expedition to failure. Aside from inexact calculations of the moon's position, the effect of the earth's rotation, the friction of the atmosphere, gravitational influences, and similar technical details, the experts hold that the shock of departure would have been fatal to the projectile's passengers. According to Verne, the rocket attained a velocity of 54,000 feet per second in traveling about 700 feet. At this speed, the three men would have been crushed to a film, as would all objects in the projectile and the rocket itself.

Such technical flaws have not detracted from Verne's influence on inventors and scientists, an amazing number of whom have acknowledged his inspiration. Simon Lake, inventor of the submarine, credited Verne's books for many of his ideas concerning undersea craft. La Cierva, inventor of the autogiro (now the helicopter), expressed his indebtedness to the author.

Several years after Verne's death, General Louis Hubert Lyautey, French marshal, was describing proposed radical improvements in armaments. An official listening to the plans commented, "But, General, that sounds like something out of Jules Verne!" General Lyautey nodded in agreement and replied, "Yes, it *is* like Jules Verne, but for twenty years the nations that have progressed have done little else but follow Jules Verne."

86. FOUNDER OF ANTISEPTIC SURGERY

Joseph Lister's *On the Antiseptic Principle in the Practice of Surgery*

1867

Medical historians are virtually unanimous in holding that Joseph Lister represents the beginning of a new era in medicine, and that he was directly responsible for extraordinary progress in the control of human suffering.

No novelist describing an imaginary chamber of horrors could surpass in gruesome detail the actual conditions prevailing in mid-nineteenth-century hospitals. A charnel-house odor pervaded them, a stench referred to by the old surgeons as "a good healthy surgical stink," caused by the saturation of wounds with pus. Four diseases took a heavy death toll: septicemia, a form of blood poisoning caused by pathogenic bacteria in the blood stream; pyemia, with abscesses spread throughout the body; hospital gangrene, characterized by mortification of the tissues; and erysipelas, a contagious skin disease. The death rate from operations ranged from 25 to 40 per cent and was even higher for amputations. In military hospitals, fatalities were as much as 90 per cent. Napoleon's surgeon, Larrey, reported only two survivals in several thousand amputations at the hip. Excessive overcrowding led to complications in diseases. A Paris hospital had only 1,200 beds for 3,000 patients.

Joseph Lister, then a young surgeon in a Glasgow hospital, was appalled at the prevailing situation. Why, he asked, did every wound in the surgical wards become infected and suppurate? Why did so many of the surgeon's patients die, and what could be done to save them? One distinguished surgeon declared that "a man laid on the operating table in one of our surgical hospitals is exposed to more chances of death than the English soldier on the field of Waterloo."

Lack of sanitation, Lister suspected, might be one source of infections. Surgical instruments were cleaned only casually; silk threads used for stitches were carried in the surgeon's lapel or pocket; when his hands were otherwise busy, the surgeon held the operating knife in his teeth; his coat, covered with stains and blood, was seldom if ever washed; and the surgeon did not trouble to wash his hands when going from one type of disease to another or from an autopsy to a living patient. Naturally, microorganisms flourished and multiplied to claim their victims. Acting upon the theory of better sanitation, Lister's wards became models of cleanliness. Still the death rate did not decrease.

Among Lister's colleagues at Glasgow was Dr. Thomas Anderson, Professor of Chemistry. One day in conversation, Anderson drew Lister's attention to an article written by a Frenchman, Louis Pasteur, on the processes of fermentation and putrefaction. Immediately after reading the article, Lister was convinced that he had found a solution to the questions that had continually perplexed him. The germs Pasteur had discovered causing fermentation in wine could perhaps contaminate wounds, causing fermentation or pus formation in infections. "It occurred to me that decomposition in the injured part might be avoided, without excluding the air," Lister

wrote, "by applying as a dressing some material capable of destroying the life of the floating particles."

How could the deadly little organisms be killed off and excluded
from wounds? Lister learned that municipal authorities at Carlisle
had successfully used a new German invention, carbolic acid, to
disinfect and deodorize the sewage system. From his chemist friend
Anderson, Lister was able to obtain a supply of the acid for experimentation.

On August 12, 1865, Lister's great opportunity arrived. An eleven-
year-old boy had been run over by a cart and was brought to the
Glasgow hospital with a compound fracture. Lister had the wound
dressed with a piece of lint saturated in carbolic acid, set the bones,
and applied another carbolic acid dressing. The boy made a rapid
recovery, with none of the customary inflammation, pus formation, or
other complication. "This, no doubt, was a favourable case," Lister
wrote in his famous 1867 paper, "and might have done well under
ordinary treatment. But the remarkable absence of suppuration, and
the immediate conversion of the compound fracture into a simple
fracture [a fracture with unbroken skin] with a superficial sore,
were most encouraging facts."

Delighted with his success, Lister began to use carbolic acid on
everything that came into contact with the patients. Bandages, instruments, and ligatures were dipped in it; the operating table was
washed with it; the surgeon and his assistants scrubbed their hands
in a dilution of the acid; and even the air in the operating room was
sprayed with it by means of a complex apparatus. The odor of carbolic acid replaced the smell of decay and death.

Certain now that he was on the right track, Lister turned from
accident wounds to abscesses, again using the carbolic acid technique. The results obtained from treating abscesses antiseptically
were even more astonishing than those obtained from the antiseptic
treatment of compound fractures. Patients who previously almost
certainly would have succumbed from their infections made quick
and satisfactory recoveries.

The results of his experiments were reported by Lister in his notable article "On the Antiseptic Principle in the Practice of Surgery,"
published in *The Lancet,* 1867. He described the successful application of his methods in cases of compound fractures and other severe
injuries, in the antiseptic treatment of abscesses, and for the improvement of hospital sanitation. Concerning the last, he wrote:

Since the antiseptic treatment has been brought into full operation, and wounds and abscesses no longer poison the atmosphere with putrid exhalations, my wards, though in other respects under precisely the same circumstances as before, have completely changed their character; so that during the last nine months not a single instance of pyemia, hospital gangrene, or erysipelas has occurred in them.

In common with virtually all great discoveries, Lister's findings at first met with violent criticism and opposition from conservative members of his profession, especially from the senior surgeons who disliked change and who clung to the old methods of treatment. Acceptance came more readily from German, French, and other Continental physicians than from the English diehards. But long before his death, at the ripe age of eighty-five, Lister had seen world-wide approval and adoption of his ideas. Among numerous honors conferred upon him were those of being raised to the peerage by Queen Victoria in 1897 and election to the presidency of the Royal Society from 1894 to 1900.

Lister himself was responsible for continual improvements in medical practice after his original discoveries. The advances in surgery since his day have, of course, been phenomenal. Sir St. Clair Thomson, eminent London physician, pointed out that "Listerism is the foundation of the vast edifice of hygiene and preventive medicine. The investigations leading to the discovery of the control of epidemic disease; the rapid disappearance of typhoid, cholera and plague; the investigation of tropical diseases; the establishment of blood transfusion and other remedial measures were made possible by the methods of Listerian surgery."

87. PLUCK AND LUCK, OR, HOW TO MARRY THE BOSS' DAUGHTER

Horatio Alger, Jr.'s *Ragged Dick*

1867

In American folklore two concepts are firmly fixed in the national imagination. First, great statesmen are born and reared in log cabins, and, second, successful businessmen—through scrupulous honesty, tireless diligence, and unfailing loyalty—have progressed from poverty-stricken youth to wealth and eminence.

The image of Abraham Lincoln is clearly discernible in the first tradition. The other is primarily the creation of a phenomenally popular writer of books for boys in the second half of the nineteenth century. Horatio Alger, Jr., described by one critic as "the most successful writer of boys' stories in the whole of American literature," thoroughly indoctrinated millions of young Americans, in the period between the Civil War and World War I, with the belief that virtue unfailingly brings financial rewards.

In a highly materialistic sense, though on the lowest literary level, the steady stream of books that flowed from Alger's facile pen portrayed the great American dream. Every immigrant landing on our shores, the poor farm boy remote from great cities, and the ragamuffin on the street were convinced, through reading Alger, that America was the land of opportunity. By pluck and luck they could conquer poverty, defeat any villain, marry the boss' beautiful blonde daughter, and live happily ever after. Alger's influence on the formation of American youth, at the height of his popularity, has been compared with that exercised on British boyhood by a contemporary rival, George A. Henty, in the latter's demonstrations of Anglo-Saxon superiority.

Nobody knows how many books Alger really wrote. His name is found on the title pages of 135, but dozens ascribed to him were written after his death. Alger himself claimed about seventy. Likewise unknown, because of lost publishers' records, is the total number of copies sold. Estimates range from 10 million to the fantastic figure of 250 million. One fact is certain: the circulation was enormous and enough to influence the attitudes of at least two generations of American boys.

Alger began turning out juvenile books as early as 1856, but it was not until about a decade later that he found his true niche. In 1867, his *Ragged Dick; Or, Street Life in New York,* appeared serially in Oliver Optic's magazine, *Student and Schoolmate.* Considered by some critics the best of all the many Alger yarns, *Ragged Dick* caught the public fancy immediately and became immensely popular. The story is a moral but lively one, dealing with the rise to respectability of a homeless bootblack. With the luck characteristic of Alger heroes, Dick was on the Brooklyn ferryboat when he heard a distracted father, whose son had fallen overboard, exclaim in anguish, "My child! Who will save my child? A thousand—ten thousand dollars to any one who will save him!" By happy coincidence,

Dick was an expert swimmer, and he plunged in the East River immediately when he saw little Johnny rise to the surface. Soon, "strong hands seized Dick and his youthful burden, and drew them into the boat, both dripping with water."

Here began Dick's rise in the world. He received an outfit of clothes and was asked to call at the counting room of James Rockwell on Pearl Street. There he entered Mr. Rockwell's employ at the then munificent salary of ten dollars a week. Dick is early made to realize the advantage of education. A young chum, Frank Whitney, son of a gentleman of wealth who has befriended Dick, tells him, "You began in the right way when you determined never to steal, or do anything mean or dishonorable, however strongly tempted to do so. That will make people have confidence in you when they come to know you. But, in order to succeed well, you must manage to get as good an education as you can." To which Dick replies, "That's so. I never thought how awful ignorant I was till now."

On another occasion, Dick had told his patron, Mr. Whitney, that he yearned for an education, adding "I ain't always goin' to black boots for a livin'." Mr. Whitney mildly reprimanded him with the remark, "All labor is respectable, my lad, and you have no cause to be ashamed of any honest business." Thus was the spirit of the Alger books epitomized: prosperity comes with hard work, saving money, being honest, and showing proper respect for one's superiors.

The sure-fire, rags-to-riches formula developed by Alger in *Ragged Dick* was applied with no important modifications to the scores of books that followed. The hero might be a fiddler, a peddler, a newsboy, or be engaged in any of a variety of other humble occupations, but he was always a handsome lad with a cheerful, friendly disposition. His mother was invariably a widow, persecuted by an avaricious landlord. By saving a stranger's child from drowning, or from a mad dog, or a runaway horse, the hero meets a rich businessman, who proceeds to adopt him as a son. Success, of course, was constantly measured in terms of money and a home on Fifth Avenue.

Alger himself was anything except an heroic figure. The son of a tyrannical Unitarian clergyman, he, too, was trained for the ministry but showed little aptitude or liking for that calling. After several aimless years of drifting, he took up residence in and helped for a long period to manage the Newsboys' Lodging House in New York City. Through a warm-hearted, sympathetic nature, Alger won the confidence of the boys, became familiar with details of their lives, and drew upon their experiences, in highly idealized and sentimental-ized form, for his stories.

Although the hackneyed plot of an Alger book may seem inane and trite in the telling, there were enough "self-made" men in Alger's time to lend more than a shade of reality to his theme. As Alger's principal biographer, Herbert R. Mayes, observed, when Alger was writing, James B. Duke, the tobacco king, was peddling tobacco planted by his father; James A. Farrell, later president of the United States Steel Corporation, was a laboring boy in a wire mill; Henry Ford was working for two-and-a-half dollars a week as a polisher of steam engines; Julius Rosenwald, later head of Sears Roebuck, was selling chromos from door to door; George Eastman worked for three dollars a week in an insurance office; Thomas A. Edison was earning a precarious living as a newsboy; and John D. Rockefeller was out of a job. Who can say how many of these individuals and many others who started low on the ladder and climbed to dizzy heights of success were influenced and inspired by the writings of Horatio Alger, Jr., even if during their ascent they failed occasionally to adhere strictly to the elevated code of ethics constantly reiterated by Alger and his heroes? Certainly, all would have acclaimed Alger's laissez-faire philosophy for American business.

88. GREAT DEMOCRAT

Walt Whitman's *Democratic Vistas*

1871

"I can conceive of no better service in the United States hence-forth by democrats of thorough and heartfelt faith," declares Walt Whitman, "than boldly exposing the weaknesses, liabilities, and in-finite corruptions of democracy." This statement exactly describes Whitman's intention in writing *Democratic Vistas*, which one critic termed "a prose invocation to the free man in a just society."

In *Leaves of Grass* and other early writings, Whitman had been almost ecstatic in describing "the great future of this western world . . . involving such unparalleled human happiness and rational free-dom, to such unnumbered myriads, that the heart of a true *man* leaps with a mighty joy only to think of it." He dreamed of a democracy that would produce a new perfect race representing the highest standards of civilization.

By the time Whitman wrote *Democratic Vistas,* he had become disillusioned and more pessimistic about the political development of the United States. The tract was not written on any sudden impulse. Since the eighteen forties the author had been examining the failures as well as praising the victories of democracy. Corruption was rampant throughout the fifties, but the Civil War created a spirit of idealism, saved the Union, and proved that Americans on both sides were of heroic stature. Despite such promise, however, in the inevitable postwar reaction America became a mockery of Whitman's dream. Though Edgar Lee Masters may have overstated the case, there is a large element of truth in his denouncement:

> America was at this time in its foulest period. The South had been crushed and was being devoured by political buzzards. Liberty was dead in the land. A riot of crooked finance had crazed and demoralized the people. The Credit Mobilier sent forth its stink. The banks got what legislation they wanted in order to pick the pockets of the nation. Monopolies began to rise like giant poisonous weeds in the soil enriched by the blood of the youths whom Whitman had nursed.

In *Democratic Vistas,* Whitman repeatedly condemns the falsities and shortcomings of American democracy in his time. A famous passage contains both his indictment of contemporary society and indirect expressions of his hopes and ideals for the future:

> Are there, indeed, *men* here worthy the name? Are there athletes? Are there perfect women to match the generous material luxuriance? Is there a pervading atmosphere of beautiful manners? Are there crops of fine youths, and majestic old persons? Are there arts worthy of freedom and a rich people? Is there a great moral and religious civilization—the only justification of a great material one? Confess that to severe eyes, using the moral microscope upon humanity, a sort of dry and flat Sahara appears, these cities, crowded with petty grotesques, malformations, phantoms, playing meaningless antics. Confess that everywhere, in shop, street, church, theatre, barroom, official chair, are pervading flippancy and vulgarity, low cunning, infidelity—everywhere the youth puny, impudent, foppish, prematurely ripe—everywhere an abnormal libidiousness, unhealthy forms, male, female, painted, padded, dyed, chignon'd, muddy complexions, bad blood, the capacity for good motherhood decreasing or decreased, shallow notions of beauty, with a range of manners, or rather lack of manners, (considering the advantages enjoyed) probably the meanest to be seen in the world.

Government at all levels—national, state, and municipal—except the judiciary, Whitman also found "saturated in corruption, bribery, falsehood, mal-administration"; and even the judiciary was "tainted." In business the sole object was pecuniary gain.

On the strength of his examination, Whitman is forced to admit that, of various forms of government, "democracy grows rankly up the thickest, noxious, deadliest plants and fruits of all," and "in its social aspects" democracy in the New World was at that stage "an almost complete failure."

Nevertheless, Whitman did not despair or lose faith in the ultimate triumph of democracy. The ills were temporary, and he had unwavering confidence in the heroic character of the people. The American people's great potential capacity for democracy, he felt, was still unexpressed. Democracy, remarks Whitman, "is a great word, whose history, I suppose, remains unwritten, because that history has yet to be enacted." In his judgment, "the fruition of democracy, on aught like a grand scale, resides altogether in the future."

The progress of democratic institutions in America is divided by Whitman into stages: first, establishment of "the political foundation rights of immense masses of people"; the second "relates to material prosperity, wealth, produce, labor-saving machines, iron, cotton, local, State and continental railways, intercommunication and trade with all lands, steamships, mining, general employment, organization of great cities, cheap appliances for comfort, numberless technical schools, books, newspapers, a currency for money circulation, etc." The third stage, yet to come, is the development of a great national culture, an indigenous national literature, and the "growths of language, songs, operas, orations, lectures, architecture," accompanied "by a sublime and serious Religious Democracy . . . from its own interior and vital principles, reconstructing, democratizing society."

In spite of its defects, Whitman was convinced that "political democracy as it exists and practically works in America, with all its threatening evils, supplies a training school for making first-class men." He agreed with Carlyle as to the infinite value to the race of great men, and he believed that it was for the creation of great personalities that democracy exists. Commenting upon the practical workings of politics, Whitman says, "I know nothing grander, better exercise, better digestion, more positive proof of the past, the triumphant result of faith in human kind, than a well-contested national election." Young men were urged "to enter more strongly yet into politics."

A theme running through *Democratic Vistas* is that national life can never become illustrious without a national literature, and it is here, Whitman maintains, that America is sadly deficient. "America," he insists, "has yet morally and artistically originated nothing . . . I say that democracy can never prove itself beyond cavil, until it founds and luxuriantly grows its own forms of art, poems, schools, theology, replacing all that exists, or that has been produced anywhere in the past, under opposite influences." What America required, as Whitman viewed the situation, was "a new founded literature, not merely to copy and reflect existing surfaces, or pander to what is called taste—not only to amuse, pass away time, celebrate the beautiful, the refined, the past, or exhibit technical, rhythmic, or grammatical dexterity—but a literature underlying life, religious, consistent with science, handling the elements and forces with competent power, teaching and training men."

Quite apart from the question of whether people in the mass are sensible or good, or of the right of the majority to rule, Whitman concludes "that good or bad, rights or no rights, the democratic formula is the only safe and preservative one for coming times." He is both critical and idealistic. Because he had no doubt of the essential rightness of the democratic principle, Whitman's censure of its failings and shortcomings was rendered doubly effective.

89. GREATEST AMERICAN SCIENTIST

Josiah Willard Gibbs' On the Equilibrium of Heterogeneous Substances

1876–1878

Josiah Willard Gibbs is ranked by historians of science as probably the greatest of American scientists, and by world standards some would place him beside Newton and Maxwell, on the ground that he did for thermodynamics and physical chemistry what they did for mechanics and electromagnetics.

Gibbs' name means little or nothing, however, to the man on the street, and a majority of scientists recall only that he discovered a principle of great importance called the "phase rule" and expressed it in terms which hardly any of his contemporaries could understand.

Why, in view of his lofty rank in the world of science, has Gibbs remained a relatively obscure and little-known figure? Primarily the difficulty lies in his method of expression: an application of mathematical principles to a solution of fundamental problems of chemistry and physics. Reading Gibbs with any understanding requires mathematical facility of a high order. One is reminded of Sir Isaac Newton's "glacial remoteness" of style.

Yet, Gibbs, who spent his entire active career as Professor of Mathematical Physics at Yale University (1871–1903), is universally credited with creating the systems on which much of the modern industrial and scientific world rests.

The epoch-making work that assured Gibbs a permanent niche in the hall of fame is entitled *On the Equilibrium of Heterogeneous Substances,* published in three installments (1876–1878) in the *Transactions* of the Connecticut Academy of Arts and Sciences.

The nineteenth century was the age of steam. It was natural, therefore, that Gibbs should have directed his attention to thermodynamics, the branch of science dealing with the laws of one of the forms of energy—heat. The field of thermodynamics, however, was simply a springboard or point of departure for Gibbs, who went on to work out a series of universal laws governing the conditions or "phases," as he called them, of heterogeneous matter—any matter, anywhere. In his paper, Gibbs was concerned essentially with the famous "second law of thermodynamics," which, highly simplified, states that heat must always pass from hot to cold. "Heat cannot of itself, without the performance of work by some external agency, pass from a cold to a warmer body." This is the scientific reason why it is impossible to invent a "perpetual motion" machine. The "second law" has been defined as meaning simply that hot bodies cool off, that water must be raised if it is to fall, that clocks must be wound up after they have run down, that the universe is doomed to chaos.

Gibbs followed the principles laid down by Rudolph Clausius, German mathematical physicist: "The energy of the world is constant. The entropy of the world tends toward a maximum." The term "entropy," invented by Clausius, stands for a measurable quantity; when no heat reaches it, this quantity remains constant, but when heat enters or leaves the body the quantity increases or diminishes.

Gibbs undertook to demonstrate mathematically the relations existing among temperature, volume, pressure, energy, and entropy.

Another complex term as interpreted by Gibbs is "equilibrium." In the pre-Newtonian era, equilibrium was thought of as a state of balance in which all things are motionless. The idea was expanded by Newton to include motion: for example, a planet moving in orbit. A further extension was made by Gibbs, who included in the concept of equilibrium the way in which matter changes its state and identity. For example, ice becomes water, water becomes steam, steam becomes oxygen and hydrogen. Hydrogen combines with nitrogen and becomes ammonia. In brief, every process in nature means change, and Gibbs discovered the laws determining such change. To establish the number of physical phases or states possible to a specific chemical system in equilibrium, Gibbs evolved his celebrated "phase rule" or law. The fundamental importance of the discovery may be illustrated by noting that the mathematical formulas of the phase rule made it possible to determine in advance the exact concentration of various substances that were to be used in making a required mixture. The formulas stated the temperatures and pressures best suited to produce a final mixture whose components would remain in equilibrium with each other and not separate out and destroy the mixture. Using the phase rule, an experimenter could also calculate the conditions necessary for making physical separations of one or more of the substances found in a complex mixture of salts or metals.

Though Gibbs devoted only four pages to the development of the phase rule, it has been estimated that other scientists have subsequently printed over 11,000 pages describing applications of Gibbs' phase rule to mineralogy, petrology, physiology, metallurgy, and every other branch of science.

Gibbs' paper contains, as far as general principles are concerned, practically the whole of the science which is now called physical chemistry and which had scarcely been begun when it was written. The rules formulated by Gibbs have enormously facilitated and cheapened a great variety of industrial processes—for example, in metallurgy, refrigeration, fuel and power engineering, and the manufacture of synthetic chemicals, ceramics, glass, and fertilizers. Today chemistry has become the basis of the world's greatest industries, and a substantial share of the progress in the field can be traced to Gibbs' remarkable discoveries.

90. UNIVERSAL PANACEA

Henry George's *Progress and Poverty; An Inquiry into the Cause of Industrial Depressions, and of Increase of Want with Increase of Wealth; the Remedy*

1879

Henry George's famous book, *Progress and Poverty,* was dedicated "to those who, seeing the vice and misery that spring from the unequal distribution of wealth and privilege, feel the possibility of a higher social state and would strive for its attainment." Here was the keynote of George's extraordinary career.

George's knowledge of destitution and want was gained at first hand. A native of Philadelphia, in his teens he went to sea. Soon after returning home, he settled on the Pacific Coast and there rotated among a variety of occupations: typesetter, tramp, peddler, printer, shop clerk, newspaper editor, weigher in a rice mill, ship steward, inspector of gas meters, gold-seeker, farm laborer. He married young, and family responsibilities together with the intermittent nature of his jobs caused him to lead a poverty-stricken existence, at times reducing him and his family to actual hunger.

In his travels through Australia, India, England, Ireland, New York, San Francisco, and elsewhere, George was deeply disturbed by two paradoxical social phenomena: recurring depressions and dire want in the midst of plenty. On one side, he observed a few people living in luxury, and, in contrast, the great masses barely subsisting. "This association of poverty with progress," he noted, "is the enigma of our times." On the West Coast he observed thousands of men mining, building railroads, and lumbering and the ownership of these natural and man-made resources eventually falling to a favored few. Those who held the land were rich, while those who worked it and made homes on it were poor.

Gradually, George became convinced that the concentration of land into the hands of the privileged rich was the bottom cause of depressions, the primary reason why poverty invariably accompanied a country's increasing wealth. Thus was born the theme of *Progress and Poverty.*

The writing of *Progress and Poverty* was begun by George in 1877, during a serious national depression with widespread suffering and sporadic labor strikes. The manuscript was completed in eighteen months, but then had to be privately printed because no established publisher would accept it. A short while later D. Appleton agreed to take over publication. Through several favorable publicity breaks, the book quickly caught the public fancy, and it ultimately became one of the most widely distributed economic treatises of all time. How many copies have been sold in the intervening years is unknown. Estimates of world-wide circulation have varied from two to five million.

George began his book with a statement of the problem that long had "appalled and tormented" him:

> Where the conditions to which material progress everywhere tends are most fully realized—that is to say, where population is densest, wealth greatest, and the machinery of production and exchange most highly developed—we find the deepest poverty, the sharpest struggle for existence, and the most enforced idleness.

George's cure-all for this dilemma was to free the land, returning its ownership to the people as a whole. He argued that land is the physical foundation of the economic process and therefore its control is basic. To dominate land, he maintained, meant to dominate the entire economic structure. There was no more justification for private ownership and control of land than of air or sunshine. "The great cause of the inequality in the distribution of wealth is inequality in the ownership of land," George declared, for "the ownership of land is the great fundamental fact which ultimately determines the social, the political, and consequently the intellectual and moral conditions of a people."

George suggested that men should be allowed to use land in any amount they could reasonably manage, but never be permitted to hold it after their use of it had ceased. Rentals for use would be paid to the community for the expense of government. The anticipated yield would be fully adequate to make possible the abolition of all other forms of taxation—import duties, personal property taxes, inheritance taxes, and income taxes. Here would be the one and only tax—the Single Tax, a concept popularly associated with George's name. The fruits of the recommended reform were thus glowingly described by George:

> What I propose, therefore, is the simple yet sovereign remedy, which will raise wages, increase the earnings of capital, extirpate pauperism, abolish poverty, give remunerative employment to whoever wishes it,

afford free scope to human powers, lessen crime, elevate morals, and taste, and intelligence, purify government and carry civilization to yet nobler heights, is—to appropriate rent by taxation.

George's later years were spent in active promotion of his economic theories, in England, Ireland, Australia, and of course the United States. He gained a tremendous following at home and abroad, and he narrowly missed election as mayor of New York City. George was largely responsible for the rise of socialism in England, a fact confirmed by George Bernard Shaw, who wrote that "five-sixths of those who were swept with me into the great socialist revival of 1883 had been converted by Henry George."

Borrowing a phrase from Theodore Roosevelt, Gerald W. Johnson in a recent series of biographic studies categorized Henry George as belonging to "the lunatic fringe." Despite this unflattering description, Johnson concluded that George was "in many respects remarkably right" and praised his reliance "on the eventual triumph of the good sense and innate decency of the masses of men." It is George's diagnosis of the ills from which the modern economy suffers rather than his solution which remains of permanent interest and importance. His greatest accomplishment was to awaken in thinking people everywhere a hope for the abolition of poverty through public control of natural resources.

91. BIRTH OF THE NEW WOMAN

Henrik Ibsen's *Et Dukkehjem* (A Doll's House)

1879

Rebels against convention, like prophets, are seldom honored in their own countries or their own times. Society frequently exacts a high price for their refusal to conform. Henrik Ibsen, nineteenth-century dramatist, is a case in point. Few men have been so violently attacked and condemned by their contemporaries for holding unorthodox views. One consequence was that Ibsen spent twenty-seven years in voluntary exile from his native Norway.

The wrath of public opinion was brought down on Ibsen's head by his social problem plays, especially his *Pillars of Society,* exposing much ugly hypocrisy under the veneer of middle-class respectability;

Ghosts, dealing with the effects of venereal disease on heredity; and *An Enemy of the People,* revealing the spiritual laziness, backwardness, and dishonesty of a majority of citizens when their material interests are imperiled. But none of these was so fiercely resented as *A Doll's House,* in which Ibsen exploded the notion that marriage is a sacred institution. It has been noted that the slamming of the door in the final scene, when Nora departs from her husband's house, reverberated throughout Europe. "*A Doll's House* stands in relation to modern drama," comments M. C. Bradbrook, Ibsen biographer, "as Queen Victoria to the royal families of Europe. The strong divorce play and the social drama are alike descended from it."

As *A Doll's House* opens, Torvald and Nora Helmer seem an ideally happy young married couple. Nora is the spoiled pet of her husband, a vain but conscientious lawyer and a model family man. For eight years Nora has been a doll-wife, living in a doll's house, playing with her three doll-children, and treated as a child by her husband, who is quite certain that she is incapable of a serious thought. Her individuality and will are wholly subordinated to Torvald's superior masculine judgment. Nevertheless, Nora well knows the secret of her power over men, her husband in particular, and how to get what she wants by coquetry. She is as irresponsible as a child, little lies drop from her lips with the greatest of ease, and concealment and prevarication are her normal behavior.

For some time Nora has had a skeleton hidden in her closet. Its eventual exposure precipitates the crisis that wrecks the Helmers' charming home life. During the first year of their marriage, Torvald had been critically ill, and to save his life it had been necessary to take him to Italy. So opposed had he been to incurring debt that he would have died before borrowing the necessary funds. Nora had proceeded to obtain the money from a moneylender, giving the latter a promissory note, to which she had forged her father's name, and telling her husband that the money was a gift from her father. Since then she had worked at small tasks, unknown to her husband, until the debt had nearly been paid off.

Now Torvald has been appointed manager of the bank in which he is employed, and he decides to dismiss the man, Krogstad, who made the loan to Nora. Krogstad has discovered the forgery on the note and blackmails Nora by threatening to reveal the secret to her husband if he loses his job. Her intercession with Torvald on Krogstad's behalf is futile because of a forgery once committed by the moneylender himself. Furthermore, Torvald uses the occasion to lecture his wife on the heinous crime of forgery and expresses the opinion that commercial dishonesty is generally to be traced to the influence of bad mothers. Nora, her self-confidence badly shaken, realizing the seriousness of her act in the eyes of the world, begins to doubt whether she is a fit person to rear her children, and she contemplates suicide.

To redeem the forged note, Nora resolves to borrow the balance due from an old friend of the family. In her interview with him, she resorts to the feminine artifices so successful with her husband and is startled by an unexpected declaration of love. Suddenly, Nora realizes the real source of her power at home. She sees herself revealed as a silly woman and a dangerous mother, kept solely for her husband's pleasure.

Through a letter from Krogstad, which Nora is unable to intercept, Torvald eventually learns of the forgery. And with the disclosure comes Nora's final disillusionment. Instead of showing appreciation for her loyalty and struggle, as she had anticipated, Torvald turns on her in selfish fury and heaps abuse on her for disgracing him. "During all these eight years," he exclaims, "she who was my pride and my joy—a hypocrite, a liar—worse, worse—a criminal!" To which Nora retorts, "It appears that a woman has no right to spare her dying father or to save her husband's life! I do not believe that. . . . I must make up my mind which is right—society or I." Torvald indignantly declares, "No man sacrifices his honor, even for one he loves," and Nora makes the profound reply: "Millions of women have done so."

Utterly appalled by her husband's self-righteousness and his harsh judgment of her as an unscrupulous, irresponsible woman, Nora realizes that throughout her life, both with father and husband, her own personality had been subjugated and her worth as an individual ignored. Her home had been simply a doll's house. Marriage, she felt, should not be such a degradation, and there can be no true marriage where the man is everything, the wife nothing. The drama ends as Nora leaves her husband and her children, to support herself and to learn to do her own thinking.

A Doll's House brought Ibsen into wide notoriety, and the play was branded as "immoral," "an affront to all the decencies," and "full of sophistries tending to domestic misunderstandings and open insurrection." According to Janko Lavrin, another Ibsen biographer, "the morality of the period was shocked by even such a comparatively mild catastrophe of married life as Nora's flight." In Germany, a happy ending had to be substituted.

Ibsen was an ardent champion of feminine rights, and *A Doll's House* was doubtless inspired by his conviction that organized society was trying to keep woman in a state of virtual slavery—a condition completely at odds with his own profound beliefs in freedom and individualism. Despite immense progress since Ibsen's day—an emancipation which he did much to further—the status of women in the world at large remains ambiguous, unequal, and unsatisfactory.

In writing *A Doll's House*, Ibsen may have had a larger design in mind than merely a feminist propaganda play. The husband, Torvald, it has been suggested, is meant to represent conventional law and morality, and Nora represents the spirit of Ibsen himself. Supporting the theory are such lines spoken by Nora as these: about religion, "I know nothing but what the clergyman told me when I was confirmed"; about law, "I hear that the laws are different from what I thought, but I can't believe they are right"; about morality, "I am all at sea about these things," adding, "I only know that I think quite differently from you about them." These remarks appear irrelevant and remote in a debate on the inequality of the sexes—as though the dramatist was using the play as a vehicle for stating ideas broader in their implications.

92. BACILLUS HUNTER

Robert Koch's *Die Aetiologie der Tuberculose*
(The Etiology of Tuberculosis)
1882

Both Louis Pasteur and Robert Koch are frequently referred to as the "father of bacteriology." Each unquestionably is entitled to share that high honor. The difference between their respective achievements in this field is that Koch was a great research bacteriologist and Pasteur was perhaps the greatest of applied bacteriologists.

A striking similarity may be noted in the early careers of Koch in

Germany and of Edward Jenner in England. They began as country doctors, with only the crudest laboratory apparatus available for
experimental purposes. Both were extraordinarily keen observers
with a passion for scientific research. Jenner, however, was content
to spend most of his years in the rural environment where he started,
while Koch was called to Berlin, in his early thirties, and thereafter
the world was his stage.

Koch's first significant research, commenced before he gave up his
country practice at Wollstein, was on the bacteria of anthrax, a disease that had occupied much of Pasteur's time. Other bacteriologists
had noted that the blood of animals dying of anthrax contained
numerous minute, rod-shaped bodies. Working in his poorly equipped
laboratory, Koch cultivated the anthrax germs outside the animal
body, using broth as a culture medium. The artificial cultures of
anthrax bacilli were then used to inoculate mice and rabbits.
In a short time, the laboratory animals exhibited the typical symptoms of anthrax. Here was the first demonstration in medical annals
that specific bacteria or bacilli caused a specific disease.

His investigations into anthrax and other diseases, as well as researches by later scientists, were vastly aided by two new laboratory
techniques developed by Koch.

The first technique was a method of obtaining pure cultures. Before Koch, bacteriologists experienced great difficulty in separating
one variety of bacteria from another. Cultures were grown in test
tubes, usually in a beef, chicken, or mutton broth, but it was impossible to separate one kind of organism from another or to avoid
contamination from the air. One day Koch observed numerous spots
different in color and shape on a piece of potato left on his laboratory
table. Examination by microscope revealed that each spot represented a distinctive colony of bacteria. Later, Koch substituted a
sterile meat extract containing liquid gelatine for the potato. This
mixture solidified when poured on a glass plate.

A second highly valuable technique perfected by Koch was the
use of aniline dyes for staining bacteria for easier identification, a
laboratory method followed to the present day.

The scientific discovery that will always be most closely associated
with Koch's name is the isolation of the tubercle bacillus, *Mycobac-
terium tuberculosis*, the cause of the "white plague." Infinite patience had been required, for the tuberculosis germ grows slowly,
developing over a period of weeks in contrast to hours characteristic

of most bacteria. In reporting the discovery to the Berlin Physiological Society on March 24, 1882, Koch stated that he had found the rodlike bacillus present in every case and type of tuberculosis examined; the bacillus had been isolated from the human body and grown in a pure culture; and with this culture he had been able to give the disease to healthy animals. The complete story of his investigations and findings is contained in Koch's *Die Aetiologie der Tuberculose.* "In future," he asserted, "the fight against this terrible plague of mankind will deal no longer with an undetermined something, but with a tangible parasite, whose living conditions are for the most part known and can be investigated further."

Prior to Koch's epochal discovery, it was believed that tuberculosis was caused by bad heredity or weakened constitutions. Over the centuries it had established itself as the most ruthless killer in human history. In the fourth century, B.C., Hippocrates wrote that of all diseases tuberculosis caused the most suffering and the greatest number of deaths. In the nineteenth century, it was estimated that fourteen million people died in war, while thirty million succumbed to consumption. During the period of Koch's discovery, tuberculosis was the leading cause of death throughout the Western world.

By demonstrating that tuberculosis is an infectious disease caused by a specific bacillus and spread from man to man, Koch laid the groundwork for public health measures that have immeasurably reduced the incidence of the disease throughout the world.

Aged only thirty-nine when the tuberculosis discovery was announced, Koch turned his brilliant research abilities to other major diseases. During outbreaks of cholera in Egypt and India, he isolated and identified the comma-shaped bacillus causing the disease, then showed how it was transmitted by drinking water and, therefore, how it might be prevented.

For the remaining years of an extremely active life, until his death in 1910, Koch carried on teaching and research at home and engaged in scientific expeditions abroad. In the course of a dozen years, he and his assistants discovered the causes of ten important diseases. In addition to tuberculosis and cholera, these included typhoid fever, diphtheria, erysipelas, tetanus, glanders, pneumonia, epidemic meningitis, and bubonic plague.

Early in his career, Koch developed four "postulates" or rules which he and later investigators found infallible in the study of disease-producing organisms. A parasite cannot be regarded as the cause of a disease unless all these conditions are met: first, the germ must be found in large numbers in the blood and tissues of a diseased animal; second, the germ must be grown outside the body of the animal in a pure culture; third, the pure form, when injected into other animals, must produce the same disease; and, fourth, the germs must be recoverable from the blood and tissues of the second animal.

Koch covered a wide field of medical investigation and made solid contributions to many phases of his profession. Methods developed by him or his followers for the control of bacterial infections in man, animals, and plants play a major role in making modern life possible, notably through such practices as the purification of water supplies, disposal of sewage, sterilization of food supplies, measures to insure a supply of pure and clean milk, cleanliness in personal living, and techniques for the prevention of specific diseases.

93. RUGGED INDIVIDUALIST

Herbert Spencer's *The Man versus the State*

1884

Herbert Spencer and his social theories have been the source of innumerable controversies. Sociologists are now inclined to discredit or at least heavily discount his ideas; nevertheless, they recognize his pervasive influence in the history of social thought. Right or wrong, Spencer enjoyed a tremendous reputation throughout the world in the latter part of the nineteenth century, his fame transcending even that of Charles Darwin, whose evolutionary ideas he shared.

At the age of twenty-two, Spencer published his first book, *The Proper Sphere of Government*, preaching a virtually absolute laissez-faire doctrine: no meddling by the state with religion, no regulation of industry and commerce, no poor relief, no control of education, no enforcement of sanitation, no encouragement of colonization, no waging of war. The sole concern of government should be to administer justice and enforce contracts. With minor modifications, these principles were the keynote of all Spencer's voluminous writings on political and social affairs until his death at the age of eighty-three.

Forty-two years after his first book appeared, Spencer wrote *The Man versus the State,* his most famous book on politics, and a definitive summing-up of his uncompromising convictions on individualism. This work still represents one of the most effective statements ever penned of extreme laissez-faire doctrines. The work is divided into four parts, the titles indicative of the contents: "The New Toryism," "The Coming Slavery," "The Sins of Legislators," and "The Great Political Superstition."

In "The New Toryism," Spencer bitterly criticizes the English Liberals for departing from their traditional support of individualism and for having been won over to ideas of social reform and the welfare state. Historically, he points out, the Liberal consistently stood for reducing the state's power over the citizen, whereas the Tory was equally insistent upon increasing the state's prerogatives. According to Spencer:

> Dictatorial measures, rapidly multiplied, have tended continually to narrow the liberties of individuals; and have done this in a double way. Regulations have been made in yearly-growing numbers, restraining the citizen in directions where his actions were previously unchecked, and compelling actions which previously he might perform or not as he liked; and at the same time heavier public burdens, chiefly local, have further restricted his freedom, by lessening that portion of his earnings which he can spend as he pleases, and augmenting the portion taken from him to be spent as public agents please.

Spencer notes that even the Tories had become alarmed by the steady tendency toward socialism, from which he concludes that "if the present drift of things continues, it may by and by really happen that the Tories will be defenders of liberties which the Liberals, in pursuit of what they think popular welfare, trample under foot."

In the second essay, "The Coming Slavery," Spencer deplores the trend of the times toward regimentation, bureaucracy, excessive taxation, and socialism. Most social legislation, he contends, interferes with the natural process of the survival of the fittest, thus helping to perpetuate the weak and unfit. He describes the "tens of thousands" of idlers on the London streets as "simply good-for-nothings, who in one way or other live on the good-for-somethings." As people get used to the idea that the state will provide for them, individual initiative and enterprise are lost. "And obviously," says Spencer, "the more numerous governmental interventions become, the more confirmed does this habit of thought grow, and the more loud and perpetual the demands for intervention . . . the more there is generated in citizens the notion that everything is to be done for them, and nothing by them." Social welfare programs, asserts Spencer, inevitably lead down the road to socialism, and "all socialism is slavery."

Discussing "The Sins of Legislators," the author cites numerous examples of the disasters that have resulted from the meddling and muddling of politicians. Legislation and other governmental activity in social and welfare matters, in Spencer's view, do not produce progress:

> It is not to the State that we owe the multitudinous useful inventions from the spade to the telephone; it was not the State which made possible extended navigation by a developed astronomy; it was not the State which made discoveries in chemistry, physics, and the rest, which guide modern manufacturers; it was not the State which devised the machinery for producing fabrics of every kind, for transferring men and things from place to place, and for administering in a thousand ways to our comfort.

Spencer's concluding essay, "The Great Political Superstition," begins, "The great political superstition of the past was the divine right of kings. The great political superstition of the present is the divine right of parliaments." Furthermore, the author refuses to accept, as an unalterable principle, the concept of majority rule—what John Stuart Mill called "the tyranny of the majority." Neither parliaments nor majorities, maintains Spencer, have divine rights. "The fundamental assumption made by legislators and people alike, is that a majority has powers which have no bounds," but this is rejected as being incompatible with "natural rights," with the inalienable rights of the individual.

Though insisting upon narrowly circumscribing the activities of the state, Spencer is willing to concede it certain limited functions. The primary business of government, he believes, is to protect life and property. Resistance to foreign invasion is also a legitimate sphere. In general, however, along with Jefferson and Thoreau, Spencer holds that the least government is the best government.

Spencer's influence both in England and the United States was strongest in the last quarter of the nineteenth century, the era when William H. Vanderbilt could say "The public be damned." The Spencerian doctrine of irreconcilable lassez faire and elimination of the unfit in life's struggles hit a responsive chord among success-ful business and industrial leaders. *The Man versus the State* sup-plied them with ample ammunition to defend the practices of ruth-less competition and to oppose social reform. As viewed by such rugged individualists, Spencer was simply stating the true principles of social evolution and progress. And today, with increasing govern-mental control in virtually every field of human activity throughout the world, in democratic as well as totalitarian states, adherents of the Spencerian philosophy remain numerous.

94. BLOND BEASTS AND SUPERMEN

Friedrich Nietzsche's *Jenseits von Gut und Böse* (Beyond Good and Evil)
1886

Friedrich Nietzsche is the only philosopher in history accused of furnishing the philosophical basis for two world wars. In Nietzsche's condemnation of utilitarianism and democracy, his attacks upon the ethical concepts of pity and love of one's neighbors, his exaggerated praise of strong, ruthless individuals and races, and his prediction of their ultimate triumph over inferior peoples and nations, Kaiser Wilhelm II, Adolf Hitler, and Benito Mussolini found justification and support for their deeds and misdeeds.

Before World War I, German nationalists, inspired by Nietzsche, were obsessed with dreams of power, the "Will to Power," and re-ferred constantly to themselves as a "Sovereign Race." The rise of National Socialism, with its concentration camps and mass execu-tions, brought the fanatical Hitler to the top and his Nazi hordes hurled themselves upon the Third Reich in the manner, as Nietzsche expressed it, "of some herd of blond beasts of prey, a race of con-querors and rulers, which organize for war, and, through the power of organization, plunge their terrible talons into a population which, even if enormously superior in numbers, is still utterly unorganized." Hitler saw his storm-troopers as the personification of Nietzsche's Nordic man, the "blond beast," who was to found a new master race.

Nevertheless, it is highly questionable whether Nazism would have held any appeal for Nietzsche. He disliked intensely the type of industrial civilization to be observed in nineteenth-century Germany, and Nazi methods would have made the entire system even more repellent to him. Furthermore, he was a European rather than a nationalistic German, and he urgently wished for a united Europe. Nietzsche viewed with loathing the growth of Prussian militarism and the narrow chauvinism supporting the new German Empire. Thus, though his ideas were appropriated by Hitlerites and other disreputable German nationalists, their misuse was completely contrary to their author's intent.

Nietzsche himself is chiefly to blame for this paradoxical situation. Illustrative of the confusion he has created is the fact that different critics have characterized him as a poet, a prophet, a philosopher, a psychologist, a Fascist, a socialist, a radical, a conservative, an intellectual, an anti-intellectual, a Christian, a freethinker, and an atheist. Nietzsche can be quoted on either side of a variety of controversial issues. His writings are chiefly in the form of short statements, a sentence or a paragraph, presenting a single thought or brief argument, frequently as an aphorism. Often he is ambiguous, contradictory, and inconsistent.

An example is Nietzsche's views on the Jewish people:

> Among present-day Germans there is alternately the anti-French folly, the anti-Semitic folly, the anti-Polish folly, the Christian-romantic folly, the Wagnerian folly, the Teutonic folly, the Prussian folly . . . and whatever else these little obscurations of the German spirit and conscience may be called. . . . The anti-Semites do not forgive the Jews for having "spirit" and money. Anti-Semites—another name for "failures" . . . endeavor to work up all the blockhead elements of the people.

Nietzsche also praises the Jews for having produced in Jesus the "noblest man," in Spinoza the purest sage, and in the Bible the most effective moral code in the world. Elsewhere, however, he refers to the Jews as "that instinctively crafty people," and, attacking Christian ideals of morality, declares that "sin is a Jewish sentiment and a Jewish invention. . . . The Jews are the worst people in the world."

Insofar as any consistent threads can be traced through Nietzsche's writings, he was bitterly opposed to democracy, to the idea of equality, to concern for the welfare of the "herd," to Christianity (considered the morality of the weak), and to mediocrity in all forms. He was profoundly concerned with culture, especially as represented in music, art, and literature. His fertile ideas are scattered through numerous works, including *Thus Spake Zarathustra* (1883–85), a collection of discourses and sermons delivered by a mythical Persian prophet. *Beyond Good and Evil* is less obscure and somewhat broader in scope, touching upon most of the doctrines in philosophy, sociology, literature, morals, and religion for which Nietzsche is noted.

Nietzsche abhorred nationalism of any sort and preferred to think of himself as " a good European" rather than as a German. "State is the name of the coldest of all cold monsters," he maintained. "Coldly it tells lies, too; and this lie crawls out of its mouth: 'I, the state, am the people.' That is a lie!" Nietzsche admired Napoleon for his internationalism: "When Napoleon wanted to bring Europe into an association of states (the only human being who was strong enough therefor) they botched everything with their 'Wars of Liberation,' and conjured up the misfortune of the insanity of nationalities with the consequence of race-fights in such long mixed countries as Europe."

Accepting the Darwinian theory of the survival of the fittest, Nietzsche believed that the fittest of men to survive are those with the strongest wills, the aristocracy or supermen whose irresistible "will to power" is "beyond good and evil." The driving instinct of all life is the "will to power"—an instinct fully realized only in superior personalities, whose victories are gained through self-discipline and self-torture. These individuals are destined to be the supermen forming the ruling caste, without regard to nationality, though Nietzsche believed that the will to power is more inherent in some races than in others. The instinct is developed to a certain extent in everyone: "Wherever I found a living thing, there I found Will to Power; and even in the will of the servant found I the will to be master. The Will to Power—the unexhausted, procreating life-will."

One of Nietzsche's interpreters, Irwin Edman, suggests that "by 'will to power' he [Nietzsche] meant will to excellence . . . the will to aristocratic greatness . . . vulgarized by many of his later readers into a will toward brute domination. . . . By reaching 'beyond good and evil,' he meant the reaching beyond the conventional good and evil of timid, middle-class, provincial households and of village mentalities."

Certainly Nietzsche detested what he called Herd Morality, the triviality and vulgarity of nineteenth-century bourgeois life, the timid little hypocrisies of his age, mass uniformity, "the ant-hill swarming of the mongrel populace." But his image of the superman (popularly represented as a blond beast and ruthless tyrant) is unclear, nor is it made any more precise or meaningful by Nietzsche's statements that the superman has not yet existed and centuries may elapse before he appears.

Peering into the future, Nietzsche foresaw a "classical era of wars and revolutions in the twentieth century," leading to general exhaustion and the bankruptcy of all belief. The most momentous event of the future, he prophesied, would be Russia's emergence as a world power and force in shaping civilization. Ultimately, Europe would recover its strength, a stronger race of Europeans would rise from the holocaust, and from these superior individuals would evolve the superman.

95. SOCIALISM WITHOUT MARX—A DREAM OF UTOPIA

Edward Bellamy's *Looking Backward, 2000–1887*

1888

Descriptions of an ideal social state, providing happiness for all and bringing mankind into a new golden age, began at least as early as Plato's *Republic,* and the concept has inspired such works as Campanella's *City of the Sun,* Francis Bacon's *New Atlantis,* Sir Thomas More's *Utopia,* and William Morris' *News from Nowhere.* Of the numerous American writers who have tried their hand at utopian themes, only Edward Bellamy caught the public fancy to any considerable degree.

Bellamy, a native of Massachusetts, born in 1850, was a descendant of a long line of ministers. His thinking on social problems was undoubtedly influenced, at age eighteen, by a trip to Germany. "It was in the great cities of Europe," he wrote, "that my eyes were fully opened to the extent and consequences of man's inhumanity to man." Similar conditions were equally evident in the Massachusetts mill towns a few miles from Chicopee Falls, where Bellamy was reared.

When Bellamy sat down to write his masterpiece, *Looking Backward,* he had in view "a literary fantasy, a fairy tale of social felicity," but as it progressed, he said later, the novel "became the vehicle of a definite scheme of industrial reorganization."

Looking Backward, 2000–1887, tells the story of a fashionable young Bostonian, Julian West, who, after calling on his fiancée, Edith Bartlett, goes home to bed. A chronic sufferer from insomnia, he has had an underground chamber specially constructed in order to be able to sleep without being disturbed by the noises of the town. On this night of May 30, 1887, his doctor sends him into a deep sleep by mesmerism. While he remains in that comatose state, his house burns down, and West lies hidden in his hypnotic trance until the year 2000, when he is found in the course of some excavations. He is awakened by a Dr. Leete, who becomes his host. From here on, the tale is concerned with Julian West's reactions to the amazing world of the year 2000 and his romance with Dr. Leete's young and beautiful daughter, Edith, who happily turns out to be a great-granddaughter of West's nineteenth-century love.

West discovers that during the period of 113 years in which he has slept America has become a co-operative commonwealth, where all work and share alike. Private enterprise has been completely abolished; everything is run by the state. The economic situation is strikingly unlike that of 1887, for labor troubles are unknown, as are private monopolies, wasteful, competitive, and profit-seeking production, the concentration of wealth, and the accompanying social inequalities characteristic of Bellamy's nineteenth-century America. There is national ownership of all resources, and agencies of production and distribution included even food preparation and house-cleaning service. Until age 21, every citizen is in the process of education. From 21 to 45, he is a member of an industrial army, paid not in money (which has been abolished), but in vouchers accepted at state warehouses. Each person has his allotted trade or profession, assigned as far as possible on the basis of individual choice and aptitude. At 45, because of the immense advantages of the co-operative system, all except a few leaders retire and spend the rest of their lives occupying themselves as they wish.

In the model world of the year 2000, society is classless, all social inequalities have disappeared, men and women have identical status, crime is virtually unknown, peace reigns everywhere, armies and navies are no longer needed, the race has been improved eugenically, and individual security is complete.

To dramatize the virtues of his ideal republic, Bellamy used a parable depicting the absurdity of the economic system prevailing in 1887:

> By way of attempting to give the reader some general impression of the way people lived . . . I cannot do better than compare society . . . to a prodigious coach which the masses of humanity were harnessed to and dragged toilsomely along a very hilly and sandy road. The driver was hungry, and permitted no lagging. . . . Despite the difficulty of drawing the coach at all along so hard a road, the top was covered with passengers who never got down, even at the steepest ascents. These seats on top were very breezy and comfortable. Well up out of the dust, their occupants could enjoy the scenery at their leisure, or critically discuss the merits of the straining team. Naturally such places were in great demand and the competition for them was keen, every one seeking as the first end in life to secure a seat on the coach for himself and to leave it to his child after him.

A significant feature of *Looking Backward* is Bellamy's wholehearted acceptance of scientific and technological progress. Unlike some other utopian writers, he assumed that the machine is not the enemy but the potential servant of mankind. The mechanical conquest of Nature, with its immense economies in the use of human energy, has, through social control, finally placed mankind by the year 2000 in a secure world, surrounded by plenty. Bellamy's exposition of the benefits of science and invention, a belief almost universally shared by the American people, helped to make real his visualization of a utopia based on efficiency.

From the beginning *Looking Backward* was a best seller. Since its first appearance, over a million copies have been sold. As evidence of its continuing appeal, an edition of 100,000 copies was issued as recently as 1945. The work has been translated into every important language, and it has inspired innumerable other utopian writings. By 1890 the enthusiasm for Bellamy's socialistic theories resulted in the creation, in the United States and abroad, of scores of Nationalist Clubs and Bellamy Societies, some of which are still flourishing. Among Bellamy's contemporary admirers were Mark Twain, William Dean Howells, Edward Everett Hale, Frances E. Willard, Thomas Wentworth Higgins, and Thorstein Veblen.

Bellamy's theories, as set forth in *Looking Backward,* have been called "socialism without Marx, the class struggle, or the dictatorship of the proletariat." Though perhaps influenced by European socialism, Bellamy's dream was basically American, highly simplified, and appealing to the imaginations of millions who would regard

Marxist dogma with abhorrence. His voice was authentically that of the American middle class protesting against plutocracy.

The validity of Bellamy's views is still widely debated. Since his day, collectivist forms of society and the role of government have vastly expanded throughout the world, but for the most part in forms of which Bellamy would have thoroughly disapproved. Still, his writings have indicated the nature and possible extent of future governmental social controls. The central theme of *Looking Backward*— the full social use of our resources and productive powers—remains one of the great unresolved problems of modern civilization.

96. PROGRAM OF PERMEATION AND PERSUASION, OR, THE INEVITABILITY OF GRADUALNESS

George Bernard Shaw, Sidney Webb, and Others, *Fabian Essays in Socialism*

1889

It is unlikely that the Fabian Society could have come into existence anywhere except in England. While Karl Marx, Friedrich Engels, and other extremists on the Continent were preaching class war, revolution, and violence to gain their ends, the founders of Fabianism were holding to unshaken faith in gradual evolution, peaceful infiltration of the ruling classes, and strictly constitutional methods to achieve their program of economic and social reforms.

The name of the Society itself was an index of its character. The title was inspired by the Roman General Quintus Fabius Maximus Cunctator, "the Delayer," who refused to risk a direct attack on, but harried the flanks of, Hannibal's invading army. An early motto of the Fabian Society reads: "For the right moment you must wait as Fabius did, most patiently, when warring against Hannibal, though many censured his delays; but when the time comes you must strike hard, as Fabius did, or your waiting will be in vain and fruitless."

A year after Marx died, the Fabian Society was founded, in 1884. Within a short space of time it had attracted an extraordinary little group of intellectuals: George Bernard Shaw, Sidney and Beatrice Webb, Graham Wallas, Sydney Olivier, and others scarcely less distinguished. The particular form which British socialism has since taken was in large measure due to the work of these few brilliant individuals.

A clear line of descent can be traced from the late-eighteenth-century Benthamites, proclaiming the principle of "the greatest happiness for the greatest number," to the Fabians. Frank H. Underhill points out that "Bentham had set out to provide a social philosophy for the moderate practical reforming Englishmen which could take the place of the romantic revolutionary doctrines of the French Revolution; the Fabians set out to provide an alternative to the revolutionary catastrophic doctrines of Marx." The Benthamites were primarily interested in legal, constitutional, and political reform, much of which had been accomplished by the last quarter of the nineteenth century, while the first concern of the Fabians was social and economic reform.

A realistic view of British temperament and traditions likewise influenced the Fabians. They perceived the average Englishman's intense dislike and suspicion of utopian socialist schemes. George Bernard Shaw, writing about the origins of the Fabian Society, says, "We set ourselves two definite tasks: first, to provide a parliamentary program for a Prime Minister converted to Socialism as Peel was converted to Free Trade; and second, to make it as easy and matter-of-course for the ordinary respectable Englishman to be a Socialist as to be a Liberal or a Conservative."

Slow evolution from current institutions is the prevailing note in the Society's most famous publication, *Fabian Essays in Socialism,* a work based upon public lectures by Shaw, Webb, Wallas, Olivier, William Clarke, Annie Besant, and Hubert Bland. In Shaw's contribution, "The Transition to Social Democracy," discussing "the humdrum programme of the practical Social Democrat today," he mildly suggests:

> There is not one new item in it. All are applications of principles already admitted, and extensions of practices already in full activity. All have on them that stamp of the vestry which is so congenial to the British mind. None of them compel the use of the words Socialism or Revolution: at no point do they involve guillotining, declaring the Rights of Man, swearing on the altar of the country, or anything else that is supposed to be essentially un-English.

According to Shaw and other historians of the movement, a direct stimulus to Fabian Socialism came from across the Atlantic: Henry

George's *Progress and Poverty*. George's vivid descriptions of the misery of the wage earners as a class and his prescription of political methods to remove social ills provided concrete ideas for the Fabians' guidance. Firsthand acquaintance with George on his triumphant lecture tour of England stirred up further enthusiasm for his theories, though he won little support for his single-tax doctrine.

The program of action presented in *Fabian Essays in Socialism* called for reconstruction of the existing social system "in such manner as to secure the general welfare and happiness." Socialism was held to be the next step in the progress toward complete democracy. "Democracy," writes Hubert Bland, "holds socialism in its womb," and Sidney Webb adds, "Socialism is the economic side of the democratic ideal." The Fabians' most important function, they felt, was to educate English public opinion to acceptance of socialism as the logical and inevitable culmination of the democratic tide that had been running strongly since the Reform Act of 1832.

From the date of its original appearance *Fabian Essays in Socialism* has been a best seller, reprinted again and again and translated into numerous foreign languages. Though the Fabian Society's members produced hundreds of other books and tracts, the *Essays* have never been revised, except for new introductions by Shaw and Webb. In his 1908 preface, Shaw was apparently reflecting the Society's sentiments when he wrote, "Fortunately, in the main we have nothing to withdraw, nothing to regret, nothing to apologize for, and much to be proud of."

Subsequent events in the history of the Fabians and British socialism form a stirring sequel to the story of the *Fabian Essays in Socialism*. For a long time the Society had only a few hundred members and never more than a few thousand, but among these were some of the ablest propagandists using the English language—Shaw, Sidney and Beatrice Webb, H. G. Wells, and later Harold Laski and G. D. H. Cole—exercising an influence far beyond their limited numbers. Working through the leaders of the Independent Labor Party, the Fabians established close contacts with the masses of organized labor. After the First World War the Fabian program was adopted in its entirety by the Labor Party. G. D. H. Cole writes that "the recent comparative inactivity of the society is largely due to the fact that the Labour party is a larger reincarnation of Fabianism." When Labor controlled the British government in 1946, 229 of 394 Labor members of the House of Commons were members of the Fabian Society.

97. EXPONENT OF MARITIME MIGHT

Alfred T. Mahan's *The Influence of Sea Power upon History, 1660–1783*

1890

Skeptics who question whether any book can have any tremendous impact on actual events should have cited to them Admiral Alfred T. Mahan's *The Influence of Sea Power upon History*. Historians agree that the Mahan work has played a principal role in shaping the modern navies of the world.

Mahan's celebrated book was based upon a series of lectures on tactics and naval history presented in the late eighteen eighties at the newly established War College at Newport, Rhode Island.

Throughout recorded history, Mahan demonstrates, sea power has been the deciding factor in world dominion. Command of the sea is essential for any nation aspiring to leadership in world affairs and to maximum prosperity and security at home. Land powers, no matter how great, are doomed to eventual collapse and decay without access to the sea. The land, Mahan points out, "is almost all obstacle, the sea almost all open plain." A nation capable of controlling this plain by its naval power and of maintaining a strong merchant marine can exploit the world's wealth.

The Influence of Sea Power upon History is, in essence, a narration and explanation of the rise and progress of British sea power from the middle of the seventeenth century to the close of the Napoleonic wars. In the beginning, Mahan traces in broad outline the rise and decline of the great maritime powers, reviewing the elements necessary for a nation aiming to achieve first rank at sea. The prime conditions he reduces in number to six: geographical position, physical conformation, extent of territory, number of population, nature of the people, and character of the government.

Elaborating upon these elements of sea power, Mahan shows in each instance how Britain has gained strength as against her enemies. According to his interpretation, sea power is far more than naval might, comprising not only a military fleet but commercial shipping and a strong home base. It is continually emphasized that navies, campaigns, and battles are only means to an end. Neither a flourishing merchant marine nor a successful navy is possible without the other. National prosperity depends upon the combination.

In considering geographical position, a matter of first importance, Mahan stresses the vast advantages accruing to a nation so located "that it is neither forced to defend itself by land nor induced to seek extension of its territory by way of the land." A great strategic asset also is a central position with ports near major trade routes and strong bases for operations against potential enemies.

Concerning physical conformation, Mahan notes the vital significance of numerous and deep harbors. In defining extent of territory, the author means "not the total number of square miles which a country contains, but the length of its coast-line and the character of its harbors."

After describing the three natural conditions affecting sea power—geographical position, physical conformation, and extent of territory—Mahan turns to consideration of the people and their government. The size of the population is stressed, though "it is not only the grand total but the number following the sea" or available for maritime occupations that must be counted. National character and aptitudes have a direct bearing upon the development of sea power, for "almost without exception, history shows that aptitude for commercial pursuits must be a distinguishing feature of the nations that have at one time or another been great upon the sea." The ability to establish healthy colonies is likewise essential. Further, Mahan believes that the form of government and the character of rulers "have exercised a very marked influence upon the development of sea power."

Following examination of the basic features affecting sea power, Mahan devotes the remainder of his book to a detailed analysis of European naval wars of the seventeenth and eighteenth centuries. His main thesis, recurring throughout, is that, as between sea power and land power, a relentless sea blockade has always proved more decisive than an invincible land army. Mahan's objective, too, is to demonstrate the interrelation of naval and political history; he is fully convinced that the economic power which accompanies control of the sea gives its possessor a dominant position in world affairs.

World recognition for *The Influence of Sea Power upon History* came immediately upon publication, though more quickly abroad than in the United States. Within a short period, translations were available in German, Japanese, French, Italian, Russian, and Spanish. Mahan's dictums on the significance of maritime might fell upon fertile soil, fitting perfectly the belligerent tendencies of the age.

The great powers were flexing their muscles for a disastrous naval race and for the acquisition of new colonial possessions.

Under the impact of Mahan's teachings, Britain began an extensive naval reorganization program to modernize and strengthen its fleet. Kaiser Wilhelm II reported, "I am just now not reading but devouring Captain Mahan's book. It is on board all my ships." Mahan's work became the inspiration for the new German Navy. Likewise in Japan, every captain of a Japanese ship of war was served out a copy of the book as part of his equipment, and, taking their cue from Mahan, the Japanese set out to become the supreme naval power of the Far East. Through two of his disciples, Theodore Roosevelt and Henry Cabot Lodge, the influence of Mahan on the huge program of naval construction in the United States, beginning in the eighteen nineties, is also clear and marked.

Thus did Mahan live to witness the triumph of his philosophy that "whoever rules the waves rules the world," with the major nations engaged in a mad competition for sea power—all heading directly toward World War I.

98. INTERPRETER OF MAGIC AND MYTH

Sir James G. Frazer's *The Golden Bough*

1890; 1911–1915

One of the leading anthropologists of the twentieth century, Bronislaw Malinowski, states that "there are no peoples however primitive without religion and magic." As defined by Malinowski, these are "the traditional acts and observances, regarded by the natives as sacred, carried out with reverence and awe, hedged around with prohibitions and special rules of behavior. Such acts and observances are always associated with beliefs in supernatural forces, especially those of magic, or with ideas about beings, spirits, ghosts, dead ancestors, or gods."

Sir James Frazer's *The Golden Bough*, "the great codex of primitive magic," is the most comprehensive effort to date to present an integrated description and explanation of magic, religion, cults, and folklore throughout the world. For this monumental compilation, which in its final edition grew to twelve massive volumes, Frazer drew upon every available source, including especially ancient and modern literature, the researches of anthropologists, and accounts by missionaries associated with peoples of low cultural levels.

The original inspiration for *The Golden Bough* appears to have come to Frazer from reading Virgil's *Aeneid*. When Aeneas visited "the place that hath no road for living men," he carried in his hand a golden bough. Four hundred years after the *Aeneid*, Servius, a commentator, illustrated the passage by referring to a tradition, current in his time, that the bough was to be found in a wood near Aricia, by the Lake of Nemi. As told by Frazer, at the time of Imperial Rome, in a sacred grave by Lake Nemi in the green Alban hills was a hoary oak. Around it day and night prowled a grim, wary figure with sword in hand. He was Diana's priest and the King of the Woods. He was also a murderer. He had succeeded to the priesthood by plucking from the sacred oak a branch of mistletoe, the golden bough, and then slaying his predecessor. And in turn he would grow weak or unwatchful and himself be slain.

Why, asked Frazer, was this priesthood transmitted from one king to another by mortal combat? And why did the challenger first have to pluck a bough from the sacred oak? The pursuit of answers to these riddles occupied Frazer in one way or another for the greater part of a long lifetime, as he explored primitive magic, tree worship, the divinity of kings, taboo, human sacrifice, the symbol of the scapegoat, fertility rites, myths, and festivals of fire.

At the beginning of *The Golden Bough*, Frazer promises his readers "the interest and charm of a voyage of discovery, in which we shall visit strange foreign lands," and he does not disappoint them. Before the voyage is completed, the reader has ranged from Egypt to the Mexico of the Montezumas, from the Creek Indians of the American Northwest to the rice farmers of Bali. He has witnessed the black Mass of Saint Sécaire, Sicilian peasants punishing their saints for failure to end a drought, the priests of the sanctuary of Cybele gashing their bodies and bespattering the altar with their blood, hunters of India begging the elephant's pardon before killing him, the propitiation of the whale in Madagascar, a black man in Africa smearing himself with red paint so that the ghost of his victim will not recognize him, villagers of Bohemia throwing the image of death into the water to drown, the Wotyaks beating every corner of their houses to expel Satan, a scapegoat being hurled from the precipice at Cape Leucadia, a priest in ancient Mexico at the Toxcatl festival tearing the heart from the breast of a victim, and the tragic spectacle of fire festivals.

The dominant theme of *The Golden Bough* proves to be the mythology of vegetation and fertility. The priest who slays the murderer in the woods at Aricia is enacting the annual mystery of the succession of the seasons. All the green things upon the earth die in the winter and come to life again in the spring. Starting with the strange ritual of Nemi, Frazer depicts a bewildering variety of magical and religious cults devised by primitive man to stimulate and control the fertilizing work of sky, earth, sun, and rain.

Wherever the reader wanders in *The Golden Bough,* among the Babylonians, Greeks, Saxons, Sioux, Bushmen, Samoans, Eskimos, and dozens of other peoples, from the ancient world to the modern age, he encounters the Vegetable God. The mystery of the golden bough was in essence the mystery of all sacrificed gods of myth and legend: Adonis, Attis, Osiris, Odin, the Aztec Texcatlipoco, and perhaps the gods of higher religions.

The charming concept of the carefree, happy savage, imagined by Rousseau and other nature worshipers, was thoroughly demolished by Frazer. He showed primitive man living in an unbelievably complex world, harassed by taboos, besieged by demons, hopelessly entangled in ritual, and engaged in a life-or-death struggle with untamed nature.

His exhaustive researches into magic, mythology, and primitive religions convinced Frazer that man is not a rational creature. *The Golden Bough* he considered "a melancholy record of human error and folly," and he was certain of "the permanent existence of a solid layer of savagery beneath the surface of society."

The Golden Bough has been ranked as "one of the twentieth century's most influential books," leaving a lasting mark on science, literature, and the history of Western thought. Though some of Frazer's anthropological theories have been rejected by later scholars in the field, *The Golden Bough* and his other prolific writings remain invaluable source books. Among numerous writers who have drawn freely from this wellspring are Sigmund Freud, Carl Jung, James Joyce, D. H. Lawrence, W. B. Yeats, T. S. Eliot, and Robert Graves. One of the effects of *The Golden Bough* was to popularize the study of comparative religion. At the same time, the work was attacked by conservative religious leaders because of its implication that certain accepted Christian doctrines were based upon savage superstition.

99. THE GREAT WIDE OPEN SPACES

Frederick Jackson Turner's *The Significance of the Frontier in American History*

1893

"One July day in 1893, members of a learned society heard a young man in Chicago read a paper which was destined to have a more profound influence on thought about American history than any other essay or volume ever written on the subject." Thus did Charles A. Beard, one of the most highly-esteemed of American historians, evaluate Frederick Jackson Turner's *The Significance of the Frontier in American History,* originally presented before an American Historical Association meeting during the Chicago World's Fair of 1893.

The point of departure for Turner's famous essay was a statement by the Superintendent of the Census for 1890: "Up to and including 1880 the country had a frontier of settlement, but at present the unsettled area has been so broken into by isolated bodies of settlement that there can hardly be said to be a frontier line. In the discussion of its extent, its westward movement, etc., it can not, therefore, any longer have a place in the census reports." Here, as Turner saw it, was the close of a great historical epoch, the end of a four-hundred year period of continuous western advance and settlement.

In a charming, almost poetic style, Turner pictures the process of colonization: "The Atlantic frontier was compounded of fisherman, fur-trader, miner, cattle-raiser and farmer. . . . Each passed in successive waves across the continent. Stand at the Cumberland Gap and watch the procession of civilization, marching single file—the buffalo following the trail to the salt springs, the Indian, the fur-trader and hunter, the cattle-raiser, the pioneer farmer—and the frontier has passed by. Stand at South Pass in the Rockies a century later and see the same procession with wider intervals between."

According to Turner's thesis, the wilderness deeply affected the colonist. When he entered the frontier area he was a European in dress, manners, industries, and ways of thinking. Gradually, as he transformed the wilderness, it also transformed him, resulting in a distinctly American product. The ideas and ideals of the inhabitants of the frontier regions constantly reacted upon the older settled areas, dramatically altering their culture also. "To study this advance, the men who grew up in these conditions, and the political, economic, and social results of it," declared Turner, "is to study the really American part of our history."

Because of the frontier environment, Turner believed, Americanization was rapid among immigrant groups, the frontier having the effect of a great melting pot; democratic institutions were strengthened and feelings of nationalism accentuated; and such essentially American traits developed as coarseness and strength, acuteness, inventiveness, restless energy, optimism, materialism, receptivity to new ideas, masterful grasp of material things, dominant individualism, and wastefulness of natural resources. Free land acted as a magnet to attract men westward, serving as a safety valve to draw off the adventurous, the discontented, and the economic failures from the East. In Turner's words, "the existence of an area of free land, its continuous recession, and the advance of American settlement westward, explain American development."

Turner's definition of the frontier is somewhat vague. First, there was the explorer's frontier, followed immediately after by the frontiers of the missionary, the soldier, and the trader. Later came the farmer, and finally the frontiers of trade, of manufacture, and of organized communication. Most basic of all was the agricultural frontier.

The Turner "frontier hypothesis" was widely acclaimed both by historians and by scholars in other fields, and soon caught the popular fancy. A host of Turner disciples in the ensuing years produced a flood of books and articles developing the western frontier theme. Woodrow Wilson was among those fully convinced of the validity of the concept, writing, "When the great western migration began everything was modified." As late as 1932, Franklin D. Roosevelt, defending the philosophy of the New Deal, declared: "Our last frontier has long since been reached, and there is practically no more free land. . . . There is no safety valve in the form of a Western prairie to which those thrown out of work by the Eastern machines can go for a new start." The argument that the United States no longer possessed an open frontier has also been used by politicians to justify imperialist expansion and restriction of immigration.

In recent years, however, numerous critics have pointed out serious defects in the Turner thesis, especially as a complete explanation of American historical development. Doubts are expressed that democracy sprang from the forest environment of the United States, rather than being inherited from English institutions. Turner is condemned as an isolationist for failure to acknowledge the continued impact of Europe, as well as of the East Coast, on western America. The safety-valve theory has been largely discredited, as relatively few depressed industrial workers migrated from urban centers in the East to the free land of the West. Furthermore, there was little desirable free land; the best was grabbed by speculators and railroads and was available at prices beyond the means of the eastern "proletariat." Actually, census records of the past one hundred years demonstrate a steady tide of migration from the farm to the city. The American historian Fred Shannon estimated that "at least twenty farmers moved to town for each industrial laborer who moved to the land." Also questioned is Turner's claim that "in the crucible of the frontier, immigrants were Americanized, liberated and fused into a mixed race, English in neither nationality nor characteristics." In actuality, again, racial differences persisted on the frontier, as elsewhere, and were the source of serious economic and political problems.

Despite these caveats and reservations, strong support exists for Turner's basic premise that the influence of the frontier is an essential tool, though only one of many, for interpreting American history.

A fascinating new frontier conception has lately come from the pen of Walter Prescott Webb in his *The Great Frontier*. Webb's contention is that "the American frontier was but a small fragment of the Great Frontier." The Great Frontier, as defined by Webb, began with Columbus' landing in the New World. For the next four centuries practically the entire earth—"three new continents, a large part of a fourth, and thousands of islands"—was Europe's frontier, with an immeasurable impact on world history.

100. MOST CIVILIZED ENGLISHMAN

Havelock Ellis' *Studies in the Psychology of Sex* 1897–1928

When, as a young man growing up in Australia, Havelock Ellis resolved to become a physician and to devote himself to a lifetime study of sexual phenomena, the subject was surrounded by social taboos. Ellis became the first notable English writer to discuss sex openly and with detachment. Starting with Ellis and Sigmund Freud, late in the nineteenth century, human physiology began to be seriously investigated and sex to be studied not as if it were a disgraceful function but as something normally common to the human race. That everything relating to sex can be freely discussed in the mid twentieth century is owing largely to the work of these two trailblazing scientists.

Among Western peoples attitudes toward sex during the nineteenth century were doubtless conditioned by the Victorian reaction against the frank language and easy morality of the preceding century. The study of sex was the one field still shunned by scientists. Actually, the need for sexual enlightenment was as great among the medical profession as among laymen. Ignorance was equated with morality. When Thomas Henry Huxley wrote his *Elementary Lessons in Physiology* (1866), for example, he was compelled to omit the fact that the human body possessed sexual organs. Normal sexual interests and attributes were assumed to exist only among the "low," such as professional prostitutes and country boys and girls. Nevertheless, it was in such an atmosphere of severe legal restrictions, public prejudice, professional attacks, and social ostracism that Ellis carried on his research and writing.

In the Preface to his monumental *Studies in the Psychology of Sex* Ellis states the motives that impelled him to undertake the work:

As a youth, I had hoped to settle problems for those who came after; now I am quietly content if I do little more than state them. For even that, I now think, is much: it is at least the half of knowledge. In this particular field the evil of ignorance is magnified by our efforts to suppress that which can never be suppressed, though in the effort of suppression it may become perverted. I have at least tried to find out what are the facts, among normal people as well as abnormal people; for, while it seems to me that the physician's training is necessary in order to ascertain the facts, the physician for the most part only obtains the abnormal facts, which alone bring little light. I have tried to get at the facts, and, having got the facts, to look them simply and squarely in the face. If I cannot, perhaps, turn the lock myself, I bring the key which can alone in the end rightly open the door: the key of sincerity. That is my one panacea: sincerity.

After returning to England and completing his medical training, Ellis began the investigations for his *magnum opus* that were to be his chief occupation for the remainder of a long lifetime. The first volume, dealing with *Sexual Inversion,* of the seven-volume work was issued in London in 1897. Almost immediately, the publisher, George Bedborough, was arrested and charged with "having unlawfully and wickedly published and sold, and caused to be procured and to be sold, a wicked, bawdy, and scandalous, and obscene book." Found guilty, Bedborough was released on condition that he destroy the stock and publish nothing further of a similar nature. Because of the savage stand taken by the English courts, Ellis determined to issue none of the succeeding volumes in England. Instead, the entire set was brought out by F. A. Davis Company of Philadelphia, with the sale limited to members of the legal, medical, and educational professions.

While Ellis undertook a certain amount of original investigation for *Studies in the Psychology of Sex,* his writings are based chiefly upon already published work scattered through hundreds of learned journals and innumerable books, many of them exceedingly obscure. To the study of sex, Ellis proposed to apply the same objective research methods followed by other scholars in anthropology, politics, and the social sciences. His seven-volume work was directed primarily at the education of normal people—the general public—to persuade them that a rational attitude toward sex is essential to human happiness. Only incidentally was Ellis concerned with the problems of medical practitioners and with sexual abnormalities.

Studies in the Psychology of Sex has been termed "the world's first scientific encyclopedia of sexual information." Ellis' purpose, as stressed in his preface, was to discover the facts—the socially tabooed facts, knowledge of which was forbidden by church and state, the "real natural facts of sex apart from all would-be moralistic or sentimental notions."

Though he began his series with a monograph on homosexuality, Ellis emphasizes the normal expressions of sex and documents his study with a wide background of historical, psychological, and anthropological data. The physiological and psychological aspects of sex are treated as inseparable parts of a single process. Ellis was convinced that men's capacity to love sexually should be valued, developed, and educated, and is as basic to his happiness as the capacity to think, to play, to create, or to exercise any other function belonging to normal existence.

Summing up Ellis' achievements, the American psychiatrist Karl Menninger concludes:

Substantially, he did three things. In the first place, he made a careful, thorough, and honest collection of data relating to a phase of biology which the hypocrisy and prudery of medical science had, until Ellis, caused to be ignored for the most part. In the second place, he evolved and advocated a hedonistic philosophy of life tempered if not determined by the sane, scientific attitude toward sex which his studies engendered. In the third place, he presented his scientific findings and philosophical beliefs to the world with that artistic combination of directness and delicacy which made them acceptable to nonscientific readers.

H. L. Mencken described Ellis as "undoubtedly the most civilized Englishman of his generation," a judgment that has won wide concurrence. Ellis has been more responsible than any other man for lifting the Puritan taboo upon sex, for bringing the subject into the clear light of science, and for preparing public opinion for objective research in the field of sex and marriage. He paved the way for the reception of Freud and Jung in psychological theory, for such literary figures as Joyce and Proust, and for such further investigations in his own chosen field as those of Alfred Kinsey.

101. SOCIAL DARWINISM IN REVERSE

Thorstein Veblen's *The Theory of the Leisure Class*

1899

Social criticism was approached by Thorstein Veblen, remarked one commentator, "as if he were some expert envoy-extraordinary sent from a distant planet to report on human behavior." His *The Theory of the Leisure Class* is one of the most scathing criticisms of the American social order ever made by an American writer. His ruthless dissection of the behavior of the wealthy and powerful and their emulators has been compared to the scientific objectivity of a zoologist examining a cageful of monkeys. To Veblen, human behavior was the most fascinating puzzle in the world.

Veblen, the child of Norwegian immigrants, was congenitally a nonconformist, a rugged individualist, always the square peg in a round hole. Throughout his life he was plagued by poverty—probably an influence reflected in his caustic literary style. Veblen's cross-grained personality led him into continual conflict with his environment. Nevertheless, there is little dissent from the view that he was one of the, most remarkable intellects produced by America. He has been called "the last man who knew everything," and he wrote freely upon such diverse fields as history, literature, anthropology, biology, technology, and the physical sciences.

Veblen's aim in the first of his dozen books, *The Theory of the Leisure Class,* was "to discuss the place and value of the leisure class as an economic factor in modern life." The economic history of mankind is traced from the primitive cave man to the social elite of our own time. In the beginning was the Peaceful Savage, living in a Golden New Stone Age, peaceful, lazy, with few material needs or desires, and lacking any urge to compete with his neighbors for the ownership of property. This Eden was followed by the Predatory Barbarian, as population grew and hunting grounds were extended. Conflicts occurred with members of strange tribes, and enemy women were captured and brought home. With the coming of handicraft and agriculture, women, being the weaker sex, were assigned the drudgery of preparing food and clothing. Establishment of the marriage custom resulted in households with male heads. Since strength, bravery, and warlike ability were needed to conquer enemy men and to take their women, the possession of multiple wives won prestige for their owner among his fellows.

Here was Veblen's theory of the origin of individual ownership, of the idea that all useful work except hunting should be assigned to women and other inferiors and that therefore all productive labor is beneath the dignity of the lordly male. "Conspicuous leisure," as Veblen called it, was a mark of the idler's superiority, setting him apart from persons forced to work for a living.

Because man is born with an "instinct for workmanship," however, he is dissatisfied with mere idleness. Accordingly, occupations were sought that did not carry the stigma of productive industry. Natural energies, consequently, have been expended on hunting, warfare, government, priestly service, and sports. Because they brought success in achieving leisure and wealth, such characteristics as ferocity, ruthlessness, selfishness, clannishness, shrewdness, and trickery came to be admired by mankind.

Accompanying conspicuous leisure, continued Veblen's analysis, was "conspicuous consumption," the accumulation of material things, not for need, but to impress one's neighbors. Chiefs, kings, and nobles competed for more servants, more elegant palaces and castles, more expensive and showy clothes and jewels, and more exotic food and drink. The net result was "conspicuous waste," which Veblen believed to be the ruling canon of leisure-class life. Under the conspicuous-waste code, the more useless an activity, service, or article, the greater the consumer's prestige. Fox hunting, for example, is superior to deer hunting, because the deer can be eaten; a butler or footman ranks ahead of a cook; and handicrafts are preferred to the machine-made product because they are scarcer and cost more.

Eventually the benefits of conspicuous leisure, consumption, and waste were extended vicariously to women, as the chiefs came to recognize that their wives should not lower the prestige of their masters by stooping to any form of useful labor.

With the passing of time, the values of the idle aristocrats were accepted by the middle class, who set out to emulate them by every feasible means. The consequences are minutely described by Veblen. Among them were the vogue for nonfunctional but ostentatious houses, uncomfortable but fashionable clothes, lavish entertainment, and the prestige of useless learning, such as a knowledge of Greek and Latin. A glaring instance is women's fashions primarily designed to show that the wearer cannot engage in any productive activity while wearing them: the corset, the long skirt, the bustle, the hoop skirt, the high heel, the towering coiffure. In the same category are the bound feet of Chinese women and the old Russian aristocratic custom of allowing nails to grow so long and curved that all work with the hands was impossible. Styles must be continually changed to provide fresh opportunities for conspicuous waste.

The principle of conspicuous waste is illustrated also by domestic pets, such as caged birds, cats, dogs, and fast horses. Of these, the dog is the favorite; it is not only completely useless but has "special gifts of temperament" which feed the human ego. The dog, asserted Veblen, "is the filthiest of the domestic animals in his person and the nastiest in his habits. For this he makes up in a servile, fawning attitude towards his master, and a readiness to inflict damage and discomfort to all else."

So Veblen continues his dissection of human institutions. Productive pasture land is turned into a nonproductive park, and the useful cow is replaced with a herd of useless deer. Old china and silverware are collected, chiefly because they are handmade and very expensive. College sports perpetuate the "archaic virtues" of ferocity, trickery, and clannishness. Religious observances lead to the building of conspicuously wasteful churches: castlelike, large, costly, and richly decorated. Elsewhere in architecture, Veblen saw a continual conflict between beauty and pretentiousness, between simple utility and conspicuous waste. A scathing discussion of the "higher learning" concludes his social analysis.

Veblen's influence on later economists and social thinkers has been pervasive and far-reaching. As *Fortune* noted: "Every American who is skeptical of business glories, suspicious of great enrichment, contemptuous of social climbing and wealthy ostentation, dubious of the merits of keeping up with the Joneses, probably owes something to Thorstein Veblen's intellectual adventuring." Using effectively the weapon of satire, Veblen attacked such enemies of a good society as class pride and distinctions, the unsocial behavior of the wealthy, ostentation in displays of material possessions, and placing property and privilege ahead of humanity.

102. EDUCATION IN A DEMOCRACY

John Dewey's *School and Society*

1899

John Dewey has been described as the man who saved school children from dying of boredom by changing the schools of his time from places where children "prepared for life" to places where they lived. Dewey was among the first, and unquestionably the most influential, of the educational thinkers who placed primary emphasis upon the child instead of the subject matter.

The prevailing teaching method when Dewey's educational activities began in the last quarter of the nineteenth century, and against which he led a rebellion, was the ancient puritanical "pumping-in" system, in vogue for hundreds of years. As the contemporary humorist Mr. Dooley aptly summed it up: "It don't make much difference what you study, so long as you don't like it."

The times were exactly ripe for Dewey and his educational theories when, in 1894, he joined the University of Chicago faculty and established an elementary laboratory school. In the university itself and the city of Chicago, among both professional educators and the lay public, there was deep interest in educational issues. Widespread disillusionment existed about the quality of public education, and in particular many persons were concerned over widespread criticism of the Chicago schools. The era reveled in reform movements. Labor unionists, civil-service advocates, woman suffragists, free silverites, and Populists were in their heyday. Social, political, and economic dissatisfactions spilled over into attacks on an educational system that had failed to prevent serious maladjustments and dislocations. In this critical examination, chief attention was directed at the curriculum and teaching methods. The stage was set for Dewey's experimental approach, and a sympathetic audience awaited him.

The educational philosophy guiding Dewey and his followers became popularly known as "learning by doing." Instead of attempting to stuff the students' minds with facts, as if they were sponges soaking up knowledge for its own sake, and instead of ignoring individual needs or talents, Dewey stressed bodily activity, manual dexterity, the ability to do and make, individual initiative and self-reliance, the satisfaction of natural needs and desires, and the development of habits of social co-operation. Three concepts which had dominated the pre-Dewey elementary schools—the religiously motivated moral aim, the disciplinary aim, and the informational aim—were ruled out in Dewey's scheme of things.

Dewey held to the firm conviction that the foundations of a democratic way of life must be provided by the school system. Accordingly, children should not only learn facts and skills but should also become accustomed to take part in projects for the common good and learn to appreciate democratic values. Meaningless discipline would be replaced by expert guidance by teachers, under whose direction students would soon develop habits of self-discipline. The school, in Dewey's view, is primarily a social institution, and its chief function is to help the individual to discover the powers, capacities, and skills with which he is endowed and to use his talents with the greatest satisfaction to himself as well as to others.

Basic to Dewey's methodology is the idea of interest, first stated in an early work, *Interest as Related to Will*. The theory is that education must be directly related to the child's experiences and expanding concerns. Facts, figures, and ideas were not to be thrust upon him until he became curious about them. All teaching should consist of presenting practical problems to be solved by the child himself. Young children should deal with problems of personal family life, and older ones with the problems of society.

These general doctrines were presented in 1899 in *The School and Society,* one of the first and probably the most famous of dozens of books to come from Dewey's prolific pen and the most widely influential. *The School and Society* laid the groundwork for the philosophy of education which Dewey was to elaborate and extend during the next half century.

Simply linking the words "school" and "society" in the title of Dewey's book had great impact on the minds of teachers and interested laymen. It dramatized the close relationships existing between the two. Changes in teaching methods and curricula, according to Dewey, should have as their sole aim meeting the constantly changing needs of society. The twentieth-century world, with its application of scientific techniques to the means of production and distribution, great manufacturing centers, and rapid systems of communication, had in effect created a new society. It was the duty of the school to recognize the changed social situation and to modify its program to encourage vocational interests or special interests of any kind that would promote the general welfare. Also emphasized by Dewey was constant experimentation to learn more about child nature in order that the school might most effectively aid in its development.

Dewey's influence on educational thought and practice in the twentieth century is many-faceted. He materially modified the prevailing ideas of education at home and abroad. A majority of the educational principles championed by Dewey were so radical that at first they were summarily rejected. Within a few decades, however, they had become the accepted guidelines for elementary and secondary schools in the United States and in numerous foreign countries.

Nevertheless, controversies continue to rage over the validity of certain Dewey theories, in part because of misinterpretation and misunderstanding among both laymen and professional educators. For example, misapplying Dewey's idea that children should be encouraged to follow their natural interests, some "progressive" educators have carried unlimited freedom to absurd extremes. Dewey himself was not naive or softly sentimental, and he was the first to deplore the extremists in the application of his philosophy. Much of what called itself progressive education was just a travesty of what Dewey intended. His fundamental contribution to education is insistence on the principle that human beings learn to live by living and his demonstration that the inexhaustible native curiosity of the young, if properly channeled, can immensely facilitate the learning process. In an oft-quoted statement, Dewey maintained that "what the best and wisest parent wants for his own child, that must the community want for all its children."

103. WEDDING OF GEOGRAPHY AND POLITICS

Halford Mackinder's *The Geographical Pivot of History*

1904

No more improbable setting could be conceived for the dissemination of revolutionary theories than the meeting of the Royal Geographical Society in London in 1904, at which Sir Halford Mackinder, English geographer, read his famous paper, *The Geographical Pivot of History*. Filling only twenty-four printed pages, the work was no more than an ordinary pamphlet in length. But its remarkable analysis of the interrelations of geography and politics, past and present, introduced concepts that subsequently swayed the thinking of political and military leaders, economists, geographers, and historians everywhere. The paper laid the foundation for the study of geopolitics, the combination of geography and political science.

In *The Geographical Pivot of History*, Mackinder first presents his theory of closed space. He believes that "the Columbian epoch," a period of four centuries of geographic exploration and expansion, had ended at the beginning of the twentieth century. The map of the world was complete, no more important discoveries were possible, and the frontier had vanished throughout the world. Accompanying the closed system was almost limitless mobility on land and in the air, from which Mackinder concludes that the age of dominant sea power has passed and that a new age of land power has arrived.

The natural center for the new epoch, in Mackinder's view, is the greatest of land masses, the immense area of Eurasia, "the pivot region of the world's politics." The key, he says, is the inner area extending roughly from the Himalayas to the Arctic Ocean, and from the Volga to the Yangtze, stretching 2,500 miles north and south, another 2,500 miles east and west—remote from and beyond the control of sea power.

According to Mackinder's historical analysis Europe and the rest of the world have for centuries been under constant pressure from the pivot area, the "Heartland." "European civilization," declares Mackinder, "is, in a very real sense, the outcome of the secular struggle against Asiatic invasion. . . . All the settled margins of the Old World sooner or later felt the expansive force of mobile power originating in the steppe."

Projecting his story to our own times, Mackinder sees the pivot area, now occupied by Soviet Russia, as increasing its weight in world affairs, coincident with its growth in economic and military power. The geographical significance of the pivot position, he thinks, would not be altered if it were inhabited by some other people than the Russians.

Pursuing further the idea of the pivot area, Mackinder points out that the Heartland is set in the center of the "World Island." Europe, Asia, and Africa are not three continents but one: the World Island. Except for its vast dimensions and the impossibility of circumnavigating it, the World Island does not differ from other islands. Two thirds of the earth's land area and seven eights of its population are contained in the World Island.

Mackinder reduces his arguments concerning the fundamental importance of the Heartland and World Island to a formula: "Who rules East Europe commands the Heartland; Who rules the Heartland commands the World Islands; Who rules the World Island commands the World."

To prevent any one nation, especially Russia or Germany, from becoming supreme in the Heartland following World War I, Mackinder advocated setting up a barrier of buffer states from the Baltic to the Black Sea. The Paris Peace Conference led to the establishment of such a chain of independent states, but the buffer zone failed to accomplish its purpose. First Germany and then Russia broke through the barrier.

Nowhere were Mackinder's theories more avidly seized upon than in Nazi Germany. As interpreted by Karl Haushofer, prolific writer on geopolitical subjects, Mackinder's root idea of the Heartland set in a World Island dominated German political thought for two decades, 1925–1945. From Haushofer's pen came innumerable books, pamphlets, and articles expounding upon two key words in Nazi ideology: *Geopolitik,* dealing with the dynamics of world political change, and *Lebensraum,* the German people's need for living space, for room to grow and expand.

Haushofer freely admitted his debt to Mackinder, on one occasion describing the 1904 paper as "the greatest of all geographical world views," adding that he had never "seen anything greater than these few pages of a geopolitical masterpiece." Haushofer was obsessed with the conviction that Germany must win control of the Heartland, and his teachings were strongly endorsed and supported by the German General Staff. The signing of the Nazi-Soviet Pact in 1939 seemed to make his dream come true, but the whole policy was tossed overboard when Hitler ordered his generals to attack the Soviet Union.

The spread of geopolitical doctrines has not been confined, of course, to Germany. The Russians, for example, have been no less active. A flourishing geopolitical bureau, Moscow's Institute for World Economy and Politics, has long concerned itself with the conflict between the United States and the World Island, which the Soviet Union hopes to dominate.

The validity of Mackinder's geographical theories has been frequently debated, and flaws have been shown in his arguments. An obvious defect is the author's failure to take into account the immense potentialities of air might. Another blind side is his lack of realization of the increasingly powerful place occupied by the United States; Mackinder could see the Americas only as peripheral, "merely satellites of the old continent."

Unquestionably, details of Mackinder's views are susceptible to criticism and refutation, but without destroying his essential premises. He was the first geographer to provide a global concept of the world and its affairs. Upon Mackinder's ideas of the world and its regions, the foundations of modern geography are laid.

104. EFFICIENCY EXPERT

Frederick Winslow Taylor's *Principles of Scientific Management*

1911

William James, noted psychologist, once wrote that " a man who energizes below his normal maximum fails by just so much to profit by his chances in life; and a nation filled with such men is inferior to a nation run at higher pressure. *The problem is then, how can men be trained up to their most useful pitch of energy?"* Finding an answer to the question posed by James occupied most of the active career of Frederick Winslow Taylor, "Father of Scientific Management." The findings are reported in Taylor's *Principles of Scientific Management* and numerous other writings.

During Taylor's lifetime (1856–1915), American industry had grown from small pioneering units to consolidated, nationwide combinations. Conflicts between organized capital on one hand and organized labor on the other were increasingly acute. Despite vast industrial expansion and accompanying great wealth, the manual worker's position was little improved.

Taylor's intimate firsthand acquaintance with industrial processes was an invaluable asset to him in formulating scientific principles of management—a virgin area when he began. As a young man, he entered the Midvale Steel Works, where for eleven years he worked successively as laborer, shop clerk, head of toolroom, gang boss, assistant foreman, foreman of machine shop, master mechanic, chief draftsman, and chief engineer. At Midvale, the workmen planned how fast each job should be done and limited the speed of the machines so that the output was actually about one-third of the potential production.

With his promotion to foreman, Taylor began the first of thousands of experiments designed to increase the workers' efficiency. His methods were sufficiently successful for him to be asked to introduce them into the Bethlehem Steel Company operations. At the Bethlehem plant was a great yard, over two miles wide, in which six hundred men shoveled sand, coal, and ashes. After systematic analysis of the work, Taylor concluded that a shovel holding a twenty-one pound load was ideal; a lighter load required too high speed, and a heavier load placed too great a strain on the worker. Further, a man could load his material more quickly and easily from an iron or wooden floor than from the ground. Time, distance, and motion studies were applied to these and other aspects of the job. By determining accurately the elements of the work, selecting and training the men, offering bonuses to workmen who fully co-operated, and planning each day's work in advance, Taylor achieved spectacular results: the number of laborers was reduced from 600 to 140; the average number of tons handled per day per man was increased from 16 to 59; the average earnings per man per day rose by 60 per cent; the average cost of handling a ton decreased from 7.2 to 3.3 cents.

Later, the same principles were applied to bricklaying, to the folding, sealing, and stamping of letters in a publishing house, and to innumerable other business and industrial processes, with similar striking improvements in production.

Taylor's guiding rule, as stated by him, was: "When starting an experiment in any field question everything, question the very foundation upon which the art rests, question the simplest, the most self-evident, the most universally accepted facts; prove everything."

Drawing on his experience and experiments at the Midvale Steel Works and at Bethlehem Steel Company and as a consultant for many corporations, Taylor developed a formula that industrial engineers have continued to follow: first, specify a given task (there should be no room for misunderstanding by the worker of the results expected of him, determined by an analysis of the sequence of operations through which the whole job must pass); second, allow a definite time—determined by a stopwatch time study or from standard data; third, prescribe a definite method for the worker to follow in performing his operation.

To guarantee high wages for workers and a profit for employers, it is essential, Taylor argued, to determine as exactly as possible just how much the average man ought to be able to accomplish under given conditions. Workmen who perform above the average of their class should receive a higher rate of pay, while the workman who does less than the average should be dropped. The maximum industrial production can be achieved by finding out, to a split second, the best time for every operation and the ideal speed for each machine for each kind of work and then basing standards for a fair day's work, timetables, and pay rates on mathematical formulas developed therefrom. Taylor recognized that production is a complex of tools, machinery, materials, power, workers' skills, and managerial direction and that all these factors must be taken into account in the science of management.

On several occasions, Taylor attempted to define the term "scientific management." The following appears in his 1911 work:

Scientific management, in its essence, consists of a certain philosophy, which results in a combination of four great underlying principles of management: First, the development of a true science. Second, the scientific selection of workmen. Third, their education and development. Fourth, intimate friendly cooperation between the management and the men.

In his first years, Taylor met bitter opposition at every step. Conservative managers refused to believe that raising the pay of superior workmen could lower the cost per unit of work, or they disliked sharing increased profits with workers. But the most unyielding resistance came from the labor unions. The American Federation of Labor went on record, officially opposing "Taylorism" as a "diabolical scheme" that treated men like machines. The United States House of Representatives appointed a Special Committee to Investigate the Taylor and Other Systems of Shop Management. One of the consequences was a rider in every military appropriation bill for almost forty years prohibiting the use of funds for any "timestudy with a stopwatch or other time-measuring device."

In certain quarters Taylor's name is still synonymous with the exploitation of manual workers, speeding up, wage-rate cutting, and monopolizing of jobs, though Justice Louis D. Brandeis is quoted as saying of Taylor that it was the workers "for whom he labored most." Repeatedly Taylor found himself opposed not only by labor and management but also by banking and promoting interests. In general, he insisted that the interests of the employer and of the employee were identical, but he felt that the employer who had his eye on dividends alone was unsympathetic to the principles, methods, and results of scientific management.

The tremendous advance made since Taylor's day in the field of management is demonstrated by the fact that the Society for Advancement of Management, founded in 1912, has grown to 13,500 members. Historians of business and industry are agreed that the Taylor system, now spread throughout the world, has profoundly influenced twentieth-century industrial development.

105. CONQUEST OF FREEDOM

Woodrow Wilson's *The New Freedom*

1913

Among notable events in American political history, the 1912 Presidential campaign ranks high. The personal quarrel between Theodore Roosevelt and William Howard Taft split the Republican Party between progressives and conservatives, assuring the election of the Democratic candidate, Woodrow Wilson. As the three-cornered fight proceeded there began to take shape in Wilson's mind, apparent from an analysis of his speeches, a political philosophy that would determine the nature of his domestic reform program after his election to the Presidency. This philosophy was termed by Wilson "The New Freedom."

Theodore Roosevelt was the first President to recognize and to attempt to cope with the impact of industry and great corporations on government and politics. His administration had undertaken a moderate reform program, but his more conservative successor, Taft, had failed to follow through or to support needed additional legislation to regulate trusts, banks, labor, and other economic factors. Both Roosevelt and Wilson campaigned in 1912 on aggressive platforms for further economic reform, though with basically different approaches.

At the beginning of the campaign, Wilson had not fully developed all the principles of the New Freedom. As governor of New Jersey, he had successfully carried through a series of important reform measures at the state level: a primary election law, a public utilities act, a corrupt practices act, an employers' liability act. Now the Presidential race forced him to turn his thoughts to the problems of the nation. Within a few months, in a series of brilliant speeches, Wilson developed, revised, and strengthened his fundamental principles, establishing himself as the unquestioned leader of American liberalism.

Shortly before he assumed the Presidency, the major Wilson speeches were published under the title *The New Freedom,* subtitled "A Call for the Emancipation of the Generous Energies of a People." In a brief preface, Wilson explains that he "did not write this book at all. . . . It is the result of the editorial literary skill of Mr. William Bayard Hale, who has put together here in their right sequences the more suggestive portions of my campaign speeches. . . . It is a discussion of a number of very vital subjects in the free form of extemporaneously spoken words. . . . It is an attempt to set forth what must be done if we are to restore our national life to its purity, its self-respect, and its pristine strength and freedom."

The essence of the program presented in *The New Freedom* was to revitalize American democracy and readjust the American economy. The government, acting as umpire, declared Wilson, must set men free of restraints on their trade and their economic life. He was eager to return to the common people equality of privilege currently threatened by the "interests" of industry, finance, and commerce. The rather simple formula proposed was to smash the trusts, destroy special privilege, restore competition, and let the full light of publicity beat in on all the activities of business and government. As a first step, the nation should be liberated from the political influences that had made the federal government a dispenser of special favors. As Wilson viewed it:

> American industry is not free, as once it was. The man with only a little capital is finding it harder to get into the field, more and more impossible to compete with the big fellow. Why? Because the laws of this country do not prevent the strong from crushing the weak. . . . What this country needs above everything else is a body of laws which will look after the men who are *on the make* rather than the men who *are already made.*

Decentralization of business and industry was urged by Wilson. He spoke eloquently against "a network of control that will presently dominate every industry in the country, and so make men forget the ancient time when America lay in every hamlet, when America was to be seen in every fair valley, when America displayed her great forces on the broad prairies, ran her fine fires of enterprise up over the mountainsides and down into the bowels of the earth, and eager men were everywhere captains of industry, not employees." In that happy era, said Wilson, men did not have to look "to a distant city to find out what they might do," but now no sizable enterprise could be started without "obtaining the good-will of large allied capitalists." That, he asserted, "is dependence, not freedom."

Governmental paternalism was equally deplored by Wilson—reflecting an individualistic philosophy that is a far cry from the extensive social welfare legislation of later administrations: "If any part of our people want to be wards, if they want to have guardians put over them, if they want to be taken care of, if they want to be children, patronized by the government, why, I am sorry, because it will sap the manhood of America. But I don't believe they do."

Concrete reform measures proposed by Wilson included Congressional legislation for revision of the tariff, for reorganization of the banking and currency system, for destruction of monopoly, and for dealing with social problems. A basic aim of the New Freedom was to achieve free enterprise by regulating competition. This platform was substantially enacted in the early years of the Wilson administration by passage of the Underwood Tariff Act, providing for lower tariff schedules; the first federal income tax law; the Federal Reserve Act, designed to facilitate the flow of capital through twelve regional reserve banks; a law creating the Federal Trade Commission; and the Clayton Antitrust Act, to prevent interlocking directorates.

The coming of World War I in the second year of Wilson's administration marked the effectual end of Wilson's program of domestic reform. Henceforth, despite his primary concern with matters of domestic reform affecting individual freedom, Wilson was forced to center his attention on international affairs. Nevertheless, Wilson had already demonstrated the power of the Presidency in dealing with social problems. The reforms initiated by Wilson have become a permanent feature of the American governmental structure, and the New Deal, Fair Deal, New Frontier, and other evolutionary developments in governmental philosophy have continued to draw inspiration from Wilson's New Freedom.

106. HARBINGER OF THE ATOMIC AGE

Albert Einstein's *Über die Spezielle und die Allgemeine Relativitätstheorie* (Relativity, the Special and General Theory)

1917

The theory of relativity, universally associated with the name of Albert Einstein, has doubtless influenced the thinking and the lives of twentieth-century men more than any other scientific concept. Since the theory deals with the relationship between physical and mathematical events, it can be adequately expressed only in abstract mathematical language—placing it beyond the comprehension of the layman. Nevertheless, certain features of the Einstein cosmos can be suggested without resort to mathematical symbolism.

Einstein published his first paper on the theory of relativity while serving as a member of the staff of the Swiss Patent Office. What is now known as the special theory of relativity was presented by him, in 1905, in a paper entitled "The Electrodynamics of Bodies in Motion," in the *Annalen der Physik*. Eight years later, Einstein put forward the general relativity theory and published the whole in his

Relativity, the Special and General Theory. By 1917, the combined theory had been extended, verified, and accepted, and, with the quantum theory, it now forms the essential basis of modern physics.

The special theory of relativity is so called because it is concerned with a special kind of motion: uniform motion in a straight line, that is, with constant velocity. In describing the motion of a body, it is necessary to refer to another body, e.g., the motion of a railroad train with reference to the ground, of a planet with reference to all visible stars. The motion of each is relative to the other. In his conception of space, Einstein added a fourth dimension, time, to the three classical dimensions of length, breadth, and height.

A major principle on which the special relativity theory rests is that of the constancy of the velocity of light in a vacuum. The speed of light is constant as measured by all observers anywhere and with all possible varieties of motion with respect to each other. According to the special theory, no material body can move with a velocity greater than that of light—186,000 miles per second. Further, any measuring rod for length, such as a yardstick, if moving with a speed approaching that of light as a limit, would become shorter and shorter approaching zero in length as that speed was approached. Likewise, a clock moving with a speed approaching that of light would slow down and stop at the speed of light. Mass also is changeable. As velocity increases, the mass of an object becomes greater. Particles of matter speeded up to 86 per cent of the speed of light weigh twice as much as when at rest—a fact that had tremendous implications for the development of atomic energy.

In a brief sequel to his original paper, Einstein introduced the most famous equation in history: $E = Mc^2$, energy equals mass multiplied by the square of the velocity of light. Energy and mass are thus demonstrated to be identical, differing only in state. The formula shows that the energy in a single uranium nucleus would be 220,000,000,000 electron volts if all its mass could be converted into energy. Only one-tenth of one per cent of the total energy content is released by splitting the uranium nucleus, or fission.

In his general theory of relativity, Einstein advanced a new concept of gravitation. Gravity had been regarded by Isaac Newton as a "force." Einstein proved, however, that the space around a planet or other celestial body is a gravitational field similar to the magnetic field around a magnet. A massive body, he said, causes a distortion of space and time. To check Einstein's general theory, an expedition was sent out by the Royal Society in 1919 to observe an eclipse of the sun; as Einstein predicted, photographs revealed that light rays bend toward the sun. When a planet is closest to the sun in its orbit and the gravitational field greatest, the planet reaches its greatest speed. This fact was used by Einstein to explain a constant shift in the orbit of Mercury, nearest planet to the sun, again confirmed by experimental evidence.

Einstein suggested that the universe may be finite and that space itself may be curved, though no definite boundaries can be established. An alternative hypothesis is that space may be curved but still is infinite. Also a matter of speculation is the shape of the universe: a plane surface, a sphere, or a cylinder, the last theory preferred by Einstein.

Einstein's equation stating that mass can be converted into energy or energy into mass has formed the basis of today's atomic reactors and thermonuclear releases of energy. The title of "the father of the release of atomic energy" was disclaimed by Einstein. In his *Atomic War or Peace* he writes, "My part in it was quite indirect. I did not, in fact, foresee that it would be released in my time. I believed only that it was theoretically possible. It became practical through the accidental discovery of chain reaction, and this was not something I could have predicted." Despite this modest denial, it was Einstein's letter to President Roosevelt in 1939, describing the incredible power of atomic energy, that led to the construction of the Manhattan atom-bomb project.

Einstein's later years were devoted to a unified field theory, attempting to discover a completely inclusive explanation of the energy in all scientific phenomena, including electric, magnetic, and gravitational fields of force. According to his view, physical laws for the minute atom should be equally applicable to immense celestial bodies. The unified field theory, he felt, would demonstrate the existence of a well-ordered universe. Einstein's final statement of the theory, published in 1953, two years prior to his death, has failed to find support among leading physicists.

Concerning the present status of relativity, an international conference of theoretical physicists, at Berne, Switzerland, recently agreed that the foundations of the special and general theory have been universally accepted. Experiments have conclusively confirmed the special theory and are convincing for the general theory. The special theory has been incorporated into general physics and is used continually in atomic and nuclear physics.

For a number of years, the general theory was applied mainly to cosmology and cosmogony, but lately relativity is being applied to microphysical problems. The relationship to the quantum theory is still quite undetermined. It is apparent that general relativity provides a new approach to the ultimate properties of space and time. If true, the theory may have as much bearing on the physics of the very small as of the very large. The increasing world-wide interest in general relativity indicates that scientists believe the theory may add further to our understanding of the universe as an organic whole.

107. DICTATORSHIP OF THE PROLETARIAT

Nikolai Lenin's *The State and Revolution*

1918

As the storm clouds for the Bolshevik Revolution in Russia began to gather, its key figure was residing in Switzerland, a refugee from the czarist government. His career had been a long succession of arrests and escapes, long concealments, and sudden emergencies.

Since about 1907, Nikolai Lenin, christened Vladimir Ilich Ulyanov, had had in preparation a set of notebooks called by him "Marxism and the State." After the outbreak of World War I, foreseeing the imminence of revolution in Russia, Lenin applied himself diligently in the libraries of Berne and Zurich to completion of his work. The revolutionary explosion in his homeland came, however, before the writing could be finished, and Lenin immediately arranged to have himself smuggled back into Russia. The remainder of *The State and Revolution* was written while Lenin was in hiding in Petrograd and later across the Finnish border in Helsingfors. A final chapter outlined by the author was never written.

The importance attached by Lenin to his manuscript is revealed by a note to his representative, L. V. Kamenev; if he were killed, he evidently intended that the book should be his legacy to the revolutionary movement:

If they get me I ask you to publish my little notebook, "Marxism and the State" (stranded in Stockholm). Bound in a blue cover. All the quotations are collected from Marx and Engels, likewise from Kautsky against Pannekoek. There is a whole series of notes and comments. Formulate it. I think you could publish it with a week's work. I think it important, for it is not only Plekhanov and Kautsky who got off the track.

To Lenin belongs the credit for formulating, for the first time, a corpus of Marxian political theory. Marx had provided an economic theory in *Das Kapital,* while Marx and Engels' *The Communist Manifesto* had supplied a theory of history and the class struggle. In *The State and Revolution,* Lenin proposed to remedy the deficiency.

But in keeping with the Communist critique, all theory had to be based upon the sacred writings of the founding fathers: Karl Marx and Friedrich Engels. No theologian ever searched his scriptures more assiduously to support his text and to confound his enemies than did Lenin in combing the writings of Marx and Engels for the purpose of underpinning his arguments in *The State and Revolution.* Lenin saw his role as a synthesizer and interpreter, with no pretense to originality. He wished also to refute the Mensheviks, the Social Democrats, the Social Revolutionaries, and others who, in his view, had distorted and misrepresented the true faith.

The state, asserted Lenin and his mentors, is nothing more than a machine for the oppression of one class by another, whether in a democratic republic or in a monarchy. "The existence of the state proves that class antagonisms are irreconcilable." To maintain control over the oppressed workers, the state's chief instruments are a standing army, the police, the judiciary, and a burdensome bureaucracy. All the "trappings" of republicanism, such as universal suffrage, cannot conceal the fact that democracy in a capitalist society is for "an insignificant minority, democracy for the rich."

Lenin, Marx, and Engels unanimously insisted that the power of the bourgeois state can only be overcome and the chains of the oppressed workers thrown off by violent revolution. Lenin quotes approvingly Engels' panegyric on "the immense moral and spiritual impetus which has resulted from every victorious revolution."

Bourgeois-dominated government, according to Communist theory, will be followed by the dictatorship of the proletariat. The old machinery of the state will be broken up and annihilated (rather than being simply seized and possessed), while new forms will be created, with the proletariat organized as the ruling class. The transition from capitalism to communism is marked by an evolutionary stage. The proletariat needs the state for a while. "Temporary use," said Lenin, "must be made of the instruments, means, and methods of the state power *against* the exploiters, just as the dictatorship of the oppressed class is temporarily necessary for the annihilation of classes." After its conquest of political power, when the resistance of the capitalists has been completely broken, the capitalists have disappeared, and there are no classes, "the proletarian state will begin to wither away, because in a society without class antagonisms, the state is unnecessary and impossible." Engels confidently stated that "a new generation, reared under new and free social conditions, will be able to throw on the scrap-heap all this state rubbish." Meantime, all officials would be elected and subject to recall at any time and their salaries reduced to "workingmen's wages."

Lenin anticipated no difficulty in having the proletariat assume all essential functions of society, with the united workers supplying their own technicians, managers, and bookkeepers. Such operations, he contemptuously declared, were "within the reach of anybody who can read and write and knows the first four arithmetical rules."

Following the disappearance of the proletarian state, a higher phase of Communist society will have arrived. The withering away of the state will come, asserts Lenin, when society has realized the rule: "From each according to his ability; to each according to his needs."

In the perspective of more than forty years of Communist rule in the Soviet Union, Lenin's utopian predictions appear ironic. Features of bourgeois society to which the pure Marxists take particular exception—a huge standing army, a great sprawling bureaucracy, a ubiquitous police system, and clearly defined classes—are solidly established in "the workers' paradise." Though Lenin was careful not to attach any time limit to the state's "withering-away" process, it is patent that even after four decades not the slightest evidence can be detected of such a development in the "Socialist Fatherland," the U.S.S.R.

The State and Revolution first appeared in print in 1918, and it has since been widely translated. Editions in millions of copies have been printed and sold in the Soviet Union and in other Communist lands. The successful establishment of the Soviet state has naturally added tremendously to the book's prestige and reputation.

108. THE VERSAILLES PEACEMAKERS

John Maynard Keynes' *The Economic Consequences of the Peace*

1919

His authorship of *The General Theory of Employment, Interest and Money,* with its immense influence in shaping American New Deal philosophy and British government fiscal policies, has somewhat overshadowed the reputation of John Maynard Keynes' earlier *The Economic Consequences of the Peace.* Few, if any, books, however, have had a more immediate or decisive impact on their time than did the latter in the post-World War I years.

Keynes, a Cambridge University economist, was responsible for British financial relations with the Allied Powers during the 1915–18 period. Following the Armistice, he was the chief representative of the British Treasury at the Versailles Peace Conference. Keynes soon found himself in violent disagreement with the decisions of the conference. He deplored the economic features of the treaty being evolved there and believed that the Big Four (Clemenceau, Lloyd George, Woodrow Wilson, and Orlando) were completely blind to the economic structure of European society. Accordingly, Keynes resigned his post and returned to England. *The Economic Consequences of the Peace,* records show, was written at the suggestion of General Jan Christiaan Smuts, South African representative, who was also in opposition to certain aspects of the treaty. The General advised Keynes not to make the book "too long or technical, as we may want to appeal to the plain man more than to the well informed or the specialist."

Keynes begins with an idyllic picture of Europe between wars, the half-century before the outbreak of World War I, when the Continent had achieved economic equilibrium, the population was reasonably well fed, frontiers and tariffs interferred little with the flow of goods and people between countries, national currencies were stable, the world's natural resources were being freely drawn upon, and "there was an almost absolute security of property and of person." Keynes' nostalgia for this lost paradise, the yearning to put Humpty Dumpty back on the wall intact, is a strong motif through his book. At the peace conference for several months Keynes had an opportunity to observe the treaty makers in action. His brilliant, though cruel, characterizations of the leading figures are memorable. As Keynes saw it, the conference was primarily a conflict for mastery among three great personalities: Clemenceau, Lloyd George, and Wilson. Clemenceau is pictured as silent and remote, sitting enthroned on a brocaded chair, wearing gray suede gloves, "dry in soul and empty of hope, very old and tired . . . surveying the scene with a cynical and almost impish air. He had one illusion: France; one disillusion: mankind." Lloyd George was "this extraordinary figure of our time, this syren, this goat-footed bard, this half-human visitor to our age from the hag-ridden magic and enchanted woods of Celtic antiquity . . . watching the company with six or seven senses not available to ordinary men."

Keynes' sharpest thrusts were reserved for the American President. Woodrow Wilson is depicted as a "blind and deaf Don Quixote" being rounded up, manacled, and strapped down by the agile minds around him. Instead of being "the man of destiny" or "the philosopher-king" Europe had expected, Wilson "was not a hero or a prophet; he was not even a philosopher, but a generously intentioned man, with many of the weaknesses of other human beings." Here was a man, Keynes was convinced, who constantly compromised his high principles and was invariably outmaneuvered by "the subtle and dangerous spell-binders," Clemenceau and Lloyd George.

The main body of *The Economic Consequences of the Peace* is devoted by Keynes to the proposition that the peace terms imposed upon Germany and her Allies, both territorial and economic, violated the surrender agreement, were overly harsh to the vanquished, and were impossible of execution. The sums demanded for reparations, he argued, were far in excess of what Germany could conceivably pay, and in any case it would be impracticable for her to transfer such huge sums through currency barriers. A conquered enemy country could not be kept in a state of weakness, as the Peace Conference envisaged, and at the same time be expected to pay large damages. Both reparations and war debts could be paid only with goods. "The policy of reducing Germany to servitude for a generation, of degrading the lives of millions of human beings, and of depriving a whole nation of happiness should be abhorrent and detestable," maintained Keynes, "even if it were possible, even if we enriched ourselves, even if we did not sow the decay of the whole civilized life of Europe."

The appearance of Keynes' book roused a storm of controversy in Europe and America. In its principal aim, the revision of the reparations agreement, the book widely influenced public opinion. After five years of fruitless efforts to collect full reparations from Germany, more lenient terms were arranged under the Dawes and Young Plans. In actuality, loans from America exceeded Germany's total reparation payments, until the world slump and the emergence of Hitler, when her obligations were suspended. Keynes' critics have insisted that the Allies were never under any illusions about their ability to collect immense indemnities from Germany but fixed harsh terms in the treaty at first to satisfy strong public sentiment at home, represented by such slogans as "Hang the Kaiser" and "Make the Boche Pay."

Two other Keynesian "remedies" for Europe's ills were proposed: cancellation of war debts and establishment of a free-trade union. The first was largely accomplished by a series of debt defaults and moratoriums. Progress toward the second has been made recently through creation of the European Economic Community.

The Economic Consequences of the Peace, in the eyes of at least some historians, did more than any other writing to discredit the Treaty of Versailles. It has been suggested further that the book contributed powerfully to the political defeat of President Wilson, to the refusal of the United States to accept the peace treaties and the League of Nations, and to the strengthening or revival of American isolationism. The German Foreign Office, of course, found strong support in Keynes for resisting the reparations demands of the Allies. Later, Adolf Hitler drew ammunition from Keynes for his diatribes against the iniquities of the Treaty of Versailles—a platform which aided his rise to power in Germany.

In his *The World Crisis,* Winston Churchill essayed a thoughtful appraisal of Keynes and his work:

He showed in successive chapters of unanswerable good sense the monstrous character of the financial and economic clauses. On all these matters his opinion is good. Carried away, however, by his natural indignation at the economic terms which were to be solemnly enacted, he wrapped the whole structure of the Peace Treaties in one common condemnation. His qualifications to speak on the economic aspects were indisputable; but on the other and vastly more important side of the problem he could judge no better than many others.

109. DER FUEHRER

Adolf Hitler's *Mein Kampf* (My Battle)

1925–1927

When the Nazi Party under Adolf Hitler's leadership took over the reins of government in Germany in 1933, after a decade of agitation and violence, the world was appalled by its ruthless methods of establishing control, its abolition of all vestiges of democracy, its merciless suppression of dissenting views, its persecution of Jews, and its territorial threat against friendly neighboring nations.

Yet, if non-Germans had read Hitler's *Mein Kampf*, they would have found the entire program spelled out in all its shocking detail. Der Fuehrer was completely frank about his intentions and plans for Germany and Europe. But, thanks to the protection of international copyright, the full story had been restricted to the original German. A great nation and her allies committed themselves to carrying out the book's fantastic ideas. Prior to the outbreak of World War II, five million copies had been distributed in Germany alone.

The German people in the early thirties were in a mood that made them dangerously susceptible to the Fascist infection. For a century, high-pressure nationalism and ideas of race superiority had been drilled into them, and after World War I and the Treaty of Versailles they suffered from an acute persecution complex. To many, order and security seemed to matter more than a political freedom that had become synonymous with street brawls and bloodshed. Hitler, aided by a phenomenal capacity for organization and by the readiness of Germany's great industrialists to finance his campaign, shrewdly utilized the prevailing attitude to establish his power.

Mein Kampf's theme song, recurring again and again, is race, race purity, race supremacy, though nowhere did Hitler attempt to define race. Mankind, he says, is divided into three groups: the culture creators, of whom there is only one example, the Aryan or Nordic; the culture bearers, such as the Japanese; and the culture destroyers, such as the Jews and Negroes. It was never intended by Nature, Hitler claims, that all races should be equal, any more than individuals are equal. Some are created superior to others. The Germans, as the world's strongest race, should rule over the inferior races of the earth.

Fanatically believing in the innate superiority of the "Aryan" race over all others, Hitler preaches that it is the duty and privilege of the master race to conquer, exploit, dispossess, or exterminate other races for its own advantage. All humanity in the long run would benefit through having the habitat of the highest race extended and scattered Germanic peoples united under one rule. The vast expansion visualized by Hitler would take place principally at the expense of Russia. According to *Mein Kampf:*

> Frontiers are made and altered by human agency alone. The fact that a nation succeeds in acquiring an unfair share of territory is no superior reason for its being respected forever. It merely proves the strength of the conqueror and the weakness of those who lose by it. This strength alone constitutes the right to possess.

To attain the objectives set by his soaring ambition, Hitler proposes three methods: propaganda, diplomacy, and force. Nowhere in *Mein Kampf* is the author more revealing of himself and his tactics than in his discussion of propaganda techniques—correctly believed by him to be one of the Nazis' most effective and formidable weapons. To perfect his own understanding of the propaganda art, Hitler studied the techniques of the Marxists, the organization and methods of the Catholic Church, British propaganda during World War I, American advertising, and Freudian psychology.

The importance of concentration and repetition is stressed by Hitler. The masses can only assimilate a small amount, because their intelligence is limited and their forgetfulness great. Therefore effective propaganda must be confined to a very few points and these hammered home until even the most stupid hearers will comprehend them. Propaganda must be "aimed always and primarily at the emotions and very little at man's alleged reason." Hitler's frequently expressed belief is that mankind in the mass is lazy, cowardly, feminine, emotional, and incapable of rational thought.

The ultimate in Hitlerian propaganda technique is the principle of the big lie. The doctrine is wholly correct, Hitler declares, "that the very greatness of the lie is a factor in getting it believed. With the primitive simplicity of the masses a great lie is more effective than a small one, because they often lie in small matters, but would be too ashamed to tell a great big lie."

Another major propaganda principle is that of the single devil. Do not confuse the populace by offering too many enemies for it to hate at the same time. Concentrate upon one adversary and focus the people's hatred upon this enemy. For Hitler, of course, the Jew served as the universal scapegoat.

The task of the propagandist is facilitated, Hitler says, by state control of education. Too much book learning is an error. Physical education and physical health should take first place. Second is the development of character, especially the cultivation of military virtues such as obedience, loyalty, strength of will, self-control, capacity for sacrifice, and pride in responsibility. Girls must be trained for motherhood. Always the guiding principles are that the child belongs to the state and that the sole object of education is to train tools for the state.

Rejecting democracy, Hitler substituted the leader principle, dividing mankind into leaders and the herd. "Only a fraction of mankind," he concludes, "is energetic and bold." The rest are cowards and dupes.

Viewing *Mein Kampf* retrospectively, historians insist that Hitler had no understanding of history, anthropologists say that his racial views are nonsense, educators declare that his theories of education are altogether medieval and reactionary, political scientists protest his authoritarian doctrines of government and his misrepresentation of democracy, and literary experts state that he did not know how to write a paragraph or organize a chapter. One critic, Weigert, summed up:

> The half-educated Hitler was a mosaic of influences: the amoral statecraft of Machiavelli, the mystic nationalism and romanticism of Wagner, the organic evolution of Darwin, the grossly exaggerated racialism of Gobineau and Houston Stewart Chamberlain, the messianic complex of Fichte and Hegel, the military braggadocio of Treitschke and Bernhardi, and the financial conspiracy of the Prussian Junker caste.

Nevertheless, despite such glaring defects, the American editor Norman Cousins has called *Mein Kampf* "by far the most effective book of the twentieth century. For every word in *Mein Kampf*, 125 lives were to be lost; for every page, 4,700 lives; for every chapter, more than 1,200,000 lives."

110. DOYEN OF EXPERIMENTAL PHYSIOLOGISTS

Ivan Petrovich Pavlov's *Conditioned Reflexes: an Investigation of the Physiological Activity of the Cerebral Cortex*

1927

George Bernard Shaw and Ivan Petrovich Pavlov were strikingly similar in appearance, each sporting a luxuriant beard, and their long lifetimes were almost exactly contemporaneous. Shaw, the uncompromising antivivisectionist, exhibited no fraternal feeling, however, for his twin. His *Black Girl in Search of God* is represented as encountering "a very short-sighted elderly man in spectacles [Pavlov] who was sitting on a gnarled log." The man addressed the black girl as follows:

In running away you were acting on a conditioned reflex. It is quite simple. Having lived among lions you have from your childhood associated the sound of a roar with deadly danger. Hence your precipitate flight when that superstitious old jackass brayed at you. This remarkable discovery cost me twenty-five years of devoted research, during which I cut out the brains of innumerable dogs, and observed their spittle by making holes in their cheeks for them to salivate through instead of through their tongues. The whole scientific world is prostrate at my feet in admiration of this colossal achievement and gratitude for the light it has shed on the great problem of human conduct.

The black girl ridicules the old gentleman by remarking that she could have told him as much in twenty-five seconds without hurting any dogs, and points out that he is sitting on a crocodile mistakenly taken for a log. But despite the Shavian satire, the description of Pavlovian methods is not greatly exaggerated.

Pavlov, perhaps the outstanding scientist produced by Russia in modern times, devoted his early years to investigating the functions of the alimentary tract. Most of the facts relating to digestion now known either had their origin, or were established, in Pavlov's laboratory. For these researches, he received the Nobel Prize for Physiology and Medicine in 1904.

From 1902 until his death in 1936, Pavlov went on to explore a new branch of knowledge—the physiology of higher nervous activity. In his own words:

For many years previously I had been working on the digestive glands. I had studied carefully and in detail all the conditions of their activity. Naturally I could not leave them without considering the so-called psychical stimulation of the salivary glands, i.e., the flow of saliva in the hungry animal or person at the sight of food or during talk about it or even at the thought of it.

During Pavlov's work on the digestive system he had observed that a dog secretes saliva and gastric juice not only as the result of being fed, but even in response to the sight or smell of food or to signs that it is about to be fed. Here was the beginning of his experiments extending over many years.

Pavlov's primary aim was to understand the working of the human brain. For laboratory purposes he chose dogs because of the simplicity of their mental processes and because they are close enough to man in the evolutionary scale to have brains essentially comparable.

The Pavlovian experiments were centered around reflex actions. Reflexes were divided into two groups: natural and conditioned. The ordinary inherited reflexes, sometimes referred to as "instincts," were called *unconditional,* and such acquired responses as those of the burnt child or the beaten dog, *conditional* reflexes.

Pavlov's basic method was to take a hungry dog and place it in a room from which all outside distractions of sight, sound, or smell were shut out. In one experiment, a metronome, an instrument with an audible tick, was used. When the metronome had ticked a few seconds, a plate of food was swung down to the floor, the dog ate the food, and the plate was pulled out of sight. At intervals, the ticking of the metronome followed by the appearance of food was repeated until the two became closely associated in the dog's mind and its salivary glands became active at the sound of the metronome. This is a simple example of a conditioned reflex. In other experiments a flash of light, the ringing of a bell, a touch upon a certain part of the body, the twang of a tuning fork, or squares of black and white cloth were used as signals. Soon the dog would learn that a certain sign meant food; its tail would wag and its mouth water before the food actually appeared.

Succeeding Pavlov experiments were designed to decondition a conditioned reflex. An animal conditioned to the ringing of bells would be subjected to a series of rings but no food would follow. At first the dog's mouth watered and its tail wagged. After a number of disappointments, however, it would no longer lick its lips. The dog had unlearned its original lesson. This process was termed *inhibition* by Pavlov. Inhibition takes various forms. To illustrate, dogs learned to discriminate that a flash of light with a noise meant food but a flash alone did not.

On the basis of experiments with numerous dogs, Pavlov found that animals varied greatly in the speed with which conditioned reflexes were formed and in the permanence of the reflexes. Some dogs became greatly excited during the experiments and developed nervous disorders. The neurotic states were evidently caused by conflicts between the reflexes that excited and those that inhibited. The dogs showed different temperaments and individual peculiarities, not unlike human beings. Confronted by insurmountable obstacles, the animals succumbed to nervous breakdowns, but the symptoms of the emotional strains, worries, or shocks were shown in diverse fashions: intense excitement comparable to insanity, a state of deep depression characterized by sleepiness, etc.

Pavlov's findings led psychologists to conduct extensive investigations of experimental neuroses. New approaches to phenomena of mental instability were suggested by the Pavlovian discoveries. As interpreted by Pavlov, fears, phobias, hates, and other irrational behavior are caused by reflexes conditioned by some earlier happenings, such as those associated with frightening or disturbing experiences. Near the end of Pavlov's life a psychiatric and psychoneurological clinic was added to his laboratories. Here an effort was made to analyze various cases of human neuroses by applying the criteria revealed in experiments on animals.

The first full account of Pavlov's work to appear in English was his *Conditioned Reflexes: an Investigation of the Physiological Activity of the Cerebral Cortex.*

It is generally agreed that in the development of modern psychology, conditioned reflexes have played a major part. Important trends of psychological investigation now in progress are based largely on the accomplishments of the Pavlov laboratories. The behavioral school founded by two Americans, Watson and Yerkes, in great vogue during the nineteen twenties, though now somewhat passé, was inspired by the Russian. Unquestionably, the study of conditioned reflexes has made fundamental contributions to an understanding of the nature of sleep, neuroses, and temperament. To Pavlov belongs the honor of being the first scientist to investigate the functions of the whole central nervous system from a physiological point of view. Some of his theories have been rejected by physiologists and neurologists, but his basic facts remain beyond dispute.

Pavlov's extraordinary achievements and influence are widely acknowledged among psychologists, psychiatrists, medical practitioners, and other specialists whose fields were touched by his researches. Because of Pavlov, psychology is now a branch of science rather than a subdivision of philosophy. Physiologists are indebted to him for developing a method of studying the brain in healthy animals, and psychiatrists for his investigations in experimental neurosis.

Critics of Pavlov's teachings have pointed out certain sinister aftermaths of his discoveries. Since his viewpoint was completely mechanistic, Pavlov concluded that even such concepts as freedom, curiosity, and religion were conditioned reflexes of the brain. Psychologists under authoritarian regimes have endeavored to apply these principles to the conditioning or "brainwashing" of masses of the population.

111. EROS AND DEATH

Sigmund Freud's *Das Unbehagen in der Kultur* (Civilization and Its Discontents)

1930

The theories of Sigmund Freud, founder of psychoanalysis and modern psychiatry, have exerted a profound influence on twentieth-century thought. Scarcely any facet of contemporary life and culture has remained unaffected by Freud's explorations of the subconscious regions of the mind. Such Freudian concepts as the influence of the subconscious on consciousness, the sexual basis of neuroses, the existence and importance of infantile sexuality, the function of dreams, the Oedipus complex, repression, resistance, and transference are now accepted as commonplace.

In his old age, Freud became interested in the application of psychoanalytic principles to society and its problems. One of the results was the writing of *Civilization and Its Discontents,* a searching analysis of modern civilization and its besetting ills. After a lifetime of specialized scientific investigations and experiments, Freud, in this general work, presents the broad impressions which his immense knowledge of innumerable individual cases had given him. The over-all effect is highly pessimistic.

Civilization as we know it, says Freud, is made possible only by man's heroic sacrifice of instinct. The instinctive life of man is one of unrestrained aggression and egoistic self-satisfaction. But civilization is built upon prohibitions and curbs of the natural impulses. From infancy, man is trained to become a member of a community organized for mutual assistance and is inhibited against murdering the man who stands in his way or raping the woman he desires. Thus in every civilized individual there is developed a force commonly called conscience, termed by Freud "the super-ego," to censor and judge every act and every desire. Without this mechanism, there could be no civilization.

The renunciation by individuals of instinctive gratifications, however, has created intense inner antagonisms and conflicts in mankind, accounting, according to Freud, for the turmoil of present-day civilization. Freud attaches high importance to the sexual privations, but places chief emphasis on the universal instincts of aggression and destruction. Countering the instinct of self-preservation, he believes, is a "death instinct," from which the instinct of aggression is derived. The instinct of aggression is the most powerful obstacle to culture and frequently threatens its destruction.

Assuming that the purpose of human life is the pursuit of happiness, Freud considers the principal barriers to its attainment:

> Suffering comes from three quarters: from our own body, which is destined to decay and dissolution, and cannot even dispense with anxiety and pain as danger signals; from the outer world which can rage against us with the most powerful and pitiless forces of destruction; and finally from our relations with other men. The unhappiness which has this last origin we find perhaps more painful than any other.

Yet, though our goal of happiness appears unattainable, the struggle to realize it continues. Among the means enumerated by Freud as ordinarily utilized to reduce unhappiness are powerful diversions of interests, leading us to forget our miseries; substitute gratifications, such as art, "illusions in contrast to reality"; intoxicating substances, making us insensitive to hard facts; personal delusion or religions, which "must be classified as mass delusions"; or the seeking of happiness through loving and being loved.

In his endless and restless search for happiness, man has gone far toward conquering nature. "In the last generations," Freud points out, "man has made extraordinary strides in knowledge of the natural sciences and technical application of them, and has established his dominion over Nature in a way never before imagined. . . . But men are beginning to perceive that all this newly won power over space and time, this fulfillment of age-old longings, has not increased the amount of pleasure they can obtain in life, has not made them feel any happier." This is no reason, though, in Freud's view, for concluding that technical progress is worthless from the standpoint of happiness. It merely means that power over Nature is not the only condition of human happiness, nor is it the only goal of civilization's efforts.

The hostility of men toward one another, declares Freud, is a perpetual menace threatening the disintegration of society. His review of Marxist socialism's solution for the problem is of interest:

> The Communists believe they have found a way of delivering us from this evil. Man is whole-heartedly good and friendly to his neighbor, they say, but the system of private property has corrupted his nature. . . . If private property were abolished, all valuables held in common and all allowed to share in the enjoyment of them, ill-will and enmity would disappear from men. . . . I cannot enquire into whether the abolition of private property is advantageous and expedient, but I am able to recognize that this theory is founded on an untenable illusion. By abolishing private property one deprives the human love of aggression of one of its instruments, a strong one undoubtedly, but assuredly not the strongest. To do this in no way alters the individual differences in power and influence which are turned by aggressiveness to its own use, nor does it change the nature of the instinct in any way.

The moral conscience is dwelt upon at length by Freud. Conscience in the child is a relatively simple affair, usually manifested by dread of losing the love of its parents. In the adult, the phenomenon is more complicated, marked by tension and conflict between the strict "super-ego" and the "ego," the latter defined as the sense of guilt. Freud stresses the basic significance of this factor, because he wishes "to represent the sense of guilt as the most important problem in the evolution of culture, and to convey that the price of progress in civilization is paid in forfeiting happiness through the heightening of the sense of guilt." The feeling of guilt, while causing the multiple discontents of civilization, increases our sense of responsibility to the community. Out of guilt comes not only wretchedness but progress.

The meaning of the evolution of culture, as defined by Freud, is clear: "It must present to us the struggle between Eros and Death, between the instincts of life and the instincts of destruction, as it works itself out in the human species. . . . The evolution of civilization may be simply described as the struggle of the human species for existence." Freud concludes his treatise with these penetrating observations:

> The fateful question of the human species seems to me to be whether and to what extent the cultural processes developed in it will succeed in mastering the derangements of communal life caused by the human instinct of aggression and self-destruction. In this connection, perhaps the phase through which we are at this moment passing deserves special interest. Men have brought their powers of subduing the forces of nature to such a pitch that by using them they could now very easily exterminate one another to the last man. They know this—hence arises a great part of their current unrest, their dejection, their mood of apprehension. And now it may be expected that the other of the two "heavenly forces," eternal Eros, will put forth his strength so as to maintain himself alongside of his equally immortal adversary.

BIBLIOGRAPHICAL NOTES

AGASSIZ, JEAN LOUIS RODOLPHE (1807–1873)
Études sur les Glaciers. Neuchâtel: Jent et Gassmann, 1840. 2 vols.

ALGER, HORATIO, JR. (1832–1899)
Ragged Dick; or, Street Life in New York with the Boot-blacks. Boston: Loring, 1868. 296 pp. First published serially in Oliver Optic magazine *Student and Schoolmate,* 1867.

BACON, SIR FRANCIS, BARON VERULAM, VISCOUNT ST. ALBANS (1561–1626)
The Twoo Bookes *Of the Proficience and Aduancement of Learning, Diuine and Humane.* London: H. Tomes, 1605. 2 pts. in 1 vol.

    The *Advancement of Learning* was intended as an introduction to *Instauratio Magna,* an encyclopedia of all knowledge—a project never completed—but was revised and expanded in a Latin version, *De Augmentis Scientiarum* (1623). In *Novum Organum* (1620), Bacon discussed the uselessness of the older philosophies and the traditional errors of mankind and held out science as the hope of the future. The *New Atlantis,* published posthumously (1627), is a fragmentary sketch of a utopian community of scientists engaged in research for the betterment of mankind.

BAYLE, PIERRE (1647–1706)
Dictionnaire Historique et Critique. Rotterdam: R. Leers, 1697. 2 vols.

BECCARIA, CESARE BONESANA, MARCHESE DI (1738–1794)
Dei Delitti e delle Pene. [Livorno] 1764. 104 pp.

BELLAMY, EDWARD (1850–1898)
Looking Backward, 2000–1887. Boston: Ticknor, 1888. 470 pp.

    Looking Backward is known to have inspired at least a hundred other utopian fantasies, including Morris' *News from Nowhere,* Schindler's *Young West,* Michaelis' *Looking Further Forward,* Vinton's *Looking Further Backward,* Cirkel's *Looking Beyond,* Roberts' *Looking Within,* and Giles' *Shadows Before.*

BENTHAM, JEREMY (1748–1832)
An Introduction to the Principles of Morals and Legislation. London: T. Payne, 1789. 435 pp.

BLACKSTONE, SIR WILLIAM (1723–1780)
Commentaries on the Laws of England. Oxford: Clarendon Press, 1765–69. 4 vols.

BODIN, JEAN (1530–1596)
Les Six Livres de la République. Paris: J. Du Puys, 1576. 759 pp.

BOYLE, ROBERT (1627–1691)
The Sceptical Chymist: or Chymico-Physical Doubts & Paradoxes. London: J. Crooke, 1661. 442 pp.

BUNYAN, JOHN (1628–1688)
The Pilgrim's Progress. London: Nathaniel Ponder, 1678. 232 pp.

Among Bunyan's prolific writings (some 60 titles in prose and verse were published), two other allegorical works attained considerable fame and popularity: *The Life and Death of Mr. Badman* (1680), a realistic portrayal of coarse and vulgar provincial life, intended to be a contrast to *The Pilgrim's Progress;* and *The Holy War* (1682), which would be the best allegory ever written, it has been said, if *The Pilgrim's Progress* did not exist.

BURKE, EDMUND (1729–1797)
Reflections on the Revolution in France, and on the Proceedings in Certain Societies in London Relative to that Event. In a Letter Intended to Have Been Sent to a Gentleman in Paris. London: J. Dodsley, 1790. 356 pp.

CALVIN, JOHN (1509–1564)
Christianae Religionis Institutio. Basel: T. Platteru and B. Lasium, 1536. 514 pp.

CARLYLE, THOMAS (1795–1881)
On Heroes, Hero-Worship, and the Heroic in History. London: J. Fraser, 1841. 393 pp.

In his *The Letters and Speeches of Oliver Cromwell* (1845) and his monumental six-volume *History of Frederick the Great* (1858–65), Carlyle continued to set forth his conviction that the important work of the world is accomplished through "heroes" or natural leaders.

CERVANTES SAAVEDRA, MIGUEL DE (1547–1616)
El Ingenioso Hidalgo Don Quixote de la Mancha. Madrid: Juan de la Cuesta, 1605–15. 2 vols.

CLAUSEWITZ, KARL VON (1780–1831)
Vom Kriege. Berlin: F. Dümmler, 1832–34. 3 vols.

COLUMBUS, CHRISTOPHER (1451–1506)
De Insulis Inuentis; Epistola Cristoferi Colom. Basel, 1493. 10 ff. The first edition, the only known copy of which is in the New York Public Library, was printed in Spanish in Barcelona in the same year.

For nearly fifty years after the Columbus discovery, Europeans continued to think of the northern region of the New World as Asia, applying the name America only to the southern continent. The first surviving map to label both of the new continents "America" was drawn in

1538 by Gerardus Mercator, Dutch cartographer, who also showed an
ocean between America and Asia.

COMTE, ISIDORE AUGUSTE MARIE FRANÇOIS (1798–1857)
Cours de Philosophie Positive. Paris: Bachelier, 1830–42. 6 vols.

CONDORCET, MARIE JEAN ANTOINE–NICOLAS DE CARITAT,
MARQUIS DE (1743–1794)
L'Esquisse d'un Tableau Historique des Progrès de l'Esprit Humain.
Paris: Agasse, 1795. 389 pp.

COPERNICUS, NICOLAUS (1473–1543)
De Revolutionibus Orbium Coelestium. Nuremberg: Johann Petrus,
1543. 196 ff. The first accurate and complete edition was published in
1873, at Thorn (Torun), Poland, by the Copernicus-Verein für Wissen-
schaft und Kunst.

The first written account of his theories, entitled *Commentariolus,*
"Little Commentary," was circulated by Copernicus among students of
astronomy perhaps as early as 1510, but was not published in the author's lifetime. The first printed account, *Narratio Prima,* written by a
fervent admirer, George Joachim Rheticus, appeared in 1540.

DALTON, JOHN (1766–1844)
A New System of Chemical Philosophy. Manchester, 1808–27. v. 1,
pt. 1, 1808; v. 1, pt. 2, 1810; v. 2, pt. 1, 1827; v. 2, pt. 2, not published.

DARWIN, CHARLES ROBERT (1809–1882)
*On the Origin of Species by Means of Natural Selection, or the Preser-
vation of Favoured Races in the Struggle for Life.* London: J. Murray,
1859. 502 pp.

Darwin's *Journal of a Naturalist* (1839), later expanded into *A
Naturalist's Voyage Round the World in H.M.S. Beagle* (1860), describes the beginning of his life work. The theme of the *Origin of Species* was subsequently developed in detail in *The Descent of Man, and
Selection in Relation to Sex* (1871), *The Variation of Animals and
Plants Under Domestication* (1868), *Expression of the Emotions* (1872),
The Effects of Cross and Self-Fertilization in the Vegetable Kingdom
(1876), *The Power of Movement in Plants* (1880), and other specialized works.

DEFOE, DANIEL (1661–1731)
*The Life and Strange Surprizing Adventures of Robinson Crusoe of
York, Mariner.* London: W. Taylor, 1719. 364 pp. Part II: *The Farther
Adventures of Robinson Crusoe.* London: W. Taylor, 1719. 373 pp.

In addition to the inspiration furnished by Alexander Selkirk's adventures, the story of *Robinson Crusoe* drew extensively upon William
Dampier's *A New Voyage Round the World* (1697).

DESCARTES, RENÉ (1596–1650)
Discours de la Méthode pour Bien Conduire sa Raison et Chercher la Verité dans les Sciences. Leyden: J. Maire, 1637. 413 pp.

DEWEY, JOHN (1859–1952)
The School and Society. Chicago: University of Chicago Press, 1899. 125 pp.

William James' *Principles of Psychology* (1890) early stimulated Dewey's thinking along pragmatic lines, or, as the latter preferred to call it, in the direction of instrumentalism or experimentalism. Both James and Dewey were also influenced by the writings of Wilhelm Max Wundt, German physiologist and psychologist, who in 1878 at Leipzig founded the first laboratory for experimental psychology.

DICKENS, CHARLES (1812–1870)
Hard Times for These Times. London: Bradbury and Evans, 1854. 352 pp.

Dickens' impact on social reform was also felt through *Oliver Twist* (1837–39), an indictment of orphanages and of the London slums; *Nicholas Nickelby* (1838–39), describing the brutal country schools; *David Copperfield* (1849–50), expressing hatred of debtors' prisons; *Bleak House* (1852–53), a satire on the workings of the law; *Little Dorrit* (1856–57), also concerned with imprisonment for debt; and *Our Mutual Friend* (1864–65), protesting against the poor laws.

DIDEROT, DENIS (1713–1784), Editor
Encyclopédie ou Dictionnaire Raisonné des Sciences, des Arts et des Métiers. Paris: Briasson [etc.] 1751–72. 28 vols.

EINSTEIN, ALBERT (1879–1955)
Über die Spezielle und die Allgemeine Relativitätstheorie. Braunschweig: Vieweg, 1917. 70 pp.

The Special Theory of Relativity was first set forth by Einstein in an article "On the Electrodynamics of Moving Bodies" in *Annalen der Physik*, in 1905. Shortly afterward, the same journal published a second article, "Does the Inertia of a Body Depend on Its Energy?" stating the basic principle for the release of atomic energy. The General Theory of Relativity was presented in Einstein's *Die Grundlagen der Allgemeinen Relativitätstheorie* (1916).

ELLIS, HENRY HAVELOCK (1859–1939)
Studies in the Psychology of Sex. Philadelphia: F. A. Davis, 1900–1928. 7 vols. Volume I originally published in London, 1897, and suppressed.

EMERSON, RALPH WALDO (1803–1882)
Essays. Boston: Munroe, 1841. 303 pp. Second series, Boston: Munroe, 1844. 313 pp.

ERASMUS, DESIDERIUS (1466–1536)

Encomium Moriae. Paris: Gilles Gourmont, c. 1509–11. 96 pp. First dated edition: Strassburg: Mattheus Scheurer, 1511. 94 pp.

In much the same spirit as the *Praise of Folly* is Erasmus' *Colloquia Familiaria* (1500), "The Adages, Familiar Quotations from the Classics," containing over 3,000 sayings or maxims, a compendium of satirical comments on women, monks, lawyers, and anti-humanist forces. The *Colloquies* was immensely popular in its time, passing through 120 editions before 1570.

FARADAY, MICHAEL (1791–1867)

Experimental Researches in Electricity. London: R. and J. E. Taylor, 1839–55. 3 vols. Reprinted from the *Philosophical Transactions,* 1831–52.

James Clerk Maxwell's *Electricity and Magnetism* (1873), based on Faraday's experimentation and research, developed the theory of the electromagnetic field on a mathematical basis and made possible a greater understanding of the newly discovered phenomena.

FICHTE, JOHANN GOTTLIEB (1762–1814)

Reden an die Deutsche Nation. Berlin: In der Realschulbuchhandlung, 1808. 490 pp.

FRANKLIN, BENJAMIN (1706–1790)

Mémoires de la Vie Privée. Paris: Chez Buisson, 1791. 207 pp. The first complete and accurate edition in English: *Autobiography of Benjamin Franklin,* edited by John Bigelow. Philadelphia: Lippincott, 1868. 409 pp.

FRAZER, SIR JAMES GEORGE (1854–1941)

The Golden Bough. London: Macmillan, 1890. 2 vols. Definitive edition (3rd): London: Macmillan, 1911–15. 12 vols.

FREUD, SIGMUND (1856–1939)

Das Unbehagen in der Kultur. Vienna: Internationaler Psychoanalytischer Verlag, 1930. 136 pp.

Freud advanced and developed his theories in a long series of publications, of which the most important are *The Interpretation of Dreams* (1900), *Three Contributions to the Theory of Sex* (1905). *Introductory Lectures on Psychoanalysis* (1916), and *The Ego and the Id* (1923). He was indebted to the French neurologist, Jean Martin Charcot's *Lessons on the Maladies of the Nervous System* (1880); to the writings of Pierre Janet, French physician and psychologist; and to James Braid, nineteenth-century English writer on hypnotism and magic.

GALILEI, GALILEO (1564–1642)

Dialogo . . . sopra i Due Massimi Sistemi del Mondo Tolemaico, e Copernicano. Florence: G. B. Landini, 1632. 458 pp.

Galileo's second major work, *Dialoghi delle Nuove Scienze*, "Dialogues of the New Sciences," was issued in 1638, four years before his death, by the Elzevirs at Leyden. Generally considered his most valuable work, the *Dialogues* reviews the results of Galileo's earlier experiments and his meditations on the principles of mechanics.

GEORGE, HENRY (1839–1897)
Progress and Poverty; An Inquiry into the Cause of Industrial Depressions, and of Increase of Want with Increase of Wealth; the Remedy. San Francisco: Wm. M. Hinton, 1879. 266 pp.

GIBBON, EDWARD (1737–1794)
The History of the Decline and Fall of the Roman Empire. London: W. Strahan and T. Cadell, 1776–88. 6 vols.

GIBBS, JOSIAH WILLARD (1839–1903)
"On the Equilibrium of Heterogeneous Substances." Connecticut Academy of Arts and Sciences, *Transactions* (New Haven, 1874–78), pp. 108–248, 343–524.

GILBERT, WILLIAM (1540–1603)
De Magnete, Magneticisque Corporibus, et De Magno Magnete Tellure; Physiologia Nova. London: P. Short, 1600. 240 pp.

GODWIN, WILLIAM (1756–1836)
An Enquiry Concerning the Principles of Political Justice, and Its Influence on General Virtue and Happiness. London: G. G. J. and J. Robinson, 1793. 2 vols.

GROTIUS, HUGO (1583–1645)
De Jure Belli ac Pacis. Paris: Buon, 1625. 3 pts.

HAMILTON, ALEXANDER (1757–1804), MADISON, JAMES (1751–1836), JAY, JOHN (1745–1829)
The Federalist: A Collection of Essays, Written in Favour of the New Constitution. New York: J. and A. M'Lean, 1788. 2 vols.

HARVEY, WILLIAM (1578–1657)
Exercitatio Anatomica de Motu Cordis et Sanguinis in Animalibus. Frankfort: William Fitzer, 1628. 72 pp.
    Harvey had predecessors: Vesalius' *De Humani Corporis Fabrica* (1543) noted that the septum between the right and left ventricles is complete; Servetus, in his *Christianismi Restitutio* (1553), stated his belief that the blood circulates through the lungs, but he did not recognize the heart as the pumping organ; Realdo Colombo, author of *De Re Anatomica* (1559), anatomy professor at Rome, correctly taught that blood passes from the right to the left ventricle through the lungs; Fabricius of Padua, Harvey's teacher, author of *De Venarum Ostiolis* (1603), discovered and described the valves of the veins.

HEGEL, GEORG WILHELM FRIEDRICH (1770–1831)
Der Philosophie des Rechts. Berlin: Nicolai, 1821. 355 pp.

HELMHOLTZ, HERMANN VON (1821–1894)
Über die Erhaltung der Kraft. Berlin: G. Reimer, 1847. 76 pp.

HITLER, ADOLF (1889–1945)
Mein Kampf. Munich: F. Eher, 1925–27. 2 vols.

The principal precursors of the Hitlerian racial theories were Joseph Arthur Gobineau's *Essay on the Inequality of the Human Races* (4 vols., 1853–55) and Houston Stewart Chamberlain's *The Foundations of the Nineteenth Century* (1911), both attributing to Teutonic genius all advances in European civilization and attacking mixed races and Jews.

HOBBES, THOMAS (1588–1679)
Leviathan, or The Matter, Forme, & Power of a Common-Wealth Ecclesiasticall and Civill. London: A. Crooke, 1651. 396 pp.

HOOKE, ROBERT (1635–1703)
Micrographia: or Some Physiological Descriptions of Minute Bodies Made by Magnifying Glasses with Observations and Inquiries Thereupon. London: J. Martyn and J. Allestry, 1665. 246 pp.

HUGO, VICTOR MARIE (1802–1885)
Les Misérables. Paris: Pagnerre, 1862. 10 vols.

HUMBOLDT, FRIEDRICH HEINRICH ALEXANDER VON 1769–1859)
Kosmos. Stuttgart and Tübingen: J. G. Cotta, 1845–62. 5 vols.

Humboldt shares with Karl Ritter the title of founder of modern scientific geography. The latter's monumental *Die Erdkunde im Verhältnis zur Natur und zur Geschichte des Menschen* (10 vols., 1822–59) emphasized the relationship between man and the physical features of the earth and the influence of these features on history. The seventeenth-century German geographer, Bernhardus Varenius, in his *Geographia Generalis* (1650), had paved the way for Humboldt and Ritter and for such later writers on geopolitics as Friedrich Ratzel and Sir Halford Mackinder.

HUTTON, JAMES (1726–1797)
Theory of the Earth; or An Investigation of the Laws Observable in the Composition, Dissolution, and Restoration of Land upon the Globe. Edinburgh and London, 1795–1899. 3 vols. Original paper read 1785 and printed in *Transactions* of the Royal Society of Edinburgh. Edinburgh, 1788, vol. 1, pt. 2, pp. 209–304.

William Smith, English geologist and the founder of modern stratigraphy, furnished irrefutable proof of Hutton's theories on the age of the earth by his study of fossils in rocks, the beginning of the science of paleontology. Smith's findings were reported in *Order of the Strata and Their Imbedded Organic Remains, Examined and Proved Prior to 1799* (1799) and in his renowned *Geological Map of England and Wales, with Part of Scotland* (1815).

IBSEN, HENRIK (1828–1906)
Et Dukkehjem (A Doll's House). Copenhagen: F. Hegel, 1880. 180 pp.

JEFFERSON, THOMAS (1743–1826)
A Summary View of the Rights of British America. Williamsburg: Printed by Clementine Rind, 1774. 23 pp.

JENNER, EDWARD (1749–1823)
An Inquiry into the Causes and Effects of the Variolæ Vaccinæ, a Disease Discovered in Some of the Western Counties of England, Particularly Gloucestershire, and Known by the Name of the Cow Pox. London: S. Low, 1798. 75 pp.

JOHNSON, SAMUEL (1709–1784)
A Dictionary of the English Language. London: J. and P. Knapton; T. and T. Longman; C. Hitch and L. Dawes; A. Millar; and R. and J. Dodsley, 1755. 2 vols.

KANT, IMMANUEL (1724–1804)
Zum Ewigen Frieden; ein Philosophischer Entwurf. Königsberg: F. Nicolovius, 1795. 104 pp.
One of the greatest of modern philosophers, Kant originated the transcendental method of philosophy in his three critiques: *Kritik der Reinen Vernunft* (*Critique of Pure Reason,* 1781), *Kritik der Praktischen Vernunft* (*Critique of Practical Reason,* 1788), and *Kritik der Urtheilskraft* (*Critique of Judgement,* 1790).

KEPLER, JOHANNES (1571–1630)
Astronomia Nova. Prague, 1609. 337 pp.
Harmonices Mundi. Linz, 1619. 255 pp.
Kepler's Laws were based chiefly on the mass of observations made over a twenty-year period by the Danish astronomer Tycho Brahe, whose works included *Astronomiae Instauratae Progymnasmata* (Prague, 1602–3) and *Epistolae Astronomicae* (Uraniborg, 1596).

KEYNES, JOHN MAYNARD, 1st BARON (1883–1946)
The Economic Consequences of the Peace. London: Macmillan, 1919. 279 pp.
In his later years, Keynes' economic theories, as elaborated in his *The General Theory of Employment, Interest, and Money* (1936), had an international influence, especially on the New Deal philosophy in the United States and on British official economic and social policies.

KOCH, ROBERT (1843–1910)
"Die Aetiologie der Tuberculose." *Berliner Klinische Wochenschrift* (Berlin), XIX (1882), pp. 221–30.

LAPLACE, PIERRE SIMON, MARQUIS DE (1749–1827)
Traité de Mécanique Céleste. Paris, 1798–1805. 3 vols.; supplements, 1823–25. 2 vols.

LAVOISIER, ANTOINE LAURENT (1743–1794)
Traité Élémentaire de Chimie. Paris: Cuchet, 1789. 2 vols.

LEEUWENHOEK, ANTON VAN (1632–1723)
Epistolae ad Societatem Regiam Anglicam. Leyden: J. A. Langerak, 1719. 429 pp.

LENIN, NIKOLAI (1870–1924) (Pseudonym of Vladimir Ilich Ulyanov)
Gosudarstvo i Revolyutziya. Petrograd, 1918. 113 pp. First English edition: *State and Revolution.* London: Allen and Unwin, 1919. 123 pp.

   Lenin's prolific writings on Marxian ideology and related subjects have been collected in Russian (Moscow, 1941–50, 4th ed., 35 vols.), and partly translated into English, e.g., *Selected Works* (London, 1936–39, 12 vols.)

LINCOLN, ABRAHAM (1809–1865) and DOUGLAS, STEPHEN ARNOLD (1813–1861)
Political Debates Between Hon. Abraham Lincoln and Hon. Stephen A. Douglas, in the Celebrated Campaign of 1858, in Illinois. Columbus [Ohio]: Follett, Foster and Company, 1860. 268 pp.

LINNAEUS, CAROLUS (1707–1778) (Swedish form: Carl Von Linné)
Systema Naturae. Leyden: T. Haak, 1735. 11 pp. Definitive edition (10th): Stockholm: L. Salvii, 1758–59. 2 vols.

LISTER, JOSEPH, 1st BARON (1827–1912)
"On the Antiseptic Principle in the Practice of Surgery." *The Lancet* (London, 1867), pp. 741–745.

LOCKE, JOHN (1632–1704)
Two Treatises of Government. London: Awnsham Churchill, 1690. 467 pp.

   Locke's political writings are derived from his empirical views, set forth in detail in his *Essay Concerning Human Understanding* (1690), wherein are examined the nature of knowledge, the basis for judging truth, and with what questions the human understanding is best fitted to deal. Almost all knowledge, Locke held, emanates from experience. The *Essay* was the most widely read philosophical book of its generation.

LUTHER, MARTIN (1483–1546)
An den Christlichen Adel Deutscher Nation. Wittenberg: Melchior Lotter, 1520. 94 pp.

LYELL, CHARLES (1797–1875)
Principles of Geology, Being an Attempt to Explain the Former Changes of the Earth's Surface, by Reference to Causes Now in Operation. London: J. Murray, 1830–33. 3 vols.

McGUFFEY, WILLIAM HOLMES (1800–1873)
Eclectic Readers. Cincinnati: Truman and Smith, 1836–37. 5 vols. (Includes Primer, First, Second, Third, and Fourth Readers).

In the history of early American elementary textbooks, the only works comparable in popularity to McGuffey's are the *New England Primer*, the first edition of which was issued before 1690 and of which some forty editions are known, and Noah Webster's *The American Spelling Book* (1783) and *An American Selection of Lessons in Reading and Spelling* (1785).

MACHIAVELLI, NICCOLÒ (1469–1527)
Il Principe. First edition: Rome: Antonio Blado, 1532. 53 ff.

Machiavelli's *Discourses on the First Ten Books of Titus Livius* (1521) gives a better rounded and more complete statement of his views on political organization than does *The Prince.* His *The Art of War* (1521) and *History of Florence* (1532) are also primarily concerned with politics, ancient and contemporary.

MACKINDER, SIR HALFORD JOHN (1861–1947)
"The Geographical Pivot of History." Royal Geographical Society, *Proceedings,* January 25, 1904 (London). *Geographical Journal,* XXIII (1904), p. 431–37. Definitive edition: *Democratic Ideals and Reality.* London: Constable, 1919. 272 pp.

Karl Haushofer, German geographer and political adviser to Hitler, wrote voluminously on geopolitics, directly inspired by Mackinder's theories. Among his widely-circulated works are: *Bausteine zur Geopolitik* (1928), *Weltpolitik von Heute* (1934), *Geopolitik des Pazifischen Ozeans* (1924), *Wehr-Geopolitik* (1932), and *Weltmeere und Weltmächte* (1937).

MAHAN, ALFRED THAYER (1840–1914)
The Influence of Sea Power upon History, 1660–1783. Boston: Little, Brown, 1890. 557 pp.

Mahan continued his writings on sea power in a series of specialized works, notably *The Influence of Sea Power upon the French Revolution and Empire, 1793–1812; Sea Power in its Relations to the War of 1812;* and biographies of Farragut and Nelson.

MALTHUS, THOMAS ROBERT (1766–1834)
An Essay on the Principle of Population. London: J. Johnson, 1798. 396 pp. Five revised and enlarged editions were printed during author's life-time, 1803–26.

MARX, KARL (1818–1883) and ENGELS, FRIEDRICH (1820–1895)
Manifest der Kommunistischen Partei. London, 1848. 23 pp.

The economic and social theories outlined in *The Communist Manifesto* were developed by Marx in much greater detail in *Das Kapital,* the first volume of which was issued in 1867. The second and third volumes, edited by Friedrich Engels, were published in 1885 and 1894, after Marx's death. In *Das Kapital,* Marx sets forth at length the doctrine of value and surplus value, i.e., that the value of a commodity is determined by the amount of human labor going into its production. Later communist theoreticians, notably Trotsky, Lenin, Stalin, and Mao Tse-Tung, have written voluminous interpretations and modifications of Marxian dogma and ideology.

MENDEL, GREGOR JOHANN (1822–1884)
"Versuche über Pflanzen-Hybriden." *Verhandlungen des Naturforschenden Vereines in Brünn* (Brünn), IV (1866), pp. 3–47.

MILL, JOHN STUART (1806–1873)
On Liberty. London: J. W. Parker, 1859. 207 pp.

MILTON, JOHN (1608–1674)
Areopagitica: a Speech of Mr. John Milton for the Liberty of Unlicenc'd Printing, to the Parlament of England. London, 1644. 40 pp.

Milton's activities and influence as a social reformer appear also in his *Doctrine and Discipline of Divorce* (1643), interpreting marriage as a contract that could be dissolved; *On Education* (1644), recommending a vital system of linguistic training and practical knowledge in place of the dull grind of Latin grammar; and *Eikonoklastes* (1649), *Pro Populo Anglicano Defensio* (1651), and other pamphlets defending the republic as the best form of government.

MONTAIGNE, MICHEL EYQUEM DE (1533–1592)
Essais. Bordeaux: S. Millanges, 1580. 2 vols., Paris: A. L'Angelier, 1595. 2 vols.

MONTESQUIEU, CHARLES LOUIS DE SECONDAT, BARON DE LA BRÈDE ET DE (1689–1755)
De L'Esprit des Lois. Geneve: Barrillot, 1748. 2 vols.

MORE, SIR THOMAS (1478–1535)
Libellus vere Aureus nec Minus Salutaris quam Festivus de Optimo Reipublicae Statu Deque Insula Utopia. Louvain, 1516. 54 ff.

Utopian dreams flourished long before and after More, e.g., Plato's *Republic* (4th century, B.C.), Campanella's *The City of the Sun* (1623), Bacon's *New Atlantis* (1627), Andreae's *Christianopolis* (1619), Harrington's *The Commonwealth of Oceana* (1656), Fénelon's *The Adventures of Telemachus* (1699), Mercier's *Memoirs of the Year 2500* (1770), Spence's *The Constitution of Spensonia* (1803), Cabet's *A Voy-*

age to Icaria (1840), Edward Bellamy's *Looking Backward* (1888), and H. G. Wells' *A Modern Utopia* (1905).

NEWTON, SIR ISAAC (1642–1727)
Philosophiae Naturalis Principia Mathematica. London: Printed by Joseph Streater for the Royal Society, 1687. 510 pp.

Newton's researches on light—the composition of light, the nature of color and of white light—which occupied his early years, were summed up in his *Opticks* (1704).

NIETZSCHE, FRIEDRICH WILHELM (1844–1900)
Jenseits von Gut und Böse. Leipzig: C. G. Naumann, 1886. 271 pp.

OWEN, ROBERT (1771–1858)
A New View of Society, or Essays on the Formation of the Human Character. London, 1813–14. 4 vols. in 1.

PAINE, THOMAS (1737–1809)
Common Sense, Addressed to the Inhabitants of America. Philadelphia: R. Bell, 1776. 79 pp.

Paine's political ideas were developed further in his *Rights of Man* (1791), written in defense of the French Revolution and answering Edmund Burke's hostile *Reflections on the Revolution in France.* His *Age of Reason* (1794–96), a deistic work sometimes unfairly described as the "atheist's Bible," was written, Paine maintained, to counteract the trend toward atheism among the French Revolutionary leaders.

PASTEUR, LOUIS (1822–1895)
"Mémoire sur la Fermentation Appelée Lactique." Académie des Sciences, *Comptes Rendus* (Paris), XLV (1857), pp. 913–16.

PAVLOV, IVAN PETROVICH (1849–1936)
Conditioned Reflexes; an Investigation of the Physiological Activity of the Cerebral Cortex. London: Oxford University Press, 1927. 430 pp. First published in Russian, 1926.

Nearly a century before Pavlov's experiments, a Scottish physiologist Sir Charles Bell, had pioneered in research dealing with the anatomy and physiology of the nervous system. His findings were reported in *New Ideas of the Anatomy of the Brain* (1811) and *The Nervous System of the Human Body* (1830). Bell's discoveries have been compared in historical importance with those made by William Harvey on the circulatory system.

PESTALOZZI, JOHANN HEINRICH (1746–1827)
Wie Gertrud Ihre Kinder Lehrt. Bern and Zurich: Heinrich Gessner, 1801. 390 pp.

Pestalozzi was the successor of Rousseau in the field of education. The latter's *Émile* (1762), the story of a boy reared apart from other children and the subject of experimental methods, was highly influential in the development of modern elementary education. Following immediately after Pestalozzi were Johann Friedrich Herbart, noted for the application of psychology and ethics to educational systems and methods, and Friedrich Froebel, founder of the kindergarten movement. The evolution to John Dewey's progressive theories of education, nearly a century later, formed a natural sequence.

PROUDHON, PIERRE JOSEPH (1809–1865)
Qu'est-ce que la Propriété? ou Recherches sur le Principe du Droit et du Gouvernement. Paris: Brocard, 1840. 244 pp.

ROUSSEAU, JEAN JACQUES (1712–1778)
Du Contrat Social, ou, Principes du Droit Politique. Amsterdam: M. M. Rey, 1762. 324 pp.

Comparable in influence to *Du Contrat Social* were Rousseau's *Émile* (1762), setting forth his ideas of education, and the *Confessions* (1781), which inaugurated a new school of autobiographic writing.

SHAKESPEARE, WILLIAM (1564–1616)
The Tragicall Historie of Hamlet, Prince of Denmarke. London: Nicholas Ling and John Trundell, 1603. 33 ff. More complete edition: James Roberts and Nicholas Ling, 1604, 51 ff.

SHAW, GEORGE BERNARD (1856–1950), WEBB, SIDNEY (1859–1947), CLARKE, WILLIAM (1852–1901), OLIVIER, SYDNEY (1859–1943), BESANT, ANNIE (1847–1933), WALLAS, GRAHAM (1858–1932), and BLAND, HUBERT (1856–1914)
Fabian Essays in Socialism. London, 1889. 233 pp.

Shaw's Fabian ideas and ideals were subsequently carried over into his plays concerned with social problems, e.g., *Arms and the Man* and *The Devil's Disciple,* witty satires on military heroism; *Mrs. Warren's Profession, Candida,* and *Man and Superman,* on social attitudes toward sex relations; *The Doctor's Dilemma,* a satire on some aspects of the medical profession; *Major Barbara,* on organized charity; and *Pygmalion,* on high society and the Cinderella theme.

SMITH, ADAM (1723–1790)
An Inquiry into the Nature and Causes of the Wealth of Nations. London: W. Strahan and T. Cadell, 1776. 2 vols.

SPENCER, HERBERT (1820–1903)
The Man versus the State. London: Williams and Norgate, 1884. 113 pp.

In his first important book, *Social Statics* (1851), Spencer began to advocate extreme individualism. This doctrine is the key to all of his work, and came to full flower in *The Man versus the State.*

STOWE, HARRIET BEECHER (1811–1896)
Uncle Tom's Cabin; or Life among the Lowly. Boston: J. P. Jewett, 1852. 2 vols. First published serially in the *National Era,* June 5, 1851–April 1, 1852.

1 LONG

Two other works on slavery came from Mrs. Stowe's pen: *A Key to Uncle Tom's Cabin* (1853), written to prove that the original work was not exaggerated or "a tissue of lies," as some detractors charged; and *Dred, A Tale of the Great Dismal Swamp* (1856), picturing the evil effects of the slave system upon the white man.

SWIFT, JONATHAN (1667–1745)
Travels into Several Remote Nations of the World [Gulliver's Travels]. London: Benjamin Motte, 1726. 2 vols. in 4 pts.

TAYLOR, FREDERICK WINSLOW (1856–1915)
Principles of Scientific Management. New York: Harper, 1911. 77 pp.

THOREAU, HENRY DAVID (1817–1862)
"Resistance to Civil Government." *Aesthetic Papers*, edited by Elizabeth P. Peabody (Boston, 1849), pp. 189–211.

In his most famous book, *Walden, or Life in the Woods* (1854), which has been called the "spiritual autobiography of a rebel wearied by the machine age," Thoreau makes an appealing case for the simple life, for nonconformity and extreme individualism, and demonstrates the unimportance of material things.

TOCQUEVILLE, ALEXIS CHARLES HENRI MAURICE CLÉREL DE (1805–1859)
De la Démocratie en Amérique. Paris: C. Gosselin, 1835–40. 4 vols.

TURNER, FREDERICK JACKSON (1861–1932)
The Significance of the Frontier in American History. American Historical Association *Annual Report, 1893.* (Washington, 1894). pp. 197–227. Definitive edition: *The Frontier in American History.* New York: Holt, 1920. 375 pp.

VEBLEN, THORSTEIN BUNDE (1857–1929)
The Theory of the Leisure Class. New York: Macmillan, 1899. 400 pp.

Veblen's devastating social criticisms were aimed at various targets in a series of other remarkable books: *The Theory of Business Enterprise* (1904), *The Instinct of Workmanship and the State of the Industrial Arts* (1914), *An Inquiry into the Nature of Peace* (1917), *The Higher Learning in America* (1919), *The Place of Science in Modern Civilisation* (1919), *The Vested Interests and the State of the Industrial Arts* (1919), *The Engineers and the Price System* (1921), *Absentee Ownership and Business Enterprise in Recent Times* (1923).

VERNE, JULES (1828–1905)
De la Terre à la Lune. Paris: H. Hetzel, 1865. 170 pp.

VESALIUS, ANDREAS (1514–1564)
De Humani Corporis Fabrica. Basel: Johannis Oporinus, 1543. 664 pp.

The universal genius Leonardo da Vinci (1452–1519) preceded Vesalius in scientific studies of human and animal anatomy and muscular movement, but Leonardo's notebooks containing his anatomical, physiological, and embryological drawings were not published until modern times and therefore may be presumed to have had little contemporary influence.

VICO, GIOVANNI BATTISTA or GIAMBATTISTA (1668–1744)
Principi di una Scienza Nuova. Naples: F. Mosca, 1725. 270 pp.

VOLTAIRE. Assumed name of FRANÇOIS MARIE AROUET (1694–1778)
Dictionnaire Philosophique Portatif. Geneva, 1764. 344 pp.

WEBSTER, NOAH (1758–1843)
An American Dictionary of the English Language. New York: S. Converse, 1828. 2 vols.

Webster contributed to the development of the American language also through his *Grammatical Institute of the English Language:* Part I, *Containing a New and Accurate Standard of Pronunciation,* later known as *Webster's Spelling Book* or *Blue-Backed Speller* (1783); Part II, *Containing a Plain and Comprehensive Grammar* (1784); and Part III, *Containing the Necessary Rules of Reading and Speaking, and a Variety of Essays, Dialogues, and Declamatory Pieces* (1785)—in short, a speller, a grammar, and a reader. Of the *Blue-Backed Speller,* sixty million copies are estimated to have been sold by 1890.

WHITMAN, WALT (1819–1892)
Democratic Vistas. Washington, D.C., 1871. 84 pp.

WILSON, WOODROW (1856–1924)
The New Freedom. New York: Doubleday, 1913. 294 pp. Definitive edition of Wilson's 1912 speeches: *A Crossroads of Freedom.* New Haven: Yale University Press, 1956. 570 pp.

WOLLSTONECRAFT, MARY (1759–1797)
Vindication of the Rights of Woman. London: J. Johnson, 1792. 452 pp.

The few defenders in print of the rights of women before, and for some time after, Mary Wollstonecraft were men. There are enlightened passages in the writings of Swift and Defoe, and Holberg, Condorcet, and Holbach, among the philosophers of the French Revolution, urged equal citizenship and educational rights for women. William Thomson, socialist disciple of Robert Owen, wrote an *Appeal of One Half the Human Race, Women, Against the Pretensions of the Other Half, Men* (London, 1825). More influential was John Stuart Mill's *The Subjection of Women* (1869), which served as a text for the movement for women's rights throughout the world.

INDEX

Adams, John, 152
Adams, John Quincy, 158
Adams, Samuel, 150
Addison, Joseph, 101, 128
Address to the Christian Nobility,
xvii, 3, 17–20
Addresses to the German Nation,
206-8
Advancement of Learning, 49–52
AGASSIZ, JEAN LOUIS, 52, 172,
250; *Studies on Glaciers,* 238–41
Alembert, Jean Le Rond d', 126
Alexander VI, 9
ALGER, HORATIO, JR., 179; *Rag-
ged Dick,* 300–303
Allen, Walter, 111
American Dictionary, 218–21
American Revolution, 123, 156, 173,
177
Ampère, André Marie, 236, 250
*Anatomical Exercise on the Motion
of the Heart and Blood in Animals,*
61–64, 107
Anderson, Thomas, 298, 299
Annan, Noel, 226
*Antiseptic Principle in the Practice of
Surgery, On the,* 297–300
Aquinas, Thomas, 24, 69
Archimedes, 5
Areopagitica, 4, 71–75, 280, 288
Aristarchus, 5, 28
Aristotle, 19, 35, 50, 51, 57, 69, 79,
268
Arnold, Matthew, 247
Austin, John, 142
Autobiography (Franklin), 179–81
Avogadro, Amedeo, 211

BACON, FRANCIS, 5, 6, 42, 78;
Advancement of Learning, 49–52;
New Atlantis, 14, 323; *Novum Or-
ganum,* 50
Bacon, Roger, 41
Bailey's *Dictionary,* 129
Balzac, Honoré de, 167, 283
Barrett, Elizabeth, 265
Barzun, Jacques, 123
Baumer, Franklin Le Van, 97

BAYLE, PIERRE, 98; *Historical and
Critical Dictionary,* 95, 102–4
Beard, Charles A., 91, 158, 334
BECCARIA, CESARE BONESANA,
142; *Of Crimes and Punishments,*
100, 137–40
Becquerel, Antoine César, 284
Bedborough, George, 338
Bell, Eric T., 201
BELLAMY, EDWARD, *Looking
Backward,* 279–80, 323–26
Bellarmine, Roberto, Cardinal, 66
BENTHAM, JEREMY, 142, 167,
286, 327; *Introduction to the Prin-
ciples of Morals and Legislation,*
173–76
Bernhardi, Friedrich von, 283, 364
Berzelius, Jöns Jakob, 211
Besant, Annie, 327
Beyond Good and Evil, 320–23
Bible (King James Version), 5, 49, 87
Bill of Rights (England), 98
Bill of Rights (U. S.), 157
Bishop, John Peale, 54–55
Bishop, Philip W., 120
Bismarck, Otto von, 24
Black, Joseph, 162
BLACKSTONE, WILLIAM, *Com-
mentaries on the Laws of England,*
100, 140–143
Blaine, James G., 274
Bland, Hubert, 327, 328
Blomberg, Werner von, 229
BODIN, JEAN, 3–4; *Six Books on
the State,* 35–38
Boehmer, Heinrich, 20
Bohr, Niels, 284
Bolívar, Simón, 249, 250
Boltzmann, Ludwig, 254
Bonaparte, Napoleon, 24, 165, 169,
197, 201, 202, 206, 208, 215, 226,
227, 229, 244, 246, 250, 283, 322
Bonar, James, 199, 200
Bonpland, Aimé, 250
Borgia, Cesare, 20–21, 22
Boswell, James, 131, 183; *Life of
Johnson,* 153
Bowditch, Nathaniel, 202

387